How Capitalism Underdeveloped Black America

How Capitalism Underdeveloped Black America

Problems in Race, Political Economy and Society

Manning Marable

SOUTH END PRESS   BOSTON, MA

Library of Congress Catalog Card Number: 82-061153

ISBN 0-89608-165-6 paperback

ISBN 0-89608-166-4 cloth

Cover design by Kathy Moore

South End Press
116 St. Botolph St.
Boston, Ma. 02115

Printed In The U.S.

CONTENTS

DEDICATION

For the insights she has in the spirit of Black people, for her practical experiences as a wage laborer in the Georgia cotton fields, and for the courage she exhibits in the face of death, to my wife Hazel Ann, I owe more than I could ever say. And for his personification of praxis, for his brilliant intellect, and for his uncompromising legacy as the voice of the periphery bound up in world revolution, to Walter Rodney, the author of *How Europe Underdeveloped Africa*.

PREFACE

To be Black and a socialist in America is to be a nonconformist. Nothing presented in these pages should be accepted as holy scripture. I make no pretence that my thesis is part of some great universal Truth. My struggle for political direction and theoretical clarity has never been divorced from my deep commitment to the liberation of oppressed Black people in the United States, and of all exploited people across the world. Therefore, my judgments in certain circumstances may appear to some as too harsh, too extreme, too utopian, too subjective. Very well. The times we live in call for harsh measures, both behind the cloistered towers of the university and in the streets. The intellectual who makes a public commitment to transform society, to smash white racism and the inherently exploitative system laughingly described as "free enterprise" by its defenders, cannot plead his/her case in muted grey tones. For the Black masses to "return to their own history," we must begin by rewriting that history—but not in the language, style or outlook of the system. This book records the respective histories of the different social strata within Black political economy and society, from the political Brahmins of the elite to the industrial working class. The methodology is sociological; the questions raised, political and economic; the style, polemical; the goal: to present a critique of the strengths and contradictions which comprise Black American labor and life, with the purpose of destroying the process of underdevelopment which has imprisoned us for almost four centuries.

I have learned a great deal from the tedious research that was necessary in writing this book. Thomas Carlyle's assertion that political economy is the "dismal science" will receive no argument from me. Probably the greatest intuitive insights I achieved came from those writers who are most removed from social science—the poets. Langston Hughes' "Justice" says more than I could ever present in the form of quantitative data about the brutalization of Blacks by the U.S. criminal justice system:

> That Justice is a blind goddess
> Is a thing to which we black are wise:
> Her bandage hides two festering sores
> That once perhaps were eyes.

ix

It is impossible for me to list the number of friends and co-workers who helped me to write this book. There are a few, however, who cannot escape special acknowledgement. Two graduate students at the Africana Studies and Research Center at Cornell University, David Hatchett and Randall Brock, criticized various chapters and engaged me in a series of friendly, intellectual debates which proved to be essential in the formulation of my thesis. Mrs. Daisy Rowe and Douglas Milton typed the original manuscript, making helpful suggestions along the way. The editorial collective of South End Press provided support in turning my first draft into a real book. Williams College gave me several weeks of solitude during the bitterly cold winter of 1982 to complete research on several chapters by offering me its Luce visiting professorship in political science. David Smith, professor of English at Williams, deserves my thanks for his continued support. My ideas expressed in chapter three, "Groundings With My Sisters," were developed in my course on the political history of Black women at Cornell. Once again, all of my students—and especially Ruby Saake, Zennette Austin, Carol M. McIntosh, Karen O'Brien and Wynsome "Jackie" Davis—were important critics of a Black man earnestly attempting to develop a genuinely nonsexist Black history. The editors of *The Guardian, Socialist Review, In These Times, Science and Society, WIN* magazine, *Black Scholar* and several other journals assisted in the development of my studies. To my wife Hazel Ann, I can offer none of the standard acknowledgements: she doesn't mend my socks, and I do most of the cooking. She doesn't claim to be a feminist or a Marxist, and would prefer to be at home with our three children than out in a street demonstration. She is, however, the most important cultural force in my life and thought. She was a consistent fighter for union rights for all non-exempt employees at Cornell; she has a love for Black people, and for truth that comes from principled struggle. Hazel's courage in the face of death, in the aftermath of her brother's assassination and then, this winter, her cousin's murder by lynching in the woods of northern Georgia, has reinforced my own praxis. Despite her warning, half in jest, that with the publication of *How Capitalism Underdeveloped Black America* we would be forced to flee the country, I acknowledge everything to her.

Anyway, I responded, our bags are always packed.

Manning Marable
October 31, 1982

INTRODUCTION

INEQUALITY AND THE BURDEN OF CAPITALIST DEMOCRACY: A POINT OF VIEW ON BLACK HISTORY.

What have I or those I represent to do with your national independence? Are the great principles of political freedom and of natural justice, embodied in that Declaration of Independence, extended to us? . . . Your high independence only reveals the immeasurable distance between us. The blessings in which you this day rejoice are not enjoyed in common. The rich inheritance of justice, liberty, prosperity, and independence bequeathed by your fathers is shared by you, not by me. The sunlight that brought life and healing to you has brought stripes and death to me. This Fourth of July is yours, not mine. You may rejoice, I must mourn. . . . What to the American slave is your Fourth of July? I answer, a day that reveals to him more than all other days of the year, the gross injustice and cruelty to which he is the constant victim. To him, your celebration is a sham; your boasted liberty an unholy license . . .

Frederick Douglass, 1852, in Alice Moore Dunbar, ed. *Masterpieces of Negro Eloquence* (New York: Bookery Publishing Company, 1914), pp. 42–47.

The process of capital accumulation is a, if not the, principal motor of modern history. Structural inequality and temporal unevenness of capital accumulation are inherent to capitalism.

Andre Gunder Frank, *World Accumulation, 1492–1789* (New York: Monthly Review Press, 1978), pp. 238–239.

I

The most striking fact about American economic history and politics is the brutal and systemic underdevelopment of Black people.

1

Afro-Americans have been on the other side of one of the most remarkable and rapid accumulations of capital seen anywhere in human history, existing as a necessary yet circumscribed victim within the proverbial belly of the beast. The relationship is filled with paradoxes: each advance in white freedom was purchased by Black enslavement; white affluence coexists with Black poverty; white state and corporate power is the product in part of Black powerlessness; income mobility for the few is rooted in income stasis for the many. Many politicians, intellectuals and civic leaders condemn the United States on the grounds that white society has systematically excluded Blacks as a group from the material, cultural and political gains achieved by other ethnic minorities. Blacks are unemployed, economically exploited and politically disfranchised because they are excluded or segregated because of caste or racial discrimination. But there is another point of view on this issue: Blacks occupy the lowest socioeconomic rung in the ladder of American upward mobility precisely because they have been "integrated" all too well into the system. America's "democratic" government and "free enterprise" system are structured deliberately and specifically to maximize Black oppression. Capitalist development has occurred not in spite of the exclusion of Blacks, but because of the brutal exploitation of Blacks as workers and consumers. Blacks have never been equal partners in the American Social Contract, because the system exists not to develop, but to *underdevelop Black people*.

This different perspective raises a basic theoretical question: What is development, and what is its structural relationship to underdevelopment? Most Western scholars and the general U.S. public describe a nation as "developed" if and when it "has several political parties, widespread literacy, a high standard of living, wide circulation of newspapers and books, consensus on the fundamentals of government, a long history of peace, and .   . a white population."[1] Developed or "modern" nation-states also exhibit other characteristics, according to this view: the secularization of politics; a trained civil service; political activity which is widespread, rather than confined to the capital city; the infusion of Western political and social values into the system; the existence of constitutional government; civilian control of the military; a popular commitment to democracy; and for many, a free market economic system. Modernization then becomes the pattern by which nonwhite peoples transform themselves "through the twin processes of commercialization and industrialization," moving toward the standard socioeconomic models provided by Western Europe and the United States.[2] For most white political scientists, planners and sociologists, the road toward development for Asia, Africa, Latin America and historically disadvantaged national minorities is not unlike the Puritans' quest for the perfect "City on the Hill." For economist Robert L. Heilbronner, development is that glorious "process through which the social, political and economic institutions of the future are being shaped for the great majority of mankind."[3] Conversely, the lack of integration into the West's economic and political order means the absence of "cash, commercial credit, advanced technology, and specialized production."[4]

What all of these liberal interpretations have in common is a kind of economic amnesia. A few social scientists go so far as to discount any relationship between political development and "economic and social factors" relating to modernization.[5] An accurate understanding of underdevelopment begins with the questions raised by Marxist economist Harry Magdoff: "Where would the original accumulation of capital used in industry (in the West) have come from if not from the extraction of wealth from colonies, piracy, and the slave trade? Where would the reproduction and growth of the needed capital for investment have come from if not from sufficiently large profits arising in the operation of enterprise (in the non-western world)?"[6] The "Great Ascent" of the West since the sixteenth century was fundamentally a process of growing capital accumulation, the endless drive to control the human and material resources of the world's people. For Western Europe, Great Britain and the United States, domestic development meant the conquest of foreign markets, the stimulation of demand for Western goods within the Third World, the domination of indigenous political and social systems by the bribery of local officials, revolutions, threats, and outright colonial occupation. Development was, more than all other factors combined, the institutionalization of the hegemony of capitalism as a world system. *Underdevelopment* was the direct consequence of this process: chattel slavery, sharecropping, peonage, industrial labor at low wages, and cultural chaos.[7] The current economic amnesia of the West is therefore no accident, because it reveals the true roots of massive exploitation and human degradation upon which the current world order rests. The world "periphery" and capitalist "core" share a common history.

The U.S. state apparatus was created to facilitate the expansion and entrenchment of institutional racism in both slave and nonslaveholding states. The solidly bourgeois delegates at the Constitutional Convention held in Philadelphia in 1787 were unconcerned about the "inalienable rights" of Afro-Americans. Their chief concern was the creation of a strong national government that would guarantee property rights—slavery being counted among them. Thus, the result was the drafting of a racist manifesto which avoided the use of the words "slave" or "slavery" while protecting the institution itself. This was accomplished by three specific points: Article One, Section Two, which counted the slaves for purposes of representation and direct taxation as three-fifths of a human being; Article One, Section Nine, which mandated that Federal authorities could not interfere with the transatlantic slave trade for two decades; and Article Four, Section Two, which declared that all fugitive slaves had to be returned to their rightful owners. After the ratification of the U.S. Constitution, the Federal government adopted, even under relatively progressive administrations, a bitterly racist posture toward the rights of all Blacks, slave or free. The Fugitive Slave Act of 1793, signed by the Virginia slaveholder and plantation master George Washington, strengthened the rights of slaveowners to capture runaways in the North and to remove them by force back to the South. The banning of the slave trade in 1808 was relatively inconsequential, since 50,000 Africans were brought into the U.S. after the law took effect. Northern states led the way toward the development of white supremacy as part of local state policy. Free Blacks were barred from voting in Delaware in 1792; in Kentucky, Maryland and Ohio in 1799; in New Jersey in 1807. New York State authorized Blacks to vote only if they owned property valued above $250, while no property restrictions applied to white voters. Free Blacks were routinely excluded from juries and all public offices. This heritage of collective racial discrimination is the very foundation of what is usually heralded as American democracy.[8]

Yet every stage of Western capitalist underdevelopment, the African population resisted. Throughout the Black diaspora, resistance took the form of runaway slave communities, called maroons (French and English), palenques (Spanish), quilombos (Portuguese) and/or mocambos (Ambundu for "hideout"). In late-sixteenth-century Mexico, for example, African runaway slaves had become such a problem that the Spanish authorities ordered the castration of Black men absent for more than six months. Vigilante systems for patrolling the roads were established in rural areas. The crown granted rewards for the capture of palenque rebels and material incentives were offered to slaves and former fugitives who betrayed their brothers and sisters who were in hiding. In Veracruz, African guerillas regularly destroyed crops, attacked wagons and burned plantation houses to the ground. In the early seventeenth century, a militant palenque of Indians and Africans led by the chief Yanga fought Spanish regulars to a stalemate. Local Spanish authorities were forced to sign a peace treaty with Yanga, which established the legal town of San Lorenzo de los Negros. Between 1731 and 1781, Cuban Blacks created a palenque, Poblado del Cobre, in Oriente Province that comprised over one thousand persons. The greatest maroon of all was Palmares, a series of African quilombos founded in about 1600 and surviving armed assaults by Dutch and Portuguese troops until 1694. The Palmarista general Zambi successfully defended the territory until the combined weight of American Indian, Portuguese colonial and mestizo soldiers, skilled in guerilla tactics, were hurled against him. After a two-year siege of the major rebel city, 200 Palmarista soldiers committed suicide rather than suffer the humiliation of returning to slavery. Two hundred more Palmaristas were killed in hand-to-hand combat on the final day of fighting, with Zambi succumbing only after he was seriously wounded. On November 20, 1695, Zambi was decapitated in a public execution; his head was exhibited before Black slaves "to kill the legend of his immortality." In the United States, wherever the frontier geography permitted the possibility of maroons, Afro-American Zambis were found. At least fifty maroons existed in the U.S. between 1672 and 1864 in the swamps and Appalachian hill country of the Carolinas, Alabama, Georgia, Florida, Mississippi, Virginia and Louisiana. As late as the 1970s, "the descendants of many of those maroons who chose to cast their lot with Indians [could] still be found, largely forgotten, and often desperately poor."[9]

Where the conditions (political, social, economic) for revolt existed, Africans seized whatever arms they could find and fought desperately to assert their humanity. Along Columbia's Pata River in the 1730s and 1740s, a slave named Jeronimo incited open rebellion and refused an offer of peace rendered by Spanish authorities on the grounds that it required a return of some runaway slaves from his army. In 1647, four hundred Chilean Blacks, armed with clubs, guns and knives, staged an unsuccessful uprising in Santiago. In 1609 and 1612, rumors in Mexico City that the slaves were conspiring a bloody revolt led to extensive repression, with hundreds of Blacks arrested, imprisoned, executed and/or castrated. Gabriel Prosser and Denmark Vessey prepared plans for American slave rebellions in 1800 and 1822, respectively, that involved thousands of Black women and men. Nat Turner led a band of sixty slaves across southern Virginia in 1831, executing 57 whites in a span of two days. The Black diaspora's greatest revolutionaries, of course were the African laborers of San Domingue. The former slaves' leaders were among the most dedicated and brilliant generals who have appeared in the pages of history— Toussaint L'Ouverture, Christophe, and the ruthless Dessalines. The heroism of Haiti's soldiers between 1790 and 1804 is legendary.[10]

White planters and government officials recognized that the slavery regime could survive only with the most repressive and bestial force imaginable. The French tended to be extremely precise in their punishments of rebellious Africans. The *Code Noir* was quite specific: "The fugitive slave who has been absent for one month shall have his ears cut off and his shoulder branded with a *fleur de lis*; if he repeats his crime for a period of (at least) one month, he shall be hamstrung and branded with a *fleur de lis* on the other shoulder." Plantation managers used a variety of tortures: the "empetre" or chain, shackles three feet long with two iron rings fastened at each end to secure the slave's lower legs to impede walking; "cachots effrayants," small maximum security cells without light; the nabot, a large iron circular device weighing six to ten pounds that was cold-riveted to the slave's foot; castration, or amputation of the feet and/or limbs; forcing gunpowder into the anus or vagina of a slave and then blowing him/her up with a light—"to burn a little powder in the ass of a nigger;" burying them in the dirt up to their necks and smearing their heads with sugar so flies and ants would devour them; forcing slaves to eat animal and human excrement; roasting rebellious slaves barbeque-style over hot coals or an open fire. In the United States, however, the most popular form of labor discipline was the whip, or lash. Historian Kenneth Stampp observes that "the whip was the most common instrument of punishment—indeed, it was the emblem of the master's authority. Nearly every slaveholder used it, and few grown slaves escaped it entirely." The rawhide lash was a "savage instrument," and Stampp notes that "physical cruelty was always a possible consequence of the master's power to punish." Thoughtful white Southerners recognized the barbarism inherent in the U.S. slavery system. One Mississippi slave-owner wrote in 1846 that " a certain class of overseers" were extraordinarily cruel to Black women and men alike. "It is this unrelenting, brutalizing drive, watch and whip, that furnishes facts to abolition writers that cannot be disputed, and that are infamous." One South Carolina judge confessed in 1847 that many slaveholders "deserved no other name than fiends" because they delighted in the torture of their chattel. [11]

The ordeal of slavery was responsible for accelerating the economic and political power of Europe and North America over the rest of the mostly nonwhite world. Since the demise of slavery, and the emergence of modern capitalism, the process of Black underdevelopment has expanded and deepened. To understand this dynamic of degradation, first, is to recognize that development itself is comparative in essence, a relationship of inequality between the capitalist ruling class and those who are exploited. Underdevelopment is not the absence of development; it is the inevitable product of an oppressed population's integration into the world market economy and political system. Once "freed," Black Americans were not compensated for their 246 years of free labor to this country's slave oligarchy. The only means of survival and economic development they possessed was their ability to work, their labor power, which they sold in various forms to the agricultural capitalist. Sharecropping and convict leasing were followed by industrial labor at low wages. When Blacks performed the identical tasks that whites carried out, they were paid less than "white wages." Even when Blacks acquired technical skills and advanced educations, they were still paid much less than whites who possessed inferior abilities. At every level of employment, white capitalists accumulated higher profits from Blacks' labor than they gained from the labor of whites. Throughout the totality of economic relations, Black workers were exploited—in land tenure, in the ownership of factories, shops and other enterprises, in the means of transportation, in energy, and so forth. *The constant expropriation of surplus value created by Black labor is the heart and soul of underdevelopment.*

Another crucial aspect of underdevelopment involves the dynamics of dependency. Political parties in the U.S. are defined ideologically for the public as formations which represent all the people, rather than special interests and sectors of capital. The object of the electoral process is to achieve a majority within the voting population, and to form specific public policies with the goal of gaining majoritarian support among various constituents within the state apparatus. In the U.S. form of constitutional government, racial minorities can influence major public policies only when their agenda is sufficiently acceptable to one or both of the major white capitalist parties, which in turn assimilate the proposals into their political program for their own purposes. Since Blacks account for 12–13 percent of the U.S. population, and only 10–11 percent of the voters in most general elections, their ability to profoundly influence public policies in the broadest sense is greatly limited by the rules of the game. Blacks are pressured to become dependent on white liberals and moderates to articulate their agendas, in order to acquire majoritarian support. Historically, this has meant that many Blacks have been forced into political coalitions with whites in order to affect U.S. politics, formations which are usually directed by whites, financed by whites, and chiefly comprised of whites. During the period of abolitionist agitation, 1830–1860, many Black political activists were dependent upon the financial and political support of the Garrisonians, the early white feminists, white Free Soilers and others. In the turbulent 1890s, Black croppers were often part of Populist coalitions led by white Southern and Western farmers whose interests and commitments did not in the last analysis always coincide with their own. The NAACP, Urban League, and other civil rights groups in the twentieth century were dependent upon white foundation, corporate and political support. Without an independent capital base for self sufficiency, and operating under a political apparatus which nullifies the impact of minority pressure groups, Blacks repeatedly were trapped into alliances as dependent clients, unable or unwilling to break from the logic of a closed but supposedly democratic system.

Also decisive is the ideological dependency perpetuated among Blacks to divide and to frustrate mass-based actions against racism. The Black child attending public school is burdened immediately with an educational pedagogy which rests on the assumption of his/her cultural and intellectual inferiority. In their places of worship, most Blacks are confronted every Sunday with early Renaissance portraits of Christ, a white diety, and a form of spirituality which theoretically and historically has little direct relevancy to their unique heritage and original African belief systems. The media often carefully select and eliminate glaring contradictions which would evoke outrage and activity by Black people. The aesthetics and popular culture of racist societies constantly reinforce the image of the Anglo-Saxon ideal in the minds of Blacks, creating the tragic and destructive phenomenon of self-hatred and cultural genocide. Colleges and universities deny the legitimacy of Black history and Black studies, and propagate the illusion that U.S. democracy works for everyone regardless of socio-economic, racial and political background. The logic of the ideological apparatuses of the racist/capitalist state leads inextricably to Black accommodation and assimilation into the status quo, a process of cultural genocide which assists the function of ever-expanding capital accumulation.

Both the ideological and coercive apparatuses of white power were mediated also by yet another powerful structure—patriarchy, or institutionalized sexism. By patriarchy, I mean a sex/gender system of authoritarian male dominance and reinforced female dependency, characterized within capitalist society by certain characteristics. The first and decisive component is males' ownership of almost all private property and an absolute control over all productive resources. Second, all men are able to earn more money than women who perform identical or comparable tasks in the workplace. Men under patriarchy experience greater income mobility, and most women are identified in the ideological apparatuses as "homemakers," a vocation for which no real financial compensation is given. Third, women have few rights within the legal system. Fourth, women are either denied suffrage (prior to 1920) or are severely under-represented within the state apparatus. Fifth, various patriarchal institutions deny sexual rights for women such as abortion and birth control information. Sixth, cultural and social authority is invested in the symbolic figure of the father. The (usually white) male's penis is the necessary and logical prerequisite for power. Finally, the "coercive glue" that holds the patriarchal order in balance is systemic violence against women: rape, involuntary sterilization, "wife beatings," and the constant threat of physical punishment. Male-dominated societies existed before the emergence of capitalism, and the struggle to uproot patriarchy even in socialist or transitional states is often problematic. But under capitalism, patriarchy reinforces and converges with racism in numerous ways, affecting the daily lives of all Blacks and all women. The two groups have been historically victimized by white male violence, denied their civil rights, and their undercompensation in the workplace is accumulated in the form of higher profits for white capitalists. The existence of both systems creates a triple burden for every Black woman—for she is victimized, exploited, raped and murdered because of her class, race and sex. For the Black woman under capitalism, each rape is symbolically also a lynching.

The historical product of racist and sexist underdevelopment for Black America has been the creation of a unique national minority within the world's second-most racist state (South Africa deserving honors in this category). Blacks are an integral and necessary part of an imperialistic and powerful capitalist society, yet they exist in terms of actual socioeconomic and political power as a kind of Third World nation. As a result, Black America shares some similarities with other national minorities or oppressed nationalities within European countries; e.g., the Basques in northern Spain, the Welsh and the Irish in the United Kingdom, the Sardinians of Italy, the Corsicans of France. The critical distinction between our conditions and theirs is the factor of white racism—the systemic exploitation of Blacks as a subcaste in both the economic sphere and within civil society. Like Africans and West Indians, Black Americans are not only victims of class but also white racist exploitation. Because of its peculiar historical development, the U.S. is not just a capitalist state, but with South Africa, is a *racist/capitalist state*. The immediate task before the Black movement in this country is to chart a realistic program to abolish racist/capitalist underdevelopment. We must analyze the historical foundations of underdevelopment, and articulate a theory of social transformation which will overturn capitalism, patriarchy and white supremacy.

II

Developing a vision of an alternative, noncapitalist development for U.S. Blacks begins with a detailed critique of the American past. Throughout the first half of the twentieth century the most outstanding proponent of democracy, socialism and Black equality was W.E.B. DuBois. Contrary to the judgment of some of his biographers, DuBois' views on these issues remained remarkably consistent, despite tactical detours and modifications in his outlook caused by the Great Depression. Examining U.S. economic and political life, DuBois arrived at five theoretical positions which governed his practice and posture toward the entire panorama of public policy issues between World War I and the 1960s. His insights comprise the basic orientation of this work.

"The first and fundamental and inescapable problem of American democracy," DuBois wrote in 1921, "is Justice to the American Negro."[12] The knotty dilemma of racism was not simply a question of America's failure in race relations. Racism was at the core of every issue relating to power, economic production, culture and society. Thirty years later, writing in the *National Guardian*, DuBois argued that the twin pillars of white capitalist oligarchy were domestic racism and colonialism. Until international and domestic racism were smashed, no serious discussion of democracy could even occur in the United States.[13] For DuBois, the centrality of racism was not just a burden for nonwhites, but had to be openly and unconditionally recognized by white progressives. It was only through the development of an antiracist politics that the real material needs of all oppressed people could be addressed. The fight for Black liberation is the "realization of democracy for all . . . "[14]

Second, DuBois concluded early in his career that *no real democracy has ever existed in the United States*. The most obvious and racist manifestation of the lack of popular democracy was the segregation codes which prohibited most Blacks from participating in the electoral process from the late 1890s until the 1960s. Periodically throughout the disenfranchisement period, DuBois documented the undemocratic character of voting patterns and electoral processes in the South. Analyzing the election of 1920 in the *Crisis*, for example, he illustrated the low level of voter participation and the denial of Black voting rights.[15]

In 1948 DuBois declared that the great problem of American democracy was that "it had not yet been tried." Neither Blacks nor whites had been freed to exercise democratic principles of governance because of the powerful controls of white capitalist America's upper classes.[16] Thus any condemnation by the U.S. government of socialist and Third World countries behavior at the ballot box was the supreme hypocrisy. When South Carolina racist James F. Byrnes condemned Eastern European nations for suppressing democracy, DuBois countered correctly that Byrnes "does not understand the term."[17] Democracy is not simply "majority rule," but effective state power in the hands of the masses.[18]

The true test of democracy, DuBois argued, was always found in an examination of a nation's criminal justice and penal systems. For decades, DuBois used his newspaper columns and articles to challenge the white racist notions of Black crime and punishment. In the pages of the *Crisis* in March, 1922, he documented the tragedy of a nineteen-year-old Black man who was convicted of murder in New York City. DuBois argued convincingly that capitalist society, not the young man, was to blame for the murder, since he was the victim of ghetto education, "racist violence" and "police brutality."[19] In "The Case of Samuel Moore," written in April, 1922, he outlined the plight of a Black prisoner who had spent 37 of his 48 years behind bars.[20] In 1931 he criticized the complacency of the Negro petty bourgeoisie toward Blacks who were imprisoned, arguing that "the truth is . . . (that) we know perfectly well how often that (poor blacks) are the victims of police discrimination and judicial unfairness and that their poverty and ignorance make them the scapegoats of our present criminal law."[21] DuBois was perhaps the first American sociologist or political activist to predict the massive prison uprisings of the 1970s and 1980s. In September, 1929, he suggested, "After a time the revolt of tens of thousands of convicts all over the country may bring the attention of the philanthropists to the slavery, degradation and exquisite cruelty of the thing we call punishment for crime."[22]

The question of the U.S. claim to real democracy must be approached in the light of our history. Colonial historians have noted that the system of U.S. slavery was established to provide "freedom" and the possibility of democratic government for the white, land-owning freemen of the seventeenth and eighteenth centuries. The enslavement process was an essential guarantee to land-hungry European immigrants that their rights were protected by the state. Prior to the Civil War, white Midwest farmers opposed slavery mainly because they viewed the Kansas-Nebraska Act of 1854 as a threat to their internal freedoms and political democracy. The expansion of "the peculiar institution," as slavery was called, into the

Great Plains and upper Midwestern states would have introduced large numbers of Afro-Americans into the region and simultaneously overturned their "free" economic and political institutions. The great white American democrats, Jefferson and Jackson, owned hundreds of slaves, while political conservatives like Alexander Hamilton agitated against the expansion of slavery. During the Progressive era, Woodrow Wilson's "New Freedom" expanded racial segregation to all levels of the Federal government. Simultaneously, many of the most antidemocratic and aristocratic elements of Southern politics were the most reliable allies of Black leaders. Southern Bourbon Democrats, the commercial class, and landed gentry that dominated politics after 1877 were among the staunchest defenders of limited Black democratic rights in the face of hostile opposition from the white rural masses. As early as 1889, Julius Dreher, the president of Roanoke College in Virginia, wrote that racial tolerance and Black suffrage were essential to Southern political democracy. "If we treat (the Negro) with anything like the fairness, justice and consideration we claim for ourselves as men, we shall hear less of race antagonism in the future." Benjamin F. Riley, a Baptist minister and superintendent of the Texas Anti-Saloon League, believed that middle class Black leaders and educators were morally and culturally superior to rural white farmers and sharecroppers. "The Negro," he wrote in 1910, "has made himself an exception among the people of the earth in the rapidity of his advancement." White conservatives endorsed Black educator Booker T. Washington and state support for Black industrial and normal schools, and opposed the complete disfranchisement of all Blacks. Despite the biracial politics of populism in the 1890s and integrated unionism in isolated Southern cities, the white working class did not usually accept even minimal rights for Black people.[23]

White opponents of the Civil Rights Movement in the 1950s almost always relied upon the concept of democratic rights for the white majority. The overtly racist faction within the Democratic Party cultivated close ties with rural farmers, laborers and working class whites. But political conservatives, which included the industrialists and the banking and business establishment, usually denounced the extremist tactics of the White Citizens Councils. Most of the upper-class religious institutions, such as the Southern Presbyterians and Methodists, tended not to be the most avid supporters of the Wallaces and Thurmonds. The white working class, in general, viewed integration not within the American democratic tradition, but as an aberration of democracy imposed by liberal elites. The opposition from white workers had an impact upon the direction of the Black movement. From its beginnings until today, the movement has been overwhelmingly petty bourgeois in its leadership and dominant ideology. It has been in essence a united front, representing various factions within the Black community, all oriented toward the goal of greater democracy. In his autobiography, DuBois explained the dominant consciousness of the movement as well as his own early theoretical shortcomings:

> I was born in a world which was not simply fundamentally capitalistic, but had no conception of any system except one in which capital was privately owned. What I wanted was the same economic opportunities that white Americans had. Although a student of social progress, I did not know the labor development in the United States. I was bitter at lynching, but not moved by the treatment of white miners in Colorado or Montana. I never sang the songs of Joe Hill, and the terrible strike at Lawrence, Massachusetts, did not stir me, because I knew that factory strikers like these would not let a Negro work beside them or live in the same town.[24]

The left tendency within the movement, from A. Phillip Randolph's National Negro Congress in the 1930s to Student Nonviolent Coordinating Committee (SNCC) and radical elements within Congress of Racial Equality (CORE) in the 1960s, developed a critical perspective on society which recognized the ultimate necessity of socialism. But the dominant coalitions within the movement were simply committed to the pursuit of bourgeois democracy and increased opportunities within the capitalist system. Seldom if ever did the rank and file or leadership pose questions that transcended a limited series of political reforms which could be confined easily to a "capitalist solution to the racial crisis."

If an authentic biracial American democracy does not exist, how was it to be constructed? DuBois' thinking on this third question constitutes a series of social, cultural, political and economic prerequisites. First, democracy must of course be antiracist. It should also be committed to an antisexist society which knows no discrimination based on gender; patriarchy as a system of male authority and sexual exploitation has no place in the "new democracy."[25] Democracy should be committed to the permanent eradication of poverty and unemployment[26] A state apparatus must guarantee the right of every minority to express "unpopular opinions," and must insure civil liberties for all.[27] Educationally, the democratic state must commit itself to programs which "break down social distinctions" within the general population. Social engineering of this kind would involve increased support for national minorities' cultural, educational and social institutions.[28] Economically, democratic rule would be extended into the process of production. For DuBois, writing in 1943, this meant, "the workers in control of industry," and the abolition of ownership of the central means of production from the white ruling class.[29] DuBois had acquired such contempt for the existing political institutions that he eventually concluded that a new state apparatus needed to be constructed. In 1943 he suggested that local assemblies should be created across the nation with "actual popular participation;" these assemblies could evolve as the nucleus of the new democratic state.[30] The central popular forces needed to accomplish this ambitious agenda would emerge from a "great alliance between the darker people the world over, between (white) disadvantaged groups . . . and between the working classes everywhere." This united front of the exploited would "keep down privileges" and transform human society.[31]

DuBois was attracted to socialism early in his intellectual life, but unlike many radicals at the turn of the twentieth century, he never succumbed to a mechanistic or economic deterministic view of society. He believed that capitalism and racism were inextricably tied together, and that the Great Depression was a major but not the last of capitalism's periodic crises. He concluded that neither corporate leaders nor white racists would be able to resolve the myriad problems inherent within their economic and social systems. But he also insisted that the triumph of socialism, and the eventual destruction of white racism, were not determined or fixed by material conditions. At the outset of World War II, for example, DuBois warned his readers that "we have no right to assume that the collapse of Europe will automatically free Asia and Africa."[32] An antiracist, socialist democracy had to be fought for by progressives. Colonialism and underdevelopment would collapse only when the oppressed constructed a majoritarian political offensive against the forces of racism and capitalism. DuBois' fourth observation, then, was that socialism had to become that central vision for the Black liberation movement.

Socialism today must be placed openly and honestly on the public agenda by all American progressives. Without hesitation, we must explain that a basic social transformation within America's social and economic structures would involve radical changes that would be viewed as clearly undemocratic by millions of people. The state would assume the ownership of major corporations, and their direction would be left in the hands of those best qualified to make decisions at the point of production, the working class. Socialism would mean the expropriation of wealth from the capitalist class, and the guarantee of employment, decent housing, education and health care to all citizens. It would restrict the "democratic" rights of those who discriminate against Afro-Americans, Chicanos, women, and gays—rights that white Americans are reaffirming in recent referenda. Socialism would mean the expansion of social services for those in need. Elements of democratic political traditions in America's recent past, from Populism to LaFollette's Progressivism, might contain examples for public education on socialism. But socialism cannot be achieved simply through coalitions of "democratic movements" or united fronts with progressives of various competing interests. Our primary task as American socialists is to make the case for equality within society—a principle that cannot be achieved without the total reconstruction of American civil society. We should assume what Antonio Gramsci often called the "long view" of socialist transformation. Democratic socialism can and must become the "common sense" of the working class, the brown and Black populations, and critical elements of the petty bourgeoisie. Through our efforts to compete with bourgeois ideologists in existing cultural and intellectual institutions and simultaneously in coalition with liberal petty bourgeois social forces, socialists will have the opportunity to establish their "legitimacy" to govern in both civil and political societies. Throughout this long historical process, coalitions must occur within the Democratic Party, and with reformist progressive groups like NOW, the NAACP and the National Association of Neighborhoods. But unless we place the necessity of socialism as the solution in the struggle for human equality, the battle for socialism will again be lost for another generation. An "invisible socialist movement" of the kind once characterized by Michael Harrington is actually no movement at all.

The possible common ground between the Black movement—in both its integrationist and Black nationalist tendencies—and predominantly white progressive movements, is the principle of equality. By equality I do not mean "equal opportunity" as defined by the Urban League and the Federal bureaucracy, as a means toward integrating minorities and women into the hierarchies of the state and civil society. Equality implies a theory of justice which assumes that all parties within the state should have free access to the state apparatus, can reform existing economic and social institutions, and can enact laws that promote a more humane society. A society committed to equality would require a political system that would promote affirmative action and racial quotas as a means toward a more equitable socioeconomic status for Blacks and women. As Julius K. Nyerere observes, "the basis of socialism is a belief in the oneness of man and the common historical destiny of mankind. Its basis, in other words, is human equality." Despite Tanzania's ongoing political problems and Nyerere's other contradictions, his observation is central to our own situation. "Without an acceptance of human equality there can be no socialism." Similarly, as we establish a dialogue with various sectors of society around the principle of equality, we will be able to provide the foundation essential for transforming capitalism, the economic system that rests upon inequality. [33]

From the perspective of Black history and experience, the practice of bourgeois democracy in America has consistently worked in favor of special propertied interests and against the promise of equality. In *The Education of Black People*, DuBois complained that democracy viewed as a commitment to human equality and emancipation has never existed for Black people or other minorities. "In theory we know" [the real meaning of democracy] "by heart: all men are created equal and should have equal voice in their own government," he wrote in 1938. Democracy should mean "the opening of opportunity to the disinherited to contribute to civilization and the happiness of men." DuBois believed that the quest for equality was central to all related struggles in abolishing *de jure* and *de facto* segregation and obtaining political suffrage. "Given a chance for the majority of mankind to be educated, healthy and free to act," he noted, "it may well turn out that human equality is not so wild a dream as many seem to hope." [34]

DuBois' fifth point was more of a prediction than an assessment of contemporary socioeconomic problems. DuBois recognized that the actual practice of socialism in other countries, especially in the Soviet Union, left much to be desired. Even after reading Soviet party leader Khrushchev's revelations of Stalin's crimes against his people, however, DuBois still could write in 1957 that the Soviet Union was closer to his ideal of democracy than his native land had ever been.[35] During the Cold War, and perhaps even during World War II, DuBois concluded that the road toward democracy and an antiracist society must also lead toward socialism. One could not struggle decisively against racism and remain a proponent of capitalism. From this perspective, DuBois recognized that America would eventually and inevitably come to a basic decision—either it would move toward worker self-management, antiracism and a new democratic state apparatus, or it would lapse into authoritarianism, racial barbarism and militarization of the work force. Speaking in 1951, DuBois declared, "Either in some way or to some degree, we must socialize our economy, restore the New Deal and inaugurate the welfare state, or we descend into military fascism which will kill all dreams of democracy, or the abolition of poverty and ignorance, or of peace instead of war."[36]

III

DuBois' theoretical conclusions, taken from a rich lifetime of research and struggle, form the basic point of view for *How Capitalism Underdeveloped Black America*. The study of Black social stratification and political economy departs from an appreciation of the contours of Black history. Yet where we stand in the past largely determines our understanding of what a people have been, and what they intend to become. Beneath history, and all social science research, exists explicitly or implicitly a philosophy or world view that tends to explain or to justify phenomena. All history conceals an *a priori* superstructure which promotes the interests of certain social classes at the expense of others. Thus intellectual work becomes a kind of cultural propaganda that serves the ideals or aims of certain racial and class groups within particular historical epochs. The absence of a clearly articulated ideology, so often the hallmark of objectivists in the liberal academic tradition, neither minimizes nor obscures the political function of all intellectual work. Intellectuals are the vanguard or ideological proponents of both well-entrenched and nascent social orders. It is their task to explain what has been, to justify or to overturn what now exists, and to chart what must become tomorrow.

All social transformations begin with a criticism of existing social forces, the material and ideological components which comprise social reality. The liberation of historically oppressed and underdeveloped peoples takes as its point of departure a revolutionary critique of the integral social classes which constitute that national minority or nation. For Black America, that means an assessment of the evolution of the Black petty bourgeoisie, the Black entrepreneurs, a general overview of the impact of capitalist development upon Black educational and social institutions, and the relations between Black women and men under the system of exploitation. Criticism leading to political praxis must include evaluations of the ambiguous legacy of the Black church within Black society and the pattern of police brutality, lynchings, convict labor and imprisonment of Black workers by the state and racist elements within white civil society. Finally, this criticism must address the questions of ultimate power within a biracial "democracy," and what forces now exist that will become part of the new hegemony within a nonracist, nonsexist socialist society in America. This book will hopefully establish a necessary discourse among activists and intellectuals alike, who are now and will in the future determine the course of that struggle to transform the United States.

SECTION ONE

THE BLACK MAJORITY: THE DOMESTIC PERIPHERY.

CHAPTER ONE

THE CRISIS OF THE BLACK WORKING CLASS.

So long as white labor must compete with black labor, it must approximate black labor conditions—long hours, small wages, child labor, labor of women, and even peonage. Moreover it can raise itself above black labor only by a legalized caste system which will cut off competition and this is what the South is straining every nerve to create . . . It is only a question of time when white working men and black working men will see their common cause against the aggressions of exploiting capitalists.

W.E.B. DuBois, "The Economic Revolution in the South", in B.T. Washington and DuBois, *The Negro in The South* (London: Moring, 1907), pp. 114–115, 117.

Unless organized labor transforms itself into a social movement with broad goals and a new concept of union membership that goes beyond dues-payers in a collective bargaining unit, it will continue its current decline. And if it is transformed, the character of a new dynamic labor movement will be expressed most significantly in its active and special concern for the problems of racial minorities and women at the work place and in the community.

Hebert Hill, "The AFL-CIO and The Black Worker," *Journal of Intergroup Relations*, Vol. 10 (Spring, 1982), pp. 5–78.

I

The central character and participant of Black U.S. history is the Afro-American. This is not a particularly surprising statement: the central focus of Irish history is the Irish people; Japanese history examines the people of Japan, and so forth. Yet there is a hidden problematic here for the political economist. The presumption here is that the *people* share a common social history, a collective experience, and perhaps even a collective consciousness. This is the first assumption that must be challenged.

Black people in the U.S. are the direct product of massive economic and social forces which, at a certain historical juncture, forced the creation of the early capitalist overseas production of staples (rice, sugar, cotton) for consumption by the Western core. The motor of modern capitalist world accumulation was driven by the labor power of Afro-American slaves. In the proverbial bowels of the capitalist leviathan, the slaves forged a new world culture that was in its origin African, but in its creative forms, something entirely new. The Afro-American agricultural worker was one of the world's first proletarians, in the construction of his/her culture, social structures, labor and world view. But from the first generation of this new national minority group in America, there was a clear division in that world view. The *Black majority* were those Afro-Americans who experienced and hated the lash; who labored in the cane fields of the Carolina coast; who detested the daily exploitation of their parents, spouses and children; who dreamed or plotted their flight to freedom, their passage across "the River Jordan;" who understood that their masters' political system of bourgeois democracy was a lie; who endeavored to struggle for land and education, once the chains of chattel slavery were smashed; who took pride in their African heritage, their Black skin, their uniquely rhythmic language and culture, their special love of God. There was, simultaneously, a *Black elite*, that was also a product of that disruptive social and material process. The elite was a privileged social stratum, who were often distinguished by color and caste; who praised the master publicly if not privately; who fashioned its religious rituals, educational norms, and social structures on those of the West; who sought to accumulate petty amounts of capital at the expense of their Black sisters and brothers; whose dream of freedom was one of acceptance into the inner sanctum of white economic and political power.

Both the Black majority and the Black elite were often divided by language, politics, economic interests, education and religion. That both groups were racially Black escaped no one's attention, least of all the white authorities. Yet both had created two divergent and often contradictory levels of consciousness, which represented two very different kinds of uneven historical experiences.

Malcolm X, the greatest Black revolutionary of the 1960s, recognized the essential conflict in the history and class consciousness of Afro-America. Speaking before civil rights activists in Selma, Alabama, only three weeks before his assassination, Malcolm characterized this pivotal contradiction as the division between the house and field Negroes:

> The house Negro always looked out for his master. When the field Negroes got too much out of line, he held them back in check. He put them back on the plantation. The house Negro lived better than the field Negro. He ate better, he dressed better, and he lived in a better house. He ate the same food as his master and wore his same clothes. And he could talk just like his master—good diction. And he loved his master more than his master loved himself. If the master got hurt, he'd say: "What's the matter, boss, we sick?" When the master's house caught afire, he'd try and put out the fire. He didn't want his master's house burnt. He never wanted his master's property threatened. And he was more defensive of it than his master was. That was the house Negro.
>
> But then you had some field Negroes, who lived in huts, had nothing to lose. They wore the worst kind of clothes. They ate the worst food. And they caught hell. They felt the sting of the lash. They hated this land. If the master got sick, they'd pray that the master'd die. If the master's house caught afire, they'd pray for a strong wind to come along. This was the difference between the two. And today you still have house Negroes and field Negroes.[1]

Historians might disagree with Malcolm's portrait of the plantation, pointing out that most slaves worked on farms with fewer than twenty Blacks. There were relatively few large plantations in the United States that were comparable to those of pre-revolutionary San Domingue, Bahia or Pernambuco, and the actual social and material conditions which usually separated Black house servants from field hands in the U.S. experience were insignificant. Yet the strength of Malcolm's commentary is essentially ideological and political. The embryonic Black elite was the product of the enslavement process, those New World Africans who culturally assimilated the world view of their exploiters. Resistance tended to come from those who had suffered the most, physically and mentally, at the hands of the masters. Some slaves docilely accepted their plight; others did not.

The Black majority was confronted with two decisive political options which, as we shall explore later, form the crucial axis of Black history: *resistance and accommodation.* Slavery and colonialism created the material conditions which forced an oppressed people to leave the surroundings of their previous history. That is, the external constraints demanded by coerced labor and a rigid caste/social hierarchy redirect the forces of a people's history. The slave could not live for him/herself at any particular moment during the productive process; the slave was viewed by the master as a cog in the accumulation of capital. Many slaves responded to the daily exploitation of the work place by resisting—running away, destroying machinery, burning crops, killing the master and his family. Others protested in more subtle ways, such as work slowdowns. But all faced the inevitable wall of reality from which there was no real escape. Rape, murder and the terrorization of their communities would continue as a logical and necessary part of capitalist society. One could stand against the weight of the exploiter's history, and suffer the inevitable concequences. Many chose to die this way. But the path of resistance contained no guarantees that one's lover, spouse, parents or children would escape brutal retribution for one's act of glorious defiance. One could make one's own history, but no single act of protest would overturn the powerful machinery of the racist/capitalist state, unless that action took a collective form involving others. Institutional safeguards usually blocked this option of mass-based resistance.

For the Black majority after slavery, the long night has continued. Historians traditionally concentrate on the lives of "exceptional" men and women whose political actions were different from those of the masses in certain respects. This is a mistake. The fabric of Afro-American life has been woven from the contradictory strands of faith and doubt, courage and fear, resistance and acquiescence. The collective Black life and labor in America has taken place in the context of penal-type conditions and restraints. The very nature of struggle under these totalitarian conditions is underscored by a series of seemingly futile protests, failures and disasters—all of which culminate in an inevitable success in which the central characters never witness. A prisoner from another political environment, Antonio Gramsci, describes this long process in brutal detail:

> All (want) to be the ploughmen of history, to play the active parts. . . Nobody wished to be the 'manure' of history. But is it possible to plough without first manuring the land? So ploughmen and 'manure' are both necessary. In the abstract, they all admitted it. But in practice? Manure for manure, as well draw back, return to the shadows, into obscurity. . . There is not even the choice between living a day as a lion, or a hundred years as a sheep. You don't live as a lion even for a minute, far from it: you live like something far lower than a sheep for years and years and know that you have to live like that. (Imagine) Prometheus who, instead of being attacked by the eagle, is devoured by parasites.[2]

The oppressed recognize, implicitly perhaps, the weight of oppression, the terrible contradictions imprinted by centuries of slavery, agricultural and industrial labor. After emancipation, the Black majority struggled to attain critical self-consciousness, a return to their own history-for-themselves. W. E. B. DuBois wrote of the postbellum Negro:

> He began to have a dim feeling that, to attain his place in the world, he must be himself, and not another. For the first time he sought to analyze the burden he bore upon his back, that deadweight of social degradation partially masked behind a half-named Negro problem. He felt his poverty: without a cent, without a home, without land, tools or savings, he had entered into competition with rich, landed, skilled neighbors. To be a poor man is hard, but to be a poor race in a land of dollars is the very bottom of hardships. He felt the weight of his ignorance,—not simply of letters, but of life, of business, of the humanities; the accumulated sloth and shrinking and awkwardness of decades and centuries shackled his hands and feet.[3]

Each member of the Black majority is a prisoner, and shares the marks of oppression upon his/her shoulders. Each Black worker is a representative of the collective patterns of exploitation, the series of murders, the lynchings, the mutilations. Each has been touched by starvation and unemployment. Each has experienced through his/her own life or through the lives of others, destitution, illiteracy, prostitution, disease and death at an early age. Acceptance of bourgeois illusions provides no temporal salvation; the crushing blows of the workplace, the police and the racists form a chorus which proclaims to the Black majority: *you are not human beings.* The ringing of the racist chorus resounds in the oppressed's ears from cradle to grave. That shrill ringing is the cold aesthetic expression of white capitalist America.[4]

So the basic social impulse of Afro-American workers is more than the search to find meaning within the tedious, often boring labor they are forced to perform to survive. It is a struggle, in part, for retaining collective self-respect in the face of degradation. It is the effort to create the material possibility of a better and more affluent life for future generations. "People are not fighting for ideas, for things in anyone's head," Amilcar Cabral observed. "They are fighting to win material benefits, to live better and in peace, to see their lives go forward, to guarantee the future of their children."[5] Without these daily sacrifices and battles, no terrain for successful resistance would be created. Even the compromises and accommodations made by Black workers' organizations during moments in history help to prepare future Black revolutionaries by illustrating tactics which cannot circumscribe the power of capital. Sometimes the courage it takes to survive is infinitely greater than the suicidal impulse to fight when the odds are not in one's favor. As Sartre reminds us, "life begins on the other side of despair."

This section examines the evolution of the Black majority since slavery, concentrating on four key groups: the Black working class; the Black reserve army of labor, or the permanently unemployed and poor people; Black women; and Black prisoners. Each has a special role in the making of Black civil and political societies. The only period when Black employment approached 100 percent was during slavery; since the end of World War II, the numbers of Black unemployed have soared. Poor Blacks are the most brutally victimized and exploited sector of the Black majority. If the projected labor force figures for the next two decades become reality, the Black reserve army or "ghettoclass" will soon comprise the majority population within the Black masses. Black women are not a class, but their history cannot be explored properly in the same context with that of Black males. Capitalist patriarchy, combined with racism, shackles the majority of Black women more firmly to the process of exploitation than any group of Black men. Black prisoners, the necessary human sacrifices to the capitalist criminal justice system, are also cogs in the productive process. Without criminal records, how else could the masses of poor Blacks be segregated in the modern labor force? Lynchings and their contemporary equivalent, capital punishment, are a prime means to discipline the entire Black labor force and the unemployed. Police brutality in the late twentieth century has simply perpetuated the coercion of the "patrol roaders" and white vigilantes of the mid-nineteenth century. Black urban workers comprise the first group under consideration, because of their still decisive position within the political economy of capitalism. Each of these group's overlapping historical experiences, its failures and contradictions as well as its militant moments of organized social protest, form the life and spirit of the Black majority. Their collective history and struggles constitute the necessary basis for revolutionary change, not simply for Blacks, but for the entire society. They represent the domestic nonwhite periphery in the core of capitalist accumulation, in the protracted process of social transformation.

II

Over fifteen years has now passed since the major upheavals of Black workers, youth and students which was termed the Black Power and Civil Rights Movements. Black political militancy spread from streets and lunch-counters to factory shops and production lines across the country. Black unrest at the point of production created new and dynamic organizations: the League of Revolutionary Black Workers in Detroit; the Black Panther Caucus at the Fremont, California General Motors plant; and the United Black Brotherhood in Mahwah, New Jersey. In the Deep South, civil rights activists from the Southern Christian Leadership Council helped to organize sanitation workers' strikes in St. Petersburg, Florida, Atlanta, Georgia, and Memphis, Tennessee. Ralph D. Abernathy, Hosea Williams, Coretta Scott King and A. Philip Randolph supported the vigorous unionization efforts of the American Federation of State, County and Municipal Employees (AFSCME) in the Deep South. Abernathy, Williams and Andrew Young were arrested in Sepember, 1968, for nonviolently blocking the path of garbage trucks in Atlanta. On June 21, 1969, Abernathy and Williams were arrested in Charleston, South Carolina, for supporting AFSCME's Local 1199 attempts to unionize hospital employees. By September, 1972, hundreds of Black trade unionists, led by AFSCME Secretary-Treasurer William Lucy and Cleveland Robinson, president of the Distributive Workers of America, created the Coalition of Black Trade Unionists in Chicago. By its second annual convention, held in Washington, D.C., May 25-27, 1973, 1,141 Black delegates representing 33 unions were in attendance; 35-40 percent were Black women.[6]

It cannot be overemphasized that the Civil Rights and Black Power Movements were fundamentally working class and poor people's movements. From the very beginning, progressive unions were involved in the desegregation campaigns. The United Auto Workers, United Packinghouse Workers, District 65, Local 1199 in New York City, and the Brotherhood of Sleeping Car Porters all contributed funds to Martin Luther King Jr.'s Montgomery County bus boycott of 1955-56. And in rural areas of the Black Belt, small independent Black farmers risked their families' safety by opening their homes to freedom riders and Student Nonviolent Coordinating Committee (SNCC) workers. Black farm workers, sharecroppers, service workers and semi-skilled operatives were the great majority of those dedicated foot soldiers who challenged white hegemony at Selma's Pettus Bridge and in the streets of Birmingham.[7] SNCC understood well the importance of Black working class support for the Civil Rights Movement and thus recognized the need to develop an employment strategy for Blacks.

Labor unions also understood the connection. In November, 1963, a number of labor unions financed a conference at Howard University that brought democratic socialists, trade union organizers and radical civil rights activists together.[8] Civil rights workers, Black and white, recognized by late 1964 that demands simply for desegregating the South's civil society lacked economic direction. In 1965 Jessie Morris, SNCC's field secretary in Mississippi, helped to establish the Poor People's Corporation. Serving as its executive secretary, Morris funnelled financial aid for various labor projects initiated by poor Black workers. That same year, the Mississippi Freedom Labor Union

(MFLU) was created by two Council of Federated Organizations staff members. Historian Clay Carson relates that "within a few months, the MFLU attracted over a thousand members in several counties through its demands for a $1.25 an hour minimum wage, free medical care, social security, accident insurance, and equality for blacks in wages, employment opportunities, and working conditions." MFLU relied upon the fund-raising resources of SNCC and "by that fall had developed its own sources of financial support."[9] As "We Shall Overcome" gave ground to "Black Power" in the mid-1960s, a wave of nationalist activism seized the new generation of Black urban workers and students. Militant Black construction unions were formed, such as the Trade Union Local 124 in Detroit, and United Community Construction Workers of Boston. Black steelworkers at Sparrows Point, Maryland, formed the Shipyard Workers for Job Equality, pressuring Bethlehem Steel to halt its policies of hiring and promotion discrimination against Blacks. In most of the protest actions, there was the recognition that racism in the plants also undercut the "economic status of white workers. For example, when the United Black Brothers struck at Mahwah's auto plant in April, 1969, they urged white workers to "stay out and support us in this fight."[10]

By the 1980s much of the political terrain had shifted to the right. White blue collar workers voted strongly for Ronald Reagan in 1980. The League of Revolutionary Black Workers, The Black Panther Labor Caucuses and other revolutionary nationalist organizations within the Black working class no longer existed. The late A. Philip Randolph had campaigned for the election of a white racist, neoconservative, Daniel Patrick Moynihan, to the U.S. Senate in 1976. Andrew Young, running for mayor in Atlanta in 1981, advised patience to the Black community's demands in ending the murders of its children. Abernathy and Williams supported Reagan's candidacy. An entire class of Black farmers, sharecroppers and rural laborers almost completely disappeared, eliminating part of the social foundation for the civil rights struggles in the Deep South a generation ago. As an activist in the Amalgamated Clothing Workers Union, Coleman Young led the creation of the fiercely independent National Negro Labor Council in the 1950s; years later, as mayor of Detroit, he forged a conservative political alliance with corporate capital at the expense of Black and poor constituents.

Mahwah's huge automobile plant, the site of Black labor militancy, has been shut down permanently, along with hundreds of other industrial plants in the Northeast and Midwest.

In a recent essay, labor historian Philip S. Foner outlines the dimensions of the organic crisis confronting Black workers. Despite considerable gains, Black workers in the early 1970s were largely concentrated in the lowest paid, semi-skilled and unskilled sectors of the workforce. Those Blacks in skilled trade union positions usually had low levels of seniority. According to Foner, the recession of 1973—1975, combined with the political drift to the right in national politics, greatly worsened the position of the Black working class in several ways. The exportation of capital and jobs, especially by multi-national corporations, reduced the number of available jobs. Capital-intensive industries, particularly auto and steel, sharply cut back the number of workers with low levels of seniority. Despite the creation of pressure groups like the Coalition of Black Trade Unionists, Foner notes, Blacks still have "an infinitesimal percentage" of top to middle-level representatives within the trade union bureaucracy. In 1977 the Supreme Court reinforced racism and sexism within unions by insist-ing that Blacks and women must prove that seniority systems were designed to "intentionally discriminate" against them. For these rea-sons the tenuous relationship between Black progressive groups and organized labor was increasingly antagonistic and bitter.[11]

The acceleration of Black unemployment and underemployment, the capitulation of many civil rights and Black Power leaders to the Right, the demise of militant Black working class institutions and labor caucuses, and the growing dependency of broad segments of the Black community upon public assistance programs and transfer payments of various kinds, are not mutually exclusive phenomena. These interde-pendent realities within the contemporary Black political economy are the beginnings of a new and profound crisis for Black labor in America. As Harold Baron once noted, the capitalist class historically has needed "black workers, yet the conditions of satisfying this need compel it to bring together the potential forces for the most effective opposition to its policies, and even for a threat to its very existence. Even if the capitalists were willing to forego their economic and status gains from racial oppression, they could not do so without shaking up all of the intricate concessions and consensual arrangements through which the State now exercises legitimate authority."[12] Despite the destruction of *de jure* segregation, the white capitalist class has not abandoned racism. Instead, it has transformed its political economy in such a way as to make the historic "demand for black labor" less essential than at any previous stage of its development. In the production of new goods and services, from semi-conductors to petroleum products, the necessity for lowly paid operatives, semi-skilled laborers and service workers becomes progressively less with advances in new technology. Simultaneously it has succeeded in developing a strong Black political current against Black participation in unions. Leading representatives of the Black petty bourgeoisie are in outspoken opposition to public sector union activities in metropolitan centers dominated by newly elected Black officials. These immediate political and economic problems, and the prospects for the Black working class beyond the 1980s, are the concern of this chapter.

III

The making of the Black industrial working class is a relatively recent historical phenomena, spanning only three generations. Throughout this period of Black proletarianization, advocates of Black economic equality and civil rights maintained an uneasy and ambiguous relationship with the labor movement. At most times, the overtly racist practices and policies of white labor leaders proved to be major obstacles to biracial labor unity. A brief historical sketch of the evolution of this uneasy relationship indicates the ideological and political tensions which comprise part of the contemporary crisis for Black labor in the U.S.

The longest and most durable labor Blacks have performed within the American experience was, of course, in the area of agriculture. From the American Revolution until the eve of World War I, about 90 percent of all Black people lived in the South. As late as 1940, 77 percent of all Blacks resided in the former slave states, while only 27 percent of all white Americans lived there. The majority of Black male workers ploughed and planted the fields, harvesting the annual yields of cotton or corn, usually for the benefit of an absent white landlord. In 1910, 57 percent of all Black men and 52 percent of all Black women workers were farmers. Eight percent of the men and 42 percent of the women were employed as domestics or personal servants. Only one sixth of the Black population worker in manufacturing or industries.

During the early decades of the twentieth century, the disparity in income between Blacks and whites was nothing but extraordinary. This was particularly the case in the burgeoning commercial districts of Southern and border states, industrial and urban centers where the rural Black immigrants first arrived in their trek north. In Atlanta during the winter months of 1935-36, the median income for Black husband-wife families was $632; the median for white husband-wife families in the city was $1,876, creating a Black-white income ratio of 34 percent. Income disparities below 25 percent were not uncommon. Black families headed by women in Atlanta earned median incomes in 1935-36 of $332. In Columbia, South Carolina, these families earned only $254 per year. [13]

The actual beginnings of the Black industrial working class are found with the massive migrations of Black humanity from the Deep South to the North after 1915. Most economists explain Black migrations after 1915 and again subsequently in 1940s as a result of the pull of wartime production in the factories of the North. However, the collapse of the cotton market and the epidemic of Black-owned bank failures in the autumn of 1914, combined with the curse of the boll weevil and the omnipresent fear of white lynch mobs, were also powerful factors pushing Blacks out of Dixie. The number of Black people who left the South rose from 454,000 from 1910-1920, 749,000 from 1920-1930, to 1,599,000 from 1940-1950. Most of these rural farmers and sharecroppers settled in the crowded yet bustling ghettoes like Cleveland's Hough district and Chicago's Southside. This was the first generation of Black workers who earned a living primarily from manufacturing, industrial and commercial labor. In 1940, 28 percent were service workers. Farm employment had dropped to 32 percent. Twenty years later, blue collar employment increased to 38 percent, and the number of operatives more than doubled. Thirty-two percent were service workers and only 8 percent of all Blacks employed worked on farms. [14] (See Table I)

Labor unions were slow in their efforts to help organize the new Black proletariat. Until the Civil Rights Movement, the percentage of Black workers within organized labor was always significantly lower than the percentage of Blacks within the general U.S. population. In 1902, about 30,000 Blacks were in the AFL, only 3 percent of its total membership. During the Great Depression, Black membership actually declined to 2 percent. As the Congress of Industrial Organizations (CIO) recruited members in basic industries—electrical, auto, steel, rubber—the number of Black trade unions increased dramatically. Black membership in trade unions exceeded 700,000 in 1945, 5 percent of all members. In the early 1950s A. Philip Randolph initiated the Negro-American Labor Council to force all-white craft unions to desegregate and to abolish racially segregated locals. With the rapid expansion of public sector employment, where the percentage of Black workers was particularly high, more Blacks became members of unions. By 1970 Black trade union membership totalled 2 million, one-tenth of all union members. Ironically, even this figure does not indicate a historic breakthrough in biracial labor cooperation. In the late 1880s and 1890s the Knights of Labor had practiced a policy of building an effective biracial organization, and claimed Black workers as almost 15 percent of its 600,000 membership. In the assessment of political economist Victor Perlo, the Knights of Labor "represented a high point of an approach in industrial unionism and of black-white labor unity." In short, organized labor had only begun to reach the level of numerical parity for Blacks within its own ranks, an equality that had existed for a brief moment a century before. [15]

Yet many instances of biracial cooperation within the labor movement occurred, even during the long night of Jim Crow. In September, 1920, between 12,000 to 15,000 bituminous coal miners, mostly Black, led an Alabama-wide walkout in demand for higher wages. The state militia was called to break the strike, and thousands of Black members of the United Mine Workers were beaten, arrested, or evicted from company houses. Coal company executives vowed to "fight for their property rights on high social, moral and legal grounds" and to crush the UMW, a union guilty "of associating the black man on terms of perfect equality with the white man."[16] During the Depression, the Communist Party succeeded in establishing the Sharecroppers Union. By 1934, the mostly Black union acquired six thousand members in the Carolinas, Alabama, Florida and Georgia.[17] CIO affiliates created in the South usually required integrated locals, and Blacks were encouraged to participate in local union decisions. A few Southern unions in the 1940s followed the example of the UMW, developing "a standard pattern of mixed locals in which the two races shared the offices."[18] In a totalitarian social environment that was implacably hostile to both racial desegregation and labor organizing, it was abundantly clear to most Blacks at that historical moment that trade unions, for all their faults, were a positive force in the struggle for civil rights and Black economic advancement.

But as more Blacks occupied positions in industrial production, working conditions seemed to become worse. On the job accident and death rates were particularly high for Black workers, who were relegated by unions and bosses alike to the most unsafe and lowest paid work. As the number of Blacks increased in Detroit's automobile plants, for example, demands for higher productivity levels were made by management. In 1946, 550,000 Detroit auto-workers produced three million automobiles; by 1970, 750,000 workers were making over eight million automobiles every year. White union leaders were generally unsympathetic to demands raised by Black union members to improve the desperate workplace situation.

Management declared that this rapid increase in productivity was achieved by technological advances, "management techniques," and automation. Black Detroit workers responded, in turn, that these brutal methods of industrial exploitation were not "automation but Niggermation."[19] After labor unions purged leftists from their ranks in the Cold War, they lost their "innovative dynamism and became narrowly wage-oriented," writes Harold Baron. Shop grievances were neglected, and "the black officials who arose as representatives of their race were converted into justifiers of the union administration to the black workers." Black labor leaders like Randolph and Bayard Rustin actually subordinated Black militancy "to maneuvers at the top level of the AFL-CIO."[20]

And as in their domestic policies, the labor aristocracy pursued foreign policies in nonwhite countries that were overtly racist. The AFL-CIO played a major role, for example, in the CIA-sponsored subversion of Guyana and the Peoples Progressive Party of Cheddi Jagan. In 1964 the AFL-CIO sent Gene Meakins, former vice president of the American Newspaper Guild, to coordinate propaganda for the anti-Jagan forces. Between 1958 to 1964 the American Federation of State, County and Municipal Employees (AFSCME), then under president Arnold Zandler, received $60,000 or more annually from the CIA—much of which was spent "in the campaign of rioting and sabotage against the Jagan government." When Jagan was finally defeated in 1966, George Meany authorized the American Institute for Free Labor Development to initiate a housing project with loans from U.S. union coffers.[21] Throughout the 1940s and 1950s, white labor leaders voiced opposition to the immediate independence of African nations. In a *Federationist* editorial published in July, 1952, for example, AFL leader William Green supported white minority rule in Northern and Southern Rhodesia and Nyasaland, declaring that only whites were "competent in government." The best that the "natives" could achieve was colonial patronage and "gradual development." In the 1960s the AFL-CIO helped to establish a school to train "moderate" African trade union leaders in Kampala, Uganda. Progressive African nations were attacked by Meany for their "totalitarian methods in labor relations."[22]

By the late 1960s many Black activists concluded that most white-dominated unions would continue indefinitely to be unsympathetic to Blacks' economic plight. In *Black Awakening In Capitalist America,* Black social theorist Robert Allen predicted that many unions in the future would become more hostile to Federal government-sponsored "training programs for the hard-core jobless." Unemployed minority workers were, in their view, the "economic enemies" of white workers:

> Labor leaders increasingly stress the need for protecting and preserving the existing jobs held by union members. The unemployed are seen as a great mass of potential strike breakers and scabs, ready on a moment's notice to take the union member's job and upset the wage scales for which the unions have so bitterly fought. That this narrow-minded policy is ultimately self-destructive has not occurred to most union leaders and their rank-and-file followers. The labor unions perceive the advance of automation and mechanization as a threat to their interests, but the union leaders, once militant fighters for social change, have no program other than a panicky defensive reaction for meeting this challenge. Pleas to labor leaders to organize the jobless go unheeded as the unions watch their power base erode; the prospect of their eventual impotence seems ever more certain.[23]

A consensus began to emerge among many Black middle-class leaders, many of whom were veterans of civil rights struggles, that unions were at best unreliable allies, and perhaps even structural impediments to Black socioeconomic advancement under capitalism. This growing hostility is particularly evident in the relationship between Black elected officials in municipal governments and the mostly white leaders of public service unions. Although many public sector workers are nonwhites in urban areas, Black mayors and city officials tend to rely on management techniques to limit wage demands. As Paul Johnston notes, "the union serves as a convenient political scapegoat for public officials caught between relatively declining tax revenues, spiraling demand for public services, and the taxpayers' rebellion. The union as villain takes the heat off management for its ineptitude, its criminal priorities, corporate profiteering, etc."[24] The classic example of the budding unity of Black politicians—chamber of commerce vs. Black public employees occurred in Atlanta in 1977. Atlanta's 900 Black sanitation workers, members of AFSCME, had campaigned aggressively to elect Maynard Jackson as that city's first Black mayor. Under Jackson's tenure in office, the sanitation workers averaged annual salaries of $7,500, and received no wage increases in three years. After negotiations failed, the Black public employees went out on strike. Jackson's immediate response—to fire the Black workers— won the praise of Atlanta's corporations, media and leaders of the Black petty bourgeoisie. AFSCME president Jerry Wurf, a social democrat with a history of support for civil rights causes, was condemned as a "racist manipulator" who sought the demise of Black political power in Atlanta. Reverend Martin Luther King, Sr., informed the media that Jackson should "fire the hell out of" the Black public employees.[25]

However, the most conservative Black expression of this anti- union view was published in 1980 by the Lincoln Institute for Research and Education, a Black think-tank in Washington, D.C. Two of the authors of the widely-circulated monograph, entitled *Black American and Organized Labor: A Fair Deal?* were Walter E. Williams, economics professor at George Mason University and a leading proponent of Black Reaganism, and Wendell Wilkie Gunn, assistant treasurer of Pepsi Corporation. The authors argue that capitalism is inherently demo- cratic and amiable to Black advancement. The primary source of racism in the workplace comes from labor unions. The monograph implies that Black equality cannot be achieved unless trade unions are abolished. Failing that, Black workers should resist joining unions wherever possible. "It is only by providing real freedom of choice to workers with regard to whether or not they wish to join a labor union," the Institute declared, "that black workers will be given an opportunity to advance."[26] Williams also has suggested that Blacks' interests would be better served in an alliance with Reagan Republicans and corporate interests. High Black unemployment rates are not the responsibility of business, in any event, since the Blacks' lack of educational preparation and low productivity are almost as much to blame as union racism.[27]

Although progressive labor historians would dissent from this interpretation, many leftists would agree that labor's long prejudice towards Blacks was the direct result of the fact that all white workers have benefited in absolute terms from racism. A "whites-only" labor strategy supposedly increases the wages and ultimately the bargaining power of white union members at the expense of superexploited Blacks. Paul L. Riedesel argued in 1979 that census data indicates "an overall pattern of white gain" in spite of great income dispersion within the white group. White racism is "endemic" to the AFL-CIO, and racially divisive policies and practices of the white labor aristocracy are designed consciously to promote the interests of all whites.[28] It is true that segregationist policies can benefit whites in some unions, particularly racial restrictions in certain crafts or highly technical skills sectors. Craft unions historically discriminated against all Blacks with the desired intent to increase their own bargaining power.[29] But even this does not prove that white workers as a group benefit in absolute, rather than in relative terms, from the perpetuation of racism. In a critique of Riedesel, Marxist economist Al Szymanski writes that where racism is dominant in labor relations, working class cohesiveness declines, creating a net loss in incomes for all whites, although less in real terms than to Black labor.[30] But even after the election of Ronald Reagan, and the successful Solidarity demonstration in Washington, D.C., involving the coordinated efforts of both Black and labor groups in September, 1981, the issue was not resolved—at least not within the Black community.[31]

The historic evolution of the Black working class in advanced capitalism, and the ambiguous relations between Blacks and organized labor, raise a series of difficult questions. Is there any real basis for Black-white working class unity within the trade union movement, and more generally, within American politics? Does unionization help or hinder Black economic advancement vis-a-vis whites? Are unions "structurally racist" in a racist/capitalist state, unable by their very existence to advance the material interests of Black laborers? To arrive at some conclusions, one must assess whether any real gains in Black income were derived in part from unionization.

IV

There is no question but that the large majority of the Black working class supports unions. Both in public opinion polls and in their support for "pro-labor" political candidates, most Blacks continue to express support for legislation favorable to union growth, despite organized labor's shoddy record on racial issues. The central reason for this is that the majority of Afro-American people—blue collar and service workers, public sector employees and clerical workers—understand that unionization has historically produced higher wages, both in absolute terms and in relative terms compared to white employees with similar educational backgrounds and skills. Unionization means improved working conditions, and a greater likelihood of upward income mobility. An analysis of the percentage of median earnings of Black male workers to the median earnings of all male workers for selected industries in 1969 illustrates this point. In industries with heavy union representation, the income disparity between Black and white males is relatively low: automobile industries, 84 percent; iron and steel, 83 percent; rubber products, 78 percent; primary nonferrous metals, 82 percent. In industrial sectors dominated by craft unions, or in industries that remain largely unorganized, the median income gap between Black and white males is more severe: yarn, thread and fabric mills, 75 percent; furniture and fixtures, 69 percent; printing and publishing, 68 percent; professional and photographic equipment, 67 percent. By comparison, the median income ratio of Black to white males for all workers in 1969 was 58 percent. Racism still exists within all unions, and most white union leaders tolerate if not encourage the systemic exclusion of their Black members from the highest paid and skilled positions. Nevertheless, it remains clear that "the relative wages of black workers to those of white workers are considerably better in industries where powerful industrial unions with a militant tradition embrace the majority of production workers, than in industries where craft unions, or weak industrial unions, or no unions at all prevail."[32]

Another way of viewing the impact of unionization as a factor in reducing the economic inequality of Blacks is evident in census data comparing the relative incomes of nonwhite full-time male workers both in and outside labor unions. The ratio of nonwhite males' to white males' median incomes for all occupations in 1970 was 83 percent in unions, and 62 percent outside unions. For blue collar male workers, the ratio is 90 percent in unions, 72 percent outside unions. For white collar employees, the ratio is 85 percent in labor unions, 70 percent outside unions. Only for service workers are the figures for nonunion members higher than those of union members, 77 percent to 73 percent. The ratio for nonwhite females' to white females' median incomes for all occupations in 1970 was 91 percent for union members, and 82 percent for nonunion employees.[33]

There is also a substantial body of research indicating the egalitarian or progressive effects of trade unionism on the dispersion of wages and fringe benefits. The option for personal wage differentials based on favoritism or white racism within specific job categories is greater in nonunion firms than in the unionized sectors of the economy. Harvard economist Richard B. Freeman argues that union wage policies which are designed to set standard rates across and within firms "significantly reduces wage dispersion among workers covered by union contracts and that unions further reduce wage dispersion by narrowing the white collar/blue collar differential within establishments." The dispersion of compensation "is also lower among establishments that are unionized than among those that are not."[34] Because unions are fundamentally political institutions which are "sensitive to the intensities of preference," unionism raises the fringe shares of all workers. Union workers are usually more knowledgeable about retirement policies in their companies than nonunion workers, and generally expect to "receive a pension higher than that expected by" nonunion employees.[35] Particularly in capital intensive industries, unions are able to achieve significantly higher wage increases for workers—so long as political unity exists between Blacks and whites within specific unions.

The divergent attitudes expressed by some Black petty bourgeois leaders as opposed to the great majority of Black workers towards unionization and biracial labor alliances can be explained in part by unemployment statistics. Blacks with college educations and professional degrees, who are employed in white collar work as professionals, technicians, managers and administrators, uniformly experience relatively low rates of unemployment. During the recession year of 1975, when the overall unemployment rate stood at 14.7 percent for Black men and 14.8 percent for Black women, only 7.4 percent of Black males employed as professional or technical workers were out of work. Black males and females employed as managers and administrators had unemployment rates in 1975 of 4.7 percent and 5.9 percent respectively. By contrast, white males and females working as managers and administrators experienced 1975 unemployment rates of 2.6 percent and 4.3 percent. The greater burden of joblessness always falls squarely on the shoulders of Black blue collar and service workers. The unemployment rates for Black male craft workers was 13.1 percent; Black male and female operatives, excluding transport equipment workers, 17.3 percent and 21.9 percent; Black male nonfarm laborers, 19.2 percent. The pattern of permanent Black working class unemployment persists. In 1977, the unemployment rates for Black male and female workers in wholesale and retail trade were 15.9 percent and 21.6 percent, while white males and females in this sector had unemployment rates of 6.1 percent and 8.6 percent, respectively. The immediate spectre of unemployment forces most Blacks in blue collar and service jobs, both within unions and outside of them, to view unionization as a step toward greater job security. Elements of the Black elite, reasonably comfortable in their own job positions, can afford the luxury of exigent condemnations of the future political utility of unions to the Black movement.[36]

The critical irony here is that neither the material interests of white workers nor those of labor unions as a whole are advanced by white racism. There are at least several ways to document this. Perhaps the simplest is the lower rate of unionization in the South in virtually every industry. The strength of racial segregation both within the civil society as a whole as well as within broad elements of the trade union movement in the region is commonly recognized by historians as the major reason for Southern labor's failure to organize.[37] Second, racism dilutes the bargaining power of unions for higher wages, fringe benefits and better working conditions. White workers who have greater seniority than many Blacks often accept contracts with decreasing benefits simply to maintain their own positions vis-a-vis Blacks within the labor market. In the long term, however, this racist strategy inhibits "union bargaining strength and militancy," according to economist Michael Reich, "thereby reducing the total income share of labor."[38] Again, the political economy of the South provides an example. By the 1970s 75 percent of all textile workers in the U.S.

worked in the Southern states. Only ten percent of this workforce of nearly 600,000 was unionized. The average hourly wage of Southern textile workers in the late 1970s was $3.46, near the bottom of the national wage scale for all industrial workers.[39]

Probably the greatest negative impact of racism upon the material interests of labor and more generally of all workers is in the area of public policy. The massive spending reductions of the Reagan Administration are "racist" in that they have a disproportionately higher affect on Blacks as a group than upon all whites. It is crucial to observe, however, that by far the largest population targeted for cutbacks is the lower income, white working class.

Three illustrations will suffice to document this claim—food stamps, public housing and Medicaid. The 1977 Food Stamp Act was originally designed to "permit low-income households to obtain a more nutritious diet." According to the Bureau of the Census research, about 5.9 million households in the U.S. received food stamps in 1979. The median annual income of these families was a meager $5,300. Seventy-Seven percent had total personal incomes below $10,000 a year. The average face value of food stamps received in 1979 was only $810 per household. Sixty -three percent of all household recipients of food stamps were white, 3.7 million families; 2.1 million, 35 percent, were Black; another 600,000 families were Latino, 10 percent.* One million householders were 65 years or older. Two-thirds of these households had children 18 years old and under.[40]

The first public housing act passed by Congress in 1937, was initiated "to remedy the unsafe and unsanitary housing conditions and the acute shortage of decent, safe, and sanitary dwellings for families of low income." Rents for public housing are set not to exceed 25 percent of net monthly incomes for families or individuals served. In 1979, about 3 percent of all U.S. households, 2.5 million families, lived in federally subsidized or public housing. The median annual income for these households was $4,980. Almost half of all families living in public or subsidized housing had incomes below the official poverty line. 1.5 million households, 59 percent, were white; 1.0 million households, 39 percent, were Black; 200,000 households, 8 percent, were Hispanic. Two-thirds of these households were maintained by women householders without husbands present; one-third had householders who were 65 years or older.[41]

---

*The percentages total to greater than 100% because Latinos are also included as subsets of both the white and Black percentages.

Medicaid was created by the Federal government in 1965 "to furnish Medical assistance on behalf of needy families with dependent children, and of aged, blind, or permanently and totally disabled individuals whose incomes and resources are insufficient to meet the costs of necessary medical services." 18.1 million individuals, 8.0 million households, were enrolled in the Medicaid program in 1979— that is, they had a Medicaid assistance card or had medical bills which were paid for by Medicaid. Of these, 68 percent were white; 30 percent were Black; 700,000 or 9 percent were Latino. 36 percent were 65 years or over; 61 percent of all householder recipients had not worked during the year.[42]

The chief beneficiaries of several decades of liberal and reformist Federal intervention programs have been individuals and families with annual incomes below $20,000 (1982 dollars); those without post-secondary education or technical skills, national minorities; blue collar and service workers; and the elderly. Mathematically these diverse groupings have the potential for becoming, in the new age of fiscal austerity, a left-of-center coalition that could be forced to articulate minimally a left social democratic public policy agenda, simply for their own survival. Yet the centrifugal forces of white racism, cultural conservatism and political reaction, embodied in the emergence of the New Right and the election of Reagan, now threaten the realization of such a majority.

The basic issue here is an old problem which can be traced to the very beginnings of U.S. history. White populists, labor leaders and leftists have long made the argument that racism actually reduces the absolute living standards of white workers, retards their unions, and undermines the institutional stability of their communities. Racial divisions within the working class accelerate the processes of exploitation in the workplace for Blacks and whites alike. Yet given clear political options, white workers have frequently sacrificed their own material and political interests to engage in the mass-mania of racist violence, terrorism and prejudice. White workers have organized lynchmobs, raped Black women, mutilated Black children, engaged in strikes to protest the employment of Black co-workers, voted for white supremacist candidates in overwhelming numbers (e.g., George Wallace in the Democratic Party's presidential primaries in 1972), and have created all-white unions. How and why does this process happen? We can gain some insights here from Georg Lukács. In *History and*

Class Consciousness, Lukács writes that "Marx repeatedly emphasized that the capitalist is nothing but a puppet. And when, for example, he compares his instinct to enrich himself with that of the miser, he stresses the fact that 'what in the miser is a mere idiosyncrasy, is, in the capitalist, the effect of the social mechanism, of which he is but one of the wheels.' "[43] In a racist/capitalist state and economy, the instinct among whites to exhibit racist behaviors and practices is not a psychological aberration. To be racist in a racist society is to be normal; to reject racism, denounce lynchings, and to fight for Black political and economic rights is to be in a symbolic sense "abnormal." Racism benefits the bourgeoisie absolutely and relatively; working class whites are usually part of the larger "social mechanism" of racist accumulation and Black underdevelopment, serving as uncritical cogs in the wheels of Black exploitation.

For many working class whites, the Afro-American is less a person and more a *symbolic index* between themselves and the abyss of absolute poverty. All whites at virtually every job level are the *relative* beneficiaries of racism in the labor force: Blacks, Puerto Ricans, Chicanos, etc., supply the basic "draftees" in the permanent and semi-permanent reserve army of labor. In the capitalist economy's periodic downturns, whites benefit relative to Blacks by not being Black. Moreover, lowly paid white workers, particularly in semi-skilled occupations, can "justify" their low wages, poor working conditions, and deteriorating standards of living with the racist view, "At least I am not living like the niggers." Another perspective on this process is provided by Jean-Paul Sartre. Anti-Semitism in the West, Sartre suggested, is "a poor man's snobbery. By treating the Jew as an inferior and pernicious being, I affirm at the same time that I belong to the elite."[44] The philosophical foundations of "redneck racism" are the same dynamic. For generations, many white American workers refused certain menial jobs on the principal that they refused to do "nigger work." Psychologically, the Black was not simply a cultural "symbol of Evil and Ugliness," as Frantz Fanon attests. "The Negro (also) represents the sexual instinct (in its raw state). The Negro is the incarnation of a genital potency beyond all moralities and prohibitions."[45] At a level of the collective unconscious, the Negro's demands for decent jobs, healthcare and voting rights could be opposed by the question, "Do you want your daughter/son to marry one?" In the workplace, labor union unity across the color line could be opposed as a contradictory coalition between white workers vs. beings who were somehow "less than human." The continued suppression of Blacks within the economy and across civil and political societies becomes the means through which many oppressed whites can derive cultural and psychological satisfaction without actually benefiting in an absolute material sense in super profits of racism.

The sad irony is that certain sectors of the white working class are *also* targeted for elimination and radical transformation. The identical processes which threaten the Black proletariat are confronting white autoworkers, steelworkers, rubberworkers, textileworkers, laborers and many millions more. Whether white workers as a self-conscious mass will *perceive* that their own "benefits" from racism are only relative to the oppressed conditions of Black labor, and that the social and psychological image of the Blacks-as-inferior beings actually promotes their own exploitation as well as that of Blacks, cannot be predetermined. A majoritatian bloc against the New Right and the interests of capital must at some initial point call for the protracted cultural and ideological transformation of the white working class.

V

The question of organized labor's relations with the Black movement acquired even greater significance with the recessions of 1980 and 1981-82. U.S. capitalism is in the midst of a major economic crisis. The serious character of the crisis has forced corporations to reevaluate their own assumptions about the internal workings of the capitalist system. The capitalist prognosis for restoring profits at the expense of the working class is old hat. However, it is how they plan on doing it and what sectors of the working class it will affect that is revealing. This strategy was spelled out in fine detail in *Business Week* (June 1, 1981).[46]

In this special issue the editors observed that the American economy since 1977 "has been far stronger than anyone expected, it has refused to go into recession when predicted, it has been more inflationary than forecast, and it has created more new jobs than imagined." The reason for this, *Business Week* argued, is due to a radical transformation of the industrial and commercial economy since the 1960s. "The economy has developed into five separate economies that no longer act as one; these subeconomies do not grow together in periods of prosperity, nor do they decline together in periods of recession." The five subeconomies cited are: 1) old-line industry, which includes automobiles, steel, textiles, appliances, construction, electrical and non-electrical machinery, food and tobacco manufactures; 2) agriculture—livestock, vegetables, food grains, forestry, fishery products, cotton, and poultry; 3) energy—coal, oil, natural gas and utilities; 4) high-technology—semiconductor and computer technology, office machines, aircrafts, dental and optical supplies, surgical supplies, radio and television equipment; and 5) services—finances, personnel, consulting, information processing, education, healthcare, hotels and apartments, real estate, media, insurance and other social services.[47]

Business Week noted that the rates of capital investment, relative prices and profits were strikingly divergent from one sector of the capitalist economy to another. Old-line industries employ about one-third of the U.S. work force, and once constituted the foundation for corporate growth. This is no longer true. Projected real growth in steel, autos and other older industries, with "Reagan's reforms" allowing for accelerated depreciation allowances, will be two percent, less than half the rate of growth achieved during the previous two decades. In 1975, the average return on equity for older industries was 14 percent; by 1980 return on equity was below 8 percent. Since 1973, 23 tire plants have shut down in the U.S.; 11 percent of America's steelmaking capability was "phased out" between 1977 and 1980. Defense-related firms, chemical food processing and steel industries will continue leaving the industrial Northeast and Midwest to pursue tax abatements and lower labor costs in the "sunbelt" or abroad. In New York City alone in the 1970s between 40-50,000 jobs in apparel and textile industries disappeared. About 400,000 U.S. workers, mostly employed in old-line industries, lost their jobs in 1979 alone because of plant closings or relocations.[48]

Sectors of the private economy expected to do well in the 1980s include energy, high technology and many services, according to *Business Week.* Industry analysts predict that oil prices, currently about $34/barrel, will range between $77-$117/barrel by 1990. Despite reductions in the rate of U.S. petroleum consumption and an expansion of U.S. drilling, domestic oil and gas prices will go even higher. 1980s record profits for the U.S. oil and gas corporations, $37.7 billion, will reach $100 billion by 1990. In semi-conductor and computer production, also, profits will be staggeringly high. With a growing worldwide demand for technology, annual sales of semi-conductor corporations alone should reach $40-50 billion. Many human service-oriented corporations, particularly in the fields of advertising, travel, banking, credit, insurance and health care, will expand. Others, such as public education, automobile services, etc. will contract sharply in the next years. Government employment, particularly in lower paid white collar and blue collar service positions will be reduced significantly.

Perhaps the greatest rise in prices and profits in the 1980s will occur in agriculture. During the 1970s, U.S. exports of soybeans, corn, rice, wheat and truck produce reached all-time highs. Gross farm income rose 6 percent to almost $140 billion in 1980. But rising costs for fuel, pesticides and real estate have severely reduced agribusiness' profits. *Business Week* noted that "real profits plunged to $13.4 billion in 1980, from $31.5 billion in 1973." Farm liabilities tripled from $54 billion in 1970 to $180 billion in 1980. "Debt has jumped from 6 percent of overall cash flow in 1970 to about 19 percent today." Because of an accelerated demand for farm products and a growing debt, economists predict that agricultural prices will "explode" in the 1980s. Prices for food should increase about twice the rate of inflation. The continued high cost of commercial capital means that hundreds of thousands of small farmers will go out of business. *Business Week* observed, "the total number of farms will drop 25 percent to 1.8 million, and the largest 50,000 farms, about 3 percent of the total—will account for 58 percent of total cash sales." Overall farm assets will triple to an amount of $3.3 trillion by 1990.[49]

What will be the position of the Black workers within the new capitalist macroeconomy? Blacks are being concentrated in exactly those industries that are undergoing rapid decline and conversely are excluded from the sectors of the economy targeted for growth. This labor force projection can be illustrated by a brief examination of Black employment patterns. (See Tables II, III) Of the eight and one-half million Blacks who found employment during the year 1977, 24 percent were in manufacturing. About 2 percent were employed in motor vehicle production; 12 percent made other durable goods, such as steel; 5 percent were in construction; 2 percent made food products.[50] All of these sectors will experience harsh reductions in hiring, and hundreds of thousands of transport equipment operatives and nonfarm laborers will lose their jobs. In areas of potential economic growth, however, Blacks are underrepresented. 11 percent of all Black workers are in retail trade, and another 2 percent are in wholesale trade. Their numbers amount to only 8 percent of repair services, 7 percent of the employees in real estate, insurance and banking. 8 percent of all Black workers comprise 13 percent of the total work force in public administration or government—a sector targeted for major reductions in hiring in the wake of Proposition-13 style cut-backs.[51]

At the same time the level of permanent Black unemployment, which increased from 8.1 percent in 1965 to 14.7 percent in 1975, will probably exceed 20-22 percent by the end of the 1980s. Black youth unemployment, which was only 16.5 percent in 1954 and 26.2 percent in 1965, will exceed the 51 percent figure of 1982. Growing numbers of Blacks, especially youth and adults under the age 35, will find few positions available to them in the work force. (See Table IV)

The economic plight of the Black labor force is symbolized best by the ironies of agricultural production. Only forty years ago, 41 percent of all Black male workers were either farmers or farm laborers. In 1949, Blacks owned 80,842 commercial cotton farms in Mississippi, a total of 66.0 percent of the segregated state's total. The number of Black-owned and operated cotton farms in 1949 ranged from 30,807 in Arkansas to 9,727 in North Carolina, an amount that was still 45.4 percent of that state's cotton farms. Even as late as 1964, there were 21,939 Black-owned cotton farms in Mississippi, 61.7 percent of the total number. But by 1969, Black farmers were effectively swept from the fields. Only one thousand Black-owned cotton producing farms remained in Mississippi that year. In North Carolina, there were only 18 Black-owned cotton farms left. Between 1965-80, the amount of Black-owned agricultural land had been reduced by more than half. Thus, precisely as agricultural production has become as potentially profitable as high technology or natural gas production, Black agricultural workers/owners have been reduced to insignificance.[52]

The fiscal projections of U.S. corporations have been wrong in the past, and nothing in the discussion above suggests that they will not be wrong in the immediate future. Little analysis in *Business Week, Fortune* or within the Council of Economic Advisors has been given to the central reason for the American economy's superficial vitality between 1976-80; the unprecedented explosion of public and private debt. In 1960, for example, the total net debt of all farms, banks, business, consumers and government amounted to $38.5 billion. This figure was equal to 7.6 percent of the nation's gross national product. By 1977, net additions to public and private debt came to $378.3 billion, about 20 percent of GNP. Much of this growth has been the indebtedness of consumers. Of the $378.3 billion figures, $107.7 billion was public debt, $103.1 billion was owed within business, and $130.0 billion debt was that of the consumer. Furthermore, the percentage of consumer debt vs. consumer income has grown from 4.4 percent in 1975 to 9.9 percent in 1977. The structural debt of even the most profitable sectors of the macroeconomy will continue to escalate. In agriculture alone, liabilities are projected to reach $600 billion by 1990. The upswing in the capitalist economy, in short, will be financed by borrowed funds, paid for at interest rates that will oscillate between 12 and 22 percent.[53]

Surveying all possibilities, two conclusions can be drawn. First, there is a practical limit to the amount for mortgages and credit that individual and corporate consumers will be able or willing to pay for. Cutting the number of operatives, manual laborers and service workers will inevitably ease the pain for corporations, as they attempt to expand profit margins at the expense of growing unemployment. But as Paul Sweezy has observed, growth "rests on the continuous rise in consumer spending, mainly on durable goods, (and) an increasing flow of consumer credit will eventually—and sooner rather than later—turn back on itself as the stream of accompanying repayments grows inexorably larger."[54] The second point is that one segment of the work force that is most vulnerable to these shifts in the macroeconomy is the Black working class. As many as one million could lose their jobs with the flight of capital in the form of plant closings in the "Frostbelt." Thousands of former Black farmers will not take part in the unprecedented expansion of agribusiness' profits, because they now lack the land and capital for reinvestment. Advancements in technology will replace thousands of manual laborers and service workers. Many white collar workers within government and those hired by affirmative action policies in the private sector may find it difficult if not impossible to keep the positions they have. As the economic crisis deepens, corporations will seek more innovative strategies to weaken unions, exacerbate differences between Black and white workers, and threaten financial chaos for entire cities. A number of predominantly working class communities are already subject to what United Auto Workers president Douglas Fraser has termed "industrial blackmail," where corporations threaten to leave an area if the local government does not grant extraordinary tax breaks. Union members are told that they must lower their expectations for wage increases and fringe benefits at contract negotiations, in order to keep the plant alive. The climate of fiscal austerity creates new tensions between those employees with greater seniority and those who have only recently entered the job market—often young people, women and Blacks.[55]

An analysis of the evolution and current status of the Black working class leads us to several conclusions. More than any other social stratum within American society, Black workers would be the direct and immediate beneficiaries of the reorganization of the U.S. political economy. The contemporary and historical crisis which confronts the Black working class primarily, as well as the Black majority, cannot be resolved unless worker self-managed factories and the public ownership of the central means of production, transportation and the distribution of goods and services is won in our generation. There are two basic contradictions which present barriers to such a solution. The first, and most obvious, is the great (and still unanswered) question: will labor unions and the white working class wage unconditional war against its own contradictory history? The primitive bigotry, cultural exclusivity, social norms and explicit ideology of white supremacy have repeatedly undercut Black-white labor unity.[56] If there is no attempt on the part of white labor to engage in extensive self-criticism, and to construct a common program for struggle against capital with non-whites, the final emancipation of the American working class will be unattainable. The second problem relates to a more recent development within the overall political economy—the growth of a massive number of permanently unemployed men and women. The reserve army of labor is swelling the ranks of the American poor, and has created the socioeconomic conditions for an unpredictable "ghetto-class" whose political interests are not always identical to those of employed workers. As the contradictions within the capitalist economy and civil society deepen, millions of unemployed and desperate Americans may continue to ignore socialist alternatives for something that can promise jobs, food and domestic tranquility. That authoritarian alternative could be some form of fascism, as we shall discuss in chapter nine.

CHAPTER TWO

THE BLACK POOR: HIGHEST STAGE OF UNDERDEVELOPMENT.

The economic relations of the ghetto to white America closely parallel those between third-world nations and the industrially advanced countries. The ghetto also has a relatively low per-capita income and a high birth rate. Its residences are for the most part unskilled. Businesses lack capital and managerial know-how. Local markets are limited. The incidence of credit is high. Little savings takes place and what is saved is usually not invested locally. Goods and services tend to be 'imported' for the most part, only the simplest and the most labor-intensive being produced locally. The ghetto is dependent on one basic export—its unskilled labor power.

William K. Tabb, *The Political Economy of the Black Ghetto* (New York: W. W. Norton, 1970), p. 22.

I

The citadel of world capitalism, the United States, has never liked to admit that millions of its citizens are poor. Yet the hub of international financial markets, Wall Street, is only blocks from some of the worst urban slums in the world. Atlanta's Omni and glittering convention center is walking distance from delapidated shanties that are mirror images of eighteenth and nineteenth century slave quarters. The White House and the posh residential district of Georgetown are respectively less than twenty city blocks from rat infested, crime filled squalor. The percentage of the total U.S. population defined as impoverished increased from 11.1 percent in 1972 to 13.0 percent in 1980, the highest figure recorded by the Bureau of the Census since 1966. 1.3 million New York City residents were defined as poor in 1978, 18.7 percent of the city's populace. Chicago recorded 667,000 poor persons in 1978, 18.4 percent of its total population, and Philadelphia had 336,000 poor people, 19.8 percent of the city's total population. There were 2.6 million Latinos, 7.6 million Blacks and 16.3 million whites who were classified by the Federal government as poor in 1978. In a racist society, poverty is alloted unequally: 31 percent of all Blacks in the U.S. are poor, 22 percent of all Hispanics, but only 9 percent of all whites.[1]

Poverty must be understood properly as a comparative relationship between those segments of classes who are deprived of basic human needs (e.g., food, shelter, clothing, medical care) vs. the most secure and affluent classes within a social and economic order. It does relatively little good to compare and contrast the family of a Puerto Rican welfare mother in the South Bronx with a poor family in Lagos, Saõ Paulo or Bombay. Black American living conditions may be superior in a relative material sense to those of working class families in Poland—but we are not Poles. The process of impoverishment is profoundly national and regional, and it is in the light of capitalist America's remarkable success in producing an unprecedented standard of living for the majority of its indigenous white population that Blacks' and Hispanics' material realities must be judged.

The first dilemma confronting the researcher who explores the dimensions of American poverty involves the definition of class. Traditionally, American bourgeois social scientists have defined one's class status as a function of annual earned income, and not in terms of one's relationship to the means of production. Upper class Americans are not individuals who own the factories and the corporations, and who live without selling their labor power in the marketplace for a wage. Rather, the capitalist elite is delineated by its annual income of, let us say, $200,000 or more. Of course, this definition could include any number of persons who are not capitalists—from highly successful physicians to lucrative (and illegal) drugs dealers. Conversely, the Federal government has established a rather elaborate theoretical construct to define poverty, based again on an individual's or family's annual income—"the sum of the amounts received from earnings; Social Security and public assistance payments; dividends, interest and rent; unemployment and workmen's compensation; government and private employee pensions, and other periodic income." Certain non-monetary tranfers, such as healthcare benefits and food stamps, are not counted as income.[2] The Federal government makes a distinction between "nonfarm" and "farm" residence in determining poverty status, weighs its analysis according to the number of persons who are in a particular family, and even considers whether a female is the nominal "head" of a particular household. Thus, widely varying standards emerge on what constitutes "the poor." An eighteen year old Black woman with a small child in Atlanta was considered poor in 1978 if her annual income was $4,268 or less. If she and her child lived in rural Georgia, her "poverty threshold" was $3,614. A Black family of seven persons in Chicago with both male and female parents would be poor at $11,038 or less. If their father was killed by the police, and the family returned to rural North Carolina, its poverty threshold would be $7,462; if it stayed in Chicago, $8,852. A blind and partially crippled 66 year old widow, living in a dangerous and drafty rowhouse in the slums of North Philadelphia, would not be considered poor if her yearly income exceeded $3,253. Sensible people of all political persuasions would have to admit that no single person can survive on an annual income of under $10,000 in a metropolitan area except at the precipice of despair and hunger. But as everything else in capitalist America, the state defines "poverty" to suit its own needs.[3] Thus, the assertion that the percentage of all Americans who are "poor" declined from 22.4 percent in 1959 to 11.1 precent in 1973 must be viewed with a healthy degree of skepticism.[4]

Even when one accepts the Federal government's definition of poverty, the general situation for millions of Americans becomes strikingly apparent. For the year 1978, there were 9.7 million children under the age of 18 who lived in families existing below the poverty level. 3.2 million persons 65 years or older were poor. 10.3 million poor persons, about 42 percent of the nation's total poor population, resided in the South. 62 percent of all poor people lived in metropolitan areas, and 62 percent of this population resided in the ghetto or central city. 5.4 million unrelated individuals over 14 years old, residing in the homes of nonrelatives or living alone, were poor. Most of these unrelated persons, 4.2 million, were white. 1.4 million white families with no husbands present were classified as poor, 23.5 percent of all such families. 15.7 percent of all families, Black, white and Hispanic— who lived in central cities were below the poverty level. 38.5 percent of all married women age 25 to 44 whose spouse was absent from the home in 1979 were poor, and 80.8 percent of all American women over 65 who are widowed are poor.[5]

Statistically, the poor Black family differs from the impoverished white family in a number of critical respects. From 1959 to 1978, the number of whites classified by the Federal government as below the poverty level declined from 28,484,000 to 16,259,000. In terms of percentage to the general white population in the U.S., the decline cut the white poverty rate from 18.1 percent to 8.7 percent. During the same period, the number of poor Blacks also declined both in real numbers and in terms of their percentage to the Black population, but not as much as the whites' figures—9,927,000 persons and 55.1 percent in 1959 to 7,625,000 persons and 30.6 percent in 1978. In real terms, the number of poor Blacks actually increased slightly after 1969, from 6,245,000 that year to the current level. The number of poor white males with families declined from 4,952,000 to 2,132,000 between 1959 and 1978, for a drop in percentage terms of from 13.3 percent to 4.7 percent of all such white families. For Black male households, the decline was more marked, from 1,309,000 to 414,000. Even so, 13.4 percent of Black household heads were poor in 1979, a figure that exceeds the level of white male householders twenty years before.[6]

Black families throughout the U.S., in every region and city, assume the unequal burden of poverty. In suburban districts outside the ghetto, 21.3 percent of all Black families are poor, vs. only 5.9 percent of white families. In central cities Black and white families below the poverty level comprise 28.6 percent vs. 7.6 percent of their total populations respectively. Outside metropolitan areas, 39.1 percent of all Black families are poor, while only 11.2 percent of white families are.[7] When all American families are divided into fifths according to income, a much higher proportion of Blacks and Hispanics are located in the bottom two-fifths, and virtually disappear in the highest fifth of U.S. income earners. Using 1977 figures, 39.6 percent of all U.S. nonwhite families were in the lowest fifth of all income earners. 22.6 percent were located in the second lowest fifth. Only 9.4 percent of all nonwhite families earned yearly incomes to rank in the highest fifth, by way of contrast.[8]

Although Blacks' incomes have increased over the past ten years, earners generally have not kept pace with inflation. One way of viewing the illusion of Black income mobility is by comparing Black median incomes between 1970 and 1977 in current dollars and in constant 1977 dollars. The median Black family income in 1970 was $6,279. Seven years later, Black family median income was $9,563, an increase of $3,284. In constant 1977 dollars, however, $6,279 was worth $9,799. Thus, the median Black family income actually declined—2.4 percent in the period 1970 and 1977. Using constant 1977 dollars, a pattern of growing impoverishment becomes clear. The median Black family incomes in Northeastern states declined by 15.2 percent between 1970 and 1977, from $12,132 to $10,285 annually; in the North Central States, the decline was 11.2 percent, $12,045 to $10,690; in the West, 20.6 percent, $12,487 to $9,917. Those families that suffered most were located in urban metropolitan areas. In central cities in excess of one million persons, Black median family income declined 13.6 percent, from $11,589 to $10,012. Even in the suburbs of major cities, Black median family income dropped 7.1 percent, $14,111 to $13,104. For Black families with no husband present, median incomes increased marginally, from $5,581 in 1970 to $5,598. Simultaneously, white median family incomes between 1970 and 1977 increased in constant 1977 dollars by 4.8 percent, and whites suburban families' median incomes passed the $20,000 mark by 1977.[9]

Although the majority of Black poor families earned something between $3,000 to $5,000 in 1978, a frightening number of Blacks exist on virtually no financial reserves or resources. 78,000 Black families reported annual incomes between $1,000 and $1,499; 45,000 families earned between one dollar to $999 during 1978; 31,000 additional families actually had no cash income at all. For the most oppressed and destitute sector of the permanently unemployed, social services and public programs have provided little in the way of real additional income. Inside poverty areas, residential districts containing at least 20 percent of the population living below the official poverty level, 220,000 Black families survive solely on public assistance plus their meager salaries. 31,000 families in poor communities depend primarily on Social Security income. About one-third of a million Black poor families live in public housing, which reduces the amount of money they must pay toward their rent. 770,000 other Black poor families, however, are forced to find private accommodations usually at exorbitant rates.[10]

Demographically, Black poor people are distinguished from poor whites by certain social characteristics: they are largely more female, younger, and usually reside in the urban ghetto. At all ages, Black women are much more likely to be poor than white females, white males, or Black males. Several examples can be used to illustrate this. Consider four categories of unmarried persons between the ages of 15 to 19: white males, white females, Black males and Black females. For these groups, the percentage of their total populations who would have been below the poverty level in 1978 was the following: white males, 8.5 percent; white females, 14.8 percent; Black males, 36.0 percent; Black females, 40.0 percent. For divorced women between the ages of 25 to 29, the poverty rates are white females, 19.7 percent; Black females, 41.2 percent. Among married women who are legally separated but not divorced, between age 35 to 44 years, those below the poverty line are white females, 40.6 percent; Black females, 52.5 percent. Overall poverty rates for all household heads 15 years and over, by race are white males, 5.3 percent; white females, 9.5 percent; Black males, 11.8 percent; Black females, 31.1 percent. For all persons of both sexes, the percentages of those in poverty are white males, 7.3 percent; white females, 10.0 percent; Black males, 26.5 percent; Black females, 34.1 percent.[11] (See Table V)

Subproletarian status for Black women creates oppressive social conditions that inevitably include an absence of adequate birth control information and support services for young children. In residential areas where at least twenty percent of all persons exist below the poverty level, both birth and infant mortality rates are exceptionally high. In impoverished central cities, the number of Black children under 3 years old per 1,000 Black women between the ages of 15 to 44 was 327.93. In rural poverty areas, the rate is a staggeringly high 441.66. Again, these rates must be contrasted with both white and Black women who live above the poverty level, 173.61 and 184.69, respectively. There is a direct relationship between the number of children that are within a Black family with a sole female householder and family's likelihood of being below the poverty level. Only 14.8 percent of all Black women householders without children are in poverty. That percentage increases with each dependent: one child, 42.2 percent in poverty; two children, 59.8 percent; three children,

63.4 percent; four children, 82.5 percent; five children, 86.0 percent. [12]

Poverty is also reinforced within the Black community by educational underdevelopment and academic inequality. By 1978, as an illustration, 74 percent of all Blacks between the ages of 22 to 34 were high school graduates, with 12.6 median years of school completed. 86.1 percent of all whites in this age group were high school graduates, with 12.9 median years of education. For Blacks below the poverty level between 22 and 34, both figures were significantly lower—53.0 percent high school graduates, with 12.1 years of schooling. Overall educational statistics for poor Blacks are much worse. The average poor Black person has completed only 10 years of school. Only 26.8 percent have been graduated from high school. Impoverished Blacks between 45 to 54 years of age recorded only 9.3 years of education, and Blacks between 55 to 64 years of age have but 8.4 years. Not a single Black man between age 60-64 in 1978 who lived in poverty had a high school diploma. 118,000 Black poor people have never attended school in their lives, 491,000 completed under five years, and another 585,000 had only a sixth or seventh grade education. [13]

The strongest roots of Black poverty are anchored firmly in the capitalist marketplace, contrary to the opinions of most social scientists. The process of income erosion for Black families since the 1960s can be examined several ways. Perhaps the most effective is an assessment of the number of salaried workers per family by race, and the ratio of persons to income earners per family. (See Table VI) In 1967, the Black families were significantly larger than white families (4.35 persons vs. 3.59 persons). However, the economic conditions of the period allowed a relatively larger number of Blacks to enter the job market to support family members. The percentage of families with two income earners that year was 41.8 percent for Blacks and 38.4 percent for whites. 11.1 percent of all Black families had three earners, and 5.3 percent had four or more. There were overall slightly more income earners per family for Blacks (1.76) than for whites (1.67). By 1977, both Black and white families had dropped in size (3.74 persons vs. 3.25 persons). The percentage of white families having no earners increased during the decade, from 8.2 to 11.8 percent. For Black families without salaried workers, the percentage jumped about 70 percent, from 10.2 to 17.2 percent. The percentage of Black families with one only wage earner increased from 31.6 to 36.2 percent, while the figure for whites dropped, 39.5 to 31.7 percent. The percentage of Black families with two or more earners decreased, 58.2 to 46.6 percent, whereas the whites' percentage increased 52.3 to 56.5 percent. Only 3.8 percent of all Black families had four or more income earners by 1978. Most significantly, the ratio of persons to earners per family had remained roughly the same for Blacks, while the ratio declined for whites. These figures imply that the recessions of 1969-70 and 1973-75 forced at least 550,000 Black workers permanently out of the job market; that Black families who depended upon a second or third job to maintain their homes lost the opportunity to acquire employment; and that whites took the places of Blacks in most of these jobs.[14]

Unemployment statistics provide another key in explaining the steady deterioration of Black economic life. In 1961 the official rate of unemployment for nonwhites and whites in the U.S. was 12.4 and 6.0 percent respectively. In the mid-1960s, nonwhite unemployment dropped sharply for several reasons: the continued relocation of rural Blacks to the North and West, where more jobs at higher wages were then available; the collapse of legal segregation; the Federal government's implementation of affirmative action guidelines which made jobs available to previously qualified Blacks; and a generally expanding capitalist economy. By 1969 nonwhite unemployment was 6.4 percent, and the rate for nonwhite married men who lived with a spouse declined from 7.9 percent in 1962 to only 2.5 percent in seven years. The crisis of U.S. capitalism in the 1970s contracted the number of available jobs in the labor market, with Black workers usually the first to be dismissed. In 1972 nonwhite unemployment reached 10 percent, and by 1975 the figure was almost 14 percent. (See Table VII) Nonwhite married men in 1975 had an unemployment rate of 8.3 percent, 170 percent higher than that for white married males. In 1975, 33 percent of all unemployed nonwhites were out of work for 15 weeks or more; 16 percent were jobless for more than half the year. Blacks below the poverty level were particularly victimized. Only 1.6 million of 4.7 million poor Blacks were able to work during 1978. Of this number, less than 950,000 were employed full-time. 508,000 of the employed Black poor held jobs for 26 weeks or less, and 689,000 more could only obtain part-time work. Hardest hit were poor, young Black men and women between 16 and 21 years of age. The mean number of weeks worked in 1978 for this group was a meager 17.2 weeks. [15]

As the crisis of the capitalist economy became more severe, the rules for those unemployed workers, Black and white, to receive compensation became more restrictive. During the recession of 1973-1975, at least three-fourths of the unemployed received some sort of compensation. Workers losing their jobs because of foreign capital's growing shares of the U.S. consumer market were awarded a substantial share of their former wages for up to 18 months, with the passage of the Trade Adjustment Assistance Program. As late as December, 1980, almost one-quarter of a million unemployed workers obtained funds through the program; by December, 1981, only 12,100 were allowed to collect benefits. By the beginning of 1982, only 37 percent of the jobless were receiving any kind of compensation. Officially, Black overall unemployment reached 17.4 percent in late 1981, a percentage which does not even include those whom the Federal government calls "discouraged workers"—unemployed persons who have not looked for work actively for four weeks. Conservatively, the real rate of Black unemployment in the U.S. in the early 1980s easily exceeded 20 percent, and might surpass 30 percent under certain economic conditions. In many ghetto communities, Black youth unemployment surpassed 80 percent. [16]

The pain of unemployment is magnified still further by the growing personal indebtedness that traps the Black poor. Black families below the poverty level had a median income deficit of $2,261 in 1978, compared to a median income deficit of $1,753 for poor white families. 261,000 Black families owed $3,000-$3,999. 146,000 were in debt between $4,000-$4,999; and 182,000 were behind by $5,000 or more. For Black families with related children under 18 years of age in 1978, the median income deficit was $3,781. Black families with female householders were behind by $2,440. 215,000 of these families owed $3,000-$3,999; 262,000 more female-headed households were in debt by at least $4,000. [17]

Summarizing these statistics, one obtains at best a limited insight into the nature of Black poverty in the United States. To grasp the fact that the median annual income of a Black family consisting of one female adult and two children under 18 years of age who are below the poverty level is $3,260 does not and cannot tell us how she struggles every day to survive. Statistics report that 10,000 Black families in the

U.S. that include a female householder, no husband, and three small children, reported *no cash income* in 1978. Beyond Aid to Families with Dependent Children, and beyond food stamps, how did these 10,000 impoverished Black families purchase school books, new clothing, shoes and other necessities? Did they have the luxury of going to the cinema on a Saturday afternoon, or jumping into the family automobile to take a leisurely ride down to the beach on a warm summer day? How did they cope when a sudden health problem struck one of the children in their family? What is the possibility of them ever overcoming their massive personal debt, and escaping the harassment of creditors and finance officers? Statistics cannot relate the human face of economic misery.

II

Oppressed people learn strategies for survival: if they do not learn, they perish. The profile above indicates that in 1978 only 10.8 million out of 18.1 million Black persons over 14 years of age could find employment. What do several millions of these workers—the 2.2 million persons who have only found part-time jobs, and the 412,000 Black workers who are unemployed for more than 26 weeks during the year—do to survive? How do the other 7.3 million Black adults provide food, clothing, shelter, medical care and some measure of security to their families in the age of Reaganomics and racism? At the highest level of underdevelopment, the daily life of the Black poor becomes a continuous problematic, an unresolved set of dilemmas which confront each person at the most elementary core of their existence. The patterns of degradation are almost unrelenting, and thrust upon every individual and family a series of unavoidable choices which tend to dehumanize and destroy many of their efforts to create social stability or collective political integrity.

In recent decades, sociologists have described this growing social stratum as an "underclass" or "ghettoclass." Perhaps the best example of the literature on the subject was written by Douglas G. Glasgow, professor of social welfare at Howard University. Glasgow's *Black Underclass* examines the innercity Black youth of Los Angeles, from the Watts race uprising of 1965 to the late 1970s. Theoretically, he locates the center of Black unrest in the volatile group of 18 to 34 year olds who were unified by "their common condition":

They were jobless and lacked salable skills and opportunities to get them; they had been rejected and labeled as social problems by the police, the schools, the employment and welfare agencies, they were victims of the new camouflaged racism.

Detached from the broader white society, even largely from the seemingly complacent working Blacks around them, they drank, gambled, fought a little, but mostly just generally 'hung out.' . . . They try to keep body and soul together and maintain a job, but they remain immobile, part of the static poor. Others who could make this adaptation fail to do so, often preferring to remain unemployed rather than accept a job that demands their involvement for the greater part of each day but provides only the barest minimum of financial reward. They seek other options for economic survival ranging from private entrepreneurial schemes to working the welfare system. Hustling, quasi—legitimate schemes, and outright deviant activity are also alternatives to work.[18]

Glasgow separates the Black "underclass" from lower income Blacks by several rough social criteria: an absence of generational socioeconomic upward mobility, the "lack of real opportunities to succeed," and widespread "anger and despair" which "arises from contact with mainstream institutions, which, almost imperceptibly and very impersonally, reject them." The author also believes that "racism is probably the most basic cause of the underclass condition."[19]

Conceptually, there are some problems inherent with the term "underclass." Using Glasgow's criteria, literally millions of Black Americans would have to be included with the underclass, since as I have illustrated previously, they have absolutely no meaningful prospects for future work. Glasgow emphasizes the subjective and superstructural factors related to underclass status—lack of decent education, widespread alienation from white civil order and society, the disintegration of stability within family life, and so forth. But these factors in and of themselves do not make this massive stratum a "class" in a real and decisive sense. These "subproletarians" include both marginal elements of the working class as well as those of whom Marxists have traditionally termed the lumpenproletariat: pimps and prostitutes, small-time criminals, drug dealers and "numbers" runners. The "work" that these elements perform is defined by capitalist society as illegal, but the profits it returns for a few ghetto entrepreneurs can be monumental. Moreover, the question of class must address the issue of consciousness. A class that is neither "self-conscious" nor acts collectively according to its material interests, is not worthy of the name. The general philosophy of the typical ghetto hustler is not collective, but profoundly individualistic. The goal of illegal work is to "make it for oneself," not for others. The means for making it comes at the expense of elderly Blacks, young Black women with children, youths and lower-income families who live at the bottom of working class hierarchy. The consciousness of the subproletariat is not so much that of a "class," but the sum total of destructive experiences that are conditioned by structural unemployment, the lack of meaningful participation within political or civil society, the dependency fostered by welfare agencies over two or three generations, functional illiteracy and the lack of marketable skills.

The pimp is one typical representative of innercity underdevelopment within the subproletariat, the personification of the individualistic hustler. He accumulates petty capital by brutalizing young women, who sell their sexuality on the open market to (usually white middle class male) "consumers." Methods of "labor discipline" invariably include naked force—rape, threats, physical and psychological assaults. Women who are coerced or who accept these crude terms of "employment" are expected to deliver a certain number of tricks with "Johns" per hour, day and week. Police in the ghetto are usually an integral part of the trade, and expect a regular cut from the women's profits for tolerating the traffic in their precincts. Local Black and white entrepreneurs in the inner city motel and hotel business find room to expand and even to survive by orienting services to accommodate prostitution. The profits are also used to underwrite other illicit activities, from the ghetto's omnipresent drug traffic in elementary and secondary schools to small-time fencing operations.

Black women with young dependents are invariably touched by the process of lumpenization. A very small percentage may be forced at some point into prostitution simply to put food on the table for their children. Many more, however, supplement their inadequate incomes by a variety of illegal acts which carry relatively low levels of risk. "Boosting" or stealing clothing, shoes, small appliances and food from retail stores has become a regular and common occurence. Many poor people who maintain a high degree of public morality, and who actively participate in their churches, find little to no difficulty purchasing clothing, television sets, stereos, washing machines and even automobiles that they know are stolen. Children even below the age of twelve sometimes become numbers runners, or participate in marginal ways in the drug traffic. Teenagers who become skilled in drug transactions can accumulate literally thousands of dollars per month, and annual gross incomes above $20,000 for some high school students are not rare in major cities. In some urban Black communities, and especially in Chicago, over one-fourth of all Black youth between the ages of 14 to 25 belong to gangs, which often deal in small robberies, drugs and prostitution. A great many youth participate in gangs simply to survive daily life in urban high schools. Gang membership usually has little social stigma, and carries with it a limited guarantee of safety and security in their neighborhoods. The death of a gang member, the murder of a high school student during classes, or the random arrest of a young Black man by the police, are all integral factors of daily life. What is sad about the proliferating incidents of violence within the urban Black community's permanent reserve army of labor is that no one is surprised any more.

Substantial elements of the Black elite do not discuss the unique problems of the "underclass," either with whites or among themselves, because in doing so they would be forced to confront the common realities of racism that underlie the totality of America's social and economic order. They often do not like to be reminded that former friends and family members are on welfare, that their nieces may be prostitutes, or that their cousins peddle drugs, stolen fur coats and designer jeans. Even the expressions of popular culture among the Black ghetto poor are not seen as having any direct relationship to the Negro upper crust's aesthetics. In *Certain People: America's Black Elite*, author Stephen Birmingham recounts the acute embarrassment of one Black upper class matron from Washington, D.C. at the sight of a Black young man donning "Super Fly" pimp-type attire. " 'Disgusting', she whispered. 'There is the cause of all our problems'. Her friend, more perceptive, said, 'No, that is the *result* of all our problems.' "[20] Many Blacks who advanced into highly paid positions in the corporate world intensely dislike the mass cultural expressions of the Black poor and working classes, and refrain from any social relations with Blacks who rely on "transfer payments" to make ends meet. For several generations, the Black elite of Harlem's "Strivers' Row" effectively created a *cordon sanitaire* around their neighborhood to protect themselves and their property from contact with the Black "underclass." As late as the mid-1970s, the Strivers' Row's "two block associations (had) rigid rules which (were) rigidly enforced: no trash or litter thrown in streets; keep hedges uniformly clipped; keep brasswork polished; no children playing in the streets; no peddlers or solicitors; beautify gardens and window boxes." When well-heeled residents contemplated the plight of their distant relatives or neighbors outside Strivers' Row, the nearly universal attitude was one of contempt. The Black poor were characterized repeatedly as "lazy, shiftless, and no good." In employing low income Blacks as occasional domestic workers, the Negro elite can be every bit as paternalistic as the white ruling class. "One thing that can be said for the black upper class," one affluent Negro lady informed Birmingham, "is that we're always nice to our servants."[21]

A central focus of subproletarian life is fear. Black elderly and handicapped persons are afraid to walk or visit friends in their own neighborhoods at night or travel on public transportation because they are convinced (with good reason) that they will be assaulted. Young Black women are often uncomfortable going to parties or social gatherings by themselves because they will invariably be harassed by Black men and even male youngsters barely into puberty. Parents who live in innercities are reluctant to send their children several blocks to attend school or to play outside after dark because they are afraid they might be harmed. Black-on-Black crime usually victimizes the working and poor, but it can paralyze virtually all Black people of whatever social class or neighborhood. It produces for capitalism and the state a deep despair, a destructive suspicion we hold against each other. It thwarts Blacks' ability to achieve collective class consciousness, to build political agencies which advance our material and cultural interests, and develop ourselves economically. It forces Black innercity merchants to strap revolvers on their calves or shoulders, while serving poor patrons behind plexiglass shields. It stops Black doctors from making emergency calls to their patients who live in the midst of a tenement slum or ghetto highrise complex. It instills a subconscious apathy toward the political and economic hierarchy, and fosters the nihilistic conviction that nothing can ever be changed in the interests of the Black masses.

The permanent reserve army of Black workers, subproletarians or the "underclass," is the latest social culmination of the process of Black ghettoization, economic exploitation and urban decay. In one sense, it represents the highest stage of Black underdevelopment, because it eliminates millions of Blacks from belonging to working class organizations. The existence of a massive "ghettoclass" disrupts the internal functions of the mostly working class Black community, turning Blacks in blue collar jobs against those who have never had any job. The social institutions created by working class Blacks to preserve a sense of collective humanity, culture and decency within the narrow confines of the innercity are eroded and eventually overturned. Subproletarianization and the extension of permanent penury to broad segments of the Black majority provoke the disruption of Black families; increase the number of Black-on-Black murders, rapes, suicides and assaults; and make terror a way of life for all Blacks of every class background who live in or near the innercity.

CHAPTER THREE

GROUNDINGS WITH MY SISTERS: PATRIARCHY AND THE EXPLOITATION OF BLACK WOMEN.

ain't I a woman? Look at me! Look at my arm!. . . I have plowed, and planted, and gathered into barns, and no man could head me—and ain't I a woman? I could work as much as any man (when I could get it), and bear de lash as well—and ain't I a woman? I have borne five children and seen 'em mos all sold off into slavery, and when I cried out with a mother's grief, none but Jesus hear—and ain't I a woman?

Sojourner Truth, 1852.

We are the slaves of slaves; we are exploited more ruthlessly than men.

Lucy Parsons, 1905.

I

The first two chapters of this book, which explore the history of the Black working class and subproletariat, do not examine in any great detail the largest single group within Afro-America—Black women. As noted earlier, Black women comprise a significant minority within the Black laboring population, and have for many years experienced higher rates of unemployment than their male counterparts. (See Table IV) Over one-third of all Black women are officially classified as "poor" by

69

the Federal government. This economic profile graphically illustrates the effects of patriarchy, racism and capitalist exploitation. But it does not begin to present the unique dimensions of the Black woman's historical experience.

Black social history, as it has been written to date, has been profoundly patriarchal. The sexist critical framework of American white history has been accepted by Black male scholars; the reconstruction of our past, the reclamation of our history from the ruins, has been an enterprise wherein women have been too long segregated. Obligatory references are generally made to those "outstanding sisters" who gave some special contribution to the liberation of the "Black man." Even these token footnotes probably do more harm than good, because they reinforce the false belief that the most oppressed victim of white racial tyranny has been *the Black man*. It is true, as chapter four will cite, that the numerical majority of those Blacks who have been lynched, executed and forced to work in penal institutions have been males. But these numbers ignore a critical reality of racism and capitalist development. From the dawn of the slave trade until today, U.S. capitalism was both racist and deeply sexist. The superexploitation of Black women became a permanent feature in American social and economic life, because sisters were assaulted simultaneously as workers, as Blacks, and as women. This triple oppression escaped Black males entirely. To understand the history of all Blacks within the Black majority, the "domestic Black periphery," special emphasis is required in documenting the particular struggles, ideals and attitudes of Black women. To do less would be to reinforce capitalist patriarchy's ideological hegemony over the future struggles of all Black working people. Black male liberationists must relearn their own history, by grounding themselves in the wisdom of their sisters.

II

During the entire slave period in the U.S. a brutal kind of equality was thrust upon both sexes. This process was dictated by the conditions of slave production within the overall process of capital accumulation in the South. Black women working in the fields on rice, sugar and cotton plantations were expected to labor at least twelve hours a day without complaint, breaking their backs just like their sons, husbands and fathers. Angela Davis has recognized that "the slave system could not confer upon the Black man the appearance of a privileged position vis-a-vis the Black woman." Since slavery itself was authoritarianism in the extreme, with the white slaveowner exercising physical violence to maintain political hegemony, no "family provider" or Black patriarch could be allowed. "The attainment of slavery's intrinsic goals was contingent upon the fullest and most brutal utilization of the productive capacities of every man, woman and child. The Black woman was therefore wholly integrated into the productive force."[1]

It must be remembered that the Afro-American slave was chattel: a thing, a privately owned commodity. Some slave masters tolerated the marriages of Blacks on their own farms or on their white neighbors' property to marry each other. But even the most "humane" master, when confronted with the inevitable economic declines that are a permanent feature of capitalism, would disrupt Black families by selling off a spouse or several children. "Here and there one can find sufficient respect for basic human rights or ample sentimentality to prevent the separation of families," John Hope Franklin indicates, "but it was not always good business to keep families together." Black women were sold separately to bring a more competitive price on the open market. Children over the age of fourteen were viewed as prime field hands, and were routinely taken from their mothers and fathers. Historians disagree on the precise number of families that were divided during slavery. One fair estimate is provided by Herbert Gutman, who describes the intersectional sale of slaves as "one of the great forced migrations in world history." 835,000 Afro-Americans were moved from the Upper South to Lower South between 1790 and 1860. Most of these persons were transported in the decades immediately before the Civil War, 575,000 slaves between 1830 and 1860. No fewer than one million Blacks were sold from 1820 to 1860, roughly one percent of the total slave population every year. Estimates of the number of Black women who were sold and thereby separated from their children, parents or husbands are, of course, difficult to assess. Gutman's work indicates that anywhere from 35 to 71 percent of marriage-age Black women who were sold in the interregional slave trade were involuntarily separated from their husbands. The public sale of young Black girls above the age of 12 who were bought to satisfy the sexual needs of white racist males was notorious. A few slavers even specialized in selling Black children between the ages of 8 to 12.[2]

One decisive form of oppression which befell the Black woman was slave breeding. Here again, the overwhelming majority of white male historians insist that either slave breeding did not exist or that it was rarely attempted by white planters. Usually this volatile term is employed narrowly to describe owner-coerced matings, where little actual documentation exists. However, the concept of slave breeding should be extended to mean all and any forms of slavery which, in Kenneth Stampp's definition, "indicate that slaves were reared with an eye to their marketability." Massive evidence exists illustrating that "many masters counted the fecundity of Negro women as an economic asset and encouraged them to bear children as rapidly as possible. Masters who prized prolific Negro women not only tolerated but sometimes came close to promoting sexual promiscuity among them."[3] Some white owners voided Blacks' marriages if they suspected that the men or women were sterile. In their own literature, Southern whites were absolutely candid about the centrality of slave breeding to the accumulation of profits. One Mississippian declared that fecund slave women "are the most profitable to their owners of any others. . . It is remarkable the number of slaves which may be raised from one woman in the course of forty or fifty years with the proper kind of attention."[4] Nearly every Black woman interviewed by Fannie Kemble in her 1838-1839 journal on slavery had a number of children. One woman under thirty had borne ten children and had subsequently developed a "nervous disorder, brought on by frequent childbearing." Venus, a mulatto slave "terribly crippled with rhematism," had "eleven children, five of whom had died, and two miscarriages."[5] U. B. Phillips observed that "one phenomenal slave mother born forty-one children, mostly of course as twins; and the records of many others ran well above a dozen each."[6] One ingenious master, James Hammond of South Carolina, gave each of his Black slave mothers "a muslin or calico frock—but only when her newborn infant was thirteen months old." Another ordered that any Black "women with six children alive at any one time are allowed all Saturday to themselves."[7]

Many masters did not wait for the slaves themselves to reproduce in sufficient numbers, and took matters into their own hands. As property, Black women were expected to produce wealth for their owners. But as females, Black women were also constantly subjected to the physical and sexual assault of white males. As Angela Davis observed, "the integration of rape (into slavery) harks back to the feudal

'right of the first night,' the *jus primae noctis*. The feudal lord manifested and reinforced his authority to have sexual intercourse with all
the females." In the context of American slavery, in the United States
and elsewhere, the white man sought to reduce Black women to the
lowest level of biological being. "The act of copulation, reduced by the
white man to an animal-like act, would be symbolic of the effort to
conquer the resistance the Black woman could unloose."8 White
American historians have usually been extremely reluctant to discuss
this "normal" and universal aspect of any slave order. Brazilian sociologist Gilbert Freyre discussed the issue frankly with the initial observation that "there is no slavery without sexual depravity. Depravity is the
essence of such a regime." Freyre noted that "one favorite saying of the
planters was: 'The most productive feature of slave property is the
generative belly.' "9 Brazilian whites had a casual attitude toward
syphilis and gonorrhea and had no reservations about spreading their
affliction into Black households. From the age of thirteen, the white
boy "was subject to ridicule for not having had carnal knowledge of a
woman and would be the butt of jests if he could not show the scars of
syphilis on his body." Many older white men believed that the only
method to cure themselves of gonorrhea was to have intercourse with a
young Black virgin—"the surest means of extinguishing it in oneself."
Black women who wet-nursed white infants who were already infected
by their parents "thus convey(ed) from the Big House to the slave hut
the blight of syphilis. It killed, blinded, deformed at will."10 Sadism
and masochism were also an organic aspect of race relations, sometimes
involving even small Black boys as well as females. Freyre noted that
"the white lad was often initiated into the mysteries of "physical love"
through sexual games of submission wherein Black youths were forced
to "take a drubbing."11

White males who settled the United States lacked the cultural and
historic relations which characterize the evolution of Portuguese and
Spanish slave societies vis-a-vis Africans. Their racism was more
aggressive; their neurotic fantasies were more repressively checked by
the religious heritage of Calvinism and Puritanism; their knowledge of
Black culture was more limited; their desire for profits, greater. For the
white male American, the Black women's vagina was his private
property. Like his cotton fields, the fruit of its issue belonged to him
alone. His half-white child by the Black woman was usually treated
just like any other slave. Raping the Black woman was not unlike

plowing up fertile ground; the realities of plantation labor descended into the beds of the slaves' quarters, where the violent ritual of rape paralleled the harsh political realities of slave agricultural production. As Davis noted:

> In its political contours, the rape of the Black woman was not exclusively an attack upon her. Indirectly, its target was also the slave community as a whole.
>
> In launching the sexual war on the woman, the master could not only assert his sovereignty over a critically important figure of the slave community, he would also be aiming a blow against the Black man. . . Clearly the master hoped that once the Black man was struck by his manifest inability to rescue his women from sexual assaults of the master, he would begin to experience deep-seated doubts about his ability to resist at all. [12]

Many Black women fought these repeated sexual assaults, and an untold number sacrificed their lives to retain their humanity. Many more carried the scars of their rapes, both physical and psychological, with them for the rest of their lives. The children of such coerced owner-slave unions, and the omnipresence of white rape, is indicated in part by the swelling number of mulattoes in the South before the Civil War. By 1850 there were 245,000 mulatto slaves; by 1860, 411,000 mulattoes out of an enslaved Black population of 3,900,000. [13]

For Black women, and their men, the only means to maintain their inner strength and integrity was through resistance. Black resistance assumed, first, the form of conscious, voluntary day-to-day protest: the destruction of agricultural implements, burning crops, stealing whites' personal food and property, deliberate slow-downs in the fields, and so forth. A number of Black women, far more than most Black historians have appreciated, ran away from their plantations or farms in search of freedom. Between 1736 and 1801 in Virginia alone, there were 141 documented instances of runaway African women. There was Hannah, a young woman of 19, "who when angered flashed a 'very passionate temper' "; Sarah, a "small and courageous girl of 14" who insisted in calling herself Mindingo; Milly, described by her owner as having grey eyes, "very large Breasts," and noted for being "a sly, subtle Wench, and a great Lyar." Cicley's master warned, "Beware to secure her Well, for she is very wicked and full of flattery." Only fifteen of the 141 women ran off in the company of slave men—a piece of evidence that indicates remarkable self-reliance in a patriarchal society. Yet many white owners, blinded by their entrenched sexism, could not contemplate that Black women by themselves would thirst for liberation. In 1772, a typical master lamented about one African woman who departed with her husband, "I imagine she is entirely governed by him."[14]

The greatest indictment against slavery and white Southern patriarchy came from the voices of Black women. Jane Blake's *Memoirs,* written in 1897, provides all the evidence one needs to illustrate that slave breeding existed. Many slave women refused to have sex with men they did not love, and fought the sexual advances of their white owners. Blake wrote, if "all the bond women had been of the same mind, how soon the institution could have vanished from the earth, and all the misery belonging to it."[15] Jane Brown's *Narrative* of 1856 asserted that virtually every slave longed for freedom, and that both freed and enslaved Blacks covertly discussed rebellion.[16] Louisa Picquet was forced to become a concubine for white men. In her 1861 narrative, *Inside Views of Southern Domestic Life,* she argued that sexual exploitation of Black women constituted the core of white Southern hypocrisy. She observed that U.S. whites oppose the "heathenism of a Turkish harem. (But) is all this whit worse than what is constantly practiced, with scarce a word of unfavorable comment, in our Christian land? Our chivalrous 'southern gentlemen' beget thousands of slaves; and hundreds of children of our free white citizens are sold in the southern slave markets every year."[17] When the moment of freedom arrived, Black women understood better than anyone else the *ancien regime* of rape and labor exploitation was at an end. The story of one young Black woman named Caroline Gordon, or "Caddy," bears witness:

> Caddy had been sold to a man in Goodman, Mississippi. It was terrible to be sold in Mississippi. In fact, it was terrible to be sold anywhere. She had been put to work in the fields for running away again. She was hoeing a crop when she heard that General Lee surrendered . . . that meant that all the colored people were free! Caddy threw down that hoe, she marched herself up to the big house, then, she looked around and found the mistress. She went over to the mistress, she flipped up her dress and told the

white woman to do something. She said it mean and ugly: *Kiss my ass!*[18]

III

From the very beginning of Black political activism in the United States, Afro-American men had real difficulty in considering the "triple oppression" (race/class/sex) of Black women with any degree of seriousness. Part of the problem stemmed from the evolution of patriarchal institutions within Black civil society. Black churches in the free states were involved in a variety of reform activities, from the creation of economic enterprises to the building of a network of Black schools. But these churches were invariably dominated by Black men, who served as pastors, evangelists and deacons. Black mutual benefit societies, first started in Newport, Rhode Island and Philadelphia, gave members recreational facilities, provided families with modest economic protection in case of sickness or death, and created the foundations for Black business development. Yet the major societies were funded, directed and controlled by Black males. The Black newspapers established in the nineteenth century, including John Russwurm's *Freedom's Journal* (1827), Martin Delany's *Mystery* (1843), Frederick Douglass' *North Star* (1848) and the *Anglo-African* of New York City (1859), tended to print the antislavery speeches, manifestos and essays of articulate Black men. The Negro Convention Movement, a series of Black political conferences beginning in 1830 in Philadelphia, almost always involved only Black men.

Many Black male activists identified the cause of Black liberation with the ultimate attainment of "Black manhood." This definition of freedom was a conditioned response evoked by white patriarchy, whether the Black men of the period recognized this or not. Henry Highland Garnet's famous "Address to the Slaves of the United States," delivered at the 1843 Negro Convention specifically called upon every Black "man" to "resist aggression." "In every man's mind the good seeds of liberty are planted, and he who brings his fellow down so long, as to make him contented with a condition of slavery, commits the highest crime against God and man." Garnet's audience was reminded of the racists' transgressions upon its manhood:

> See your sons murdered, and your wives, mothers and sisters doomed to prostitution. . . And worse than all, you tamely submit while your lords tear your wives from your embraces and defile

them before your eyes. In the name of God, we ask, are you men? Where is the blood of your fathers? Has it all run out of your veins?[19]

Radical newspaper editor T. Thomas Fortune condemned whites as "the most consummate masters of hypocrisy, of roguery, of insolence, and of cowardice" in an 1887 polemic. Fortune was quick to add, however, that "many imagine that we are compelled to submit and have not the manhood necessary to resent such conduct. We shall labor as one man to wage relentless opposition to all men who would degrade our manhood."[20] Pan-African scholar and clergyman Alexander Crummell reminded Blacks that the chief aim of civilization was the creation "of a true and lofty race of men. For manhood is the most majestic thing in God's creation."[21] Even Frederick Douglass, the leading male proponent of women's rights in the nineteenth century, asserted in 1855 that the struggle for racial liberation meant that Blacks "must develop their manhood, and not be too modest to attempt such development."[22]

Douglass was exceptional among all Black male activists in his open commitment to equality for women. Soon after his flight to freedom in the North, he identified himself with militant white and Black women in their struggle for suffrage and legal rights. In the initial issue of the *North Star,* he drew the obvious political parallels between the battles against racism and sexism, declaring that "Right is of no sex." He attended the first national women's rights convention held at Seneca Falls, New York, in July, 1848, and seconded the motion of Elizabeth Cady Stanton calling for women's voting rights. Douglass was the only male of thirty-seven men in attendance who supported women's suffrage. Douglass' advocacy for feminist causes was so well-known that both Stanton and Lucretia Mott urged women to elect him as a leader of their movement only two weeks after Seneca Falls. Susan B. Anthony notified friends to purchase the *North Star* "for announcements of women's rights gatherings." Douglass' partial break with white feminists occurred after the Civil War, when Anthony, Stanton and others opposed the ratification of the Fifteenth Amendment unless it also mandated universal suffrage. Politically pragmatic, Douglass urged his followers to support the winning of Black male voting rights first. By 1869, the Equal Rights Association split, and many white feminists began to gravitate toward racist slogans to support their own cause.[23]

The struggle to destroy slavery, and the economic and political battles of Reconstruction, coincided with the entrenchment of patriarchal relations within the Black community. The rough equality of labor imposed by the brutalities of the slave regime did not extend into the slaves' quarters. Black men universally "regarded tasks like cooking, sewing, nursing, and even minor farm labor as woman's work," according to Bell Hooks. Black women after slavery seldom demanded social equality between themselves and their men. "Instead, they bitterly resented that they were not considered 'women' by the dominant culture. . ."[24] With the establishment of sharecropping, the majority of Black women farm laborers and farmers ceased work in the fields, and retreated into the kitchens and homes of their families. They expected, as a point of honor and as an element of freedom, that they would be supported by their husbands, fathers and brothers. "White plantation owners were shocked when large numbers of Black female workers refused to work in the fields."[25] Statistically this is illustrated by Census figures from 1890. Slightly less than half of all Black women between the ages of 15 to 24 years were employed in 1890; about half were domestic workers, and the remainder were field hands or farmers. Less than 40 percent of all Black women between the ages of 25 to 64 were workers, compared to 97-98 percent of all Black males. Of course, fewer white women were gainfully employed than Black women. Only 14 percent of all white women 10 years old and over were in the 1890 workforce, and the percentage dropped to 10 percent and below after age 35. (See Table VIII) Denied the right to work outside the home, the majority of Black women were expected to fulfill the "traditional" role of "mother" by giving birth to as many children as physically possible. For Black married women born between 1861 and 1865, the average number of children born to them by 1910 was 6.2. (See Table IX)

Although the Victorian era was inhospitable to intelligent and politically active females, a number of Black women succeeded in overcoming the institutional barriers of white and Black patriarchy. Frances Ellen Watkins Harper established herself as the nineteenth century's most popular Black poet/activist. Born in Baltimore of free parents in 1824, she became involved in the Underground Railroad, the illegal network by which slaves were channelled North. In September, 1854, the Maine Anti-Slavery Society recognized her talents as an orator and hired her to speak across New England. In 1857-1858 she worked for the Pennsylvania Anti-Slavery Society, speaking two or three times each day for the cause of Black freedom, attracting "large, enthusiastic audiences." In 1860 she married a Black Ohio farmer, Fenton Harper, and retired for several years to have a child. Within five months of her husband's death in 1864, Harper was again on the lecture circuit, speaking in support of the war effort. From 1865 until 1871 Harper travelled throughout the Southern United States at her own expense, living on meager donations, speaking endlessly "at Sunday schools, day schools, churches, town meetings, in homes and village squares," usually talking twice daily. During these years she also authored several popularly acclaimed books of poetry and wrote articles for the press. In the 1870s she became Assistant Superintendent of the YMCA school in Philadelphia, and was elected national officer in the National Council of Women and the National Association of Colored Women. Until her death in 1911, Harper was a noted advocate of women's suffrage, equal rights and Black freedom. [26]

Sojourner Truth was, probably only second to Douglass, the outstanding orator of Black liberation during the mid-century. Born as "Isabella" in Ulster County, New York in 1797, she was one of twelve slave children who were sold away from their parents. Married at an early age, she gave birth to five children before she was freed; one of her sons was sold by her owner to an Alabama slavemaster. In 1843, she began to speak out on her personal ordeal as a slave at abolitionist gatherings, and assumed the name Sojourner Truth. During the Civil War Sojourner lived and worked in the "contraband" camps of Washington, D.C., teaching former slaves. She aided Black women "to protect their children against white Maryland raiders who sought to kidnap them and sell them into slavery." [27] Appointed to work with the Freedman's hospital in Washington, she led the struggle to bar Jim Crow public transportation in the capital. In the late 1860s, Sojourner returned to the lecture circuit, speaking out in favor of a massive relocation of Black families from the South into the Great Plains states. In her view, no Black political solution was possible without a general reallocation of land. In 1879, Sojourner joined the wave of "Exodusters" who fled the post -Reconstruction era South and settled in Kansas City. Unlike most Black male leaders, she urged her people to buy land and to develop a sufficient economic base from which to wage their various struggles for social and political justice. One of the central tragedies of this period is that so few Black politicians listened seriously to Sojourner's ideas on Black economic development. Their ingrained sexism made it impossible, perhaps, for Black men to internalize the agenda of an eighty-two year old Black woman.

Two of the most progressive Black activists during the post-Reconstruction period of political accommodation were Ida B. Wells and Mary Church Terrell. Wells was born in 1862, in Holly Springs, Mississippi and was educated at Rust College and Fisk University. Arriving in Memphis in the early 1880s, she soon acquired the reputation as the Black South's most militant journalist. Purchasing partial ownership in the Memphis *Free Speech and Headlight,* she used the press in a campaign against Southern lynchings. In a controversial editorial, she observed that "Nobody in this section of the country believes the old threadbare lies that Negro men rape white women. If Southern white men are not careful they will over-reach themselves and public sentiment will have a reaction, or a conclusion will be reached which will be very damaging to the moral reputation of their women." Wells' documentary on the near genocidal violence against Blacks, *United States Atrocities* (1893), is a valuable precursor to the works of William Patterson and Sidney Willhelm six decades later.[28] Mary Church Terrell was the daughter of Robert R. Church of Memphis, a Southern Black real estate millionaire and political leader. Educated at Oberlin College, she taught at Wilberforce before settling in Washington, D.C. and, in 1891, marrying Robert H. Terrell, a lawyer and the principal of the District's M. Street High School. Mary Terrell was appointed a member of the Washington, D.C. Board of Education, and quickly became a leading critic of Booker T. Washington—the Black politician whom her husband closely supported. In fact, she created such a furor that one of the Tuskegeean's hacks penned a New York *Age* editorial declaring bitterly that "some one ought to muzzle Mary Church Terrell. What we now want as a race, is less agitators and more constructors." Terrell joined the NAACP and was promptly elected vice president of the Washington branch. In later years, Terrell became politically quite conservative, serving as director of the Republican National Committee's campaign to reach Black women voters on the East coast in 1920 and 1932. However, despite her support for Hoover and the Republican Party, Terrell continued to fight racial discrimination and Jim Crow laws until her death.[29]

The first half of the twentieth century produced a new generation of creative and intellectually prolific Black women in education and the arts. Jessie Redmond Fauset, born in 1886, became famous both as the translator of Black poetry from the French West Indies, and for her novels *There is Confusion* (1924), *Plum Bun* (1929), and *The Chinaberry Tree* (1931). Georgia Douglass Johnson was perhaps the most popular Black poet between Paul Laurence Dunbar and the rise of the Harlem Renaissance bards of the 1920s. Novelist Nella Larsen's *Quicksand* (1928) and *Passing* (1929) examined the "innumerable social problems of young Negro women in their efforts to struggle upward both in America and in Europe."[30] Meta Warrick Fuller became renowned as a brilliant and innovative sculptor; Laura Wheeler Waring gained fame as a painter. Actresses Ida Anderson, Edna Thomas and Laura Bowman performed to rave reviews in Harlem's all-Black Lafayette Players' group during the 1920s. Among the most creative Black minds in aesthetics during the Great Depression was unquestionably Zora Neale Hurston—cultural anthropologist, novelist, essayist and folklorist. In a brief period of twelve years she authored seven important novels. In education and politics, Black women were ably represented by Mary McLeod Bethune. Founder of Cookman College in 1905, she became a master fund raiser and proponent of higher education for young Black women. During the 1930s Bethune was named Director of the Division of Negro Affairs for the National Youth Administration. In 1945 she was one of several Blacks named as members of the United States delegation at the creation of the United Nations in April, 1945, in San Francisco.[31].

The decades after 1900 until the 1940s also produced gradual changes within both the employment patterns of Black women and in the size of Black families. More Black women were in the labor force than there were immediately after slavery: about 47 percent during the prime working ages of 20 to 54. Roughly twice the percentage of Black women were gainfully employed in 1930 as were white women (39 percent vs. 20 percent). (See Table VIII) By 1940, Black married women averaged only 2.3 children, the lowest number ever recorded for Blacks by the U.S. Census. Most married women were waiting longer to have their children, and between 22 to 29 percent of middle aged Black women were not bearing any children at all. The number of children ever born per married Black woman was reduced during this time by 53 percent. (See Table X) Black families during World War II were still slightly larger than those of whites, but as the Black woman acquired greater opportunities for post-secondary education, the number of her children dropped sharply. In 1940, married nonwhite women with one to three years of college training averaged only 1.7 children. With four or more years of college, nonwhite women had only 1.2 children—both figures that were below those for white college trained women. (See Table XI) More frequently than ever before, Black women were leaving the kitchens and earning their own wages in the labor force. Black women appeared no longer as "auxilliaries" or marginal participants in Black educational, social and political life. The leading figures of Bethune, Terrell, Hurston and others provided abundant role models for young Black girls to abandon the yoke of subordination and sexual subservience.

During these years, among Black men, W.E.B. DuBois largely filled the role of Douglass as the chief proponent of women's equality. DuBois' commitment to women's rights began as early as 1887, when as editor of the *Fisk Herald* he predicted that "the Age of Woman is surely dawning."[32] In his essays in the *Crisis* and other periodicals, DuBois emphasized that the struggle for Black freedom must inevitably include the demand for "the emancipation of women."[33] Constantly he chided Blacks for exhibiting any form of favoritism toward males over females. When one reader of the *Crisis* reported the birth of a girl, DuBois suggested "the ancient idea that boys are intrinsically and naturally better than girls is a relic of barbarism that dies a hard death . . . Be glad it's a girl and make life wider and safer and more equal in burden for all girls because of this one."[34] The patriarchal attitudes of politicians was a particularly favorite topic for this Black scholar. "Every statesman who yells about Children, Church and Kitchen," he declared in January, 1934, "ought to be made to bear twins, to listen to as many sermons as we have, and to wash dishes and diapers for at least ten years."[35] In 1912 DuBois drafted a pamphlet entitled *Disfranchisement*, published by the National American Woman Suffrage Association, which advanced women's right to vote as a necessary precondition to the realization of democracy.[36] In states where universal enfranchisement was on the ballot, DuBois encouraged Black men to cast their support behind the women's rights movement. "Is there a single argument for the right of men to vote, that does not apply to the votes for women, and particularly for black women?"[37] Although he was friendly toward feminist causes, DuBois would not hesitate to criticize the racism found within the white women's political movement. In several *Crisis* articles, he condemned some leaders of the "Suffering

Suffragettes" who advocated that white women, and not Blacks, should be allowed to vote.[38] Despite these differences, DuBois enthusiastically supported the moves of women from the kitchens into the factory and business world. In March, 1941, he pointed with pride that many more Black women were in the labor force than white women. In January, 1947, he urged Black husbands to "share housework" and to shoulder the burdens of child-rearing equally.[39] For half a century, he reminded Black men that "the hope of the Negro rests on its intelligent and incorruptible womanhood."[40]

In contrast with DuBois, however, many Black men were disturbed with the evolutionary transformation in sex roles and the creation of political, educational and economic opportunities for Black women. Marcus Garvey's political approach toward Black women's issues was a curious mixture of romanticism, sexism and race nationalism. In the 1923 edition of the *Philosophy and Opinions of Marcus Garvey*, the Jamaican militant suggested that women were necessary yet contradictory beings: "She makes one happy, then miserable. You are to her kind, then unkind. Constant yet inconstant. Thus we have WOMAN. No real man can do without her."[41] Like the Black activists of the nineteenth century, Garvey identified Black struggle with the attainment of manhood, the realization of a kind of masses' macho. He warned his followers, "There is always a turning point in the destiny of every race, every nation, of all peoples and we have come now to the turning point of the Negro, where we have changed from the old cringing weakling, and transformed into full-grown men, demanding our portion as MEN."[42] In his *Blackman* journal, he cautioned affluent Black women not to marry white men, and urged Black men not to "insult our womanhood" by having sexual relations with whites.[43] Garvey was profoundly concerned with statistics that showed a declining number of children in Black households. "By a decreasing birth rate and an increasing death rate," he warned in October, 1925, "it means the death of your race—the suicide of your race."[44] In 1934, Garvey's Universal Negro Improvement Association issued a resolution condemning birth control for Blacks. "Any attempt to interfere with the natural function of life is a rebellion against the conceived purpose of divinity in making man a part of his spiritual self," the sexist manifesto declared. "The theory of birth control . . . interfered with the course of nature and with the purpose of the God in whom we believe."[45] Simultaneously, DuBois authored a stirring statement endorsing planned parenthood in *Birth Control Review,* and invited Margaret Sanger, a "birth-control pioneer," to contribute to the pages of the *Crisis.*[46]

From the 1930s to the 1950s, a number of Black men raised serious questions pertaining to the declining birth rate among Black women. University of Chicago pathologist Julian Lewis argued in 1945 that "the survival of the black race in the United States was dependent upon "a high birth rate." In subsequent articles, Lewis attacked the Planned Parenthood Federation for attempting to "improve the quality of the human race at the cost of numbers." Blacks who condoned birth control were sponsoring "race suicide."[47] Some Blacks noted with apprehension that some states had sanctioned castrations and vasectomies on prison inmates and patients in mental hospitals in the 1890s, and suggested that racists now might be using birth control as a legal means to reduce the Black population. These fears were reinforced when a Mississippi state legislator introduced a bill in 1958 which would "provide for mandatory sterilization after a woman on welfare (had) given birth to a certain number of illegitimate children." By 1964 the Mississippi house ratified a law that "stipulated that any person who became the parent of a second out-of-wedlock child would be guilty of a felony punishable by a sentence of one to three years in the state penitentiary. A subsequent conviction would be punishable by three to five years in prison. However, a convicted parent had the option of submitting to sterilization in lieu of imprisonment."[48] White Republicans and Democrats alike, particularly in the South, proposed punitive sterilization for Black welfare mothers. These same male politicians had no reservations, however, in denying legal abortions or contraceptive information to Black (or white) teenage girls and women.

Conservative Black nationalist formations often surpassed white reactionaries in their opposition to birth control. An extreme case is provided by the Nation of Islam. Patriarch Elijah Muhammad informed Black followers that their women were unprepared for the "tricks the devils are using to instill the idea of a false birth control in their clinics and hospitals." Black women were created by God to serve their husbands and sons. "The woman is man's field to produce his nation," Elijah Muhammad observed. The Nation of Islam's ministers frequently attacked Black women and men who supported freedom of choice regarding birth control. Minister Louis Farrakhan wrote in a Black woman's publication, *Essence,* that "when the black woman kills

her unborn child, she is murdering the advancement of her nation."
One *Muhammad Speaks* article declared that population control was a
covert tactic in the general "war against the nonwhite people." Muslim
woman Shirley Hazziez wrote in *Muhammad Speaks* that every Black
woman should reject the pill as a "deadly poison," and that "Allah was
able to feed and care for black infants." Birth control was, for the Black
woman, "death for my babies and race."[49]

Well before the Civil Rights Movement, a not-so-subtle reaction
began to form within Black civil society which reinforced patriarchal
relations between men and women. The Depression and war years
produced within the popular culture the figure of Sapphire: a Black
woman who was "evil, treacherous, bitchy, stubborn, and hateful."
The Sapphire stereotype was utilized by white males, who "could
justify their dehumanization and sexual exploitation of black women,"
and by Black males, who could reasonably "claim that they could not get
along with black women because they were so evil." Black patriarchal
society employed Sapphire to explain away any Black woman who
exhibited tendencies of strength that were designated for males only.[50]
Furthermore, as greater numbers of Black women left agricultural
work for domestic service employment, many Black men leaped to the
illogical conclusion that white males "favored black women over black
men" in all levels of the job market. As Hooks observed, "white people
did not perceive black women engaging in service jobs as performing
significant work that deserved adequate economic reward. They saw
domestic service jobs performed by black women as being merely an
extension of the 'natural' female role and considered such jobs value-
less." Unemployed Black men, desperate for work, perceived their
wives' ability to gain employment an assault on their own manhood. At
another level, Black women who adopted patriarchal perspectives "saw
the black male who did not eagerly assume the breadwinner role as
selfish, lazy, and irresponsible, or in white male sociological terms,
'emasculated'."[51] These cultural, social and economic forces combined
after 1945 to produce the conditions for a fundamental reaction.

Within the U.S. economy, this reaction was apparent in civilian
labor force participation rates between 1945 and 1960. During the
early 1940s, tens of thousands of Black women went into jobs previously held by men. By the end of World War II, almost half of all
Black women (46 percent) were employed full-time, compared to only
31 percent of all white women. Fifty-one to 53 percent of Black women

between the ages of 25 and 54 were wage earners. Sixty percent of the Black women were employed as private household workers, 7 percent were blue-collar laborers, and 16 percent were farmers or farm laborers. Fifteen years later, the percentage of Black women workers outside the home had increased by only 2 percent, while white women workers increased by 6 percent. Only 22 percent of all nonwhite teenage women who were actively in the job market could find work in 1960, compared to 30 percent for white female teenagers. By 1965, Black females with an eighth-grade education or less had a labor force participation rate of only 38 percent.[52] Black men encouraged their wives and daughters to settle back, to return to the kitchen: the role of the husband was that of provider, and the task of wives was to produce offspring. After 1945, the birth rates for Black women climbed sharply. The percentage of all Black married women between the ages of 20 and 24 years who had two to four children increased from 34 percent in 1940 to 51 percent in 1960; in that same age group, those women with five or more children grew from 2 percent to 7 percent. The percentage of all Black married women between the ages of 25 and 29 who had five or more children doubled in two decades, from 11 percent in 1940 to 22 percent in 1960. Overall the number of children born per married Black woman increased from 2.3 percent in 1940 to 2.8 percent in 1960. (See Table X) Even outside of marriage, the number of Black children born during this period increased dramatically. The rate of childbirths for nonmarried nonwhite women per thousand, for women between ages 25 and 29, increased from 32.5 in 1940 to 171.8 in 1960. Black fertility rates, which declined from 3.56 in 1920 to 2.62 in 1940, rebounded to 3.58 in 1950 and reached 4.54 by 1960.[53] No Black female could become a real woman, in short, unless she had a child. Work outside the home should be a secondary goal. Black unmarried teenage girls could become women by bearing children "for the race."

IV

Sudden changes in the consciousness of oppressed people are often reflected in their poetry: the sexual and racial conflicts of the 1960s provided new directions for Black Americans in the arts. Occasionally, both Black liberation and patriarchal themes were woven together by the new Black women poets. Nikki Giovanni asked all Black men and women alike to develop their "manhood":

Can you kill
Can you piss on a blond head
Can you cut if off
Can you kill . . .
Can you splatter their brains in the street
Can you lure them to bed to kill them . . .
Can we learn to kill WHITE for BLACK
Learn to kill niggers
Learn to be Black men. [54]

In "Beautiful Black Men," written in 1968, Giovanni praised "those beautiful beautiful outasight black men with their afros . . ." Her "brand new pleasure" was observing her men "running numbers, watching for their whores, preaching in churches," and "winking at me" in their "tight tight pants that hug what I like to hug."[55] Other Black women embraced the image of the Black man as the urban guerilla, and created love poetry that expressed simultaneously their fertility and sensuality for their men:

My old man
tells me i'm
so full of sweet
pussy he can
smell me coming.
maybe i shd
bottle it and
sell it
when he goes. [56]

Along more traditional romantic lines, poet Alice Lovelace's "Wedding Song" informs her husband-to-be: "You are my man/The part I've sought that makes me whole . . . we'll raise bubbling black babies/ swathed in black culture."[57] Carolyn Rogers' "For Some Black Men" counsels her brothers to recognize the inherent dependency and submissiveness of sisters: "Woman is softness, warm of warmth, need from need."[58]

Among some Black women intellectuals, there was at one point a curious inversion of the "pedestal phenomenon," the cultural dynamic wherein white males had symbolically elevated white women to the heights of aesthetic and social predominance. These sisters not only acknowledged the innate or biological leadership of Black men, but

literally placed their faith, their ontological existence, within the
hegemonic corpus of the Black male. Romanticists were usually the
worst offenders. Poet Ann DuCille's "Lady in Waiting" combined the
African mythology of the cultural nationalists with the sexist acceptance of the woman-as-womb:

> In dreams without sleep
> I lie inside myself
> waiting to be born . . .
> I am a princess
> goddess of the Nile
> Nubian daughter of Nefertiti . . .
> unsung
> yet tuned in time
> to take the milk of man
> between my thighs.[59]

Other Black women poets who reflected critically about their own
"integrationist contradictions" sang high hosannas to the Black militant men who had delivered them from their former political beliefs.
Lucille Clifton's "apology (to the panthers)" is reminiscent of a
Catholic chant, evoking one's spiritual weaknesses before the holy
altar, requesting absolution for the remission of sins:

> i was obedient
> but brothers i thank you
> for these mannish days.
> . . . brothers
> i thank you
> i praise you
> i grieve my whiteful ways.[60]

Most Black men accepted these *mea culpas* in stride. "The role of
the black woman in the black liberation is an important one and cannot
be forgotten," Black sociologist Robert Staples wrote in 1970. "From
her womb have come the revolutionary warriors of our time."[61] Thus,
the Black woman's most significant factor to contribute to the Movement, in short, was her uterus.

But behind these glowing exhultations of the Black man there
remained the bitter embers of sexual oppression and subordination.
Half-hidden even during Black Power's hey-day, but becoming ever
more dominant into the 1970s, were the contradictory stirrings of a

Black feminist criticism. Often these expressions began in the form of an attack on all "brothers" who chose to have sexual relations with white females. Sonia Sanchez's "to all brothers" is a clear warning:

> yeah.
> they hang you up
> those grey chicks
> parading their tight asses
> in front of you.
> Some will say out right
> baby I want
> to ball you
> while smoother ones
> will integrate your
> blackness
> yeah.
> brother
> this sister knows
> and waits.[62]

And in her finest work, "Woman Poem," Giovanni illustrates the basic exploitation of Black women within a patriarchal and racist social order:

> a sex object if you're pretty
> and no love
> or love and no sex if you're fat
> get back fat black woman be a mother
> grandmother strong thing but not woman
> manseeker dick eater sweat getter
> fuck needing love seeking woman.[63]

Poet/playwright Ntozake Shange, author of *For Colored Girls Who Have Considered Suicide When the Rainbow is Enuf,* was one of the first major writers to examine the problems of abortion, alienation between Black women and men, and the hostilities between Black women over males.

> she been there for years wid this dude
> but he needed a change and well, she wd manage
> nothin gonna last forever/
> but i hesitated cuz she seemed so fragile
> i wax fulla vitality and gall
> 'get ridda that bitch or leave me alone'
> he did.
> i ignored all that talk bout the woman who tried to
> burn herself alive/waznt none of my business
> what some weak bitch did to herself.[64]

The obvious contradictions relating the issues of race and gender within these and other poems were, of course, a product of the turbulent politics of the period. The Civil Rights Movement had begun coming unglued by 1964, with the successful desegregation of Southern civil society. Young Black women and men, the vanguard of freedom fighters in the Student Nonviolent Coordinating Committee (SNCC), rejected integration as "subterfuge for the maintenance of white supremacy."[65] Black nationalism as a cultural and political expression was seized by substantial elements of the Black petty bourgeoisie and working class. Across the country, hundreds of new political and educational institutions were created that were developed within the specious theoretical framework of Black Power. Yet remarkably few Black activists elevated the question of sexism to the level of primacy, within their practical political activities or in their intellectual work. Patriarchy had been historically more compatible with most Black nationalist groupings than among cultural pluralists or even integrationists. As a result, it is not surprising that the actual practice of Black militants did precious little to overturn the rampant sexism within Black life.

The fountainhead of contemporary Black nationalism, Malcolm X, was likewise not immune from this dynamic. For many young Black militants, both in the streets and the universities, Malcolm symbolized the best that Black humanity had produced. Black actor Ossie Davis eulogized Malcolm at his funeral, declaring that he "was our manhood . . . our own black shining Prince—who didn't hesitate to die, because he loved us so."[66] Though Malcolm's views on Black women changed considerably for the better throughout his life, like so many other male leaders, he usually thought of politics as a preserve for men only; sisters were an invaluable but secondary factor in the race war. Even today, any serious criticism of Malcolm's views is akin to traitorous behavior in most Black activist circles. But it serves Malcolm's memory poorly if we simply reify the entire body of his ideas and actions without a detailed and serious analysis of his own contradictions. As Bell Hooks observes, "it is impossible to read his autobiography without becoming aware of the hatred and contempt he felt toward women for much of his life."[67] At one point in his discussions with Alex Haley, the Black novelist/journalist, Malcolm admitted that "you never can fully trust any woman":

> I've got the only one I ever met whom I would trust seventy-five percent. I've told her that. . . . Too many men (have been) destroyed by their wives, or their women. Whatever else a woman is, I don't care who the woman is, it starts with her being vain. I'll prove it . . . You think of the hardest-looking, meanest-acting woman you know, one of those women who never smiles. Well, every day you see that woman you look her right in the eyes and tell her 'I think you're beautiful,' and you watch what happens. The first day she may curse you out, the second day, too—but you watch, you keep on, after a while one day she's going to start smiling just as soon as you come in sight.[68]

Malcolm X was not the only, and certainly not the worst of the Black Power leaders with respect to the issue of gender. For Stokely Carmichael, leader of SNCC in 1966, young Black men had to assert themselves as males—politically, and sexually. "Every Negro is a potential black man," Carmichael taught nascent activists.[69] Black militants cultivated a righteous contempt for white women as a *sine qua non* of activist practice. When whites asked Carmichael if integration meant interracial marriage, he replied that "the white woman is not the queen of the world, she is not the Virgin Mary, she can be made like any other woman."[70] The revolutionary responsibilities of sisters in the cause of Black liberation were somewhat different. In a speech given at

Morgan State on January 28, 1967, Carmichael outlined his thoughts on Black women:

> Girls, are you ready? Obviously it is your responsibility to begin to define the criteria for black people concerning their beauty. You are running around with your Nadinola cream. The black campuses of this country are becoming infested with wigs and Mustangs and you are to blame for it. You are to blame for it. What is your responsibility to your fellow black brothers? So that you can become a social worker or so that you can kick down a door in the middle of the night to look for a pair of shoes? Is that what you come to college for? . . . Is it so that you can just get over? Do you not know that your black mothers scrubbed floors so you can get here—and the minute you get out, you turn your back on them?[71]

Like the Garveyites, many later-day nationalists vigorously opposed contraceptives, abortions and planned parenthood measures. In 1970, Brenda Hyson, a female leader of the Black Panthers, attacked a New York state law which made legal abortions available to Black and poor women. The "oppressive ruling class will use this law to kill off Blacks and other opposed people before they are born," Hyson warned. Voluntary abortions would lead to forced sterilization. Black women had a political responsibility to oppose "legalized murder" and forced "family planning in the guise of pills and coils." The *Black News*, a nationalist publication based in Brooklyn, described birth control for sisters as "deceptive genocide" in one 1971 essay. Black women were too frequently "duped into having unnecessary hysterectomies and surgical sterilization." For the survival of "the Black man," Black women would have to put away all forms of contraceptives—even the traditional and most unreliable device, the condom. "The hidden meaning of the Trojan," *Black News* declared, "was to emasculate the Black man by convincing him that he should throw away his living sperm into the white man's rubber contraption rather than to put it into his woman's fertile womb."[72] Haki Madhubuti, director of Chicago's Black Nationalist Institute of Positive Studies, argued that "the entire white system is geared toward the total destruction of the *Black man first*—mentally, physically and spiritually. If the Black man is not allowed to take care of and build his family, where is the Black woman?" Zero population growth campaigns and liberal abortion laws would destroy the Black race.[73]

No single Black activist was more profoundly sexist than the celebrated ex-convict/writer of the Black Panther Party, Eldridge Cleaver. His infamous and bizarre expositions against Black women, gays, and others need no recounting here.[74] What is most important about Cleaver's writing is that it falls squarely into the century-old tradition of viewing Black liberation first and last as the effort to assert one's manhood, in the sense of patriarchal hegemony exhibited by the old planter class. In a pathetic passage, Cleaver contemplates the impact of white racism upon the Black male:

> Across the naked abyss of negated masculinity, of four hundred years minus my Balls, we face each other today, my Queen. I feel a deep, terrifying hurt, the pain of humiliation of the vanquished warrior. For four hundred years I have been unable to look squarely into your eyes . . . Instead of inciting the slaves to rebellion with eloquent oratory, I soothed their hurt and eloquently sang the Blues! Instead of hurling my life with contempt into the face of my Tormentor, I shed your precious blood! My spirit was unwilling and my flesh was weak. . . . Divested of my Balls, (I) walked the earth with my mind locked in Cold Storage. I would kill a black man or woman quicker than I'd smash a fly, while for the white man I would pick a thousand pounds of cotton a day."[75]

From this standpoint, the white master had succeeded in erecting a barrier between all Black men and women. Cleaver's conclusion was to mimic the worst features of white patriarchy. "We shall have our manhood," he vowed. "We shall have it or the earth will be leveled by our attempts to gain it." This struggle for freedom did not involve Black women, since by their gender, they already possessed what Cleaver dubbed "pussy power."[76]

Robert Staples merits special commentary at this juncture, for few Black sociologists writing about the Black woman have been more consistently wrong than he has. Writing on the "Mystique of Black Sexuality" in 1967, Staples gave his views on the "guilt-free attitude towards the sex act" among sisters. In a totally bankrupt interpretation of slavery historiography, Staples insisted first that "the women of Africa were brought to this country to service the lust of the white master class." Black men were unable to shield their women from "the carnal desires" of white males. Because virtually every Black woman experienced rape, "the worth of virginity" lost all its value. "What good was it to value something one was not allowed to have?" Staples reasoned. "As a consequence the deeply rooted feelings of guilt about sex never became entrenched in the psyche of Black women as they did in her white counterpart . . . Black women receive more satisfaction in marriage and are more aggressive partners during coitus than white women." Ergo, the collective rapes of Black women were, in retrospect, a liberating force which allowed sisters to "at least salvage the spirit of eros for their own."[77] Black women were judged to have become slightly too aggressive, by Staples, as a result.

Further reflecting on the Black woman in a later publication, Staples writes: "Many black females assume that a male with an athletic build possesses large sex organs, which will guarantee them sexual pleasure." The term Staples employed to describe this process is surely a classic in the history of Black sociology: "the masculinization of female mate selection standards." "For those of us who are not built like athletes," he admitted, "this is a most disheartening trend." Describing the social phenomenon of "tipping out," or Black extramarital sex, the Black sociologist's fear of cuckoldry is plainly visible:

> The independence of the black female leads her to sexual dalliance whenever things do not go right or she feels the desire to 'make it' with another male. This practice has become quasi-institutionalized . . . Sexual dalliance must, however, be discreet so as not to damage the male ego. It is most common among black females attending college some miles away from their boyfriends and in the lower class.[78]

Regrettably, the historical legacy of racial and sexual oppression has also led some Black women to defend patriarchal definitions of manhood. In her 1968 essay in the *Liberator*, Black writer Gail Stokes denounced all Black men who were unable or unwilling to assume the role of provider and family patriarch. Stokes equated manhood with the economic function of "bringing home the bacon":

> Of course you will say, "How can I love you and want to be with you when I come home and you're looking like a slob? Why, white women never open the door for their husbands the way you black bitches do." I should guess not, you ignorant man. Why should they be in such a state when they've got maids like me to do everything for them? There is no screaming at the kids for her, no standing over the hot stove; everything is done for her, and

whether her man loves her or not, he provides . . . provides . . .
do you hear that, nigger? PROVIDES![79]

The material base that provided the impetus for such statements
was the unprecedented proliferation of Black female one-parent households and growing Black unemployment. The percentage of Black
families with no husband present increased from 21.7 percent in 1960
to 34.6 percent in 1973. The percentage of Black children who lived
with both of their parents declined from 75 percent in 1960 to 54
percent by 1975. Single female-parent households within the Black
community tended to become younger, with 42 percent of such homes
having Black female householders between the ages of 14 and 34 years
in 1975. Less than half of all Black women were married in 1975. As
unemployment rates for nonwhite married men increased by 332
percent between 1969 and 1975, even Black households with two
parents found it more difficult to provide the basic necessities of life.
Black women who viewed themselves and their children through the
prism of patriarchy could draw the conclusion that their male counterparts—unemployed, underemployed, or sometimes absent from home
for indefinite periods of time—were somehow less than real men. The
vicious cycle of sexism, fostered by white exploiters of the Black
community, would be perpetuated in the actual social practices and
relations between Black women and men.[80]

As the contemporary women's movement gained impetus during
the early 1970s, Black intellectuals and activists were forced to confront the rampant sexist traditions within their own community and
underlying their own theoretical practice. At the outset, the majority of
Blacks who wrote on feminism were decidedly hostile. In one widely
read 1971 essay published in *Ebony* magazine, Helen King denounced
"women's lib" as a white petty bourgeois fad that had little or nothing to
do with the interests of Black women.[81] In the *Black Scholar*, Elizabeth
Hood charged that white feminists had opportunistically usurped
issues such as affirmative action from Blacks. "It can be argued that
women's liberation not only attached itself to the black movement,"
Hood explained, "but did so with only marginal concern for black
women and black liberation, and functional concern for the rights of
white women." Any coalition between Black and white women was
unlikely because both groups had been socialized to perceive each other
as the "enemy."[82] Staples' view on the women's movement was

decidedly antagonistic and betrayed a pathetic inability to grasp the essential character of the economic reforms feminists proposed that would have benefited poor and working class Black women. First, he suggested that "female liberation" was tantamount to a "hatred of men." Second, any discussion of the "sex-role antagonisms extant in the black community will only sow the seed of disunity and hinder the liberation struggle." Black women must tolerate, for the time being, any sexist behavior of their brothers and the patriarchal institutions developed by nationalists. "One must be cognizant of the need to avoid a diffusion of energy devoted to the liberation struggle lest it dilute the over-all effectiveness of the movement," Staples warned. "Black women cannot be free *qua* women until all blacks attain their liberation."[83]

Perhaps the most "eloquent" assault against "white feminism" was written by Linda LaRue in 1970. Unlike other critics of the women's movement, LaRue attempted to put forward a clear theoretical argument against feminism. In her view, the basic dynamics of sexual exploitation were concretely different and secondary in nature to those of white racism. "Blacks are *oppressed,* and that means unreasonably, cruelly and harshly fettered by white authority. White women . . . are only *suppressed,*" contrasted LaRue, "and that means checked, restrained, excluded from conscious and overt activity." For LaRue, it was a farce for Black women to align themselves with white women—a social group who benefited materially from white supremacy:

> With few exceptions, the American white woman has had a better opportunity to live a free and fulfilling life. . .than any other group in the United States, with the exception of her white husband. Thus, any attempt to analogize black oppression with the plight of the American white woman has the validity of comparing the neck of a hanging man with the hands of an amateur mountain climber with rope burns. . . Is there any logical comparison between the oppression of the black woman on welfare who has difficulty feeding her children and the discontent of the suburban mother who has the luxury to protest the washing of the dishes on which her family's full meal was consumed.

LaRue's analysis rested solely on two other basic points. White women were, after all, white, and there was no reason to assume that they would be less racist or "more open-minded than their male counterparts." With millions of white housewives moving into the labor force, Black women and men would be forced inevitably to compete with them. "The black labor force, never fully employed and always representing a substantial percentage of the unemployed . . . will now be driven into greater unemployment as white women converge at every level on an already dwindling job market."[84] What is interesting about LaRue and other Black critics of feminism was their perception that all white women were inside the "middle class." Statistically, the majority of women who depended on food stamps were, and are, white; the majority of women living in Federally-subsidized public housing were, and are, white. The poverty and educational backwardness of white female householders in the Appalachian hills of Kentucky is often worse than that of the South Bronx. There exists, in short, a unity of political and economic interests between women across the color line that LaRue and others failed to recognize. Furthermore, LaRue's economic analysis was premised on the incorrect belief that all white women benefited materially from the continuation of racism—a view which is not substantially supported by economic data. (See Chapter I)

At the founding convention of the Congress of African People, held in Atlanta in September, 1970, over 2,700 delegates gathered to chart the development of new Black social, political and economic institutions. One major feature at the convention included a series of workshops relating to Black women. Coordinator Bibi Amina Baraka set the tone for the sisters' dialogue, by first quoting West Coast cultural nationalist Maulana Ron Karenga: "What makes a woman appealing is femininity and she can't be feminine without being submissive." Baraka stated that Black females had to internalize "submitting to (their) natural roles" by studying their attitudes toward their "man, house, and children." Sisters needed to take cooking classes, learn to create tasty recipes, and improve their personal hygiene.[85] In her paper on the Black family, Akiba ya Elimu suggested that Black males were the natural leaders of the Black community in all social, cultural and political relations. "He is the leader of the house/ nation because his knowledge of the world is broader, his awareness is greater, his understanding is fuller and his application of this information is wiser" than that of Black women.[86] Kasisi Washao summarized the proceedings with a few appropriately sexist remarks. The Black family was "like an organ and the woman's function must be to inspire her man, to educate the children, and participate in social development. The man must provide security. . ." Black women fortunate enough to have a man in their lives should "be humble and loving, appreciative, and resourceful, faithful, respectful and understanding . . . to provide continuous inspiration" for their husbands.[87]

Nationalists were aware of the climbing rate of Black single parent households and the economic pressures that fractured many of the relations between Black females and males. Madhubuti's *Enemies: The Clash of Races,* started from the assumption that "the destruction of the Black family was a crucial move in laying the ground for the destruction and total enslavement of Black people in America." If this destruction was a *fait accompli,* what evolved in the manner of social relations and male/female institutions among Blacks?

Madhubuti claimed that the most serious immediate effect of contemporary racism for Black women "depends upon and revolves around how they are able to effectively solve the problem of no men in their lives." The options available for Black women were unpleasant. Going "without Black men," sexual abstinence, was "unnatural and against life." Lesbianism, according to Madhubuti, "has only recently become popular among some Black women as a compensating move toward fulfilling their sexual desires, possible as a result of not having comfortable and non-frustrating relationships with a Black man." Homosexual activity among women was abnormal, "for it does not generate reproduction . . . with the opposite sex." The most dangerous option, of course, was the prospect of Black women/white men's sexual relationships. When "white men are pushed on Black women or if white men become the accepted option for Black women . . . there is a very serious consequence in terms of Black genocide." Miscegenation was a white supremacist/integrationist plot because the white man would eventually "control the reproductive process of Black women, which goes hand in hand with the physical destruction of Black men and Black families." The fourth option, prostitution, meant that the Black single woman would obtain some security by "(becoming) the property of her pimp." Within the Black community prostitution "is rampant not only for financial means but as (an acceptable) social norm" for Black females. The Black pimp was a kind of "semi-hero" for some, although the entire process "continues to degrade Black women . . . (who) end up as dead property. . ." The final option was in keeping with the African heritage of polygymy—the "quality of sharing" Black males by groups of Black females. Where a brother could economically support more than one household, and satisfy the sexual, emotional and social needs of more than one Black woman at once, such sharing agreements could be achieved for the mutual benefit of all. Sharing would "create a climate and conditions" wherein Black women would willingly permit "their men" to engage in extramarital sex and Black family-building, "while at the same time not damaging existing relationships."[88]

Even outside the boundaries of cultural nationalism, Black political activities did little to challenge institutional sexism. The continuing patterns of Black patriarchy were evident within electoral politics in the 1960s and 1970s. A few Black women politicians gained national prominence after the Civil Rights Movement, including Yvonne Burke of California, Barbara Jordan of Houston, Shirley Chisholm of New York City, and Cardiss Collins of Chicago. The percentage of Black women holding elective office increased 522 percent between 1969 and 1976. Of 508 Black delegates and alternates who participated in the 1976 Democratic National Convention, 310 were women. This "success" in challenging patriarchy was more apparent than real, however. Only 22.2 percent of all Black Federal elected officials and 13.5 percent of all Black state representatives were Black women. Black women comprised only 9.5 percent of all Afro-American judges, and 11 percent of all county officials. 80.5 percent of all Black women who were elected officials in 1976 served either at the municipal level or on boards of education. Despite the formation of the National Association of Black Women Legislators by Tennessee politician Hannah Atkins, and the activities of Nellis Saunders' National Black Women's Leadership Caucus, the effective participation of Black women in electoral politics still grossly underrepresented the potential weight of Black women nationally and regionally.[89] Both integrationist and nationalist-oriented Black men had little to say concretely about the exploitation of Black women by their own institutions. In theory and practice, the Black protest movemement was compromised and gutted by its inability to confront squarely the reality of patriarchy. Black leadership—in the workplace, in street demonstrations, in electoral politics and in the bedroom—was the province of Black men.

By the mid-1970s, a number of women emerged within the Black Movement who advocated key political and economic reforms suggested first by the feminist movement. Many, although by no means all, were also identified as socialists. Angela Davis' essays in the *Black*

Scholar, her deep commitment to an antisexist and antiracist politics, were profoundly influential for many Black women. Cathy Sedgewick and Reba Williams, young Black women who were also members of the Trotskyist Socialist Workers Party, advocated Black support for the Equal Rights Amendment as a necessary and progressive reform which aided women of all races. Advocacy of feminism, they argued, aided and enriched the struggle for Black liberation. For Black women who were pessimistic about the viability of joint political work with white feminists, they pointed out that the real political and economic advances acquired by women of color involved in the women's movement more than made up for the very real problems and personal contradictions evident among certain petty bourgeois white women's "leaders."[90]

Many of the theoretical gains achieved by Black feminists within the Black Movement and community were briefly compromised with the publication of Michele Wallace's controversial diatribe, *Black Macho and the Myth of the Superwoman.* Wallace emerged as a female version of Eldridge Cleaver, praised by *Ms.* magazine, the central publication of white liberal feminists, and exalted by pseudofeminist/ racists such as Susan Brownmiller. Her vulgar polemic combined historical truth with crude fiction, racial mythology with a neo-Freudian, psycho-sexual analysis of Black politics. "Come 1966, the Black man had two pressing tasks before him: a white woman in every bed and a Black woman under every foot," she pronounced. Wallace viewed the entire history of Black Power as "nothing more nor less than the Black man's struggle to attain his presumably lost 'manhood' ":

> To most of us Black Power meant wooly heads, big Black fists and stern Black faces, gargantuan omnipotent Black male organs, big Black rifles and foot-long combat boots, tight pants over young muscular asses, dashikis, and broad brown chests; Black men looting and rioting in the streets . . . [Stokely Carmichael] was a Black spokesman unlike any other that had come before him. He was a Black man with an erect phallus, and he was pushing it up in America's face.[91]

Wallace contended that virtually every Black male leader of the 1960s accepted and perpetuated the idea of Black Macho, the notion that all political and social power was somehow sexual, and that the possession of a penis was the symbol of revolution. "Black Macho allowed for only the most primitive notion of women—women as possessions, women as the spoils of war, leaving Black women with no resale value," Wallace charged. "The Black woman was a symbol of defeat, and therefore of little use to the revolution except as the performer of drudgery (not unlike her role in slavery)." The Black man was a pathetic failure, and "when [he] went as far as the adoration of his own genitals could carry him, his revolution stopped."[92] The obvious criticism of Wallace's work begins with her crude acceptance of Cleaver and the most blatantly sexist spokespersons of Black liberation as representative of all Black males. But the dilemma for genuine progressives was that her book served absolutely no purpose in facilitating an urgent dialogue between Black women and men on the very real and pressing questions of patriarchy within their community. *Black Macho* raised at its core several historically valid issues, but due to its distorted and acrid context, it actually reinforced sexism and a hostility towards feminism among many Blacks.

V

The emergence of a militant Black feminism since the mid-1970s, which has since continued and deepened in organizational character, is the product of the convergence of several specific social and economic factors. As illustrated previously, the actual practice of the Black Power Movement was the perpetuation of the structures of patriarchy, under the guise of "Blackness." With the passage of affirmative action legislation, many Black males drew the conclusion that Black women were now taking away newly-won middle income jobs from them. The vulgarly sexist thesis was based on the belief that Black women were indeed submissive, or less threatening to the white, male power apparatus than Black males. Their lack of a penis, in short, was an automatic ticket to employment and job advancement during economically austere times.

Black women knew better than men that the dynamics of sexist exploitation were not altered by bourgeois legislation: Black women remained at the very bottom of the income ladder within the U.S. social order. According to the 1979 Census statistics, for example, 68,000 Black males and only 8,000 Black females earned salaries between $30,000 to $35,000. 46,000 Black men and 6,000 Black women collected annual wages between $35,000 to $50,000 in 1979. 14,000 Black men and 2,000 Black women received wages between $50,000-

$75,000. Within the highest income levels, in excess of $75,000, there were 548,000 white men and 4,000 Black men. Less than 500 Black women were in this category. The illusion that Black women, even within the so-called middle class, had achieved parity or had exceded Black men's earnings was not simply false, but a gross reversal of economic reality. Black female unemployment rates were generally higher than those of Black men, especially for all blue collar workers, clerical workers and sales personnel.[93]

Responding to this chasm between Black liberation rhetoric and the harsh realities of Black women's existence, progressive Black female activists fought back. They helped to provide the political base for the fight to acquit Joanne Little, a North Carolina Black woman who was accused of murdering her jailer when he sexually assaulted her.[94] They helped to rally a majority of the national Black community in favor of the Equal Rights Amendment.[95] Progressive Black women in Boston formed the Combahee River Collective in 1974, to begin bringing together Black women who were "actively committed to struggling against racial, sexual, heterosexual, and class oppression" and who viewed as their "particular task the development of integrated analysis and practice based upon the fact that the major systems of oppression are interlocking."[96]

They criticized white feminists who tended to ignore Black women's fears about forced sterilizations and who emphasized only abortion rights. Black female activist veterans of SNCC recalled with some bitterness that a few of the white women who now championed feminism and gave lip-service to antiracist politics had eagerly slept with Black male leaders and saddled Black women with the Movement's "shit work" a decade before. Lorraine Bethel's "What Chou Mean We, White Girl? Or, The Cullud Lesbian Feminist Declaration of Independence," spoke for thousands of Black women who view themselves as the historic victims of suppression by males (white and Black) and white females:

> I bought a sweater at a yard sale from a white-skinned (as opposed to Anglo-Saxon) woman. When wearing it I am struck by the smell—it reeks of a soft, privileged life without stress, sweat, or struggle. When wearing it I often think to myself, this sweater smells of a comfort, a way of being in the world I have never known in my life, and never will. . . It is moments/infinities of conscious pain like these that make me want to cry/kill/roll my

eyes suck my teeth hand on my hip scream at so-called radical
white lesbians/feminists "WHAT CHOU MEAN WE, WHITE
GIRL?"[97]

The final history of the systemmatic exploitation of Black women
in capitalist America will not be written by whites, or by Black men, no
matter how sympathetic they might be to the struggle against racism
and patriarchy. Historically, Black women have carried the greatest
burden in the battle for democracy in this country.

Women have been the foundation of Black culture and society, yet
their contributions have been generally ignored, or relegated to second
class status by most Black male activists, historians and social scientists. They felt the sting of the lash upon their backs in Georgia's cotton
fields; they knew the pain of losing children from lack of decent medical
care; they felt the hot sun beating down upon their foreheads as they
walked to work as maids in whites' homes; they fought to preserve their
humanity from white and/or Black men's sexual abuse. The underdevelopment of Black America will end only when Black men begin to
seriously challenge and uproot the patriarchal assumptions and institutions which still dominate Black civil and political society. In the words
of Michele Barrett, the oppression of all women "is entrenched in the
structure of capitalism. Just as we cannot conceive of women's liberation under the oppression of capitalism so we cannot conceive of a
socialism whose principles of equality, freedom and dignity are vitiated
by the familiar iniquities of gender."[98] Similarly, no road toward the
ultimate emancipation of the U.S. Black working class exists outside of
a concomitant struggle, in theory and in practice, to destroy every
vestige of sexual oppression within the Black community.

CHAPTER FOUR

BLACK PRISONERS AND PUNISHMENT IN A RACIST/CAPITALIST STATE.

The Negro race . . . (has) been excluded from civilized Governments and the family of nations, and doomed to slavery. The unhappy black race were separated from the white by indelible marks . . . and were never thought of or spoken of except as property, and when the claims of the owner or the profit of the trader were supposed to need protection. Negroes were beings of an inferior order, and altogether unfit to associate with the white race, either in social or political relations; and so far inferior that they had no rights which the white man was bound to respect.

Robert B. Tawney, Chief Justice of the United States Supreme Court, the Dred Scott decision, 1857.

> *Eastern guard tower*
> *glints in sunset; convicts rest*
> *like lizards on rocks . . .*
>
> *Morning sun slants cell.*
> *Drunks stagger like cripple flies*
> *On Jailhouse floor.*
>
> *To write a blues song*
> *is to regiment riots*
> *and pluck gems from graves . . .*

Etheridge Knight, "Haiku," in Dudley Randall, ed., *The Black Poets* (New York: Bantam, 1971), p. 206.

I

The Black domestic periphery in America is essentially imprisoned behind the walls of poverty, sexism, unemployment and workplace exploitation. Sometimes the barriers to freedom seem very real, as we observe a police assault against a random Black victim. At other moments they seem quite abstract. American democracy has at certain stages relished in its passion for racist violence, and at other times, paternalistically yielded to the demands of Black and white reformers. The Civil Rights and Voting Rights Acts thus replaced the Jim Crow signs and the legal stigma of second-class citizenship. But equal opportunity programs and affirmative action did not, and could not, obscure the brutal realities of "prison life" to those who were exploited. The Black majority in America is accepted in the lowest paying jobs, tolerated in public housing, and allowed to join the unemployment lines—but it is still barred from effective power within the corporate and political ruling class. Black workers experience workplace exploitation and racist assaults against their humanity, recognizing that this country's basic democratic creed of rule by law somehow does not apply to them. But it is necessary, at this point, to describe how this bizarre juxtaposition of public rights and private brutalities, of democracy and racism, comprises no aberration, but a system to facilitate oppression and the accumulation of capital from the Black masses. At the core of the capitalist accumulation process and institutional racism is coercion.

American capitalism is preserved by two essential and integral factors: fraud and force. Fraud is the ideological and cultural hegemony of the capitalist creed: that enterprise is free and competition exists for all in the marketplace; that success is available for all who work hard, accumulate capital, and participate as voters in the electoral process; that democratic government is dependent upon the freedom to own private property. Blacks, Latinos and white workers are barraged daily with illusions about the inherent justice and equal opportunity within the American System. The educational institutions, churches, media and popular culture all in their own way participate in creating the logical framework for a system that remains irrational and inhumane.

Beneath the velvet glove of fraud exists the iron fist of force. For reasons of history, Black people are more aware than whites of this delicate dichotomy between consensus vs. coercion. The essence of slavery was coercion of the most primitive kind—the relationships between master and slave were characterized by mutual distrust, fear, hatred and undisguised force. All slaves, whether the proverbial Uncle Toms or Nat Turners, recognized that production could not take place without the daily use of physical or psychological violence. Even the most paternalistic master had to divide Black families occasionally or employ the whip to get the crop to market on schedule. Under industrial capitalism, however, the essence of production involves force of a different kind: the extraction of surplus value from the labor power of the worker. Force is generally disguised within capitalist societies with democratic forms of government. The worker never receives the actual or real value of his/her own labor power, but is technically "free" to sell his/her skills or services to the highest bidder, or employer. Blue collar and service workers are "less free" than professional workers, but all are forced to accept the conditions of employment that the owners of capital are willing to grant. Capitalists and politicians in bourgeois democracies would prefer to mask their dictatorship over labor through a variety of means. They tolerate (and at times even encourage) the activities of labor unions, so long as profit margins are not reduced seriously. Most major public decisions impacting capital are made within the established channels of bourgeois discourse and legitimacy. It is only when a capitalist society is in deep crisis, when the dictatorship of capital over labor is questioned or threatened, that capitalists are pressured to employ brute force.

The oppressed Black majority is generally more subject to the violence of American capitalism than whites because (1) it is concentrated in the lowest paid, blue collar, unskilled and service sectors of the labor force; (2) it comprises a substantial portion of the total U.S. reserve army of labor, the last hired and the first fired during periodic recessions; and (3) it is the historic target of brutality within a racist culture and society, occupying an inferior racial position which has remained unaffected since the demise of slavery. America is not simply a capitalist state, but a *racist state*, a governmental apparatus which usually denies access and power to most Blacks solely on the basis of racial background. A capitalist/racist state still attempts to resolve problems within the Black community via fraud rather than force, just

as it does for whites. Nevertheless, there remains a greater reliance on
the omnipresence of coercion aimed at Blacks than at whites, and an
even greater use of force aimed at the majority of poor and working class
Blacks than at petty bourgeois Blacks. Force is the essence of Black
underdevelopment under capitalism: to be Black in capitalist America
is to be a prisoner to the reality of coercion.

II

Both during and immediately after slavery, whites seldom
bothered to imprison Blacks for any real or imagined crimes. First, life
in the South was for most Blacks *a kind of imprisonment*. No white,
whether a drunkard, child-molester or criminal, was perceived to be
beneath any Black person, no matter how upright and financially
successful he/she happened to be. The strict racial code was an
effective barrier to keep Blacks, with rare exceptions, outside positions
of power and influence. A "salty" or "sassy" Black woman who objected
to any of segregation's insanely strict restrictions could be raped by a
white man with legal impunity. If her husband, lover, brother or son
had anything to say about the matter, he might be castrated or lynched.
Southerners established "Negro courts" which were separate from
those dealing with whites by the eighteenth century. Such courts,
according to historian Kenneth M. Stampp, "were usually less concerned about the formalities of traditional English justice than about
speedy verdicts and certain punishments." Slaves charged with petty
larceny usually did not appear in courts, but were simply lashed or
punished by their owners or overseers. In misdemeanor or noncapital
felony cases, Blacks were tried in courts that were, to say the least,
highly prejudiced. In Mississippi, for instance, Blacks charged with
noncapital felonies were tried before two justices and five slaveholders.
Louisiana Blacks in noncapital felonies were judged by four slaveowners and only one justice. Some Southern whites recognized even
then that their system of "Negro courts" was, in the words of one South
Carolina judge, "the worst system that could be devised." Nevertheless, despite its obvious contradictions, the "Negro court system"
became the basis for allocating "justice" in a biracial society.[1]

Except in those instances when Blacks were accused of assaulting
whites or stealing property, the slaveowners themselves presided over
the majority of cases involving Black infractions. Punishments varied

from the mundane to ingenious. For relatively minor offenses, field hands were forced to labor on Sundays or holidays. Black foremen were demoted to the status of field hand, and household servants were forced to leave the big house. One tobacco planter in Maryland ordered a slave "to eat the worms he failed to pick off the tobacco leaves." More serious infractions, such as failure to obey orders, meted out punishments of various kinds. Some large planters sentenced unruly slaves to spend days or even weeks in the local county jail. Others built jails ("nigger boxes") on their own plantations, small, windowless shacks in which Black workers were confined. Nearly every slave at some point in his/her life experienced the lash. Although castration was a legal and popular form of punishment in the eighteenth century, it declined in usage after 1800. A few planters resorted to the castration of a Black male, however, if they desired to take his slave wife. The greatest barrier to the imprisonment and/or execution of Black people was, ironically, slavery itself. It was not logical, in the view of most whites, for a man to "willingly destroy his own property." Racial atrocities existed in every state and on every plantation, but the loss of a prime fieldhand meant the loss of a capital investment of some importance. In rare cases, whites did not execute slaves who killed particularly brutal white foremen, especially when the white victims were from the "poor white" or lowest classes. The masters were racists, but as businessmen they also had to protect their investment. For these reasons, there were relatively few lynchings, public executions or imprisonment of Blacks prior to the Civil War. As a form of legal chattel, Blacks were the beneficiaries of a kind of perverse protection.[2]

With emancipation and Reconstruction came an inevitable reaction in Southern race relations. Technically freed from the shackles of bondage, the Black man/woman was now just another "competitor" in the labor market. White laws had to be altered to compensate for the changing status of Black agricultural workers and artisans, to ensure their continued inferior caste status. In the autumn months of 1865, a series of Black Codes were ratified to guarantee Black labor subservience. It is important to note, however, that the Jim Crow laws which imprisoned Blacks for violations were originally developed in the North, not South. Many Northern restaurants, hotels and taverns were off-limits to Blacks throughout the eighteenth and nineteenth centuries. In *North of Slavery*, historian Leon Litwack describes the general pattern of race relations in Northern states between 1790 and 1860:

> In virtually every phase of existence, Negroes found themselves systematically separated from whites. They were either excluded from railway cars, omnibuses, stagecoaches, and steamboats or assigned to special "Jim Crow" sections; they sat, when permitted, in secluded and remote corners of theaters and lecture halls; they could not enter most hotels, restaurants, and resorts, except as servants; they prayed in "Negro pews" in the white churches, and if partaking of the sacrament of the Lord's Supper, they waited until the whites had been served the bread and wine. Moreover, they were often educated in segregated schools, punished in segregated prisons, nursed in segregated hospitals, and buried in segregated cemeteries . . . Newspapers and public places prominently displayed cartoons and posters depicting (the Negro's) alleged physical deformities and poking fun at his manners and customs. Children often tormented (Negroes) in the streets and hurled insulting language and objects at them.[3]

Many Midwestern states legally excluded anyone with a "visible admixture" of Negro blood from voting. Almost every major white leader of the Republican Party declared his unconditional opposition to "Negro equality." White women were not immune from attacking Blacks. In Indiana, for instance, a large prewar political rally was led by a large cadre of young white females who carried a banner reading, "Fathers, save us from nigger husbands."[4] Thus the postbellum South after 1877 developed its public policies towards the punishment of Blacks primarily from the traditions and customs of the North.

During this period, the vast majority of Southern Blacks were legally imprisoned for three general offenses—any violation of segregation codes monitoring public behavior or activity; any violation of laws governing capitalist agricultural production; and any infraction (misdemeanors and noncapital felonies) against whites. In the first category, the most heinous crime was interracial marriage. The Mississippi Black Code of December, 1865, was specific:

> . . . it shall not be lawful for any freedman, free negro or mulatto to intermarry with any white person, nor for any white person to intermarry with any freedman, free negro or mulatto, and any person who shall so intermarry shall be deemed guilty of felony, and on conviction thereof shall be confined in the State Peniten-

tiary for life; free negroes and mulattoes are of pure negro blood, and those descended from a negro to the third generation inclusive, though one ancestor in each generation may have been a white person.

By the late 1870s, other Southern states ratified similar laws, calling marriages between the races "incestuous" and contrary to God's will. Other codes ordered Blacks off sidewalks to give way to white men, even segregating certain streets specifically for use by whites only. "Coons" were legally restricted "to keep their distance and mind their language in public gathering places," or they would find themselves behind bars. [5]

To maintain the inferior position of Blacks within agricultural production, Southern whites developed the peonage system and convict leasing. Peonage was a logical byproduct of the sharecropping system that replaced slavery immediately after the Civil War. In principle, sharecropping represented a real step forward for Black rural workers. An industrious farmer would borrow farm utensils and seeds, and would divide the proceeds from the sale of the produce at year's end. Some Black farmers used the system to accumulate small amounts of capital, eventually buying their own farms. Many bitterly discovered at the end of a harvest that they actually owed more to the white planter than their share of the crop could pay for. Since virtually all white merchants and planters inflated the cost of their supplies, and kept all business records, illiterate Black farmers were caught in a never-ending cycle of debt. "Peonage occurred only when the planter forbade the cropper to leave the plantation because of debt," writes historian Pete Daniel. "A laborer who signed a contract and then abandoned his job could be arrested for a criminal offense. Ultimately his choice was simple: he could either work out his contract or go to the chain gang." [6] Southern legislatures and courts always sided with owners in their disputes with Black sharecroppers. Once convicted of breaking their legal agreements with white planters, Black prisoners were sometimes bailed out of jail by other white businessmen, who in turn paid off the Blacks' fines and previous debts. But as convicts, these Blacks were now obliged to labor for their new "employer" in workgangs for long periods of years, often under the most brutal physical conditions.

The number of Black prisoners in Southern penitentiaries multiplied dramatically as the profitability of "convict leasing" became evident to white capitalists and politicians. In Mississippi the number of state prisoners grew from 272 in 1872 to 1,072 in 1877. Georgia's convict total increased from 432 in 1872 to 1,441 in 1877. This explosion of the Black prison population reflected an abrupt alteration of Southern laws. In 1872 Mississippi "defined the theft of any property over ten dollars in value, or any cattle or swine of whatever value, as grand larceny, with a sentence up to five years." Laws like this provided the legal foundation for a prison system that made millions of dollars for a small number of white politicians.

Colonel Arthur S. Colyar, editor of the *Nashville American* and a prominent Tennessee Democrat, who also served as director and general counsel for the Tennessee Coal, Iron, and Railroad Company, was one prominent beneficiary of the leasing program. Under Colyar's direction, the Tennessee Coal, Iron and Railroad Co. leased Black and white convicts to work in their various enterprises for a $101,000 annual fee, paid to the state. Arrangements like this were common and profitable for a number of reasons. Most states had no health or safety inspectors for the convicts, and sixteen-hour workdays were not uncommon. Leases to individual mining, railroad or other industrial companies varied from ten to thirty years. Companies often subleased their convicts to smaller white-owned firms at a profit. Prison wardens also became wealthy from the system, the beneficiaries of substantial "kickbacks" from politicians and company directors.

However, conditions for the prisoners became literally worse than under slavery. Black women who were chained together in straw bunks at night were often raped by white guards. Their children were also confined to the penitentiary with them. The annual death rates for Black convicts ranged from 11 percent in Mississippi to 25 percent in Arkansas in the 1880s. One 1887 grand jury study of a Mississippi prison hospital declared that all convicts bore "marks of the most inhuman and brutal treatments. Most of them have their backs cut in great wales, scars and blisters, some with the skin peeling off in pieces as the result of severe beatings. They were lying there dying, some of them on bare boards, so poor and emaciated that their bones almost came through their skin, many complaining for want of food. We actually saw live vermin crawling over their faces, and the little bedding and clothing they have is in tatters and stiff with filth."[7] Historian Fletcher M. Green described the South's dreaded convict-lease system in 1949 as a pattern of labor exploitation akin only to "the persecutions of the Middle Ages or in the prison camps of Nazi Germany."[8]

The general conditions in Southern penitentiaries were, of course, scandalous (or at least should have been). The major prison in Virginia in 1900 was actually designed by Thomas Jefferson in 1797. The decayed penitentiary was so overcrowded, according to one Richmond newspaper editor, that "the feet of inmates tended to stick out the windows."[9] Alabama's prisons in the 1880s were "packed with several times the number of convicts they could reasonably hold." Even that state's prison inspectors admitted that their penitentiaries "are filthy, as a rule . . . and both prisons and prisoners were infested with vermin. The convicts were excessively and sometimes cruelly punished . . . (and) were poorly clothed and fed."[10] After World War I, conditions for Black and white convicts improved somewhat, but the essential brutalities of the penal system remained. Thousands of Black peons were routinely ordered to work in county chain gangs on public roads, in work camps, or in turpentine mills and mines. In *Forced Labor in the United States,* written in 1939, Walter Wilson discovered that chain gangs were a chief means of punishing Black and white offenders. "Prison camps ranged from portable steel cages to the neat brick and wooden buildings found in the road camps of North Carolina and Virginia."[11]

Outside of imprisonment for debts owed to planters, or the "recruitment" of Blacks to replenish the numbers of convicts leased by counties or states, the frequency of arrests and imprisonment of Blacks was relatively low during the period of Jim Crow laws from 1890 to the 1930s. The reasons for this are rooted in the profoundly racist worldview most whites of all classes had adopted by this time. Writing in 1941, sociologists Allison Davis, Burleigh and Mary Gardner noted in *Deep South* that "the police, like the whites in general, believe that fighting, drinking, and gambling among Negroes are not crimes so long as they are strictly limited to the Negro group and are kept somewhat under cover. It is only when this behavior is brought out into the open and thrust upon the attention of the whites that it becomes a crime for which arrests are made." One white Southern woman of "upper middle class" origins explained to the researchers that "we have very little crime. Of course, Negroes knife each other occasionally, but there is little *real* crime. I mean Negroes against whites or whites against each other." The legal system was designed essentially for whites only, as was the rest of society. White policemen were encouraged to "pick up any Negro whose actions appear suspicious," viciously beating him/her, and then releasing the person without charges. Convinced that "formal punishments by fine or jail sentence fail to act as deterrents to Negro criminals," law-enforcement officials simply kept Blacks out of the court system entirely by "administer(ing) punishment themselves." Most Southern white police patrolmen lived in working class neighborhoods with Blacks as neighbors, and "a number of them have kept Negro women, usually on a more or less temporary arrangement, and are on a friendly footing with Negro proprietors of illegal establishments."[12] Whites were also absolutely convinced that they could judge a "bad nigger" simply by his/her appearance. Blacks were thought to be inherently so stupid that they would readily admit to any infraction they had committed when confronted by white authority.[13]

If Blacks were arrested by police for any minor or major crimes against whites, however, their eventual conviction and imprisonment were forgone conclusions. As *Deep South* explains:

> The Negro is, from the very beginning, in a position subordinate to both the police and the court. His testimony will not be accepted if contradictory to that of the police. His witnesses carry little weight with the court, and he can wield no political influence. The Negro is less apt to have legal assistance in the police court or to appeal his case to the higher courts. . . . Negroes seldom prefer charges against whites. The police usually discourage such actions; and in trying such cases, the court protects the whites by technicalities and by attacking the truth of the Negro testimony. . . . There are no Negro officers, judges, lawyers, or jurymen. The only role a Negro can take is that of defendant or witness, except in a few types of civil cases. Furthermore, the Negro has no part in making the laws which the court system enforces. As a defendant, he faces the white man's court; he is tried not only on the evidence but also on the basis of the white man's concept of how a Negro would or should act. If he is found guilty, his sentence and punishment are determined by the same factors. The law is white.[14]

Behind the peonage and convict-leasing system, behind the racist and undemocratic white court system, and behind all the powers of the brutal white police, rested what could be termed the Great Deterrent to Black crime: *lynching.* The segregationist South was steeped in violence. C. Vann Woodward documents that Alabama whites actually spent more money for rifles and pistols than they did for the state's entire supply of farming implements and tools. Into the twentieth century, white men often wore loaded revolvers "in banks, courtrooms and schoolhouses as well as in bars and ginhouses." Whites shot each other over the most "absurdly trivial" reasons.[15] In 1923, 13 of the 15 cities with the highest homicide rates were Southern or border cities. The national homicide rate of 1926, 10.1 per hundred thousand, favorably contrasts with Jacksonville, Florida's 75.9, Birmingham's 58.8, Memphis' 42.4 and Nashville's 29.2 that same year.[16] If whites in the South had few reservations about resorting to violence against each other, then the courts and police did little to protect Blacks from the wrath of that same violence. Blacks and whites alike understood that there were three crimes which would swiftly spark the flames of racist coercion: the killing or wounding of any white man; the real or suspected sexual assault against any white female; and perhaps the most serios offense of all, any overt political activity which challenged Jim Crow segregation and the basic system of caste/class rule upon which the entire economy and social order was based. Upon these acts, the massive weight of white vigilante "justice" would fall heavily upon any Black man/woman. No real trial would be held; no jail or state penitentiary would be secure enough to keep the Black man/woman from his/her certain fate. Lynching was the ultimate weapon used by whites to "keep the nigger in his place."

III

Lynching is a peculiarly American tradition. From the nineteenth to the late twentieth century, the modern *auto-da-fé* parallels the development and maturation of capitalism in an oppressive, biracial society. Technically, the term is often used to describe the hanging of a person outside the legal sanction of the police and criminal justice system. Historically, and in actual practice, it is the ultimate use of coercion against Blacks to insure white supremacy. The form it assumes—hanging by the neck, shooting, castration, burning at the stake, or other spontaneous and random forms of violence—is secondary to the actual terror it evokes among the Black masses, and the perverse satisfaction that it derives for white racists. Lynching is neither irrational nor illegal, in the sense that the white power elites tolerate and encourage its continued existence. Lynching in a racist society becomes a legitimate means to check the activities of the entire Black population in economics, culture and politics.

The creator of lynching was a Quaker, Charles Lynch, a well-to-do political leader of what is today Lynchburg, Virginia, and a member of the House of Burgesses. During the American Revolution, Lynch and his fellow patricians were disturbed with the outbreak of criminal activity in their area. Since the closest court was two hundred miles to the East, these early frontier people took legal matters into their own hands. An extra-legal court was established with Lynch presiding as chief magistrate. The arrested man was given an opportunity to defend himself. If he was declared guilty, punishments appropriate to the seriousness of his crimes were allotted: thirty-nine lashes in some cases, hanging by the thumbs in others, or in rare instances execution. These extra-legal courts became popular in the backwoods regions of Kentucky, Tennessee and the Carolinas after the Revolution. By the early 1800s, however, lynching became identified with the execution of an accused person. Southern whites of all classes tended to defend the system as honorable and as an efficient means of protecting private property. As Walter White observed, "the number of victims increased in direct proportion to the growth of the demand for cotton and to the growing sentiment in other parts of the country that slavery was not only morally wrong, but economically unsound."[17]

Surprisingly few Blacks were lynched during the greatest period of slavery expansion. Between 1840 and 1860, only three hundred persons, Black and white, were lynched in the South. Again, the perverse paternalism and self-interest that slavery created provides one explanation. White slaveowners and politicians, being racists, had few reservations about administering the harshest punishments imaginable against their own slaves. There are several documented cases where Blacks accused of rape or murder were hanged or slowly burned to death, often in the presence of other slaves. One Alabama editor defended the occasional public burning of slaves by "the law of self-protection, which abrogates all other law . . . There was no passionate conduct here. The whole subject was disposed of with the coolest deliberation and with regard only to the interest of the public."[18] After the Nat Turner rebellion of 1831, 17 slaves were lynched; other slaves were beheaded and their skulls were positioned on polls on the public roads; and Turner himself was hanged, his body given to surgeons for dissection, and souvenir purses were sewn from his dried skin.[19] But the masters of the plantations were also the masters of the larger white society, which was itself plagued with serious internal class distinctions and divisions. In *Roll, Jordan, Roll,* Genovese captures the essential ambiguities of power which trapped the planter elite: "An easy attitude toward indiscriminate mob violence against blacks would do more than threaten slave property; it would also threaten the position of the master class in society and open the way to initiatives by the white lower classes that might not remain within racial bounds. The masters felt that their own direct action, buttressed by a legal system of their own construction, needed little or no support from poor white trash. Order meant order."[20] The "compassion" that white planters felt toward Blacks was dictated not out of any abstract humanitarianism, but from simple economic self-interest. As one North Carolina planter who owned hundreds of slaves explained in 1850: "I should consider myself an unjust and unfeeling man if I did not have a proper regard for those who are making me so much money."[21]

The demise of slavery, ironically, meant the collapse of an institutional check on violence against Black people. Whites from all social positions concurred that their continued supremacy had to depend upon the practice of lynching. Between 1882 and 1903 there was an unprecedented expansion in the number of Blacks lynched across the South. In Florida alone during these years 19 whites and 115 Blacks were lynched. Figures from other states in the region include Arkansas, 61 whites and 139 Blacks; Kentucky, 64 whites and 103 Blacks; Georgia, 28 whites and 241 Blacks; Maryland, 2 whites and 19 Blacks; North Carolina, 16 whites and 48 Blacks; Tennessee, 49 whites and 109 Blacks; Virginia, 21 whites and 70 Blacks; South Carolina, 8 whites and 109 Blacks. Texas led the nation in lynchings with 324, 199 of whom were Blacks. Louisiana had the highest number of lynchings in the Black Belt South, with 53 whites and 232 Blacks. Of the 2,060 Blacks lynched in the U.S. between 1882 and 1903, only 707 were actually charged with "attempted, alleged, or actual rape." 783 were lynched for allegedly murdering whites; 208 were charged with "minor offenses;" 104 were termed "arsonists;" 101 had stolen white property. Others were killed for "striking or talking back to a white man," testifying against whites in courts, "suing whites," or other related offenses. Between 1904 and 1924 the number of lynchings declined somewhat throughout the country, but still occurred in alarming numbers in the Deep South. Furthermore, lynching had become associated as a form of punishment almost specifically for Blacks only. During this later period, 11 whites and 269 Blacks in Georgia were lynched. Louisiana vigilantes claimed 9 whites and 115 Blacks in these same years. A total of 3,513 Blacks and 1,438 whites were lynched in the U.S. between 1882 and 1927. Fourteen former slave states (Mississippi, Georgia, Texas, Louisiana, Alabama, Arkansas, Florida, Tennessee, Kentucky, South Carolina, Missouri, Maryland, Virginia and North Carolina) were responsible for 80.8 percent of all lynchings and 94.7 percent of all lynchings against Blacks. [22] (See Table XII)

White leaders justified lynching as an act to defend white racial supremacy. Most declared that rape was, in the words of Congressperson James F. Byrnes (who would later become U.S. Secretary of State), "responsible directly and indirectly for most of the lynching in America." Racist demagogue Cole Blease explained, "Whenever the Constitution comes between me and the virtue of the white women of South Carolina, then I say 'to hell with the Constitution!' "[23] Although rape accounted for only one-third of all statistics, the popular white view that Black sexuality was the sole cause of lynchings quickly was adopted at a mass level. By the 1920s, the overwhelming majority of white Southerners were convinced that the Black male was "always a potential rapist. Thus, white women are expected to fear strange Negro men, and they usually feel it unsafe to go alone in Negro districts or to stay alone at night in isolated houses." All Black men, from professionals to blue-collar workers, were regarded as "primitive being(s), emotionally unrestrained and sexually uncontrolled."[24]

At this point, it is important to distinguish between the actual number of lynchings and the psychosocial and economic function of the terror it unleashed. After 1903, the number of lynchings receded gradually to only several dozen each year in the mid-1920s. The lynching of a Black man falsely accused of a crime might evoke sorrow and outrage, and perhaps the spirit of vengeance, among the Black masses. But executions *per sé*, even accompanied with the passions of racist violence among whites, do not in themselves foster terror among Blacks. Terror is not the product of violence alone, but is created only by *the random, senseless and even bestial use of coercion against an entire population.* The coercion that takes place within a "normal" capitalist society, the exploitation of Blacks in the workplace, is insufficient to modify and control their collective behavior. Even the lynchings of thousands of Blacks across the South, for real and usually imagined crimes, could not guarantee a docile labor force. This recognition connoted a shift in racist tactics after 1900. As the absolute number of

Black lynchings decreased, the level of crude indignities and bestial acts of random violence toward Blacks increased. Terror becomes real in one's mind only when a person recognizes that, at any moment and for any reason, he/she can be brutally tortured. Slavery left many Black people and their descendants unafraid of death. But there are many things that are indeed worse than death. It is the random, limited and spontaneous use of coercion that tends to afflict the mind and spirit of the oppressed. It is the omnipresent fear of a fate *worse than death itself that creates the terror.*

The lynchings committed against Blacks in the early twentieth century were designed specifically to evoke this special kind of terror. Walter White described these murders as being "executed with a bestiality unknown even in the most remote and uncivilized parts of the world." *Between 1918 and 1927, 91.6 percent of all persons lynched in the U.S. were Black.* Eleven were Black women, three of whom were pregnant. Forty-four Blacks were burned alive, and 18 others were burned after they had been executed. Some were simply tied to the backs of automobiles and dragged across city streets until they were unconscious. Many Black men were tied down and brutally castrated with knives or axes. In some cases, the families of the intended victims were seized physically, and delivered to the site to witness the series of atrocities. The purpose of the events was not to kill the Negro quickly or painlessly, but to derive sadistic satisfaction from the suffering of something that was less than human. In the twenties, lynchings became popular cultural events, not unlike circuses and dances. Hundreds of white women and children were invited to take part in the festivities. Fingers, ears and other body parts of the Black victims were eagerly seized for souvenirs.

Two examples of such brutalities are sufficient. One account from Mississippi at the turn of the century is typical:

> When the two Negroes were captured, they were tied to trees and while the funeral pyres were being prepared they were forced to suffer the most fiendish tortures. The blacks were forced to hold out their hands while one finger at a time was chopped off. The fingers were distributed as souvenirs. The ears of the murderers were cut off. Holbert was beaten severely; his skull was fractured, and one of his eyes, knocked out with a stick, hung by a shred from the socket. The most excruciating form of punishment consisted in the use of a large corkscrew in the hands of some of the mob.

> This instrument was bored into the flesh of the man and woman, in the arms, legs and body, and then pulled out, the spirals tearing out big pieces of raw, quivering flesh every time it was withdrawn.[25]

In Georgia, a Black sharecropper was lynched for the murder of his white landlord. When word arrived that the Black farmer's wife was going to swear out warrants against her husband's killers, the mob replied, "We'll teach the damn nigger wench some sense":

> Securely they bound her ankles together and, by then, hanged her to a tree. Gasoline and motor oil were thrown upon her dangling clothes; a match wrapped her in sudden flames. Mocking ribald laughter from her tormentors answered the helpless woman's screams of pain and terror. The clothes burned from her crisply toasted body, in which, unfortunately, life still lingered, a man stepped towards the woman and, with his knife, ripped open the abdomen in a crude Caesarian operation. Out tumbled the prematurely born child. Two feeble cries it gave—and received for answer the heel of a stalwart man, as life was ground out of the tiny form.[26]

In the 1930s, the tradition of lynching and brutality was forced to submerge, and ultimately, to transform itself into a new phenomenon. Demographically, millions of Blacks left the rural South and travelled to the Northeast and Midwest, not just for employment opportunities, but to escape the reign of terror. The growth and influence of the National Association for the Advancement of Colored People in the South was another institutional safeguard that Blacks used to fight lynchings. As Black life and labor shifted toward urban and industrial areas, lynchings were made more difficult. The informal, vigilante-inspired techniques to suppress Blacks were no longer practical. Therefore, beginning with the Great Depression, and especially after 1945, white racists began to rely almost exclusively on the state apparatus to carry out the battle for white supremacy. Blacks charged with crimes would receive longer sentences than whites convicted of similar crimes. The police forces of municipal and metropolitan areas received a *carte blanche* in their daily acts of brutality against Blacks. The Federal and state government carefully monitored Blacks who advocated any kind of social or political change. Most important, capital punishment was used as a weapon against Blacks charged and convicted of major crimes. The criminal justice system, in short, became the modern instrument to perpetuate white hegemony.

Extra-legal lynchings were replaced by "legal lynchings" and capital punishment.

IV

Neither through cold design nor quiet calculation did the racist/ capitalist state choose to rely upon capital punishment as its new Great Deterrent to Black crime. Capital punishment, after all, is as old as human society. In European countries political dissidents, felons and beggars were beheaded or disemboweled by feudal governments for any number of crimes, great and small. In frontier America, the legal subtleties that separated lynchings from court-sanctioned executions were small indeed, at least so far as the populace was concerned. Both were bloody rituals evoking the worst passions (and prayers) that a culture claiming any degree of civilization can produce. At the last public execution in this nation, a Kentucky hanging in 1938, 20,000 people travelled to witness the event. But by the Great Depression, and continuing into the early 1960s, white capitalist society increasingly viewed capital punishment as its line of defense against the Negro.[27]

The racial bias within the statistics on capital punishment speaks for itself. (See Table XIII) Although Blacks comprised about nine to ten percent of the U.S. population in the 1930s, almost 50 percent of all prisoners who were executed during the decade were Afro-Americans. Though 97.1 percent of all whites executed had been convicted for murder, only 10 white men were executed for rape during the entire ten-year period. And 115 Black men were sentenced to die for rape in the 1930s—14.1 percent of all Blacks executed. After 1940, the number of Blacks convicted and eventually killed for capital crimes increased significantly relative to whites. Between 1940 and 1959 the percentage of Blacks executed for rape compared to the total number of Blacks killed steadily climbed, reaching nearly one-fourth of the total. About 90 percent of all Americans executed for rape between 1930 and 1959 were Black, and all but two of the sentences occurred in the South. Georgia, one of the leading lynching states, has also executed the highest number of prisoners since 1930, 366 persons. The most important statistic to consider may be this: "no white has ever been executed for the rape of a black" in American history.[28]

Advocates of capital punishment found themselves on the defensive in the 1960s. Research revealed that, between 1928 and 1949, the average homicide rates in states that allowed the death penalty were 200 to 300 percent higher than in states that had no capital punishment. Homicide rates in the early 1960s, when executions averaged 24 each year, were only 70 percent of the 1930s rate, when executions averaged 150 per year. Some states that switched to the death penalty actually experienced increases in their homicide rates. Confronted with mounting evidence that the death penalty was inherently racist and an ineffective deterrent against crime, white social scientists, police administrations and politicians launched an ideological "counteroffensive." The nation's leading crime stopper, FBI Director J. Edgar Hoover, spoke out repeatedly in favor of capital punishment. University of Chicago economist Isaac Ehrlich published a widely praised study which claimed that "every execution deterred approximately eight murders." Politicians in both the Democratic and Republican parties informed a budget-conscious public that executions would save taxpayers money over incarcerating prisoners for life terms. Convicted murderers were, as a group, dangerously antisocial individuals who would undoubtedly kill innocent people again once released. Evangelical white ministers even quoted Exodus 21:23–25 to justify capital punishment: You shall give "life for life, eye for eye, tooth for tooth, hand for hand, foot for foot, burn for burn, wound for wound, stripe for stripe."[29]

The solid evidence against all these pro-death viewpoints is simple enough. In the mid-1970s a group of influential econometricians examined Ehrlich's research and declared that it was "fatally flawed with numerous methodological errors." Neither Hoover nor any social scientist has ever proven a direct relationship between capital punishment and crime deterrence. The public was told repeatedly that capital punishment is less costly to the state than life imprisonment. But in 1971, for example, it was estimated that "the commutation of death sentences of 15 Arkansas prisoners saved the state an estimated $1.5 million."[30] The former assistant warden of Illinois's Cook County Jail noted that "on the average, a capital case, from the time of first commitment to the jail until the body is disposed of after an execution, costs about 25 percent more than the price of 30 years of imprisonment which, on the average, was the normal life expectancy at the age of conviction of capital cases. Capital punishment is by no means 'cheaper' than life imprisonment, and the jurisdiction that maintains it pays dearly, in both money and human costs."[31] Even the biblical justification of capital punishment was found wanting on its own terms. Black and progressive white clergy observed correctly that the Bible also sanctions capital punishment "in cases of adultery (Lev. 20:10), blasphemy (Lev. 24:15), working on the sabbath (Ex. 35:2), refusing to obey a priest or judge (Deut. 17:12), disobedient children (Deut. 21:18), fornication (Deut. 22:23) and sixteen other offenses.[32] Death penalty advocates who prided themselves on their Christianity conveniently forgot that Christ told his followers, "You have heard it said, 'An eye for an eye and a tooth for a tooth,' but I say unto you, Do not resist one who is evil." (Matthew 5:38–39) The apostle Paul wrote in the New Testament, "Beloved, never avenge yourselves, but leave it to the wrath of God; for it is written, 'Vengeance is mine, I will repay, says the Lord.' " (Romans 12:19)[33]

White America continued to be unconvinced. By 1978, almost 70 percent of all white Americans favored capital punishment. After ending the death penalty in 1967, the Supreme Court reversed itself a decade later. By June, 1981, 827 men and women were on death row, the largest number in U.S. history and probably "the largest in the world."[34] (See Table XIV) Since 1972, 62 percent of the prisoners sentenced to die "were unskilled, service, or domestic workers; 60 percent were unemployed at the time of their crimes." And again capital punishment has become a pivotal element in maintaining white supremacy. According to the Institute of Southern Studies, "in Georgia, between 1973 and 1977, over three times as many convicted defendants who had killed white victims received a death sentence as did those who had killed black victims." Three-fourths of the prisoners condemned were in the South, and almost half were Black. (See Tables XV and XVI) Blacks in the U.S. account for over half (54 percent) of all murder victims, and homicide is now the leading cause of death for Black people between the age of 25 and 34. Only 13 percent of all prisoners now on death row had Black victims. Legal activist Clare Jupiter has clearly linked racism, lynchings and the current use of capital punishment: "lynch mobs were ostensibly illegal, but the actions of juries are legally recognized as the will of the community. By their deliberations and selection of the proper victims for official murder, modern juries—especially Southern juries—echo a familiar message: white skin and wealth are still the best tools for beating the death penalty."[35]

V

In the 1960s and 1970s, white public opinion on crime took a marked shift towards an authoritarian and "law-and-order" mentality. Polls commissioned by the American Institute of Public Opinion of Columbia University, and the National Opinion Research Center of the University of Chicago indicated that the percentage of Americans who were afraid to walk within a mile of their homes at night increased from 32 percent in 1967 to 45 percent in 1977. In national surveys taken in 1965, 57 percent of all Americans responded that the U.S. justice system was not "dealing harshly enough with criminals." Since then, that troubled majority has climbed—74 percent in 1972, 85 percent in 1975, and 90 percent in 1978.[36]

Various governmental agencies responded to the anxiety of the white middle-to-upper class by increasing expenditures for public safety. Local government spending for police protection jumped from $1.8 billion in 1962 to $8.8 billion in 1977. States increased their police budgets in the fifteen-year period from $285 million to $1.6 billion. The Federal government followed suit, raising police protection spending between 1962 and 1977 from $177 million to $1.4 billion. Payments for police protection between 1962 and 1977 soared 375 percent, and annual government expenditures for prisons reached $4.6 billion in 1977. U.S. per capita expenditures for police protection jumped from $21.12 in 1960 to $34.50 in 1970 and $47.98 in 1977. States with substantial Black urban populations generally exceeded the national per capita average. In 1977, Michigan was spending $54.89; Illinois, $58.36; New Jersey, $58.82; California, $65.20; New York, $72.33. By 1974, cities with large numbers of Blacks were allotting substantial per capita sums to expand local police forces: Los Angeles, $60.51; Baltimore, $64.29; Chicago, $73.38; St. Louis, $74.11; Philadelphia, $74.98; Newark, $76.44; Detroit, $76.81; New York, $86.61; Washington, D.C., $123.60.[37]

The U.S. Right was able to manipulate the public's anxiety by propagandizing crime statistics. The number of reported violent crimes climbed from 161,000 in 1960 to 487,000 in 1978. The various types of violent crime had increased across the board. The number of murders per 100,000 population, jumped from 5 in 1965 to 10 in 1975. In the same decade, reported instances of rape per 100,000 increased from 12 to 26; robbery, 72 to 218; and aggravated assaults, 111 to 227. White male victims of homicide increased from 5 to 9 per 100,000. The number of property crimes reported to the FBI had increased to 1,726 per 100,000 by 1975. Civil libertarians and civil rights supporters pointed out frequently that the huge increases in the money spent for police were not justified. For instance, the absolute number of homicides declined 3.5 percent between 1975 and 1978. In the same period, robberies dropped 4.4 percent, and property crimes reported to the FBI declined by 1.3 percent. In 1980, the Bureau of the Census reported that "the average annual growth rate was 17 percent between 1965 and 1970, but it was only 5 percent during the next 5 years, and it actually fell by 4 percent between 1975 and 1978. Similarly, the rate of motor vehicle thefts, which had risen by some 12 percent per year from 1965 to 1970, grew by less than 1 percent per year between 1970 and 1975." The data indicates that "most reported crime is either leveling off or diminishing . . ."[38]

Crime statistics can always be interpreted in different ways, depending obviously upon one's political perspective. What neoauthoritarians failed to explore accurately was the factor of race within this unprecedented explosion of lawlessness. Several observations along the color line must be made. First and foremost, is the fact that the percentage of Black and Hispanic victims of violent crime has *always* been higher than for whites. From 1973 to 1978, white males were victimized by violent crime at rates between 42 and 45 per year per thousand. Hispanic male victims of violent crime had rates during these years between 49 to 54 per thousand. For Black men, the rate was between 53 and 57 per thousand. Nonwhite male homicide rates per 100,000 during the 1970s were between 60 and 83 annually. In other words, *any Black man in the U.S. has a 6 to 8 times greater chance of being murdered than any white man.*[39] Second, Black working class and poor people, not white, are the most likely victims of household crimes. Between 1973 and 1978, Black families earning $7,500 to $9,999 annual income experienced burglary rates per 1,000 of from 132 to 159 annually. Black families earning under $3,000 in these years reported between 129 and 155 burglaries per year, and 83 to 90 household larcenies per year. According to the Bureau of the Census, "The 1978 [burglary] rates per 1,000 households amounted to 115 (for blacks) and 83 (for whites) respectively."[40] Third, the Black petty bourgeois strata has a greater chance of being victimized in most property crimes than whites of all income groups. In 1975 alone, almost one out of every ten Black families earning more than $25,000 annually lost their cars or motor vehicles to criminals, a rate 436 percent higher than that of whites of identical income.[41] The irony of the newest "war against crime" is that white police, politicians and law enforcement officers have been nonchalant, at best, in aiding and defending Blacks' lives and personal property. The foundations of the modern U.S. police state are designed specifically to ensure that the killings, rapes and property thefts of Blacks continue unabated—so long as whites (especially in the upper classes) remain protected.

VI

Two other strategies emerged during the 1960s which increased the state's role in the suppression of Black leaders and the Black working class. The first, which involved the significant expansion of the Black prison population, was effectively used to maintain a high proportion of Blacks within capitalism's necessary reserve army of labor—a strategy not unlike that of convict-leasing in the 1800s. The second, established a sophisticated surveillance network and a police-state apparatus to blunt Blacks' criticisms of white supremacy and the political economy of capitalism. Both efforts combined to curtail the advances achieved by the Civil Rights and Black Power Movements.

In 1982, over 500,000 men, women and youths were incarcerated in more than 6,500 penal institutions of various types. Despite the growing recognition of scholars and some correction officials that mass imprisonments had not lowered the U.S. crime rate, many conservative white Americans pressed their elected officials and courts for increased jail terms for persons convicted of violent crime. A desire "to inflict severe punishment and to seek revenge and retribution," combined with the tradition of racism, sent the number of state prisoners soaring in the 1970s and 1980s. Between 1972 and 1978, for example, Florida almost doubled its state prison population. In the same six-year period, Delaware's prison population increased by 260 percent. Critics noted, without avail, that one-fourth of all persons imprisoned were alcoholics. One half million American youths every year spent some time locked away in a state reformatory or prison. Annually another 600,000 mentally ill persons are arrested and imprisoned for periods of months or even years, and few receive any psychiatric care. By the early 1980s the annual national incarceration rate of 250 per hundred thousand was the third highest in the world. Not surprisingly, the leader was South Africa, with 400; but some projections for U.S. prison growth could exceed that figure within a single decade.[42]

Like South Africa, the American prison profile reflects the brutal realities of class exploitation and racism inherent in a modern racist/capitalist state. (See Tables XVII and XVIII) Almost half of all prisoners in the U.S., at any given time, are Black. Fifty-one percent of the entire prison population is 29 years old or less; and 30 percent is between the ages of 20 and 24; several thousand convicts are not even old enough to vote. Fifty-six percent of all prisoners never completed high school, and over one quarter have an eighth-grade education or less. The great majority of prisoners are from the working class: craftsmen (23 percent), operatives (29 percent), service workers (11 percent), nonfarm laborers (17 percent), and clerical employees (4 percent). Almost one-third of these men and women (31 percent) were unemployed during the four weeks prior to their arrest. Most inmates had difficulty finding steady employment, with 46 percent working at their last job for less than six months tenure. Only 14 percent of all prisoners had $10,000 or higher annual incomes, while 60 percent earned under $6,000. Such a large pool of "idle" workers did not escape the notice of many corporations and politicians, who put forward a prison "reform" program of "rehabilitative work" in the early 1980s. Prisoners would be hired to work at manufacturing jobs while still serving their sentences behind bars. Businesses would produce commodities at lower than normal wage rates, thereby saving money. Chief Justice Warren Burger, among others, endorsed the program to convert prisons into "factories with fences."[43]

The American criminal justice system operates effectively as the conduit for enlarging the nonwhite prison population. *Every year, over 8 percent of all Afro-Americans are arrested.* As Lennox S. Hinds, former National Director of the National Conference of Black Lawyers, has observed, "someone black and poor tried for stealing a few hundred dollars has a 90 percent likelihood of being convicted of robbery with a sentence averaging between 94 and 138 months. A white business executive who has embezzled hundreds of thousands of dollars has only a 20 percent likelihood of conviction with a sentence averaging about 20 to 48 months."[44] Blacks comprise over 25 percent of all Americans arrested in a given year. (See Table XIX) Although whites are charged with about 72 percent of all criminal offenses, the criminal justice system tends to "punish" them for certain less serious crimes more so than Blacks and other national minorities. For example, in 1975 whites constituted 87.8 of all persons arrested as runaway youths, 84 percent of all charged for driving while under the influence of alcohol, 88.6 percent of those who violated state liquor laws, and 83.3 percent of all vandals. Blacks comprised more than half of all Americans charged with murder and non-negligent homicide (54.4 percent), prostitution (53.6 percent), robbery (58.8 percent) and gambling (72 percent). Blacks also accounted for 45.4 percent of all Americans arrested for forcible rape, 39.5 percent of all aggravated assaults, and 41.4 percent of those carrying and/or receiving illegal weapons. The pattern of American "justice" that emerges is obvious: white middle class Americans are arrested generally for relatively minor property crimes, whereas Blacks are arrested for violent crimes which carry substantial penitentiary sentences.

Halting the emergence of Black political activism in the 1960s could not be left solely under the aegis of the criminal justice system. To accomplish this, the state developed an extraordinarily powerful and illegal apparatus—the COINTELPRO or "Counter Intelligence Program." Begun in 1956 by the FBI as a coordinated effort to undermine the Communist Party USA, COINTELPRO mushroomed into a wide-ranging series of assaults against progressive and Black nationalist leaders and organizations.[45] In its sordid fifteen-year history of operations, the FBI sent "anonymous mailings (reprints, Bureau-authored articles and letters) to group members criticizing a leader or an allied group;" encouraged "hostility up to and including gang warfare between rival groups;" engineered the firing of SNCC, Black Panther and even Urban League officials and members; ordered "federal, state, or local authorities to arrest, audit, raid, inspect (or) deport" Black activists; interfered with "judicial proceedings" by targeting Black and white progressive attorneys sympathetic to Black liberation; and used "politicians and investigating committees, sometimes without their knowledge to take action against targets." Two hundred and thirty-three of the total 295 authorized actions against so-called "Black Nationalist Hate Groups" were targeted against the Black Panther Party, declared by Hoover in September, 1968, to be "the greatest threat to the internal security of the country."[46] Theoretically COINTELPRO ended in 1971, and the FBI was condemned by a Senate Select Committee for treading "on ground forbidden to it by the Constitution." Nevertheless, the FBI continued to operate

COINTELPRO-type actions against Black activists, and under the Reagan Administration began to terrorize individual Blacks in a brazenly open manner.[47] For example, the Black Press Institute learned in November, 1981, that the Federal government was planning a series of grand jury hearings to explore "possible linkages between respected black organizations and terrorist groups." Using a little-used regulation to investigate the Mafia, the grand jury probe targeted civil rights organizations, Black social and cultural groups, community organizations and Black student groups.[48]

VII

The plight of the Black domestic periphery is symbolized by the life and death of George Jackson. At age 15, he was convicted for breaking into a department store, and served seven months in California's Paso Robles Youth Authority. At 18, he was charged with stealing $70 from a filling station. Bourgeois democracy is generous: the state provided Jackson a white public defender. On the lawyer's advice, he agreed to plead guilty, and was promised a short sentence. Unknowingly perhaps, Jackson forfeited his legal right to any appeal. The court issued its verdice: one year to life. Jackson's "release" from the penal system did not occur until he was assassinated at the age of 31. "America cannot let a black man steal $70 without severely punishing him," wrote former prisoner Eric Mann. "A system that demands that the poor work like dogs and accept what they are given while the rich throw away better meals than the poor eat, must treat stealing $70 as an insurrectionary act. The punishment, especially if that crime against property is committed by a black person, will usually involve throwing him in a cage for from one to five years."[49]

Jackson's imprisonment and execution are mirrored in a thousand different acts of brutality that take place across the face of Black America everyday, in relative isolation and in broad daylight. These collective acts form the bars which imprison every individual member of the Black working class, every Black poor and unemployed person, and every Black woman. But George Jackson's life also provides a model for the directions of the inevitable revolutionary upsurge that must occur. Each oppressed person under capitalism must come to the realization that his/her death is a *requirement* for the continued *life of the system.* Corporate economics requires the existence of an undernourished, half-educated working class; millions of persons caught in perpetual penury, filth and disease; hundreds of thousands imprisoned, and millions more arrested annually; the development of the periphery, and the systematic elimination of the weak, the young, and the homeless. George Jackson recognized this dialectical unity as a one-sided process of death and destruction. "We always have done most of the dying, and still do: dying at the stake, through social neglect or in U.S. foreign wars. The point is now to construct a situation where someone else will join the dying," Jackson wrote. "If there must be funerals, then let there be funerals on both sides."[50] This final verdict for militant action to the Black oppressed may appear unnecessarily apocalyptic, but it squares solidly with the process of change found in the pages of social history. Revolutionary transformations are not an orderly process, and violence is always an essential "midwife" in the birth of new societies. Moral suasion and plea-bargaining will not release the thousands of Black convicts in America's penitentiaries; gradual reforms within the criminal justice system will not blunt the razor's edge of police brutality. Underdevelopment and the imprisonment of the Black masses will not die a natural death until the real criminals within America's powerful ruling class taste something of the bitter anguish that distorts and cripples the Black majority.

SECTION TWO

THE BLACK ELITE: THE DOMESTIC CORE.

CHAPTER FIVE

BLACK CAPITALISM: ENTREPRENEURS, CONSUMERS, AND THE HISTORICAL EVOLUTION OF THE BLACK MARKET.

Having attained success in business
possessing three cars
one wife and two mistresses
a home and furniture
talked of by the town
and thrice ruler of the local Elks
Robert Whitmore
died of apoplexy
when a stranger from Georgia
mistook him
for a former Macon waiter.

Frank Marshall Davis, "Robert Whitmore" in Dudley Randall, ed., *The Black Poets* (New York: Bantam, 1971), p. 121.

I

Capital accumulation in the nonwhite periphery creates a number of social and political dislocations within the indigenous society. Businesses can operate at a profit only when there are adequate transportation systems—railroads, canals, highways, airports. Modern communication systems are required to link branch offices with the metropole, to facilitate the completion of orders. A steadily growing number of women and men from the indigenous population are needed to serve in clerical and lower-level administrative posts. Thus schools are a concomitant part of the developmental process, so long as both the content of its education and its pedagogy are oriented toward reinforcing the legitimacy of capitalism and Western civil society. The incessant drive for economic growth and expansion also sparks an inevitable transition within the religious ethos of the workers, since the Puritan work ethic promotes the proper ideological outlook for a hard-working, non-disruptive labor force. It is impossible, therefore, to talk about underdevelopment as a purely *economic* process, because the human content of that dynamic is profoundly social, cultural and political.

A decisive component of this underdevelopment process within the periphery is the nonwhite elite. This small social stratum is gathered from the masses, reeducated in colonial schools, and converted to the masters' faith. In political society, it serves as a necessary yet dependent buffer between those who wield power and those who have none. Within popular culture, it is the nonwhite mouthpiece of the new order, articulating in the media and in various aesthetic forums the ideals of the masters. In the context of modern Africa, for example, one can discern a direct correlation between increased agricultural and industrial production for overseas markets and the growth of the Black elite. In the Gold Coast (Ghana), for example, between 1891 and 1911 exports and the level of production of commercial enterprises increased 400 percent; the amount of currency or monetary resources increased by 1,000 percent; the amount of investments in cocoa production soared from £3,000 to £1,573,000. Gold exports to the West increased over 5,000 percent in a ten-year period, 1901–1911. Although the lion's share of wealth was controlled by British colonialists and businessmen, underdevelopment did result in the creation of a marginal Black petty bourgeoisie. By 1945, several thousand African small farmers produced 20 percent of the Gold Coast cocoa crop from their own land. As the capital city, Accra, expanded from a colonial village into an international port, the British were forced to hire Africans in a variety of petty managerial capacities— clerks, civil servants, teachers, skilled blue-collar workers. Hundreds of Africans became lawyers, doctors, dentists, newspaper editors and held other more influential posts. At the end of World War II, about

400,000 African small entrepreneurs owned residential stores selling clothing, food and household items to the growing rural and urban proletariat. This social strata was simultaneously "nationalist" and "integrationist," to use terms perhaps more suitable to Afro-American politics. It opposed British racism, and provided critical support for the radical elitists' demands for decolonialization. Yet it had also integrated the economic and social worldview of the British into its own *raison d'être*. The elite was a *product* of capitalism, colonialism and imperialism: its activities reinforced the process of Western capital accumulation and the underdevelopment of the African masses.[1]

Across the nonwhite world, colonized elites have exhibited certain political and cultural tendencies which are, to repeat, a necessary part of the underdevelopmental dynamic. In *The West And The Rest Of Us: White Predators, Black Slavers and the African Elite,* Chinweizu observes that this stratum is primarily the product of Western capitalist "liberalism":

> African liberals, as agents of an international liberal imperialism, have a special job: to spread the liberal ideology in Africa, to maintain a black front there for a neocolonial world order run by the West, to administer the neocolonial African territories for the West, and to restore the imperialized status quo if any genuinely African nationalist regime should storm its way into power anywhere in Africa. To call them neocolonial administrators is not to say that they, like the former white colonial administrators, receive direct orders or mandatory guidelines from their masters overseas . . . But it is rather to say that, though they advertise themselves as serving Africa, they operate in an environment, with a mentality, and under conditioned attitudes and direct advice that all tend to yield policies that primarily serve the neocolonial powers, policies that often are in direct opposition to the genuine interests of the African peoples. Conditioned by a pro-western miseducation, they see their class interests as tied to those of their imperialist masters, and they readily abandon the interest of their people to protect those of their class.[2]

Although the race/class dialectic of the United States cannot be adequately or accurately described as neocolonial, it is undeniable that the process that gave birth to a Black elite here is virtually identical to that of modern Africa. When Chinweizu writes bitterly, "those whom Africa expected to liberate her from the yoke of Europe have instead chained her to that yoke, perhaps even more tightly, in exchange for crumbs of wealth and privilege," a similar verdict must be levied against their American counterparts.[3] When he dismisses neocolonial politicos as "British O.B.E.—Obedient Boys of the Empire," Black activists in the United States might include the names of Thomas Sowell, Benjamin Hooks and Vernon Jordan.[4] The Afro-American majority has been systematically betrayed by its petty bourgeois stratum.

In Reconstruction, the masses demanded universal education and "forty acres and a mule"; they received instead political leadership of an uneven quality, sharecropping and convict-leasing. In the Civil Rights Movement, they demanded an end to racial discrimination, jobs, decent housing and education; they received instead temporary employment, an end to only the most blatant forms of legal segregation, and affirmative-action programs which directly benefited the Black elite. This is not to say that the Black elite has always consciously served the interests of the exploiters and racists. The key here is not one of intentions but of historical mission—a failure of the elite to comprehend its role as a necessary social force for basic change. As Frantz Fanon noted, "each generation must, out of relative obscurity, discover its mission, fulfil it, or betray it."[5] It is here, on the scales of history, that our elites must be judged as inadequate.

Historically, within Black America, the Black elite has occupied four principal vocations—politicians, clergymen, educators, and entrepreneurs. By "politician," I mean a person who is directly involved in making, carrying out, or influencing state policies. A man/woman need not be an elected or appointed official to be described accurately as a politician. Booker T. Washington, A. Philip Randolph, Frederick Douglass and Martin Luther King, Jr., were all influential politicians, although none of these men were ever elected to public office. Even Adam Clayton Powell's profound impact within Black civil and political societies between 1945 and 1965 was perhaps only indirectly due to his position as a senior Black Congressional leader. Indeed, at the moment of the great 1963 March on Washington, there were fewer than 100 Black elected officials in the entire country. The acceptable role of a Black "politician" within a capitalist and racist society is to maximize the level of goods and services reaching the Black community. By definition, Black socialists or revolutionary nationalists are not "politicians" in this narrow bourgeois sense, because they are attempting through their practice to uproot racial hegemony and exploitative economic relations. The Negro politician is neither anticapitalist nor antiracist, except in his/her rhetoric.

The Black clergy comprise the bedrock of Black petty bourgeois politics, due to several historical and sociological reasons. The process of enslavement effectively eliminated the bonds of leadership which were part of indigenous African societies. The slaves who adopted the forms of the master's religion and who were granted the right to preach to their brothers and sisters became the ministers. These pastors were viewed by their white authorities as an ideological buffer between themselves and the often-dangerous Black masses. The Black messengers taught the Gospel of Christ to the weary, promising sweet visions of freedom in the afterlife. As in Africa, Black American preachers served a variety of roles—part-time politicians, social workers, indigenous intellectuals, spiritual comforters. Some were simply egotistical charlatans; others were reluctant revolutionaries. Because segregation eliminated any route of upward mobility for young Black men within the electoral arena between 1890 and 1960, the majority of Black would-be "politicians" ended up in the church. The church itself was, in many Black communities, the only institution in which a significant number of people regularly invested their time, energies and meager savings. The minister was particularly vulnerable to pressure from local white business and civic leaders, however, because they also recognized his central role in the daily life of his community. Through covert payments or through intimidation, the demands of white authorities were often incorporated into the political and even religious practices of many Black ministers.

The educators are still the largest single social group within the Black elite, but in many respects, they have been the least influential. During the nineteeth and early twentieth century, school for most Blacks consisted primarily of elementary level instruction. Within a patriarchal and agrarian society, public school teaching was often viewed as "women's work." The majority of Black male intellectuals were not found in the classroom; they tended to be businessmen, lawyers, newspaper editors and clergy.[6] Even with the expansion of state-supported and private Black universities in the decades after the Civil War, the number of Black male teachers was surprisingly small. The economic demands of family life pressured Black men into vocations where the greatest possible financial compensation could be achieved. It was only in the 1940s, when the relative social status of the

Black clergy had declined somewhat and the prospects for accumulating wealth through agricultural production had all but disappeared, that large number of Black males came to view teaching as a viable vocation. The status of intellectual work within the contemporary Black community still remains relatively low. This is particularly true for dissident voices among the Black intelligentsia. Revolutionary nationalists and Marxists are often *persona non grata* both at white and Black-operated universities and at white publishing houses. Mainstream Black intellectuals are usually politically integrationist and therefore more acceptable. Their Blackness is generally not part of their own intellectual praxis. The Black elite generally does not support Black institutions of higher learning as generously as other ethnic groups bankrole their own universities. Therefore, the economic terrain for Black intellectuals is always tenuous at best; Black academic institutions—particularly since desegregation—rock against the omnipresent shoals of bankruptcy; and Black education has become a marginal factor in influencing major public policy decisions that touch the lives of the Black majority.

Easily the most decisive element of the Black elite, both in the United States and in the Third World periphery, is the entrepreneur. The Black businessperson is the linchpin of underdevelopment and capital accumulation within the Black community. The goal of the Black entrepreneur is to make profits, period. How he/she accomplishes this task is secondary to the goal. The nonwhite businessperson is the personification of the legitimizing and rational character of capitalism. For white corporations, he/she serves to perpetuate the illusion that anyone can "make it" within the existing socioeconomic order, if only he/she works sufficiently at it. For the state, the Black enterpreneur represents the role model of proper civic behavior that the unruly and "nonproductive" Black masses should follow. The Black businessperson (which by definition here also includes persons involved in finance or banking, or who work as executives in a white-owned corporation) accepts and lives by the rules of the game. By nature and self-interest, the petty capitalist is profoundly individualistic. Profits can be made by exhorting Black consumers via Black nationalist appeals to "buy Black," or through NAACP-style pressures on the white private sector to subcontract goods, services or advertising through Black-owned firms: but profits *must* be made. My treatment of the elite will consist of all four major sectors described above. But it seems appropriate, writing this monograph during the period of "Reaganomics," to begin with the historical evolution of the entrepreneurs, and the theory of Black Capitalism.

Capitalism has always had proponents within the Black community. In fact, the historical evolution of the concept "Black Capitalism" provides one of the rare instances of ideological concensus among the fractious elements of the Black Movement, from the period of antebellum slavery to the present. Abolitionist leader Frederick Douglass, a strong integrationist, for example, encouraged newly emancipated Blacks to accumulate capital and to invest in their own enterprises. In 1874 Douglass even served briefly as president of the country's largest "Black" bank, Freedman's Savings and Trust Company. Racial accommodationist Booker T. Washington and Black nationalist leader Marcus Garvey developed detailed programs separately to coordinate small Black entrepreneurs. Conservative integrationists in the Urban League and nationalist-oriented members of the Nation of Islam advanced similar strategies for Black economic development within the U.S. capitalist system. At the 1968 Congress of Racial Equality (CORE) convention, leader Roy Innis, a militant Black nationalist, announced that his organization would build "a nation within a nation," attempting to develop Black community corporations and "Black ownership of capital instruments" to operate factories and to create job opportunities for thousands of unemployed Blacks.[7]

For these leaders and the majority of Black political organizations of the last 100 years Black Capitalism connotes several key concepts: the accumulation of capital by individual Black entrepreneurs; strategies designed to maintain Black control over the Black consumer market in the U.S.; collective programs to improve the economic condition of all Blacks within the overall framework of U.S. capitalism. Beneath all of this is a theory of development, rooted in the often unchallenged assumption that U.S. capitalism is not structurally racist, and that the devastated condition of most Blacks throughout history could be alleviated through the acceleration of capital accumulation in the hands of a small number of Blacks.

This chapter begins with an alternate view of Black development, a thesis articulated by sociologist E. Franklin Frazier in his 1957 book *Black Bourgeoisie*. Black Capitalism was a "social myth," in Frazier's judgment, perpetuated by individual Black entrepreneurial "success stories" and by the economic barriers established by the system of segregation.[8] The contemporary renaissance of Black Capitalist programs and ideology is fostered partially by the Reagan Administration and the emergence of a politically conservative sector of the Black elite. Beginning with Black economic history, this chapter documents some of the central components of the theory and practice of Black Capitalism, the evolution of the now highly profitable Black consumer market, and the current prospects for Black entrepreneurial activity in late capitalism. It will also reestablish that Frazier's initial critique is even more valid today than ever before in our history.

II

The origins of Black Capitalism are found in the development of a small but affluent propertied Black elite which emerged before the Civil War. In Northern cities, some Blacks owned surprisingly large amounts of real estate. Properties owned by Blacks in Philadelphia were valued at $400,000 in 1847 and $800,000 in 1856. In 1840, Blacks in Cincinnati had accumulated real property, excluding church and personal property, valued at $209,000. Real estate owned by Blacks in New York City and Brooklyn in 1853 was valued at $755,000 and $79,200 respectively. Black entrepreneurs were involved in a wide variety of antebellum commercial activities. In Manhattan, by 1840, Blacks owned one cleaning firm, two dry goods stores, two "first-class restaurants in the downtown financial district," four "pleasure gardens," six boarding houses, one confectionery and two coal yards. In the 1840s, one Black clothing and tailoring firm in Detroit, owned by James Garrett and Abner H. Frances, boasted annual gross profits of $60,000. Black entrepreneurs in Cincinnati were particularly successful. Samuel T. Wilcox, a Black boat steward on the Ohio River, initiated a wholesale grocery store in the downtown business district in 1850. Quickly he became "the largest dealer of provisions in the city," establishing commercial links with New Orleans and New York. By the mid-1850s Wilcox's annual gross profits were estimated at $140,000. In 1851 two Black businessmen acquired a contract with Hamilton County, Ohio, worth $10,000 to plaster all its public buildings. Henry Boyd, a former slave artisan, established a furniture store in the late 1830s in Cincinnati. By the 1850s he regularly employed 20 to 50 Black and white cabinet makers and workers, and was worth $26,000.[9]

Under the slavery regime Black entrepreneurial activities were difficult, but not impossible in the South. In 1860, there were 348 free Blacks in Baltimore whose total property was worth $449,000. Eight hundred and fifty-five free Blacks in New Orleans owned 620 slaves and real estate worth $2,462,470 in 1836. By the outbreak of the Civil War, conservative estimates of property and business owned by the New Orleans free Black community exceeded $9 million. The vast majority of Blacks engaged in activities which provided goods and services to white patrons—tailoring establishments, saloons, eating houses, barbering and stables. The total value of all free Black-owned establishments and personal wealth in the U.S. in 1860 was at least $50 million dollars—half of which was based in the slave South.[10]

Of course Black business was not without certain risks in a racist society. Northern and Southern whites found it difficult to tolerate the economic success of any individual Black person, fearing that even isolated instances of Black financial ability would threaten the racist order. In 1844, Virginia authorities revoked the license of mulatto innkeeper Jacob Sampson without explanation. In 1852 Maryland prohibited Black membership in building and homestead associations. Blacks who saved their money to purchase farms discovered that many white homesteaders did not want them in their states or regions. White insurance companies usually refused to do business with Blacks, and white bankers drew the color line against Blacks desiring credit. Black businessmen usually could not sue white creditors in Northern courts, and often were legally restricted from engaging in certain commercial activities. The political attitudes of wealthy Blacks were also subject to careful scrutiny. When a copy of *Uncle Tom's Cabin* was found in the possession of one Black merchant in Salisbury, Maryland, for instance, "the public hostility that resulted led to his financial ruin." In Cincinnati, white mobs periodically burned down Henry Boyd's furniture factory. "Three times he rebuilt, but the fourth blaze compelled him to yield since insurance companies refused to underwrite his risk."[11]

Despite these risks, the relatively successful record of some early Black business efforts prompted many Blacks to conclude after the Civil War that private enterprise was the only means to achieve Black economic advancement. Booker T. Washington reflected upon these isolated instances and proceeded to postulate a general theory of group upward mobility via capitalism. Writing in 1906, the Black educator insisted that Black artisans "had a monopoly of the common and skilled labor throughout the South" in 1865. "By reason of contact (between) whites and blacks during slavery," Washington stated, "the Negro found business and commercial careers open to him at the beginning of his freedom."

> In slavery, when the master wanted a pair of shoes made, he went to the Negro shoemaker for those shoes; when he wanted a suit of clothes, he went to the Negro tailor for those clothes; and when he wanted a house built, he consulted the Negro carpenter and mason about the plans and cost—thus the two races learned to do business with each other. It was an easy step from this to a higher plane of business; hence immediately after the war the Negro found that he could become a dry goods merchant, a grocery merchant, start a bank, go into real estate dealing, and secure the trade not only of his own people, but also of the white man, who was glad to do business with him and thought nothing of it.

Washington concluded, "for these reasons . . . the Negro in the South has not only found a practically free field in the commercial world, but in the world of skilled labor."[12]

But emancipation and Reconstruction did not usher in a new period of Black economic expansion. Washington's interpretation of Black economic history is sharply contradicted by the evidence of the destruction of most Black artisans after the war. Several factors limiting Black economic opportunity were present. First, the vast majority of Black millers, blacksmiths, carpenters and other potential entrepreneurs were illiterate. According to figures from the Census of 1870, probably fewer than one-third of all urban Blacks in the South who were artisans or employed in commerce were literate. Any skilled Black artisan who lacked the ability to maintain correspondence with customers, to check accounts and to supervise payments to creditors was severely crippled.[13] A second factor is suggested in DuBois' *The Negro Artisan*. Slavery permitted Blacks to develop skills as master craftsmen, but seldom permitted Black artisans to acquire training as entrepreneurs—placing advertisements in local newspapers, hiring and firing employees, purchasing supplies, and maintaining profit and loss records. The business of the Black artisan in slavery, DuBois observed, "had been to *do* work but not to *get* work."[14] A third and decisive factor was white racism. In late 1865 many Southern states passed "Black Code" regulations declaring that any Black man who did not have an employer was subject to arrest as a "vagrant." Working independently for themselves, some Black artisans were fined, jailed and even sentenced to work as convict laborers. South Carolina's legislature declared in December, 1865, that "no person of color shall pursue or practice the art, trade, or business of an artisan, mechanic or shopkeeper, or any other trade, employment or business . . . on his own account and for his own benefit until he shall have obtained a license which shall be good for one year only." Black peddlers and merchants had to produce $100 annually to pay for the license, while whites paid nothing.[15]

Historians Roger L. Ransom and Richard Sutch document that both before and immediately after slavery the number of Black artisans was extremely small. The percentage of slaves working as field hands in the Black Belt South in 1860 was between 80 and 92 percent in various states; rates for slave employment as blacksmiths ranged from under 1 to 3 percent; for all Black artisans, the percentages for states varied between 3 and 11 percent of the total slave workforce. These figures did not improve significantly by the 1890s. According to 1890 Census figures, in the five major cotton-producing states (Georgia, Alabama, South Carolina, Mississippi and Louisiana), the overwhelming majority of Black workers were employed as agricultural laborers, porters, laundresses, teamsters and personal servants. Over 90 percent of all male agricultural workers and almost 70 percent of all female agricultural laborers were Black, out of a total workforce of 594,700. The approximate number of Blacks gainfully employed in 1890 as painters in these five states was 2,272; butchers, 978; manufacturers, 256; printers, 234; bank employees, 108. More importantly, the approximate number of Black lawyers and government officials in these states was 110 and 160, respectively. Aspiring Black businessmen had few allies in postbellum state and local governments to represent their interests, and had few if any friends in the banking industry to provide venture capital.[16] The total number of Black businesses in the United States was approximately 2,000 in 1863, 4,000 in 1873, and only 10,000 in 1883. Growth rates in Black businesses declined abruptly between 1883 and 1903.[17]

The older Black business elite—barbers, butlers, caterers, tailors, blacksmiths, carpenters, furniture makers and other skilled artisans—had been dependent upon white patrons for much if not all of its business. With the expansion of racial segregation after 1890, many of these artisans disappeared. The new generation of Black entrepreneurs was a byproduct of racial segregation, developing goods and services for Black consumers, embracing Washington's rhetoric of "self help" and racial upliftment. A conservative Black nationalist ideology was promoted aggressively by Black bankers, insurance agents and small merchants precisely because they "depended upon the Negro community for their support," observed historian August Meier. "The difficulties involved in obtaining credit from white banks, the discrimination practiced by white insurance companies and real estate firms, exclusion from white restaurants, hotels, and places of amusement, (and) the gradual elimination of skilled workers from employment" all combined to force Blacks to accept the Tuskegee economic theory. "Many (Blacks) were led to believe that only racially developed and supported business would solve their economic and other problems."[18]

The number of Black Capitalist success stories multiplied with the proliferation of Jim Crow restrictions. In 1899 DuBois predicted that most Black barbers in Philadelphia would be eliminated, because they served whites. Eight years later he discovered that Black "barbers (were) more numerous than ever, but catering to Negroes." Between 1900 and 1914, the number of Black-owned banks increased from 4 to 51; Black retail merchants, 10,000 to 25,000; Black undertakers, 450 to 1,000. The total number of Black businesses in the U.S. doubled in a little more than a decade, reaching 40,000 in 1914.

Two of the most influential Black entrepreneurs of the period were John Merrick of North Carolina and Isaiah T. Montgomery of Mississippi. A former slave and brickmason, Merrick established the North Carolina Mutual Insurance Company. By 1915, the company was insuring Black customers in twelve states and the District of Columbia. Merrick and his Black partners also created Mechanics and Farmers Bank in 1908, and the Merrick-Moore-Spaulding Real Estate Company in Durham in 1910. They also briefly owned a textile mill, and managed two drug stores servicing Durham's Black population. In 1887, Montgomery, the former slave of Jefferson Davis' brother, established an all-Black town, Mound Bayou. In less than ten years the city possessed several banks and real estate firms, a trades and technical education school modeled after Tuskegee Institute, a newspaper, a power and light company and a sawmill.[19]

But if the ideology and practice of Black Capitalism was to become a national force, it required political organizations. The leading advocate of this effort was Booker T. Washington. His influence in the

Afro-American Council in the late 1890s was the beginning of the infrastructure which later became the Tuskegee Machine. The chief organization of Washington's power from 1900 to 1915 was the National Negro Business League. The original concept for the League came from the sociological studies of DuBois, who was at that time a professor at Atlanta University. In an 1899 conference, DuBois proposed "the organization in every town and hamlet where the colored people dwell, of Negro Business Men's Leagues." He also called upon Negroes to spend consumer dollars solely with Black entrepreneurs. Washington opportunistically expropriated the concept from DuBois, and within a year had created the organization. At its first annual conference in Boston, over 300 Black merchants, artisans, lawyers, doctors and newspaper editors gathered to promote the Tuskegee philosophy of self-help and Black private enterprise. For Washington, the development of the League would provide the basis for a gradual end to racial oppression and segregation. "Suppose there was a black man who had business for the railroads to the amount of $10,000 a year," he wrote. "Do you suppose that, when that black man takes his family aboard the train, they are going to put him in a Jim Crow car and run the risk of losing that $10,000 a year? No, they will put on a Pullman palace car for him." The road to eventual civil rights, in Washington's estimation, was clearly one of private capital accumulation.[20]

Much of this sudden growth of Black businesses could not have occurred without the critical assistance of the Black press. Between 1865 and 1900 over 1,200 Black-owned newspapers were established, about 70 percent of them in the South. Without adequate advertising support, most of these papers disappeared within ten years. But in the age of Black business growth after 1900, a series of Black entrepreneurs succeeded in creating a number of politically influential newspapers. Robert S. Abbott initiated the Chicago *Defender* in May, 1905, and within 15 years was printing 200,000 copies nationally. Virginia journalist P. Bernard Young started the upper South's most widely read Black newspaper, the Norfolk *Journal and Guide*, in 1909. Black lawyer Robert Lee Vann created the *Pittsburgh Courier* in 1910, which in three decades achieved a national circulation of 300,000 and became the largest Black publication in the U.S. In the Deep South, William A. Scott established a Black Republican newspaper, the Atlanta *World*, in 1928.

None of these newspapers could have survived without the continued support of Black business, since circulation revenues alone could not cover their normal expenses. As journalist-historian Henry G. LaBrie noted, "big business (in the 1920s) ignored the black press" because it was "unaware of the buying power of the black consumer."[21] Thus, it was up to Black business to support the Black press. Accordingly, the National Afro-American Press Association usually selected officials who espoused the Tuskegee philosophy. At the peak of Washington's political power, the Tuskegee Machine even subsidized a number of Black newspapers, including the New York *Age*, the Boston *Colored Citizen*, the *Colored American Magazine* and the Washington, D.C. *Colored American*. Some Black newspaper owners and editors, particularly Fred R. Moore of the New York *Age*, not only became strong polemical advocates of racial accommodation but also became affluent business leaders in their own right. With these ties to Black business, the Black press became the chief vehicle to control and to exploit the Black consumer market, as well as to promote the ideology of Black Capitalism to the masses.[22]

The "Golden Years" of Black business occurred in the decade 1919–1929, which not coincidentally was also the period of the most extensive racial segregation.[23] By 1929 the number of Black-owned firms exceeded 70,000. Virtually every Black neighborhood or town in the United States could claim a number of independent Black entrepreneurs providing goods and services to an exclusively Black consumer market: barbers and beauty parlors, laundries, restaurants, grocery stores, newspapers, shoeshine and shoe repair shops, automotive service and repair, funeral parlors, insurance companies and small banks. It was this rapid petty capitalist development within a strictly segregated society that impressed and inspired the Black nationalist leader, Marcus Garvey. After only eight months in the United States, Garvey was convinced that Washington's strategy could be combined with race nationalism and political militancy to create a self-sustaining, Pan-Africanist economic order. Writing in 1916, Garvey declared:

> The acme of American Negro enterprise is not yet reached. You still have a far way to go. You want more stores, more banks, and bigger enterprises. We (West Indians) have no banks of our own, no big stores and commercial undertakings; we depend on others as dealers while we remain customers. The file is there open and

ready for anyone who has the training and ability to become a pioneer.[24]

Garvey's Universal Negro Improvement Association (UNIA), which included commercial establishments, the Negro Factories Corporation and Black Star Line, was successful in part because it reflected the economic and political realities of the Jim Crow age. Even Garvey's harshest critics within the NAACP did not dissent from the general economic direction of the UNIA. In the *Crisis*, DuBois admitted that "the main lines of the Garvey plan are perfectly feasible. What he is trying to say and do is this: American Negroes can, by accumulating and ministering their own capital, organize industry, join the black centers of the south Atlantic by commercial enterprise and in this way ultimately redeem Africa . . . for black men. This is true. It is *feasible*."[25]

Although DuBois considered himself an avowed socialist after 1904, his militancy was compromised with the optimistic spirit of the age. The Black entrepreneurial elite was basically a progressive, potentially powerful force in the battle against Jim Crow, in DuBois' view. He praised the rapid development of the Black business class in Durham, North Carolina, in 1912.[26] In October, 1913, he commented on a conference of Black business leaders in Philadelphia, concluding that despite evidence of "a spirit of aggrandizement, lying, stealing and grafting" the general outlook for this stratum was "excellent."[27] In articles written in 1922 and 1928, he applauded the development of Black-owned and directed banks.[28] When two major Black businesses went bankrupt, Brown and Stevens Bank of Philadelphia and Standard Life Insurance in Atlanta, he urged readers of the *Crisis* not to lose confidence in Black enterprise.[29] It was not until the Great Depression and its aftermath that DuBois grew pessimistic about the long-term possibility of a "Black Capitalist Solution" to the Negro's plight. In an October, 1942 newspaper column, DuBois lamented that Black entrepreneurs as a group had absolutely no ethics or morality regarding their own people. "What American Negro businessmen have got to remember," he urged, "is that a new economic morality is facing the world, and that emancipation from unfair private profit is going to be as great a crusade in the future as emancipation from Negro slavery was in the past."[30] Again in May, 1943, he encouraged Black businesses to seek the general economic improvement of all Blacks, rather than simply the accumulation of capital at grossly high profit margins.[31]

Few if any Black intellectuals and political leaders recognized the extreme economic instability of these expanding Black firms. A National Business League Survey of 1,534 Black enterprises in 33 large cities in 1928 found that 666—43.4 percent—recorded annual gross profits below $5,000, and only 137, or 8.9 percent, had annual gross receipts above $25,000.[32]

For the Black banking industry, the Depression was disastrous. The Douglass National Bank of Chicago, which in 1929 had a capital investment of $293,212.70 and deposits totalling $1,507,336.70, failed in May, 1932, despite a $200,000 loan from the Reconstruction Finance Corporation. The Chicago African Methodist Episcopal Church lost $18,000 with Douglass' collapse; a Black fraternal order lost $20,500. Of the 134 Black banks founded between 1888 and 1934, not more than 12 were operating in 1938.[33]

Thousands of other Black businesses also went bankrupt during the Great Depression. For the survivors, many managed by illegal means. In Chicago, for example, about one-fourth of all Black firms by the late 1930s were owned or controlled by "policy syndicates"—the "numbers" daily lotteries.

In World War II the number of Black enterprises resumed their pre-Depression growth, but at very low levels of capitalization. One 1944 survey of 3,866 Black businesses in 12 cities noted that the initial amount of capital for 64.4 percent of these firms was less than $1,000. The median value for Black business initial capitalization was $549. Some 86.3 percent of all enterprises were started solely with personal savings, and only 3.3 percent were initiated with bank loans. Almost 70 percent of all Black firms comprised only six types of businesses: restaurants (627); groceries (491); funeral parlors (126); shoe repair (130); laundries (288); barber shops and beauty parlors (1,004). Not until the late 1940s did Black businesses completely recover from the trauma of economic disaster.[34]

III

As the Black sharecropper in the South became a blue collar or service worker in the East Coast and Middle West, the bulk of Black business activity moved with the massive migration North. Gradually, majority Black populations appeared where only two decades before emigrants from Eastern and Central Europe had settled. Georgia and

Carolina Blacks moved into the traditional Italian neighborhood of East Harlem. In New York's lower East Side, Blacks and Puerto Ricans replaced Eastern European Jews. From the 1870s until World War I Harlem was primarily Jewish. The "ghetto," the term used in Europe to delineate the restricted residential boundaries for Jews, became attached to the Negro for all practical purposes by the 1930s. Black entrepreneurs who travelled north discovered that small Jewish, Irish, Italian and Slavic business owners did not often sell their establishments after their old ethnic neighborhoods had been racially transformed. Most of these firms were engaged in retail trade, had stable lines of credit with small banks established by their own ethnic groups, and they had absolutely no intention of surrendering the growing ghetto consumer market to upstart Black petty capitalists. Adding insult to injury, many of these Northern stores had an informal Jim Crow hiring policy well into the 1950s.[35]

The Black response to white ethnic economic hegemony within the ghetto's retail market took distinct political form in the "Don't Buy Where You Can't Work Movement." Local Black leaders picketed white establishments first in Chicago in late 1931, demanding jobs for Blacks. The movement swept rapidly to Pittsburgh, Atlanta, Boston, Baltimore and Richmond. Blacks initiated the "Citizens' League for Fair Play of New York" and initiated selective boycotts of major white Harlem establishments. Black progressives were divided on the effectiveness of the "Don't Buy Where You Can't Work" boycotts. Adam Clayton Powell, Jr., rose to political prominence as Harlem's leading business boycott leader, and was elected to Congress in 1944. Black radical political economist Abram L. Harris thought that this Black nationalist-oriented strategy "would serve further to widen the breach between white and black labor." The boycotts "would merely meet the unemployment of Negroes with the displacement of whites. But in the final analysis it would be the hundreds of thousands of black workers in industry who would have to bear the cost of the movement's success in obtaining a few thousand jobs for Negro clerks, salesmen and managers. What would be more natural than a retaliatory movement of whites demanding that Negroes be employed only by those white capitalists whose income is mainly derived from Negro [sales]?"[36]

The aspiring Black petty capitalists profited from this racial discontent. The closing of a single Jewish grocery store in a small Black neighborhood potentially meant thousands of dollars in added gross receipts to struggling Black entrepreneurs. To many Blacks in the middle strata within Jim Crow society, the existence of white businesses in a primarily Black community seemed essentially unfair. "Denied equal competition with whites in higher positions of the capitalist set-up and thwarted in its ambition to develop a miniature capitalism within its own segregated racial domain, the Negro middle class is being driven into a position of extreme racial chauvinism toward other minorities," Harris wrote in 1936. Black peddlers, loan sharks, retail store owners and real estate dealers not infrequently blamed Jews for Blacks' higher rents and exploitative consumer prices. The picture of the "money-grubbing, cheating Jew," to quote Paul Jacobs, soon became an integral part of Black urban folklore. In Los Angeles' Black ghetto, Watts, the vulgarism employed by unemployed Black teenagers for teasing Jewish shopkeepers was "pushing peanuts up Goldberg's nose." Jews, and after 1945, Lebanese, Palestinians, Latin Americans and Chinese were often the symbolic targets of Black economic animosity, primarily because they were the most visible non-Black entrepreneurs in ghetto life. But as Harris argued, racial chauvinism was no substitute for the development of an effective program to eliminate Black urban poverty, unemployment and hunger. "If there is exploitation of the black masses in Harlem, the Negro businessman participates in it as well as the Jew, while both the Jewish businessman and the Negro are governed by higher forces that are beyond their control."[37]

In the 1950s and 1960s, the political prospects for Black Capitalism began to improve. White corporate leaders and politicians, anxious to improve their standing within the burgeoning Black urban communities of the North and West, began serious efforts to cultivate a stable and class-conscious Black elite. The general pattern that emerged was corporate and philanthropic support for local development corporations and "economic resource centers" which provided fiscal and technical assistance to Black businesses. In Los Angeles, for example, the Economic Resource Corporation was created with white corporate assistance. It guaranteed loans made by Black enterpreneurs at local banks, extended generous grants, and purchased property and machinery for Blacks. Chicago's Economic Development Corporation assisted Black businesspersons in their financial loan negotiations. The Interracial Council for Business Opportunity, a group of Black and white businesspersons in St. Louis, New Orleans, New York, Los

Angeles, Chicago and other cities, gave technical symposiums to Black would-be corporatists, created the National New Enterprise Program—which helped Black businesses needing capitalization of over $100,000—and guaranteed "up to 50 percent loans made by banks to minority entrepreneurs." The Inner-City Business Improvement Forum of Detroit helped to arrange the finances of Black firms. Rochester, New York's Business Opportunities Corporation gave technical aid to Blacks just starting in business, and also guaranteed their bank loans. San Francisco's Program for Action in Changing Times provided most of the services available in other urban corporations of the type listed above, but it also acted "as a broker between minority job-seekers and large white corporations" and gave "counseling and technical assistance on a one-to-one basis for existing and potential businessmen." New York City's International Council of Shopping Centers encouraged Blacks who aspired to initiate their own shopping malls. New York's Association to Assist Negro Businesses (AANB) provided credit to Blacks "under a mechanism whereby pledges of $10,000 were solicited from each of twenty-nine white businessmen and used this as a basis for a $290,000 line of credit for ten years to be used against loan guarantees made by AANB to black enterprises."[38]

This "benevolent" corporate strategy was actually a return to the policy of Andrew Carnegie and other business leaders vis-a-vis Washington and other Black accommodationists. It was Carnegie who financed the National Negro Business League's chapters; in 1904 the steel industrialist created a pseudo-civil rights organization, the Committee of Twelve for the Advancement of the Interests of the Negro Race, led by the politically pliable Washington.[39] Similarly, years later, Richard Nixon appointed Black millionaire real estate developer and lawyer Gloria A. Toote to serve as Assistant Secretary for Equal Opportunity in the Department of Housing and Urban Development. Nixon also selected Black Capitalist proponent Jewel Lafontant to the post as Deputy Solicitor General in the Department of Justice. As women and as Blacks, both represented the newest version of the kind of personal success stories that perpetuate the myth of Black Capitalism. After Watergate and Nixon's political downfall, both women made the transition to symbolic posts in the upper sanctum of white corporate power. Lafontant became a member of the boards of Trans-World Airlines, Continental Illinois National Bank and Trust Corporation of Chicago, Equitable Life Assurance Society of the U.S.

(New York City), Harte Hanks Communications, Foote, Cone and Belding, Jewel Companies, Inc., and the Bendix Corporation. Toote has emerged as the major Black female ideologue for Ronald Reagan and enjoys seemingly limitless access to the media to propagate her views. [40]

Despite these and other paternalistic efforts, the general pattern of U.S. Black business today still reveals a systematic underdevelopment, a paucity of capital and employees, that extends across geographical and regional boundaries. A random selection of nine moderately sized cities where at least 100 Black businesses exist—three each in the South, North, and West—provides an illustration. The towns selected ranked between 70th to 90th in their size of Black population for U.S. metropolitan areas in 1977: Chattanooga, Tennessee (48,079 Blacks), Pensacola, Florida (43,458 Blacks), and Greenville, Mississippi (37,889 Blacks), in the South; Akron, Ohio (59,441 Blacks), Bridgeport, Connecticut (35,639 Blacks), and Harrisburg, Pennsylvania (33,605 Blacks), in the North; Sacramento, California (51,953 Blacks), Phoenix, Arizona (38,561 Blacks), and Austin, Texas (36,905 Blacks), in the West. [41] Each town and region of the country exhibits different economic characteristics. Blacks comprise a higher percentage of a town's total population in middle-sized cities in the South than in the North and West. Akron, Harrisburg and Bridgeport have strong, industrial working class communities, with substantial Black membership in local trade unions. Sacramento, Harrisburg and Austin are state capitals, which traditionally have a higher percentage of Blacks employed in state government as white collar workers. Phoenix's Black community developed substantially later than in the other cities, with the sudden economic growth in the Southwest after 1950. (See Tables XX, XXI and XXII)

The data reveals some obvious divergences. The city recording the highest gross receipts in 1977 was Greenville, Mississippi, with $12,765,000. Greenville's gross receipts total is followed by Phoenix ($11,132,000) and Austin ($10,047,000). Cities with much larger Black populations, such as Sacramento ($6,920,000) and Akron ($7,666,000) actually recorded significantly lower gross profits. Greenville's Black economic development may be explained by history and geography. It is the largest town between Memphis and Baton Rouge on the Mississippi River. Situated between Arkansas and Louisiana to the Southwest, Greenville's Blacks are a high percentage of the town's population. Greenville is one of the largest commercial centers for what remains of the western Black Belt. It also retains a strong legacy of racial segregation. These points set Greenville apart from the two other Southern towns of similar size on the list. Chattanooga has some light industry, but is politically and socially more Appalachian white than Black Belt in character. Pensacola is part of the wiregrass region of western Florida and southeastern Alabama. George Wallace and his supporters still dominate the politics of the rural region, which is conservative, populist and technically outside the Black Belt. Blacks imigrating to Western cities like Phoenix and Austin after 1950 were generally better educated and more affluent than earlier Blacks who arrived between Reconstruction and World War II. Both cities, however, have recent histories of legal segregation ending only a generation ago. All three Black populations in the North have relatively small numbers of Black firms possessing paid employees, and rank fifth, seventh, and ninth in the group in 1977 amounts for gross receipts. Tentatively these figures suggest that cities with relatively high percentages of Blacks, having strong histories of legal segregation, and/or experiencing a rapid growth of middle class Blacks since 1950 will have a somewhat more developed Black petty capitalist infrastructure than towns of similar size without such characteristics. Black business communities are weakest in cities where no legal Jim Crow barriers have existed for a century or more, and/or where Blacks comprise a relatively small segment of the total metropolitan population.[42]

There are far more similarities within these Black business profiles, however, than differences. The largest number of firms in all nine cities is in the area of "selected or human services," a broad category including housekeeping, repair shops, laundries, health services, amusement and recreational concerns, automotive repair and garages, hotels and educational services. Greenville has the lowest percentage of selected services within its entire number of firms, 35.2 percent. The other towns' percentages of selected services within the total number of Black firms range from 41 to 60 percent, roughly paralleling the Black national human services figure of 44 percent. In all cities selected, the number of human service firms without a single paid employee was much larger than those with workers. In Bridgeport, only 14 out of 87 such firms have paid employees. The amount of gross receipts for firms without employees averages only $8,630 per year. Bridgeport's other 14 Black human services firms have staffs totalling 32 persons, pay annual payrolls averaging $10,214 per firm, and have average annual gross receipts of $55,714. The second leading number of Black firms in all nine cities is retail trade establishments: grocery stores, apparel and accessory shops, garden and building supply centers, general merchandise stores, restaurants, bars and furniture stores. Chattanooga and Austin have the largest number (both 108) of stores in the retail sector. The number of retail stores in both cities with paid workers is very low. Chattanooga's 79 Black retail stores without paid employees average annual gross receipts of $15,962. The city's 29 Black-owned retail establishments with employees (84 total) pay average annual payrolls of $12,689, and have average annual gross receipts of $139,931. Austin possesses 80 Black retail stores without paid workers, with average annual gross receipts of $14,925. The other 28 firms have a total of 46 employees, have average payrolls of $6,036, and average annual gross receipts of $63,679. Akron, the third ranking city (94) for Black retail firms, has similar totals: for the 77 Black retail firms without employees, average gross receipts were $10,597; the 17 other Black retail firms (43 employees) have average annual gross receipts of $130,058.

The lowest number of Black business enterprise in all of these cities is in the areas of manufacturing (food products, tobacco, lumber and wood products, electronic and electrical equipment, machinery, fabricated metal products, leather products, stone, glass and clay products, etc.) and wholesale trade (suppliers to food stores, general merchandise centers, furniture stores, etc.). Phoenix has only one Black manufacturer with paid employees, and 23 Black entrepreneurs who are wholesale merchants, most of whom (20) having no paid workers. Sacramento claims all of two Black manufacturers, neither of whom have employees, and only one out of a grand total of five Blacks involved in the wholesale business have any employees. Taken together, all nine cities listed here have a total of 2,933 Black-owned firms of various kinds. In this group, there are only 525 that have paid employees, 17.9 percent of the total number of enterprises. One thousand three hundred and seventy-one firms (46.7 percent of total) engage in human services. Some 687 businesses are in retail trade (23.4 percent). Over 70 percent of all modern Black enterprises, in summary, are in the same vulnerable sector of the segregated economy that was developed 80 years ago by Washington and the early proponents of

Black Capitalism. Relatively few have made it into the big leagues of white corporate finance, manufacturing and wholesale commercial trading.

Census research on Black-owned businesses also indicates a profound pattern of concentrated wealth and power in the hands of a relatively small number of Black capitalists. Only 164,177 workers (mostly Blacks) found employment in the 39,968 Black firms which hired personnel in 1977. Within this figure, however, 32,581 businesses (81.5 percent of firms hiring workers) employed between one to four persons during the year. These firms hired an average workforce of 1.45 employees, paid average annual gross payrolls of $9,695, and recorded average gross receipts totaling $68,831. Moving up the employment scale, a different picture emerges. Only 230 Black firms in the U.S. in 1977 hired between 50 and 99 employees. This group retained an average workforce of 67.6 employees, had average annual gross payrolls of $540,035, and average yearly gross receipts of $2,357,909. At the pinnacle of Black Capitalism were the 113 Black U.S. firms which employed 100 or more workers in 1977. This tiny elite is marginally part of the dominant U.S. capitalist class. With an average workforce of 247.5 employees, these firms met average annual payrolls of $1,960,221. Average annual gross receipts for the elite in 1977 were $8,952,469. Throughout the U.S., there were 1,060 Black-owned corporations and partnerships that hired 20 or more employees. This small fraction of all Black entrepreneurs was only one half of one percent (00.46) of all Blacks engaged in private enterprise. These 1,060 affluent Black firms had gross receipts which totalled $2,467,958,000, 38.6 percent of all gross receipts acquired by Black firms with employees, and 28.5 percent of the gross receipts received by all Black-owned businesses. Only a few enterprises earn the vast majority of profits. One hundred and three manufacturing firms out of a total of 4,243 received 67.3 percent of all gross receipts in that sector, and employed 52.8 percent of all employees. In wholesale trade, 5 percent of the firms had 75.3 percent of all receipts and 58.3 percent of all paid workers. In finance, real estate and insurance, 90 firms (0.9 percent of the total number) earned 69.2 percent of all gross receipts and had 77.1 percent of all employees. Even within the Black commercial and industrial elite, the old patterns of the segregation era were stamped clearly on these profit patterns. Three hundred and forty three of the top 1,060 firms (32.4 percent) were involved in selected services, and another 277 businesses (26.1 percent) were large retail stores. Only two Black firms in the U.S. employing 100 or more workers were in wholesale trade. Only 5 construction firms and 3 transportation companies owned by Blacks hired 100 or more employees.[43] (See Tables XXIII and XXIV)

Black Capitalism in the 1980s, whether considered as an economic force competing for a substantial share of Black consumer dollars or as a political force which advances a pro-corporate and "neo-Horatio Alger" ideology within Black society, must be subdivided into three distinct constituencies—the "proletarian periphery;" the intermediate Black petty entrepreneurs; and the Black corporate core. Over four-fifths of all Black-owned U.S. firms, 82.7 percent of the total number, belong to the proletarian periphery. These 191,235 enterprises have several common characteristics: (1) Almost all are sole proprietorships, unincorporated firms owned by a single Black individual; (2) most are started by Black blue-collar or marginally white-collar employees; (3) the firms are undercapitalized from the outset, and owners are forced to subsidize business activities by drawing upon personal savings, loans from friends and relatives, and by allocating a portion of their salaries at their other place of employment; (4) all of these firms have no paid employees; (5) the vast majority are concentrated in two traditional sectors of the segregated Black economy, human services and retail trade; (6) at least 75 percent become bankrupt within three years; and (7) their average annual gross receipts vary between $3,000 and $15,000. Economically and politically, these Blacks are essentially workers who are attempting to become small businesspersons, struggling against massive odds to leave the ranks of the proletariat.

These marginal worker-entrepreneurs must be viewed as part of the Black proletariat from which capitalism extracts surplus value. These small entrepreneurs uniformly pay higher rates for insurance, since majority-Black communities are defined as "high-risk" areas. They are exploited by banks which "redline" Black districts, making entire communities ineligible to receive loans at reasonable interest rates. The proletarian periphery falls victim to the economies of scale, wherein smaller retailers with low sales volume and a small number of commodities must charge Black consumers higher retail prices for goods or services than larger white companies. McDonalds and Kentucky Fried Chicken, for example, can sell their fast foods at nominally lower prices than the Black "mom-and-pop" chicken establishment, because of infinitely higher sales volume. Human service-oriented establishments initiated by Black workers who possess personal skills (hairdressers, cooks, barbers, caterers, etc.) can be established with little capital, but they are also extraordinarily vulnerable to capitalist recessions. Black workers and the unemployed have precious little discretionary income even during brief periods of high employment. At every periodic downturn in the capitalist economy, Black lower-to-middle income consumers cut back on their spending for services. As a result, in both 1973–75 and 1980–82 tens of thousands of small Black businesses failed.

Those fortunate enough to survive, by legal or even illegal means, became part of the Black petty bourgeoisie, the intermediate level of Black entrepreneurship. These Black businesses constitute about 38,900 firms, 16.8 percent of all Black enterprises. The common traits they share are the following: (1) All retain paid personnel, with an annual workforce between 1 and 19 employees; (2) average gross receipts are between $30,000 and $300,000; (3) almost all employers work full-time in their enterprises; (4) almost all firms receive loans from banks and savings and loan establishments to continue business expansion; and (5) a substantial minority of these firms are involved in real estate, finance, manufacturing, and other traditionally all-white sectors of private enterprise. In *Black Capitalism*, Timothy Bates outlines the financal characteristics of 285 Black "high-caliber" firms in Chicago, Boston and New York that received loans through the Small Business Administration in the early 1970s. Mean value for the group's total sales was $74,101; mean total assets, $30,029; the mean number of years of the Black owner's management experience, 8.45 years; mean total liabilities, $19,528; mean amount of Small Business Administration loan, $27,740.[44]

The corporate core of Black Capitalism is the 1,060 Black businesses with a workforce of 20 or more employees, led by *Black Enterprise* magazine's top 100 firms. Number one is Motown Industries of Hollywood, producers of soul records, films and tapes, with 1979 gross receipts of $64.8 million. Numbers two through five are Johnson Publishers ($61 million), Fedco Foods supermarkets ($45 million), H.J. Russell Construction of Atlanta ($41 million), and Johnson Cosmetics of Chicago ($35.4 million). This select group also includes Independence Bank of Chicago ($98.3 million in 1979 assets); Seaway National Bank of Chicago ($80.9 million in assets); Industrial Bank of

Washington, D.C. ($59.9 million in assets); Freedom National Bank of New York City ($57.9 million in assets); United National Bank of Washington, D.C. ($56.2 million in assets); North Carolina Mutual Life Insurance Company ($5.1 billion insurance policies in force); and Golden State Mutual Life of Los Angeles ($2.7 billion insurance policies in force). Although these figures seem impressive, all of these major Black corporations combined could be purchased, for instance, by Mobil Oil Corporation with its liquid assets. *White corporations allow these Black companies to exist for symbolic value alone*. John H. Johnson of Johnson Publishers, for instance, is a member of the Boards of Directors of Twentieth Century Fox, Greyhound Corporation, Zenith Radio Corporation and Marina City Bank. H.G. Parks, Jr., Black millionaire owner of Parks' Sausage Company of Baltimore, sits on the boards of First Pennsylvania Banking and Trust Company and W.R. Grace and Company. Former Tuskegee Institute President Luther H. Foster, the modern representative of Washington's conservative philosophy, was elected to the Boards of Directors of Sears, Roebuck and Company and Norton Simon, Inc. The modern equivalent of Fred R. Moore, *Black Enterprise* publisher Earl Graves, was rewarded with posts on the boards of International Telephone and Telegraph Corporation and the Liggett Group. Black millionaire and Atlanta Chamber of Commerce President Jesse Hill Jr. serves on the boards of Delta Airlines and Sperry and Hutchinson Company. The number of executives who truly dominate the Black corporate core within the Afro-American political economy *amount to less than 200 individuals*. They have earned the confidence of the white corporate hierarchy and the capitalist state by keeping alive the bogus illusion of Black Capitalism.[45]

IV

Undoubtedly the greatest obstacle to a present-day Black Capitalist strategy is the newly found interest of white corporations in controlling and capturing the Black consumer market. Between 1960 and 1973 the estimated amount of goods and services purchased by Black Americans increased from $30 billion to almost $70 billion annually. By 1978 the Black consumer market was the ninth largest in the world. Twenty years ago, however, at the peak of the Civil Rights Movement, few corporations seemed interested or willing to make special efforts to appeal to Black consumers. Initial advertising strategies were poorly staged and more appropriate to the racial ideologies of the 1890s. In 1960, for example, *Readers Digest* decided to reprint *Up From Slavery,* and invited the United Negro College Fund to help it sponsor a creative writing contest to promote the ideals of Washington. In 1962 Greyhound Lines, Inc., the world's most profitable transportation company, hired baseball relief pitcher Joe Black as a special markets representative in New York City, to "recognize, identify and invite black passengers" to ride its buses. With much fanfare in press released to Black-oriented radio stations and to the Black press, Black was promoted in 1967 to vice president of special markets for Greyhound, becoming the first Black vice president in the U.S. transportation industry.[46]

The white corporate strategy of gaining control of the Black consumer market occurred first with Pepsi-Cola Company. In the early 1950s the vast majority of Black soft-drink consumers purchased Pepsi, approximately three times more frequently than they selected Coca-Cola, Pepsi's chief competitor. Overall profits for Pepsi sagged from the Black market throughout the 1950s. In early 1961, Pepsi's management commissioned Elmo Roper and Associates to complete a detailed "breakout of black consumer preferences and attitudes, (giving) Pepsi its first overall picture of black consumer trends." The Roper study revealed a number of surprising facts:

1) Blacks comprised only 11 percent of the U.S. population, but made up 17 percent of the soft-drink market. Blacks purchased 300 million cases of soft drinks annually. White per capita consumption of soft drinks was 120 bottles, vs. 163 bottles for Blacks.

2) Blacks were far more "flavor-conscious" than whites. Forty-nine percent of all grape soda and over 33 percent of all orange soda sold in the U.S. was bought by Blacks.

3) Between 1951 and 1961, Blacks' consumption of Pepsi had remained constant, while Pepsi consumption among whites had increased 300 percent. "This lack of sales growth among blacks meant a loss of 60 million cases per year to Pepsi-Cola."

Reacting quickly, Pepsi elevated Harvey C. Russell as vice president of special markets. Russell's appointment, well publicized in both white and Black media, made him "the highest-ranking black executive of an international business firm." In January, 1962, Pepsi bought twelve four-color pages in *Ebony,* and ran advertisements in virtually every Black newspaper in the country. Pepsi donated money to over 30 annual Black conventions, cosponsored a tournament for Black golfers, and subsidized the casting of a special medallion for the president of the Black National Medical Association. The company urged its local bottlers to develop or expand programs for Black market development. In 1963 Pepsi hired Black historian John Hope Franklin and other prominent Black social scientists to develop an elaborate series of films and records entitled "Adventures in Negro History." By 1964, after spending several million dollars solely in Black-oriented advertising, the "bottom line" results were in. Pepsi-Cola's annual profits rose from $157.6 million to $250 million between 1960 and 1964. Market research indicated subsequently that after five purchases, six out of ten Black "heavy-user households" favored Pepsi, compared to only four out of ten white households.[47]

The Pepsi-Cola campaign not only reaped almost $100 million, but illustrated to the entire white corporate and advertising world the *enormous profits* at stake in the Black consumer market. By the mid-to-late 1960s, advertisers produced exhaustive studies of Black consumer habits, finding key differences between Blacks and whites. Researchers discovered that Black women purchased over 50 percent more home cleaning products, particularly air fresheners, garbage bags, insecticides and oven cleaners, than white women on a per capita basis. In 1966, nonwhite consumers (11.5 percent of the U.S. population) purchased 15 percent of all cereal; 18.5 percent of the flour; 39 percent of the rice; 38 percent of the cornmeal; 17.5 percent of the poultry; 26 percent of the smoked sausage; 22 percent of the canned milk; 29 percent of the green beans; 32.5 percent of the lard; 14.5 percent of the molasses and syrup; 17 percent of the salt; 22.5 percent of the wool blankets; 15.5 percent of the cooking utensils; 14.5 percent of the overcoats; and 28.5 percent of the hats sold in the United States. The list of Black consumer preferences is, of course, almost endless. The data collected by market analysts can be interpreted in a number of ways, to promote greater profits from Black sales. For example, Procter and Gambel learned from its advertising agency that 22.4 percent of Black householders used Tide to wash dishes as well as the family laundry, compared to only 3.4 percent of white householders. The company developed two different marketing strategies: in white-oriented media, "the message referred only to Tide as a laundry detergent;" in majority Black areas, Tide is advertised as "an all-purpose detergent for dishes, in the bath, for washing fine fabrics, and in the laundry."[48]

In the 1970s the level of corporate sophistication increased. Market analysts informed Pillsbury corporation that the purchasers of its "profit leader," Hungry Jack biscuits, were 46 percent Black and 54 percent white. Relatively few white householders outside the rural South regularly ate biscuits, whereas Black consumption was increasing. However, Pillsbury was dismayed to learn that only 11 percent of all Black consumers purchased Hungry Jack biscuits, which were then packaged in a ten-ounce, ten-biscuit can. Allocating $1.5 million for a new marketing strategy, Pillsbury decided to simply maintain its white consumer market while attempting to boost its sales to Blacks. A six-biscuit can was produced to appeal to smaller Black households. Black-oriented radio commercials were developed for Black stations with a "hearty endorsement of a black mother." Hungry Jack advertisements appeared in *Essence* and *Ebony*. By 1975, gross profits surged 56 percent. Brown and Williamson Tobacco Corporation of Louisville, Kentucky, hired a Black advertising firm for assistance in marketing its Kool cigarettes in the Black community. Research figures revealed that while Kool accounted for a meager 7 percent of the total U.S. cigarette market, Black smokers comprised about one-third of all Kool consumers. In the mid-1970s Brown and Williamson initiated the "Kool Jazz Festivals," featuring noted Black musicians and singers, playing only in cities where a significant number of Blacks resided. In its first year, the concerts reached 480,000 people, mostly Blacks. Much of the music presented in the Festivals by the late 1970s, ironically, was not jazz at all, but "disco." Kool producer George Wein admitted that this "has upset" some jazz artists, but "we will continue to present soul artists as long as the public wants to hear them." Authentic Black jazz or blues, in short, did not produce sufficient patrons or profits.[49]

The impact of corporate America's massive exploitation of the Black consumer market has created a profoundly negative effect within Black culture and consciousness. When Schieffelin and Company, manufacturers of Teacher's Scotch, learned that Blacks consumed a 50 percent higher per capita rate of scotch than whites, it created a film narrated by Jesse Owens, *The Black Athlete,* in 1971. The film "premiered" in every U.S. city with a large Black consumer market. "Teacher's Scotch Sports Nights" were arranged by Black liquor salesmen, and the film was displayed in bars and nightspots in Detroit, New York, Baltimore, Chicago, Washington, D.C., Cleveland and Los Angeles. Prints of *The Black Athlete* were forwarded to Schieffelin distributors for showings in bars in smaller Black communities and in Black public libraries. The same ideological techniques devised by corporations are now used with greater effect by the U.S. military and other law-and-order agencies. In the aftermath of the urban rebellions of the late 1960s, for example, the National Guard recognized that it had a major "credibility problem" within the national Black community. In 1970 only 5,000 Black Americans were members of the National Guard. The military agency hired W.B. Doner and Company to devise a media strategy to help it "to overcome negative attitudes" among Blacks. With Doner's assistance, Black Guard membership exceeded 50,000 by 1976.[50]

In addition to these specific marketing strategies, there has also been a general white corporate strategy to increase profitability at the expense of the Black consumer. The first aspect of this strategy concentrates on 50 percent of the total Black U.S. population, whose annual incomes fall below $13,000. White businessmen now recognize that the urban poor and lower-income consumers can be made to pay much higher prices than affluent white suburbanites for commodities, so long as adequate lines of credit are made available to them. In the 1960s, studies illustrated that personal debt-to-income ratios were quite high for all poor people, Blacks and whites alike. However, unlike low-income whites, Blacks' debts "tend to increase with income."[51] Blacks with incomes of $5,000 actually had greater personal debt-to-income ratios than whites with virtually no income. Black low-income consumers also suffered because of low savings rates. For Black families with incomes below $2,500 in the early 1960s, only 25 percent had savings of $100 or more. Merchants designed their Black marketing strategy to make profits not only from the sale of the commodity, but *primarily* from the terms of the credit agreements. Almost two-thirds of all poor Blacks buy their household appliances either exclusively or primarily on credit, often on terms that exceed market credit rates by over 100 percent. David Caplovitz's observation of 1963, "the poor pay more," remains true today.[52]

The second part of the profit-making corporate strategy concentrates on the 36.1 percent of the U.S. Black population with annual incomes above $15,000 in 1978. Segmented, this sector of the Black consumer market includes: the majority of Black two-parent households with both parents in the labor force, 1977 median income of $17,008; Black family heads with 4 or more years of college education, 1976 median income of $20,733; Black two-parent households under the age of 35 with both parents in the labor force, residing in the North and West, 1974 median income of $15,031. In 1974, the highest 20 percent of all Black families received 44.2 percent of the aggregate income earned by all Blacks, and the top 5 percent received 15.9 percent of all Blacks' aggregate income.[53] Corporate market analysts learned that these "middle-class" Black families spent a larger share of disposable income on travel, certain foods, entertainment and luxury furnishings than whites at identical income levels. Mediamark Research, Inc., completed a detailed study of the purchasing patterns of Black families who earned over $15,000 in 1980. The research completed indicated that Black middle-class families not only were heavy consumers, but had spending patterns that were different from lower-income Blacks. Corporations and advertisers in the 1980s began to devise class-conscious propaganda, based on this type of information, to capture this new Black elite market. (See Table XXV)

V

The modern paradox confronting the prospective Black Capitalist is the process of desegregation. No Black nation in history has acquired the economic growth potential of the total Black consumer market in the U.S. Total Black income had grown from $98.6 billion in 1978 to $125.8 billion in 1980. Almost half of the aggregate Black income, roughly $56 billion in 1980, was earned by less than one-fifth of all Black families.[54] Theoretically, Black enterprise activities should have entered an unprecedented period of capital growth in the 1970s and 1980s. But in real terms, the opposite occurred. Between 1900–1930, the number of Black firms increased 700 percent; between 1930–1969, the number of Black firms grew by 233 percent; between 1969–1977, growth was 70.5 percent. The number of Black businesses with paid employees in 1969—38,304—amounted to 23.4 percent of all Black firms in operation; by 1977, Black firms with employees totaled 39,968, only 17.3 percent of all Black businesses. Gross Black business receipts climbed from $4.5 billion in 1969 to $8.6 billion in 1977, but inflation and other factors actually reveal an overall stasis in real net profits.[55] Historically, rapid Black business growth occurred *only during the period of rigid racial segregation,* when relatively few white corporations made any attempts to attract Black consumers. The Civil Rights Movement and desegregation permitted the white private sector to develop a variety of advertising strategies to extract billions in profits from Black consumers, all in the name of "equality." The net result was the increased marginalization of the Black entrepreneur, the manipulation of Black culture and social habits by white corporations, and a new kind of economic underdevelopment for all Blacks at all income levels.

Recognizing the crucial paradox, a number of Black advocates for capitalism have stepped forward with new approaches to this dilemma. In 1968, Andrew Brimmer, a member of the Board of Governors of the Federal Reserve System (and subsequently, a member of the Boards of Directors of Bank of America, American Security Bank, E.I. DuPont, United Air Lines, and International Harvester) admitted that "the wall of segregation which cut Negroes off from many public services" provided a "wall of protection (for) the Negro businessman." Washington's ambitious strategy was doomed to failure, however, because "in those areas in which Negro customers have relatively free access to retail establishments (such as department stores, hardware, furnishings and similar outlets), Negro businessmen have not found fertile ground." Complete desegregation would destroy the entire foundation of Black Capitalism. Therefore, Brimmer concluded, would-be Black entrepreneurs should leave the ghetto and become managers and consultants to multi-billion dollar U.S. corporations. As a conservative integrationist, Brimmer views all forms of racial separatism with utter contempt. As an integral spokesperson for corporate interests, he advances the necessity to develop a stable Black stratum within the upper-to-middle ranks of the managerial elite.[56]

Other proponents of Black Capitalism are reluctant to yield to the modern realities of America's corporate system, yet they recognize that the old Washingtonian approach can no longer yield dividends. "It is obvious that black economic development, on the scale necessary, is impossible if it must rely solely on accumulated wealth possibilities in the black community," Black economist Flournoy A. Coles, Jr., wrote in 1975. "The black stock must be augmented with wealth from outside the black community—and this means wealth transfers."[57] A combination of corporate property and Federal tax revenue, or perhaps "reparations payments" from white civil society, would be used to form the basis of a Black capitalism within the overall system of "white capitalism." The most ambitious and controversial scheme outlined to date that implements this strategy was written by economist Richard America. Since Blacks comprise over 10 percent of the total U.S. population, America observed, then in a truly "democratic capitalist" society, Blacks also should own 10 percent of all U.S. corporations. The Federal government should buy 125 of the largest industrial firms and corporations over a period of 15 years at fair market rates, and subsequently resell them to Black businesspersons at below market rates. The difference in purchase and resell price, literally hundreds of billions of dollars, would be absorbed by the Federal government. Coles favors the "America plan . . . because it addresses itself to the root cause of black powerlessness and black alienation from the economic mainstream of our society." Other Black theorists have extended the proposal to include 10 percent of all corporations and firms currently owned by whites.[58]

Even when examined seriously, the America proposal is absurd. The total gross income received by all U.S. Blacks in 1980 was $125.8 billion, and the total gross receipts of all U.S. Black firms that same year was $8.6 billion. Let us assume, for the moment, that the Federal government agreed to such an arrangement—a deal that would significantly increase income tax rates and stimulate inflation tremendously. Let us assume further that every single Black income earner in the U.S. in 1980 set aside 3 percent of his/her gross income computed at $3.77 billion. Black firms with 20 or more employees would reserve 5 percent of all annual gross income ($123.4 million in 1977), and less affluent businesses with fewer than 20 workers would donate 3 percent of gross receipts ($117.9 million in 1977). The total amount of capital, excluding any costs for paperwork, etc., comes to $4 billion. The total number of all businesses in the U.S. in 1972, *excluding corporations,* was 7,053,000, of which Blacks owned 2.7 percent. Gross 1972 receipts for all businesses, again excluding corporations, amounted to $289.3 *billion.* Even if the Federal government reallocated these small-to-medium sized sole proprietorships and partnerships at fantastic budget prices, it would take probably more than one hundred years to complete the payments. But one special problem emerges. In certain very profitable economic sectors, Blacks are not currently trained in adequate numbers to assume "leadership" for their 10 percent share of that particular area. Only 2.3 percent of all construction-firm owners are Black; only 0.4 percent of all wholesale trade owners are Black; Blacks comprise only 0.8 percent of all real estate, insurance and finance company owners. Should the Federal government pay the reeducational costs of Black factory workers, for example, to become chief executive officers of metropolitan banks and public utility companies? And will the transfer of these companies mean that more Blacks from the working class will have a greater possibility of jobs, eliminating the high Black unemployment rate? What America, Coles, *et. al.*, ignore is that the U.S. is not simply a capitalist state, but a *racist state*. Everything in U.S. history indicates that *not a single major corporation* would agree to liquidate its current directors and owners, rendering itself unto the desperate Black petty bourgeoisie.[59]

There is yet another political reservation that must be registered about Black Capitalism. Historically within advanced capitalist societies it is the sector of petty capital that is often more inclined toward authoritarianism than large capital. Reactionary political movements within parliamentary democracies tend to develop their strongest support (although, I should add here, not their *decisive* support) among elements of the most economically insecure and marginal stratum within the capitalist class. Hitler's astonishingly rapid growth in Weimar Germany came not merely from the anti-Semitism of many German unemployed workers but also from the small shopkeepers and merchants of that country. In both 1976 and 1980, finance capital was extremely reserved about Ronald Reagan's candidacy for the Republican nomination. Reagan's delegates tended to be less well-educated and less wealthy than Ford's or Bush's delegates, respectively. Small business is usually less supportive of state intervention into the capitalist economy (e.g., its strong opposition to the Federal government's loan guarantees to Chrysler Corporation in 1980), and is far more hostile to unions than multinationals are. Large corporations agree to modest minimum wage laws and substantial wage and fringe benefits to workers because they desire long-term labor peace. Small corporations, sole proprietorships, and business partnerships, working with smaller profit margins, paying higher interest rates for borrowed capital for business expansion than the multinationals, cannot afford to take the "long view." The gross receipts of every single business day are much more crucial to them. Sole proprietors, Black or white, are much more likely to advocate strict laws to restrict the development of unions in their own workplace, and in their own states. The economic demands of day-to-day entrepreneurial struggle tend, in every capitalist society, to push the politics of small businesspersons to the right. This remains particularly the case for entrepreneurs engaged in human services and retail trade—the economic areas which have continued to be the decisive part of Black Capitalist development. In short, the crisis of modern capitalism may push the advocates of Black Capitalism squarely into the political camp of the most racist and conservative forces of white America. The logic of Black Capitalism could reinforce the politics of authoritarianism. The Black entrepreneurs' quest for profits could become part of the political drive to discipline the entire Black working class.[60]

CHAPTER SIX

BLACK BRAHMINS: THE UNDERDEVELOPMENT OF BLACK POLITICAL LEADERSHIP.

---

there's only two parties in this country
anti-nigger and pro-nigger
most of the pro-niggers are now dead
this second reconstruction is being aborted
as was the first
the pro-niggers council voting
the anti-niggers have guns. . .

Nikki Giovanni, *Black Feeling, Black Talk, Black Judgement* (New York: William Morrow, 1970), p. 83.

It sometimes happens in a nation where opinions are divided that the balance between parties breaks down and one of them acquires an irresistible preponderence. It breaks all obstacles, crushes its adversary, and exploits the whole of society for its own benefit. But beneath this apparent unanimity deep divisions and real opposition still lie hidden. That is what has happened in America. . . It is easy to see that the rich have a great distaste for their country's democratic institutions. The people are a power whom they fear and scorn.

Alexis De Tocqueville, *Democracy in America* (New York: Anchor, 1969), pp. 178-179.

I

There is something essentially absurd about a Negro politician in racist/capitalist America. The political apparatus was designed originally to exclude him/her. The rhetoric of the system is democratic, almost egalitarian: the practices are bluntly discriminatory. Any state cannot exist in and of itself; it rests upon the material base of a particular productive process, and in the last analysis, acts decisively to protect the propertied and powerful classes of that society. The Black majority has no real structural power, other than the productive capacity of its own hands. The Black elite retain the illusion of power, but are invested with little authority in its own right. The Black politician is locked in a world of meaningless symbols which perpetuate the hegemony of the white ruling class but that are not in themselves sufficient to maintain legitimacy. The Black elected official is essentially a vicar for a higher authority, a necessary buffer between the Black majority and the capitalist state, a kind of modern voo-doo priest, smelling of incense, pomp and pedigree, who promises much but delivers nothing. Frantz Kafka wrote of such people in this manner:

> They were offered the choice between becoming kings or the couriers of kings. The way children would, they all wanted to be couriers. Therefore there are only couriers who hurry about the world, shouting to each other—since there are no kings—messages that have become meaningless. They would like to put an end to this miserable life of theirs but they dare not because of their oaths of service.[1]

The instant that the Black politician accepts the legitimacy of the State, the rules of the game, his/her critical faculties are destroyed permanently, and all that follows are absurdities. Black petty bourgeois politics is by definition and practice an attempt to channel goods, services and jobs to Black voters. In this endeavor, not a single white corporate executive or power broker would raise a veto. The Black Brahmin, the representative of the Black elite in politics, is praised for his/her responsible activities, or is perhaps criticized for being "too liberal"; but all discourse takes place within the parameters of the system as it exists. After a period of years, the Black elected official actually believes that the meager level of services he/she provides for a constituency actually produces fundamental change for the Black masses. Perhaps bourgeois democracy is colorblind, after all. . . . The Black majority, viewing the sordid process from the bottom up, retains few illusions about its inherent equality. But real political power is not yet in its hands. So the macabre dance of the absurd continues. And the agony of the masses is increased.

The hopelessly symbolic power of Black elected officials and politicians was never more apparent than in the wake of the election of Ronald Reagan to the Presidency in 1980. Most Black leaders immediately attacked Reagan's budget cuts and gross expenditures in military hardware as socially unproductive. But on fiscal policies, no real Black political consensus emerged as to the reasons for the emergence of Reaganomics at this time which could lead towards a general critique of modern American capitalism. Indeed, most Black politicians' criticisms of Reaganomics were at best highly confused, lacking any basic comprehension of the capitalist prerogatives behind the public policies of the Reagan Administration. Testifying before Congress, Chicago Urban League director James Compton suggested that he "could support" Reagan's agenda if it created "more employ-ment opportunities for minorities."[2] The board of directors of the NAACP proposed the adoption of an alternative Federal budget which increased defense expenditures and resulted in a $55 billion deficit, but also raised the income tax exemption for a family of four to $10,000 annually. The general direction of the proposal was a fairly conserva-tive form of Keynesianism, not unlike the austere 1981 budget of Carter.[3] Some Black commentators suggested that Blacks themselves were somehow to blame for the economic mess. "With the Reagan budget cuts in full swing some middle class Blacks are beginning to feel the razor's edge inching closer and closer to their necks," columnist Joyce Daniels Phillips wrote in the *Jackson Advocate*. The solution was developing a new set of austere socioeconomic values: "cutting back on material possessions, monthly mortgage payments, exorbitant car notes, and numerous charge accounts."[4] A few Black politicians, such as Representative Harold Washington, attacked Reagan's budget cuts and tax policy as "nothing more than a transfer of wealth back to the rich from the poor," but professed no radical alternative program.[5] Some Black politicians denounced Reaganomics by declaring that the President was racist—without a concomitant explanation suggesting why neither Nixon nor Carter, who were equally racist, had not advanced these specific fiscal policies. Still others asserted that

Reaganomics was merely economic "evil," and that "Reagan is the antichrist."[6]

Many Black politicians had consoled themselves in the wake of the "Reagan mandate" with the thought that Blacks must inevitably pull together to confront the common enemy. However, it was Reagan's Black friends that seemed to pull together first.

During the 1980 Presidential campaign, Reagan's Black apologists were few and far between. But in December, 1980, barely a month after Reagan's election, 125 Black academicians and business leaders caucused in San Francisco at a conference held by the Institute for Contemporary Studies to discuss the directions for Black conservatism. Organized by black economist Thomas Sowell, the conference featured Reagan advisors Edwin Meese and Milton Friedman as honored guests. This meeting marked a significant turning point for national Black politics, for it dramatized and made public the severe contradictions on major political, economic and educational issues which divided the members of the Black elite. By the autumn of 1981, differences within the elite had become so intense that any possibility of building a consensus position on major public policy issues was lost. Dissention within the ranks was the order of the day, as Black actors opportunistically seized the subordinated roles which were given to them. A new political current was born—Black Reaganism.[7]

II

Easily the most striking thing about Black politics during the Reagan Administration was the sudden ascendancy of Sowell, Hoover Institution professor and eminent Black conservative. It occurred at a moment in history when the veterans of the Civil Rights Movement had become disillusioned and defensive in their language and public policy activities; a period when U.S. corporate hegemony was declining, and both white business and political leaders were calling for a conservative, supply side agenda. At the same time Black activists and militant nationalists seemed out of step with the masses of Black people. In the midst of this confusion Sowell stepped forward along with other Black conservatives, not to condemn the Reagan Administration, but to praise it. In a series of media events and public forums the new Black spokespersons railed against affirmative action, spending for social programs, the minimum wage law, and a host of New

Deal and Great Society programs long cherished as necessities by millions of poor and working class Black people. Sowell's calculated program of submission and silence, his bombastic attacks on the NAACP, and his conciliatory demeanor toward the interests of capital won high marks from the most bitter and vitriolic opponents of the civil rights cause. We were told that the Black American professional and business elite would soon embrace the conservatives' programs in full, and that this shift toward Black Reaganism was inevitable and even a healthy step toward Black political power.

Black conservatives do not represent a monolithic political/social force, but rather have evolved from radically different sectors of Black society. In brief, there are at least four overlapping categories of Black Reaganites: conservative Black politicians; Black philosophical conservatives; Black corporate executives, business managers and Reagan administrative appointees; and former Black Power activists and nationalists who have not fully embraced Reaganism but nevertheless have become so closely aligned with this rightist trend that they merit the obloquy "fellow travellers." Some of the most prominent Black Republicans of the past two decades have been the late W.O. Walker, publisher of the Cleveland *Call and Post* and head of the national "Blacks for Reagan-Bush" organization in 1980; James Cummings, leader of the National Black Republican Council; Art Fletcher, former executive director of the United Negro College Fund and Labor Department officer under Nixon; Samuel Pierce, Reagan's Secretary of Housing and Urban Development; and William T. Coleman, Ford's Secretary of Transportation. These Blacks were subordinates within the Rockefeller wing of the Republican Party during the 1960s and early 1970s. During the Nixon Administration they consistently supported affirmative action programs, civil rights legislation and Federal assistance to Black-owned businesses. Coleman had been part of the legal team which successfully challenged school segregation laws in the 1954 *Brown* decision. Like other liberal Republicans, notably former New York Senator Jacob Javits and Illinois Senator Charles Percy, they strived to reconcile their belief in limited Federal government and unfettered capitalism with the desegregation of white civil society and equal opportunity legislation to promote the development of a Black petty capitalist class.[8]

The philosophical conservatives properly belong to the rabid right wing of the Republican party, advocating Milton Friedman's version of laissez faire capitalism, state's rights, and a dogged hatred for left-of-center politics. This militantly rightist faction includes Walter Williams, professor of economics at George Mason University; J.A.Y. Parker, a former official of the anticommunist Young Americans For Freedom and currently president of Lincoln Institute and Educational Foundation; and Wendell Wilkie Gunn, assistant treasurer of Pepsi Corporation. The titular leader of this tendency is Sowell, Ronald Reagan's favorite "House Nigger." After serving in the Marines, Sowell attended Howard University. Considering himself a Marxist, Sowell eventually received graduate degrees at the University of Chicago and Columbia. As he moved up the academic ladder his ideological views grew increasingly conservative. By the late 1960s he had become a Goldwater Republican and a bitter opponent of the welfare state. He condemned the emergence of Black Studies and Black campus activism. By the election of Carter, Sowell had come to repudiate most of the ideals of the Civil Rights Movement. He condemned affirmative action legislation as detrimental to Blacks' interests. His prescription to the plight of poor education within the ghetto was the imposition of "strict discipline" and mandatory expulsion of "rowdies who disrupt education for the majority." Sowell attacked the NAACP/civil rights leadership as a "light-skinned elite" whose policies served to provide "access to whites" for themselves but not for the Black poor. In a major advertisement paid for by Smith Kline Corporation in 1981, Sowell praised capitalism as the vehicle for Blacks to gain acceptance and upward mobility. "The rich are a red herring used by politicians to distract our attention," he declared. "There aren't enough rich people to make any real economic difference, whether they pay high taxes or low taxes. The great majority of the government's money comes from the great majority of the people." Like Reagan, Sowell believes that inflation, not unemployment, is the real problem within America's political economy. "Balancing the budget is not enough," Sowell warns. "Whether we yearn for government giveaways as the answer to our problems, we have to realize that every giveaway is also a takeaway. Anything the country can't afford without the giveaway, it can't afford with it."[9]

Potentially the most influential faction among Black Reaganites are the coterie of Administration officials and middle level executives from major corporations. In the executive branch of government, the list includes Thelma Duggin, formerly the Republican Committee liaison to the National Black Voters Program in the 1980 election and currently serving as deputy to Presidential advisor Elizabeth Dole; Melvin Bradley, Senior Policy Advisor to Reagan, responsible for developing "public policy recommendations in the areas of food and agriculture, minority business development, urban affairs, free enterprise zones, small business administration, and Black colleges and universities"; and Thaddeus Garret, Vice Presidential assistant in charge of domestic policy and programs. Major Black corporate supporters of Reagan's policies include Gloria E.A. Toote, a New York attorney and millionaire real estate developer; William Pickard, owner of a lucrative McDonald's franchise in Detroit; Arthur McZier, president, National Business Services Enterprises, Inc.; Constance Newman, president, Newman and Associates; Abraham Venable, Vice Chairperson of the Business Policy Review Council and director of General Motor's Urban Affairs Division; Fred Blac, Business Policy Review Council Chairperson and corporate executive in General Electric; Cyrus Johnson of General Foods; Philip J. Davis of Norton Simon, Inc.; and John Millier of the United States Brewer's Association. These Black corporate executives and bureaucrats had no ideological commitment to civil rights, affirmative action, or to the defense of any traditional institutions within the Black community. They favor Reaganomics because it will generate greater profits for their client industries and monopolies. These corporate Black Reaganites are even more dangerous than Sowell, because their blatant and vigorous support for consevative public policies is rooted not in any ideological commitment, but is grounded purely in their own vicious desire for money and their hunger for power.[10]

The "fellow travellers" of the Black Reaganites include a number of would-be Black militants who are disenchanted with liberalism and protest politics. At the top of the list are Charles V. Hamilton, professor of government at Columbia, and Black media commentator Tony Brown. Both Hamilton and Brown attended the San Francisco Conference of Black conservatives. The co-author of *Black Power*, Hamilton has experienced a radical metamorphosis since his days as mentor to Stokely Carmichael (Kwame Ture). Since Blacks are a "relatively powerless minority," he informed the *New York Times*, the rise of a new Black conservative trend was essential. "Frankly," Hamilton admitted, "I'd be very worried if we didn't have them." Brown criticized the NAACP's "hostile behavior towards President

Reagan" when he appeared as a guest at their annual convention in Denver in 1981. Brown thought that Reagan really wants "to economically emancipate Black ghettos," and that the President's brutal budget cuts were tantamount to a request for Afro-Americans to "return to the fundamental nationalism of their past. Ironically," Brown explained, "Reagan's philosophy of a sound economic power base for Black America is more compatible with past Black leaders such as Marcus Garvey, Booker T. Washington, Elijah Muhammad and Frederick Douglass, than are the modern-day disciples of the Black establishment." This massive distortion of Black history by Brown scarcely masked his overt appeasement toward the forces of racism and political reaction.[11] What all four tendencies hold in common is a firm belief that racism, in words of Reagan apologist Nathan Wright, Jr., no longer has "a damn thing" to do with Black underdevelopment; that socialist, Marxist, Keynesian and/or liberal economic programs will not work; and that Black advancement is best served by initiatives of U.S. monopoly capitalism.

The emergence of a Black neoconservative tendency had not accompanied the reelection of Richard Nixon eight years before, despite the fact that Nixon had carefully cultivated a token program for Black Capitalism, and had even appointed a liberal Black Republican, James Farmer, to his cabinet in 1969. The sudden rise to prominence of the Black Reaganites can be explained, in part, by a decline in the internal organization and prominence of the Congressional Black Caucus during the interval between Watergate and the 1980 elections. In 1969, Charles Diggs, a progressive Democrat from Detroit, had initiated the process which culminated in the creation of the Caucus two years later. In the early 1970s, many Caucus members were either active or directly supportive of the Black nationalist political renaissance. Diggs served as a leader in the staging of the National Black Political Convention at Gary, Indiana, in 1972, was the influential vice chairperson of the House Committee on Africa, and chaired the House Committee on the District of Columbia. Walter Fauntroy of Washington, D.C., and Ron Dellums of Berkeley-Oakland, California, were also active at Gary; indeed, Dellums' close relationship between militant Black nationalists and the key organizers of the National Black Political Assembly, continued throughout the 1970s. The left wing of the Caucus, Dellums and Michigan Congressperson John Conyers, were open advocates of democratic socialism, and had little reservations in challenging the white leaders of their own party from the left on both foreign and domestic public policies.

Although the Caucus continued to exist (as of this writing), by the late 1970s it began to fracture internally due to ideological differences, egotistic power plays, and from external criticism from many moderate-to-conservative Black elite leaders. Critics pointed out that the Caucus was woefully inept in securing legislation favorable to minority interests. In the Ninety-fourth Congress, for example, of the 729 bills which became law, the Caucus members had sponsored only 16. Caucus efforts to identify itself as the "collective voice of the national black community" met opposition from nonelectoral Negro politicians and civil rights leaders, who jealously protected their political turf. Membership in the group was an unstable fact of life. During the Ninety-fifth Congress alone, two members resigned, one died, and another was defeated. Diggs was "forced from office by a prolonged scandal and finally a conviction for misappropriation of federal funds." The Caucus' most important achievement in their 13 year existence, the Humphrey-Hawkins Bill, was so "watered down" to meet the preferences of labor, liberals and moderates that it represented at best a defeat for the concept of universal employment. By 1980, seven Black Congresspersons had lost over 20 percent of their respective districts' populations during the decade, and were threatened with the very real prospect of losing their seats through redistricting. Shirley Chisholm's decision not to run for reelection in 1982 was dictated partially by the sobering loss of 32.1 percent of her Brooklyn constituency. By Reagan's election, a few Caucus members had climbed aboard the neoconservative bandwagon by supporting the latest corporate give-away project, the "free enterprise zones." With the outstanding exceptions of Dellums, Conyers, and Caucus newcomers such as George Crockett of Michigan, Gus Savage and Harold Washington of Chicago, the Caucus as a whole did not represent a coherent left bloc which could have pushed the Black Reaganites from media attention and public discourse. [12]

The Old Guard civil rights leadership, likewise having been challenged effectively from the right, was also forced to move to the left in the early 1980s. Jesse Jackson, Southern Christian Leadership Conference president Joseph E. Lowery and Coretta Scott King participated in demonstrations involving 9,000 people in Mobile,

Alabama on April 26, 1981, and 3,000 people in Montgomery, Alabama on August 9, 1981, to protest Congressional moves to repeal the Voting Rights Act of 1965.[13] Georgia State Senator Julian Bond and the Institute for Southern Studies led a thorough investigation of the murders of the Communist Workers Party members in Greensboro, North Carolina in 1979, charging the police with "gross negligence."[14] Benjamin Hooks, executive director of the NAACP, Vernon Jordan, Urban League head, and Coretta Scott King were speakers at the massive Solidarity march in Washington, D.C. on September 19, 1981, attracting hundreds of thousands of trade unionists and political opponents of Reaganism.[15] One of the most publicized efforts of the Old Guard was the boycott of Coca-Cola products. Jesse Jackson's PUSH organization published information on the nonexistent affirmative action record of Coca-Cola, pointing out that not a single one of Coke's 550 bottlers or its 4,000 fountain wholesalers was Black. The corporate giant had on deposit only $254,000 in ten Black banks. When Coke executives balked during negotiations, PUSH and others initiated a Black nationwide boycott of the soft drink on July 11, 1981. Coca-Cola was removed from the shelves of four Black-owned Seven Eleven franchises in Washington, D.C., and white-owned franchises in that city did the same. Gary mayor Richard Hatcher, chairperson of the Black mayors conference, authorized a move to ban Coke machines from 194 Black controlled city halls. When more than one hundred stores in Chicago's metropolitan area joined the boycott, Coke president Donald R. Keough announced his readiness to give Black entrepreneurs "a piece of the action." The agreement represented a "promise that the free enterprise system can do more to develop opportunity for all elements of society."[16]

Coke's "moral covenant" with PUSH included the following provisions: increase the number of Black-owned distributors to 32 within 12 months, establishment of a venture capital fund of $1.8 million for Black petty capitalists, the elevation of a Black to Coca-Cola's Board of Directors, double the amount of advertising capital spent with Black agencies, quadruple the amount of financial deposits within Black banks, and the hiring of 100 Black blue collar employees. The total package amounted to $34 million. Black newspapers widely publicized the boycott, calling it a "wonderful reunion fellowship" of Martin Luther King, Jr.'s old colleagues, including Mrs. King, Lowery, Hosea Williams, Andrew Young, Maynard Jackson and Jesse

Jackson. Black columnist William Raspberry, never at a loss for words, proclaimed the historical deal "as important to Black America as the boycott of the Montgomery, Alabama, bus company a quarter of the century ago."[17] The reality behind the rhetoric is somewhat different. Coke's white investors were furious with what was described as "outright blackmail" and "a $30 million giveaway plan." On September 3, Coca-Cola President Keough informed the *Atlanta Constitution* that the corporation had neither bowed to "pressure" from Black leaders, nor had given the boycott more than "two minutes attention because we never considered it a real issue." By October, 1981, Coke officials informed the media that any money lent to Blacks for venture capital would be at high market rates. No forced changes in bottling franchise ownerships would occur. Black advertising was increased to only $2 million from the previous $1.2 million figure. No loans would be made to Black-owned banks except at competitive rates. Even the one hundred additional jobs would not materialize, because Coke "might be replacing Blacks with Blacks," declared a company executive. The conspicuous failure of the Coca-Cola boycott symbolized more than ever before the utter bankruptcy of "Black Capitalism."[18]

The lack of any basic grassroots orientation or support of the Old Guard was illustrated at the 11th annual Congressional Black Caucus weekend in Washington, D.C., on September 25-27, 1981. The self-described "Black leadership family" included over 1,000 Black doctors, lawyers, politicians and bureaucrats. One participant suggested that the Black struggle in the 1980s would be led by "cadres of Black professionals." Joe Madison, an NAACP official, stated that the militancy of the old days "during the Montgomery bus boycott" were passé. "We've got to develop technical militants out of these middle class affluent Blacks who have received training, acquired good educations and have worked themselves into the mainstream of economic life."[19] Neither the multitude of fashion shows nor the $150-a-plate awards banquet could provide the cultural cohesion necessary to forge new unity among this "Untalented Tenth." Frequently they quarreled among themselves on a variety of public issues. Representative Gus Savage correctly denounced Vernon Jordan, publisher John H. Johnson, NAACP president Margaret Bush Wilson and Rev. Leon Sullivan for sitting on corporate boards and sharing in the "ill-begotten super profits" from doing business in "fascist South Africa."[20] At state levels, Black Democrats joined forces with white Republicans in reapportionment cases to increase the percentages of Blacks and/or whites within their respective Congressional districts. The most vocal advocate of the growing legislative detente between these unlikely forces is Julian Bond, a democratic socialist and the most "progressive" Black elected official in the South. The *Atlanta Constitution* charged that "the cynical coalition" of "ghetto Black politicians and country club Republicans" sought "to gut Atlanta for the sake of electing (Bond) to the Congress," while simultaneously extending GOP hegemony across the state.[21]

Although the Black Reaganites and the civil rights leaders were at odds over public policy, both factions had greater similarities than either would acknowledge publicly. Both tendencies were firmly entrenched within the Black middle class, and received the greatest percentage of their financial support from dissenting sectors of the white establishment. Both tendencies were committed to political activity within the capitalist state and economic order as it exists. Both were clients of more powerful political interests which found it necessary to develop Black constituencies for their own public agendas. Black Democrats relied on the rhetoric of resistance, but in practical terms, tended heavily to favor tactical compromises and accommodation with powerful whites. Black Reaganites parroted the slogans of Milton Friedman and the Reagan Administration to facilitate their own socioeconomic mobility, at the expense of the Black masses. Neither tendency actually embodied in practice an effective social program which called for the structural or radical transformation of the inherently racist/capitalist state. The Black Brahmins waged war against each other, but not against the system that allowed them to exist.

III

Theoretically and programmatically, the sudden prominence of the Black Reaganites raises anew the historical question of accommodation and conservatism within Black America. In the 1960s, many Black and white social scientists and activist-oriented scholars tended to identify the cultural and social tradition of Black nationalism with political independence, public protests and militancy, while integration was portrayed as inherently a conservative and gradualist strategy to separate the Black elite from the Black working masses. Much of the political literature since Black Power has described the entire evolution of Black U.S. history as a clearcut division between Black nationalists and integrationists. According to this view, Black nationalists were rooted within the bowels of oppression, the leaders of Black workers and the poor, whereas integration was the aesthetic and cultural outlook of upper class Negroes. Black nationalist movements appealed to large audiences, with the primary cornerstone being Marcus Garvey's Universal Negro Improvement Association, and integrationist organizations were elitist and small (e.g., W.E.B. DuBois' and W. Monroe Trotter's Niagara Movement or the National Urban League). Post-Black Power scholars describe integration itself as innately reformist, since its programmatic goal, the obliteration of barriers in political and social life that segregate Blacks from white Americans, is not a revolutionary demand. The nationalists identify their heroes as the real children of Martin Delany, Garvey and Malcolm X, while the integrationists remain adrift from the masses, hopelessly struggling for white recognition. [22]

This dichotomy creates more problems than it resolves. First, it does not explain the career and legacy of the influential educator/politician, Booker T. Washington. Garvey constructed his economic and social program on the philosophy of Tuskegee, as we know. But what does this tell us about Washington, when we recognize the Garveyism was the highest expression of militant Black nationalism in the first half of the twentieth century? A closer reading of the subject also calls into question the Black nationalists' rejection of Frederick Douglass and Martin Luther King, Jr. Both men were committed to social equality and a closer sociocultural relationship between the races, but neither can be termed accommodationist in their political practice or "conservative" when contrasted with their contemporaries. More problems surface when the checkered and ambiguous careers of Congress of Racial Equality leaders Floyd McKissick and Roy Innis are reviewed. In 1966, McKissick demonstrated against the Vietnam War, and stood second only to Stokely Carmichael as the most articulate proponent of militant Black separatism. By 1972 he had endorsed the reelection of the politically and racially conservative Richard M. Nixon. Innis still advances a strong race-first philosophy, but combines his activist rhetoric with a close and cordial relationship with white capitalists and conservative corporate managers. When one surveys the single organization that is closest to the masses of Black people, the Black Church, one finds that the majority of Black religious leaders from the mid-nineteenth to late-twentieth centuries have been pragmatic or accommodationist in their politics, integrationists, and at times, profoundly conservative. Few ministers would hold much credence in the exhortations of Thomas Sowell or Ronald Reagan, but not many would consider themselves the descendents of Nat Turner or Malcolm X.

The singular service that the Black Reaganites provide is a new and more accurate understanding of what exactly constitutes conservatism within the Black experience. Generally speaking, conservatives from the Civil War to the present have agreed on a philosophy which can be outlined accordingly: first, a theoretical and programmatic commitment to capitalism as an economic system in which Blacks can take part as full and equal partners. Black conservatives are traditionally hostile to Black participation in trade unions, and urge a close cooperation with white business leaders. Hostile to the welfare state, they call for increased "self-help" programs run by Blacks at local and community levels. Conservatives often accept the institutionalized forms of patriarchy, acknowledging a secondary role for Black women within economics, political life and intellectual work. They usually advocate a specific social hierarchy within the Black community, and have a pronounced bias towards organizational authoritarianism and theoretical rigidity. Black conservatism as a definite ideological force can be found within both Black nationalism and integrationism. Conversely, a militant or political activist can be integrationist, particularly during periods when the consensus of white American society swings toward strict Jim Crow or racial segregation public policies. The internal logic of a Black nationalist who also is a rigid conservative, for example, is embodied in *apartheid*. But conservatism, in itself, should not be directly corrolated with accommodation as a political style. The entire terrain of Black politics since the Civil War can be characterized by a broad and uneven distribution of nationalists and integrationists at every end of the spectrum on questions of class, economic organization and state power. (See Table XXVI)

What few historians appreciate is that the contemporary foundations of Black conservatism and accommodation are not the responsibility of Booker T. Washington alone. The Tuskegee "wizard" (as his underlings called him) was neither a political theoretician nor an original thinker. Accommodation was a definite political response to the Compromise of 1877 and the extreme racist violence that accelerated across the South in the 1880s and early 1890s. J. C. Price, the president of Livingstone College of North Carolina and an influential Black postbellum leader, advanced a program in the 1880s that proposed the "sacrifice of nonessentials," such as Black political independence. Price's "mildly conciliatory policy toward the South" was also championed by C. H. J. Taylor. A newspaper editor in Kansas City and Atlanta, lawyer and minister resident in Liberia during Grover Cleveland's first administration, Taylor condemned Black advances achieved by radicals during Reconstruction. In his 1889 accommodationist polemic, *Whites and Blacks*, he urged Blacks to "(cease) exhibiting prejudice towards whites" and to accept "the olive branch of peace" offered them by political conservatives. The root of Black oppression, he declared, was the singular disaster of Afro-American politics during the 1865-1877 period. Blacks "voted in the white political scum they thought to be their dearest friends, but who . . . proved to be their greatest enemies." Like many conservative cultural nationalists a century later, Taylor chastized Blacks for hating the race, and urged an end to bleached skin and straightened hair. "We have no reason to complain until we take more pride in our own," he stated.[23]

Black property owners, affluent small entrepreneurs and politicians helped to establish the conservative political terrain which made the subsequent rise of Booker T. Washington possible. These men adopted the aggressive, expansionist capitalist philosophy of Henry Grady by the mid-1880s. Black Mississippi planter Blanche K. Bruce resisted the "Republicans-only" politics of Frederick Douglass in 1876 by advocating the deliberate division of the Black vote in order to acquire leverage in both parties. By 1880 Bruce encouraged Blacks to deemphasize political work entirely, declaring in a series of public speeches "that the race needs now more than anything else . . . material and educational growth." In 1892, a meeting of Black educators and politicians at the Bethel Literary and Historical Association in Washington, D.C., advocated the immediate development of Black-owned banks, insurance companies and service-related businesses as a means to promote racial uplift. All too frequently, this pro-business philosophy combined with a revisionist interpretation of slavery itself, leading its promulgators into a firm political coalition with white supremacy. A typical example of this is provided by a wealthy Black Mississippi landlord, Gilbert Myers. Testifying before a Senate committee only two years after the Compromise of 1877, he defended his decision to support the conservative Democratic party: "The South has always been kind to me. My master that I lived with I nursed him and slept at his mother's feet and nursed at her breast, so I thought my interest was to stay with the majority of the country who I expected to prosper with."[24]

This is not to imply that the accommodationist philosophy was hegemonic before the demise of Populism and the Depression of the 1890s. The majority of Black Republicans and Democrats resisted whites' attempts to undermine the gains of Reconstruction throughout the period. Perhaps the leading Black militant of this era was T. Thomas Fortune. As editor of the *New York Age*, Fortune urged Blacks toward an independent political posture with the slogan "Race First: then party." Fortune condemned Isaiah Montgomery, founder of the all-Black city of Mount Bayou, Mississippi, for tacitly accepting the loss of the Black franchise in his state. He supported the creation of trade unions, and declared that "millionaires (were) the most dangerous enemies of society." As the founder of the Afro-American League in 1890, he revived the protest traditions of Martin R. Delany, declaring that "it is time to face the enemy and fight inch by inch for every right he denies us. Let us stand up like men in our own organization where color will not be a brand of odium." With the emergence of radical farmers and workers' movements, Fortune stood uncompromisingly on the side of liberation. "The revolution is upon us," he told his readers, "and since we are largely of the laboring population, it is very natural that we should take sides with the labor forces in the fight for a juster distribution of the results of labor." By the mid-1890s, Fortune's revolutionary ardor had cooled considerably. He began to accept financial contributions from the Tuskegee politician, and soon his militant voice was muted. With Fortune's active cooperation, Washington successfully plotted his election as president of the Afro-American Council and ratified an accommodationist program at the organization's meeting in St. Paul, Minnesota, in 1902. Black accommodationist Fred R. Moore was placed by Washington on the *Age's* editorial staff in 1904. Three years later, Moore became editor; Fortune's career as a progessive spokesperson in the cause of Black civil rights was effectively ended.[25]

Many historians have explored the striking prominence of Booker T. Washington, who it can be said was the most effective and influential politician that Black America has yet produced. In the light of Washington's eventual failure to achieve an "historic compromise" between the divergent interests of Southern conservatives, Northern capital, and the nascent Black middle class, he is sometimes accused of being simply the creature of white racism and oppression. His infamous Atlanta Compromise of 1895, close relationship with white millionaires like Collis P. Huntington and Andrew Carnegie, and his deprecating and even sycophantic remarks on the race question before white audiences seem to seal his fate before neo-abolitionist critics. Before we bury Booker T. as merely the compliant tool of racist reactionaries, let us make a few comments beside his grave. First, as illustrated above, Washington was the most successful practitioner of accommodation, yet the foundations of his success were forged in the years of defeatism and doubt after 1877. Without the C. J. Taylors and J. C. Prices, Washington's labor would have amounted to a futile and self-destructive errand in the political wilderness. Second, Washington's political genius was less "conservative" than tactically "accommodationist." He secretly funneled capitalists' donations for Tuskegee to a variety of civil rights causes. He paid his dues to white leaders by hiring a staff of talented ghost writers including Max Thrasher and Robert E. Park to articulate the cautious, conservative public policies of the age. For his public concessions, he achieved extraordinary influence in Federal appointments for Black members of his Tuskegee Machine. Finally, it must be emphasized the Washington was a popular figure within a significant segment of the Black community, an educator who inspired the development of schools based on the model of Tuskegee Institute in India, Panama, South Africa, Kenya, the Gold Coast and across the Black Belt South. Supporters of Washington's political organization included James Weldon Johnson, who later became Secretary of the NAACP; Benjamin J. Davis, Sr., the founder of the Atlanta *Independent;* W. H. Steward, a leading Black Baptist; and J. W. E. Bowen, president of Gammon Theological Seminary from 1906 to 1912 and senior editor of the influential *Voice of the Negro.*

The distinction between accommodation and cooptation must be emphasized here. In the light of history, we must judge the Tuskegee philosophy of tactical compromises and secret agitation against segregation a failure.[26] Its achievements in the context of that bloody era—the creation of Tuskegee Institute, the appointment of Black officials in the Roosevelt and Taft administrations, the establishment of the

National Negro Business League—should not be dismissed lightly, but in the end, do not and cannot make sufficient restitution for the forces of racist violence it also unwittingly unleashed. Washington's power was both real and an illusion; its inherent weakness was rooted not in his own body of politics, but within the racist practices of U.S. capitalism. Washington failed; but that does not make him an Uncle Tom. Had Washington's program been as servile as its critics claimed, it could not have inspired the development of Marcus Garvey's Universal Negro Improvement Association, or John Langalibalele Dube's African National Congress. Washington was a product of late nineteenth century Black cultural life, indeed as organic as the evolution of the blues at that identical historical moment.[27]

Black American history's central axis is the tension between accommodation and struggle. Most prominent Black political spokespersons have embodied both contradictory positions within their respective programs. But a few "leaders" from the very beginning, went beyond accommodation and tactical concessions with racism, into what could properly be defined as true Black conservatism: a defense of the racist status quo as it exists. The Black conservative does not desire power; he/she has no independent program worthy of the name. The interests that the Black conservative defends have little or nothing to do with the realities of Black material and social life. No public position is too extreme, no statement is too ingratiating, no act too outrageous for the Black conservative, if in some minute way it serves the interests of whites in power. Accommodation as a political tactic is genuinely foolish, because tactical concessions and quiescent rhetoric seldom achieve long term gains. "Those in power never give way," C.L.R. James wrote in *Black Jacobins*, "and admit defeat only to plot and scheme to regain their lost power and privilege." The conquest of effective power may begin within the confines of parliamentary debate and moral suasion, but inevitably must end in the streets. "The struggle of classes ends either in the reconstruction of society or in the common ruin of the contending classes."[28] Accommodation begins with the germ of doubt, a defeatist attitude which has afflicted the Black working class as well as the Black middle class. Conservatism is more clearly the attitude of sectors of the Black petty bourgeoisie, those who actively cooperate with the dominant white elites to oppress Blacks. Accommodation is "puttin' on ole massa"; conservatism for Blacks is actively doing "ole massa's" work. The former is an opportunist; the latter is a traitor.

During the "Age of Washington," the leading Black conservative was undoubtedly William Hooper Councill. After slavery, Councill became a leading Black Democrat in northern Alabama. He served as secretary for the National Equal Rights Convention in 1873, and three years later became president of the Black segregated state school at Huntsville. In 1887, he was excluded from a first-class railway car, and he appealed the case to the Interstate Commerce Commission. Alabama whites swiftly replaced Councill at the school, and he was prepared to retract his appeal. Reinstated as president, Councill began speaking out against integrated public facilities, railroads and accommodations. At the highpoint of lynchings, he praised the "love and attachment between the races at the South." He urged Blacks to accept positions as household workers, and he declared that employment discrimination toward Blacks was only "friendly advice" to start their own segregated establishments. Councill was as bankrupt morally as he was in politics: in May, 1885, he was charged with the rape of a twelve year old Black girl and the shooting of her uncle. Louis R. Harlan writes of Councill:

> At the end of Reconstruction, Councill sold his Black soul for white Conservative favor. In return for his office he agreed not merely to stay out of politics but to speak out for the Democrats. This faustian bargain gave him great power, for he fulfilled the Alabama white man's conception of a Negro leader more completely than Washington. He could condemn the Yankee radical and proclaim the Southern white man to be the Negro's best friend without the restraints that inhibited Washington. He could out-Booker Booker, and he frequently did.

Washington could hardly tolerate the man. In 1899 he even informed a colleague that he could not bear to sit at the same public forum with Councill, because he "has the reputation of simply toadying to the Southern white people."[29]

At the level of popular politics, Black electoral behavior is often characterized as monolithic behavior, with Afro-Americans casting their ballots for the Republicans between 1865 and the 1930s, and for the Democrats afterwards. In reality, the voting patterns of Blacks were uniform nowhere. The conservatives within the Black community tended to align themselves with whichever major party was ideologically and programmatically further to the right at a given time. Accommodationists, on the other hand, sought coalitions with the political party which controlled their own primary constituency's area. In the 1900s Washington quickly developed a strong national alliance with the Roosevelt administration, because the Republicans had become the majority party in the country by 1896. Locally, however, he supported Alabama conservative Democrats over Populists and the more radical agrarians from the poor white and Black classes. In the 1890s Black Republican leaders of Cincinnati threw their support to a local white Democratic boss, in order to gain petty patronage and economic development within that city. Black Republicans in Kansas City, Missouri consistently voted for the Democratic machine of Jim Pendergast, who repaid their allegiance by offering them local benefits to the city's services. For almost four decades, the Crum Democratic machine of Memphis controlled the Black vote in that city. A series of Black Republicans, the most prominent being Robert R. Church, consistently followed an accommodationist strategy by casting their weight behind local white segregationists. At the national level, a core of Black independents and former Republicans created the Negro National Democratic League in 1900, and actively attempted to increase among Blacks a new electoral loyalty for white Democrats. Even DuBois, in a rare moment of political confusion, endorsed the presidential candidacy of the Democratic governor of New Jersey, Woodrow Wilson. DuBois' support was repaid when Wilson ordered the most extreme racial segregation policies that had ever existed in the Federal government. The bitter fruits of Black accommodation to the Democratic Party during these years are illustrated by the single fact that not one Black delegate ever appeared at a national Democratic convention until 1936. It was not until 1948 that the Democratic party even took a lukewarm, public stand in favor of civil rights for Blacks.[30]

The New Deal brought a general realignment to Black politics. Local Black Republican bosses, like Atlanta's A. T. Walden, shifted their organizations behind the Democratic Party. The percentage of Black votes for the Democrats increased dramatically in a remarkably short period of time. In Chicago, Democrats obtained 7 percent of the Black vote in the mayoral election of 1927, 16 percent in 1931 and 82 percent in 1935. As early as 1932, 45 percent of Black voters in Baltimore were Democrats, 53.3 percent in Pittsburgh, and 79.8 percent in Kansas City. By 1936 the Black vote for Franklin Roosevelt exceeded 50 percent in most cities, and climbed to 75 percent in a few urban areas by 1940. As the Black working class shifted to the Democratic Party, Black accommodationists quickly followed suit. Chicago Black politician William L. Dawson had served as a city alderman from 1935 to 1939 as a Republican. Recognizing that political realities had changed, Dawson became a Democratic Ward Committeeman, and an ally of Chicago boss Edward Kelly. In 1942 he ran successfully for Congress, replacing another South Side Black Democrat, Arthur W. Mitchell. As Chuck Stone observes, "Dawson, a loyal 'organization man,' learned quickly that the organization was the wellspring from which all progress, jobs and favors flowed. Dawson exercised his power carefully, prudently and patiently. He quietly built a Black political machine that was as efficient and vicious as the city-wide Democratic machine." Like Booker T. Washington, Dawson's power was repeatedly compromised by the realities of racism and by the conformist demands that were placed upon him by whites. Dawson refused to support civil rights legislation, and was silent about the Emmett Till lynching. "As the Civil Rights Movement gathered," Stone writes, "Dawson retreated further into silence. He continued to do just three things: win re-election, control Black patronage in Chicago and keep his mouth shut." Through Dawson, the Tuskegee strategy was reborn within the Democratic Party.[31]

For white Democrats after 1940, the Negro vote was not desired out of any abstract or altruistic commitment to social justice: it was born of the realization that Blacks now constituted what Henry Lee Moon termed "the balance of power." The implications of this were apparent as early as 1944, during the Roosevelt-Dewey election. Herbert Brownell, Jr., Republican National Committee Chairman, stated that a "shift of 303,414 votes in fifteen states outside of the South would have enabled (Dewey) to capture 175 additional electoral votes and to win the presidency with an eight electoral vote margin." In over half of the states mentioned by Brownell, Blacks comprised a significant and even decisive margin for Roosevelt's victory. In Michigan, Black voters cast 41,740 ballots for the Democratic nominee and Roosevelt carried that state by 22,500 votes; in Maryland "the 50,000 votes which Negro citizens in Baltimore alone cast for F.D.R. were more than double his 22,500 state plurality."[32] Any effective power in which Blacks as a group could exercise electorally depended, of course, on whether white voters were evenly divided on the issues or candidates. In 1960 and 1976, Black voters did decide the Presidential election. About 77 percent of all Black voters supported Massachusetts Senator John F. Kennedy over Republican Vice President Richard M. Nixon in 1960, and in seven states—Illinois, Mississippi, New Jersey, Michigan, Texas, South Carolina, and Pennsylvania—the Black vote was greater than the Democratic candidate's margin of victory. Jimmy Carter received about nine out of every ten votes cast by Blacks in 1976. Democratic leaders had literally no other choice except to court the Black vote, particularly after the mid-1960s, as the New Deal coalition of organized labor and the South began drifting toward the Republican party. But white bosses, from Kelly's successor in Chicago, Richard Daley, to Democratic Senate leader Lyndon Johnson, mistrusted Blacks who expressed even modest tendencies towards political independence and militancy. They preferred to cut deals with Black pragmatists and accommodationists, Blacks clearly dependent upon the white power structure, men or women who understood and acquiesced to the rules of the game.[33]

The tradition of accommodation had become so firmly grounded within Black politics that it affected even the most progressive Blacks elected to national office. Adam Clayton Powell's entire career stands as the greatest testimony to this unfortunate fact. Like Fortune, Powell began his political life as an uncompromising militant. In the depths of the Great Depression he led a series of successful boycotts of Harlem stores that refused to hire Blacks. Powell was frequently in the streets organizing Black workers, and set in motion a successful boycott of a bus company almost two decades before Martin Luther King, Jr. repeated the tactic in the Deep South. In 1941, Powell was elected to the New York City Council, and three years later won a Congressional seat from Harlem. Between 1945 and 1965, Powell was undoubtedly the most influential Black elected offcial in the country. Unlike Dawson, Powell won the praises of almost every major sector of the Black community. For older Black nationalists, Powell's streetwise rhetoric was reminiscent of earlier Harlem nationalists, from Hubert H. Harrison to Marcus Garvey. Integrationists from the Black middle class pointed out that Powell's leadership in the House Education and Labor Committee led to the adoption of sixty major bills which included increases in the minimum wage, school lunch program, Federal aid to public schools and the war on poverty. Black men with no discernable interest in electoral politics could identify with Powell's bombastic *joi de vie,* his succession of wives and mistresses. Even the most politically advanced spokesperson that Black nationalism produced in the 1960s, Malcolm X, considered Powell a true proponent of Black independence and activism. But throughout his public life, Powell made a series of questionable tactical concessions and compromises with the white power elite. In 1956 Powell endorsed the reelection of Dwight Eisenhower, although the former general had done virtually nothing in the area of civil rights. In return for the chairmanship of his Congressional committee, Powell endorsed the Presidential candidacy of Lyndon Johnson, a political protege of House Speaker Sam Rayburn. Powell's 1959 endorsement was a shock to most Blacks, since Johnson was a known southern segregationist. Despite his erratic and sexist personal conduct, Powell's eventual undoing may have had more to do with his inexplicably infantile attitude toward power. Had he possessed the seriousness of a Washington, who made accommodating overtures towards whites without ever forgetting once that covert action resided at the center of successful petty bourgeois politics, Powell would have never fallen in disgrace. Powell was no accommodationist certainly, but his claim to the credentials of militancy seems seriously inflated.[34]

Since the Eisenhower Administration of 1953-61, many Black accommodationists and virtually every Black conservative joined the Republican Party. The most prominent Republican, and certainly the most successful, was Edward W. Brooke of Massachusetts. Brooke was "an authentic member" of the "Black bourgeoisie." After his graduation from Boston University, Brooke decided to run for the Massachusetts state legislature in both the Democratic and Republican primaries in 1950. Defeated in the former, he therefore became a Republican. After a series of electoral defeats, Brooke finally was elected Massachusetts attorney general in 1962. In 1966, Brooke campaigned and won a seat in the U.S. Senate over Endicott Peabody, a man described by observers as being "far more liberal on civil rights for black people than the black candidate himself." Of course, it may be unfair to classify Brooke as a Black politician, since he never made any attempts to identify himself as one. Stone condemned Brooke as "Mr. Non-Negro Politics," "the answer to the white man's prayers," "a political anomaly, (and) almost a political freak." After his election to the Senate, he hired only two Blacks out of a nineteen member staff. Brooke found little difficulty in campaigning for Nixon or Gerald R. Ford, despite both white politicians' antipathy toward Black political rights and socioeconomic progress. Unlike Thomas Sowell and the Black Reaganites of the 1980s, however, Brooke consistently obscured his essentially conservative economic and political philosophy by relying on the rhetoric of integration and civil rights. Even at the end of his career in 1978, when Massachusetts residents finally voted him out of office, Brooke used whatever leverage his "race" created for him within Back activist circles. Indeed, a group of Black nationalist militants from the National Black Political Assembly went so far as to campaign for Brooke that year, justifying their support solely on racial terms.[35]

In *How Europe Underdeveloped Africa*, Walter Rodney observes that the most destructive idea within the expansion of Western societies into the nonwhite world was the concept of individualism. "It is a common myth within capitalist thought that the individual through drive and hard work can become a capitalist. The acquisition of wealth is not due to hard work alone," Rodney notes, "or the Africans working as slaves in America and the West Indies would have been the wealthiest group in the world. The individualism of the capitalist must be seen against the hard and unrewarded work of the masses."[36] Individualism as an expression of Black politics is expressed as a commitment to oneself alone, a desire to transcend socioeconomic obstacles in order to become a power broker within the system. Blues artist B. B. King makes the point aesthetically: "You've got to pay the cost, to be the boss." Black accommodationists and many reformers with accommodationist tendencies such as Powell, acknowledge the centrality of individualism within their political practice. They developed a series of practical solutions, or answers, to resolve the dilemma of Black underdevelopment, from the placid politics of Dawson, to the Machiavellian agenda of Washington. Their basic flaw was that they had no theoretical or systemic analysis of what was to be done: they were asking the wrong questions. After a century of tactical compromises, Black accommodationists still retain an individualistic faith in the inherent justice of America's economic and social order.

Black conservatives from Councill to Sowell should not be considered accommodationists. They ceased asking any questions which relate to meaningful social and economic change for the Black working class and poor people. They are not willing to "pay the cost," because they do not wish to be the "boss"—that is, to transform the existing undemocratic, racist hierarchy in even miniscule ways. Like the Black radical journalist of the Harlem Renaissance, George Schuyler, some of the contemporary Black conservatives began their intellectual lives as socialists or militant reformers and gradually succumbed to anticommunism and a nihilistic view of Black activism as they reached middle age.[37] Energetically, Sowell and his fellow Black conservatives—most notably Wendell Wilkie Gunn of Pepsi corporation, Black Republican leader J.A.Y. Parker and economist Walter Williams— claim to represent a "new" and unprecedented political tendency which has the potential for becoming dominant within Black civil society in the years ahead. But the Black majority recognizes that their agendas are not ours; their "supply-side" ideas are unoriginal; and their politics are simply the program of those forces that would crush the collective life from Black America. Black Reaganism is not an accommodation to white power, but a complete capitulation to racism. Thomas Sowell's extensive theoretical work is an apology for racism and Reaganism.[38] Sowell does not even merit the mantle of Washington.

IV

History illustrates that the petty bourgeoisie of an oppressed nation or nationality is incapable by itself of struggling to achieve political and economic equality under capitalism. In *Class Struggle in Africa,* Kwame Nkrumah asserted that during national liberation efforts the Black elite responds in three ways. "Firstly, there are those who are heavily committed to colonialism and to capitalist economic and social development." The second category, the nationalists, "want to end colonial rule" but oppose "a transformation of society." The third group simply "sits on the fence," supporting the militant actions of Black workers and the peasantry when it suits their own narrow interests.[39] Politically, the Black Brahmin will go so far as to subvert its own institutions, betray its own representatives, and coalesce with the most vicious racists if conditions for progressive change seem temporarily remote. The modern "realignment" in Black politics is essentially a repetition of this classical pattern of petty bourgeois opportunism and accommodation.

The goals of the Civil Rights Movement, which promoted the necessity of social democratic reforms (e.g., food, public health care, child care, job training, free education, etc.) have been abandoned by major sectors of the Black elite. It becomes the task of Black progressives and Marxists in this period to complete this interrupted "revolution" for civil rights and social equality within the framework of the existing system. The burden of our history is two-fold. We must advance "reformist" programs within communities which reinforce Black owned socioeconomic and cultural institutions, advocating the maintenance of needed social service programs that affect the Black working class and the poor. But we must insist uncompromisingly that the social crises confronting Black people reflect a more fundamental contradiction created in part by the crisis of capital accumulation. Self-determination for the Black majority cannot be forged unless our politics, in theory and in practice, also opposes sexual exploitation, imperialism, and monopoly capitalism. The revolt for reforms within the capitalist state today transcends itself dialectically to become a revolution against the racist/capitalist system tomorrow.

Given this critique, the next logical question is—which sectors of the Black elite have the greatest potential for participating in the democratic reconstruction of capitalist America? As illustrated in chapter five, the Black entrepreneurs and executives are the greatest internal barrier to the achievement of a socialist political consensus within the Black community. The Black politicians, taken as a whole, are either clients of larger corporate interests,or excel in the electoral game for personal profit and ego gratification. We turn next to the Black Church for leadership, and find as with the politicians, a divided legacy—a history of struggle and accommodation.

CHAPTER SEVEN

THE AMBIGUOUS POLITICS OF THE BLACK CHURCH.

The history of early Christianity offers noteworthy points of similarity with the modern labour movement. Like it, Christianity was in the beginning a movement of the oppressed. It appears first as a religion of slave and freedman, of the poor without rights and of peoples dominated or dispersed by the Romans.

Friedrich Engels

Long-haired preachers come out every night,
Try to tell you what's wrong and what's right;
But when asked how 'bout something to eat
They will answer with voices so sweet:

You will eat, bye and bye,
In that glorious land above the sky;
Work and pray, live on hay,
You'll get pie in the sky when you die.

Joe Hill, "The Preacher and the Slave," in Tristram Potter Coffin and Hennig Cohen, eds., *Folklore: From the Working Folk of America* (Garden City, New York: Anchor, 1974), pp. 401–402.

I

The Black Church occupies a unique position in the evolution of Black cultural and political life in capitalist America. From Reconstruction to Black Power, many significant political figures engaged in Black liberation struggles were either ministers or were profoundly influenced by religion: Nat Turner, Henry H. Garnet, David Walker, Elijah Muhammad, Malcolm X, Andrew Young, Jesse Jackson, John Lewis and hundreds more. The most influential minister in twentieth century American society, Black or white, was Martin Luther King, Jr. The majority of Black theologians and sociologists of religion tend to make a radical separation between Black faith and the specific political praxis of Black clergy. Most political science research on the Civil Rights Movement concentrates on King's role as a centrist within the broad and often fractious united front that constituted the desegregationist campaign, and ignores the historical relationship between Black politics and faith. Few historians have seriously explored the Movement's impact on the evolution of the Black Church.

In the decades immediately preceding the Second Reconstruction, Black clergy as a group experienced a decline in political influence and social status relative to other middle-class Blacks. The Civil Rights Movement provided an historic opportunity for activist preachers to direct their working class congregations in the practical struggle to overturn Jim Crow laws, improve housing conditions and to exercise the right to vote. King and other Black ministers succeeded in their efforts to achieve democratic reforms within the capitalist democratic system, but were unable to alleviate the sufferings of the Black masses caused by institutional racism and capitalism. As the Black Power and Vietnam War destroyed the fragile consensus among the petty bourgeois leadership of the Civil Rights Movement, King was pressured to move to the left. With the courage instilled by his nonviolent convictions, he advanced a progressive human rights agenda at home and abroad, and began to make the case for economic democracy. The majority of Black clergy were then, and still are today, unable to follow King's example established in 1966–1968.

It would be an error to discuss the politics of the Black Church, however, simply by concentrating on the life and death of King. King is important for us only in two specific respects; in his skillful use of Black faith and spirituality as a lever to motivate the consciousness of the Black working-class masses towards decisive action against the interests of racists and the state, and in his devlopment of a certain praxis which was, although idealist in philosophy, clearly anticapitalist by the time of his assassination. In documenting the evolution of the Black Church, King represents the anticapitalist potential that is inherent within the Black clergy. Given the centrality of religion within the life of the Black masses, it is essential to discuss the potential and limitations of this decisive segment of the Black elite.

The foundations of modern Black politics are found within the Black Church. From the beginning periods of Afro-American slavery, the minister assumed a relatively privileged position within Black civil society, playing roles both spiritual and secular. Hundreds of Black Methodist and Baptist ministers were active in electoral politics during Reconstruction. In 1865, for example, the presiding officer of the African Methodist Episcopal Zion Church, the Reverend J.W. Hood, issued a series of radical reforms for Blacks which included the right to vote. There were a large number of Black ministers elected to their respective state constitutional conventions in the late 1860s. Some of the most influential included the Reverends Henry P. Jacobs, Baptist, Mississippi; T.W. Springer, AME, Mississippi; James Walker Hood, AME Zion, North Carolina; Richard Harvey Cain, AME, South Carolina; Francis Louis Cardozo, Presbyterian, South Carolina; and Henry McNeal Turner, AME, Georgia. In the 1880s, Black ministers like attorney T. McCants Stewart, pastor of New York City's Bethel African Methodist Episcopal Church, served on that city's school board and championed the necessity for Black political independence. Many Black religious leaders supported Black nationalist programs, including C.H. Philips, editor of the Colored Methodist Episcopal *Christian Index,* and Henry M. Turner. Without exaggeration, it can be stated that almost every Black minister was something of a politician, and that every aspiring Black politician had to be something of a minister. With the rise of Jim Crow and the electoral disenfranchisement of most Blacks after 1900, one of the few remaining roles in which articulate and militant young Black men could exercise political influence was as a preacher.[1]

The twentieth century witnessed a gradual yet unmistakable decline in the political influence and social status of Black ministers.

There were at least three basic reasons for this. The first is illustrated in U.S. Census statistics for the period 1890 to 1970. Four important vocations defined as "middle class" within American society were clergy, teachers, physicians and attorneys. In 1890 there were 12,159 Black ministers in the U.S.; that year, there were only 14,100 Black teachers, 909 doctors and 431 lawyers, out of a total Black population of about eight million. Relatively, a very large percentage of the Black intelligentsia and middle class was found within the church. By 1910 the number of Black ministers peaked at 17,495. Thirty years later, in 1940, the total number of Black clergy amounted to 17,102. That year, the U.S. Census counted 63,697 Black school teachers, 3,524 doctors and 1,052 lawyers and judges. The overall percentage of Black ministers within the Black professional stratum was greatly reduced. This decline accelerated after World War II and with the desegregation of white civil society. The U.S. Census of 1970 recorded only 12,850 Black clergy, compared to 235,436 Black school teachers, 3,728 lawyers and judges, and 6,106 physicians. The number of Black elected officials in the U.S. increased dramatically: 103 in 1964; 1,469 in 1970; and 5,003 in 1980. Many of these new and powerful representatives of the Black elite were not ministers, and owed no allegiance to the Black Church. The ministry itself ceased to be the choice vocation of the middle class, or even politically motivated Blacks. Thousands of other professional Blacks exerted, by their sheer numbers, an increasing significance within the Black community's political, social and economic development.[2]

Second, throughout the period there was a sharp decline in the per capita rate of Black ministers to the general Black population. In 1890, 14 percent of all U.S. clergy were Afro-Americans. Using Census figures, the number of Black clergy per thousand Blacks in 1890 was a very high 1.62. This figure was relatively constant for several decades. For example, in 1910 the per capita number of Black ministers per thousand Blacks was 1.56; the per capita number of white ministers per thousand whites was 1.42. After World War I and the Great Depression, the per capita rate slipped for both Blacks and whites, but the decline is more pronounced among Blacks. In 1940, the figures were .95 for Blacks and 1.11 for whites. In 1970 the per capita number dropped to .53 for Blacks, but increased slightly to 1.18 for whites. In other words, by 1970 there was about one Black minister for every 1,898 Black people—the smallest per capita figure in Black history.

Only seven percent of all U.S. clergy were Black in 1960, and this figure dropped to six percent in 1970.[3] The Census historically undercounts all Black people, so it is highly probable that the real number of Black clergy during these years was larger than reported. Nevertheless, even given a massive margin for error, there can be little doubt that both in numbers and in per capita percentage Black clergy declined after 1910.

The third and perhaps decisive factor was the escalation of Black political and social criticism levied at the Black clergy. Throughout his career as a political militant and social scientist, W.E.B. DuBois repeatedly questioned the ambiguous role of the Black preacher as a progressive factor in the liberation of Afro-American people. In "The Religion of the Negro," written in 1900, DuBois suggested that the basic spirituality of Black folk "swept irresistibly toward the Goal (of) Liberty, Justice and Right." Black ministers had the obligation to preach a theology rooted in the practical political conditions of Black humanity.[4] DuBois praised the Black Church as an expression of the "Negro's soul" and organizational ability.[5] But he criticized the tendency of major Black churches to split and engage in fractious arguments over personalities and matters of doctrine.[6] In 1928 DuBois attacked the Black ministers of Washington, D.C. for banning a lecture by Clarence Darrow because of his agnosticism.[7] DuBois understood that the shortcomings of the Black Church were small in comparison to the massive hypocrisy and blatant racism evident within white denominations. In 1913, for instance, he used the pages of *The Crisis* to condemn the segregationist policies of the Episcopal Church, declaring "the church of John Pierpont Morgan" was not "the church of Jesus Christ."[8] He denounced the Catholic Church in 1945 for maintaining "separate white and Negro congregations in the South" and for "(refusing) to receive colored students in a large number of their schools."[9] DuBois believed that all white Christian churches expressed "a double standard of truth" towards the Negro, professing the highest ideals while carrying out "the most selfish and self-seeking" practices of race hatred and oppression.[10] For these reasons, DuBois argued, the Black Clergy had no other alternative execpt to become an active agent for social justice and political transformation.

Other critics of the Black clergy were far less generous than DuBois. A. Philip Randolph and Chandler Owen, editors of the Black socialist journal *The Messenger*, declared in 1919 that the Black

Church was an utter disaster. Black preachers as a group were silent on lynchings, political disenfranchisement in the South, and Black economic exploitation by white capitalists.[11] Echoing Karl Marx, V.F. Calverton charged in 1927 that religion was a kind of "other-worldliness" among Blacks. The traditional Judeo-Christian ethic of forgiveness, submissive behavior, prayer for salvation and tolerance toward one's earthly oppressors simply perpetuated white racism and the brutal extraction of surplus value from the labor power of the Black proletariat.[12] Many Northern Black ministers were secretly on the payroll of white industrialists such as Henry Ford, using their influence among working-class Blacks to counsel patience with low wages and to reject unionism. After World War II the level of criticism increased. Writing about that "special gray death that loiters in the streets" of Harlem, LeRoi Jones condemned the Black minister as representing a drug to blind Blacks from the frustrations of urban life. "You can go to church Saturday nights and Sundays and three or four times during the week," he stated in *Home;* "or you can stick a needle in your arm four or five times a day."[13] In *The Crisis of the Negro Intellectual,* Harold Cruse suggested that the Black ministers of Harlem "vie with professional social workers and police chiefs over which brand of community uplift is best for soothing the tortured ghetto soul 'twixt Hell on earth and Heavenly hereafter. Many of them 'mean well' toward the 'masses' but they are frightened to death of power—others' and their own."[14] Many, but not all Black ministers, were silent when DuBois, Paul Robeson and other Black socialists and progressives were slandered and arrested during the McCarthy era.[15] The growing postwar successes of the NAACP and other more progressive biracial groups further reduced the power and prestige that the Black Church had once claimed.

The Black Church continued to serve its traditional function as a "refuge" and forum "to satisfy (the) deepest emotional yearnings" of Black people. However, the relationship between the first and second generation Black urban working class in the North with their Black clergy was becoming at best problematic. In *The Negro's Church,* published in 1933, the Reverend Dr. Benjamin E. Mays and Joseph W. Nicholson analyzed one hundred Black sermons at random, discovering that 20 were devoted to theological doctrine, 54 were vaguely "other-worldly" and only 26 centered on contemporary secular affairs. During the depths of the Great Depression, the Black working class had begun to "develop a more secular outlook on life" and increasingly complained "that the church and the ministers are not sufficiently concerned with the problems of the Negro race." By the dawn of the Civil Rights Movement, noted Black sociologist E. Franklin Frazier would observe that "the Negro church has lost much of its influence as an agency of social control. Its supervision over the marital and family life of Negroes has declined. The church has ceased to be the chief means of economic cooperation."[16] Growing numbers of Black ministers in the North began to be selected by white politicians and business leaders to serve on municipal health and welfare boards. "In this capacity," wrote sociologist Daniel C. Thompson, these pastors "represent(ed) the Negro community" and served "as advisors to white groups where certain problems directly affecting Negroes are concerned."[17] Nevertheless, the majority of Black clergy seemed ineffective or apathetic in the fight for meaningful economic and political reforms which would touch the daily lives of their congregations.

The *Brown* decision of the Supreme Court in May, 1954, presented new challenges to Black ministers. To the surprise and chagrin of many Negro clergy, a key element in the forces of "Massive Resistance" to desegregation were white ministers. Many more "liberal" Southern Christian clergy cautioned their white congregations to obey the law, "improve communications between races," and advocated the "full privileges of first class citizenship" for all. But even Atlanta's white ministers, who were among the most tolerant and "liberal," warned in a public statement that "we do not believe in the wisdom of massive integration." Historian Numan V. Bartley has noted that "integrationist activity was not conducive to a smoothly functioning House of God in almost any part of the South." In Montgomery, Dr. G. Stanley Frazer, leader of Alabama's white Methodists, and R. Henry L. Lyon, twice president of the Alabama Southern Baptist Convention, "were two of the most prominent ministers in the city and both were outspoken proponents of "segregation." Dr. John H. Buchanan, Birmingham's leading white clergyman, declared in 1956 that "the good Lord set up customs and practices of segregation." Throughout the 1950s and 1960s the American Baptist Association Convention annually condemned desegregation. The American Council of Christian Churches, with a total membership of one million, declared solemnly in 1958 that integration "does violence to the true gospel of Jesus Christ." Episcopalians in South Carolina proclaimed publicly in 1956 "that there is nothing morally wrong in a voluntary recognition of racial differences and that voluntary alignment can be both natural and Christian." Mississippi Presbyterians refused to carry out church directives in 1957 to desegregate. The Alabama American Baptist Convention even proclaimed in October, 1959, that integration was a "Communist" plot. White Christian clergy and laymen expressed few reservations to become involved in the fight to preserve white supremacy.[18]

The Montgomery Bus Boycott, initiated on December 1, 1955 by Rosa Parks, was the beginning of the Second Reconstruction, a massive, ethical movement by Blacks and their white liberal allies to destroy racial segregation. The idea for the nonviolent boycott had been that of E.D. Nixon, an experienced member of the 1941 March on Washington Movement and trade union activist in Randolph's Brotherhood of Sleeping Car Porters. A chief administrator in the boycott itself was Bayard Rustin, a Black Quaker and social democrat who had participated in the earliest "freedom rides," or Journey of Reconciliation in the late 1940s. Black ministers were a minority in the major Black political organization of the city, the Montgomery Improvement Association.[19] Yet it was the Black clergy which provided the moral, social and political context for the entire struggle: the Reverend L. Roy Bennett, Reverend Ralph David Abernathy, Reverend Martin Luther King, Jr., and others. King's address at Montgomery's Holt Street Church at the outset of the boycott, established the popular framework for Black resistance:

> One of the great glories of democracy is the right to protest for right . . . We are protesting for the birth of justice in the community. Our method will be that of persuasion, not coercion. Our actions must be guided by the deepest principles of our Christian faith. Love must be our regulating ideal. Once again we must hear the words of Jesus echoing across the centuries: 'Love your enemies, bless them that curse you, and pray for them that despitefully use you.' If we fail to do this our protest will end up as a meaningless drama on the stage of history, and its memory will be shrouded with the ugly garments of shame. In spite of the mistreatment that we have confronted, we must not become bitter and end up hating our white brothers. As Booker T. Washington said, 'Let no man pull you down so low as to make you hate him.'[20]

Martin Luther King's life and martyrdom, long etched in Black history, and popularized within Black and U.S. culture, require little rehearsal here. Several important social factors within King's legacy, and in the history of the Black Freedom Movement, are however grossly ignored. The emergence of King, Ralph Abernathy, and other Black clergy in the forefront of the desegregation struggle was to an extent a progressive response to white clergy who had taken up the cause of white supremacy in Alabama and across the South generally. If Christ could be portrayed by white Baptists as a Ku Klux Klansman, then He could just as easily be enlisted in the ranks of bus boycotters and Freedom Riders by Black Baptists. The Civil Rights Movement occurred at a time when the social and political role of Black preachers was steadily diminishing. By participating in their people's struggles, the Black ministers could once again set the political and moral climate for millions of Blacks who over previous decades had become alienated or disillusioned with church inactivity in secular issues. As in the years of Reconstruction, from 1865–1877, the Black Church provided the necessary social space for political discussions, strategy sessions and effective protest. With the creation of the Southern Christian Leadership Conference (SCLC) in 1957, King and other Black ministers forged an appropriate political vehicle for the battle to destroy Jim Crow. Not coincidentally, they created the political terrain essential to reclaim the prestige and class status the Black clergy had lost over the previous half century within the Negro petty bourgeoisie.

King was the most prominent Black minister of the Civil Rights Movement—yet his rise to greatness should not obscure the fact that hundreds of other Black preachers and laymen were responsible for many of the real accomplishments of the Movement. In Lynchburgh, Virginia, the SCLC affiliate led by the Reverend Virgil Wood initiated numerous nonviolent direct action campaigns. The Reverend Fred Shuttlesworth was responsible for many of the successes combating Bull Connor's racist police force and the white power structure in Birmingham. The Reverend Hosea Williams was an effective SCLC coordinator in the desegregation campaigns in Savannah, Georgia. The Reverend James Lawson assisted King in the founding conference of the Student Nonviolent Coordinating Committee (SNCC) at Shaw University, in Raleigh, North Carolina. The Reverend Matthew McCollum, one of the SCLC's founders, was a skilled veteran of desegregation struggles in Orangeburg, South Carolina. Other influential Black activist pastors included C.K. Steele of Tallahassee, Florida; C.T. Vivian, the central coordinator of the SCLC; Bernard

Lafayette of Selma, Alabama; Walter Fauntroy, director of the SCLC Washington, D.C. Bureau; Wyatt Tee Walker of Petersburg, Virginia; and a host of younger Black divinity students and pastors like Jesse Jackson, Andrew Young and James Bevel. In Northern states, Black ministers who had previously done little in the way of political or economic protest were stirred to act. In May, 1960 in Philadelphia, four hundred Black clergymen decided to pressure white-owned corporations to hire Black employees in "decent positions." Confronting the racist policies of one company, the ministers initiated a boycott of the firm's products, an act supported by virtually every Black Masonic lodge, church organization and social club in Pennsylvania.[21]

Yet it was King alone who captured the imagination of the Black masses, while earning the respect of the media and white establishment. In the early years of the sit-in movement, it was not unusual for teenage protestors to ask each other, "What do you suppose Martin Luther King would do in this situation?" King biographer William Robert Miller writes that by 1960 "King's symbolic role was supreme, his charismatic stature was universally recognized. In the flux of rapidly proliferating and chaotic events, he towered as a pillar of strength."[22] For whites, confronted with the growing radicalism of SCLC and the Congress of Racial Equality (CORE), King made the "nonviolent direct action movement respectable." Historian August Meier recognized in 1965 that "King's very tendencies toward compromise and caution, his willingness to negotiate and bargain with White House emissaries, his hesitancy to risk the precipitation of mass violence upon demonstrators, further endear him to whites. He appears to them as a 'respectable' and 'moderate' man."[23] As a minister, King constantly assumed the irreproachable posture of an ethical reformist committed to Gandhian political efforts. When white evangelist Billy Graham urged King "to put the brakes on a little bit" in the desegregation campaign in Birmingham, the SCLC leader relied solely upon Christian doctrines to justify the necessity for continued struggle. King's famous "Letter from Birmingham Jail," published in *Christian Century* and *Liberation* in June, 1963, was an eloquent rejection of white Birmingham clergymen's appeals to halt nonviolent demonstrations.[24]

III

Historical memory is selective. Most Afro-Americans now fail to recall that the support provided for Black activist-oriented clergy by more powerful Black Church leaders was hardly unanimous. The outstanding example of neoaccommodation was the Reverend Joseph H. Jackson, president of the National Baptist Convention. In 1956 Jackson applauded King's protest activities, and was one of several speakers at a rally marking the first anniversary of the Montgomery Bus Boycott. Jackson soon disapproved of King's growing influence within political circles, and cautioned his ministers not to become actively involved in the Southern Christian Leadership Conference founded in 1957. When the Reverend George Taylor and the Reverend George Lawrence challenged Jackson's faction for leadership in the National Baptist Convention in 1960–1961, King supported Taylor and Lawrence. In 1961, 800 Black activist-oriented ministers finally broke with Jackson, establishing the Progressive Baptist Convention. Subsequently, Jakcson had little to say in support of King, and took any opportunity to condemn nonviolent, direct action activities. At the 1962 National Baptist Convention, Jackson singled out fellow ministers who had assisted the SCLC drive to desegregate Albany, Georgia, criticizing the futility of their efforts. "It is hypocrisy," he charged, "for a delegation to leave Chicago and go to Albany to fight segregation." Four years later, when King, Abernathy, Jesse Jackson and other Black ministers followed his advice by staging a massive desegregation campaign in Chicago, Joseph Jackson "issued a public statement dissociating himself from the event and peppering its unnamed instigator with politely worded abuse."[25]

The success of Montgomery not only boosted the protest potential of the Black Church, but it affected the political relations of almost every left-of-center group toward the Black clergy. Harold Cruse has argued that Black members of the Communist Party in the 1930s condemned the Black Church as hopelessly reactionary. "Twenty-five years later, with the emergence of Dr. Martin Luther King, the Negro church ceased to be a reactionary, as the Communists jumped on King's bandwagon."[26] Actually, the leadership of the more conservative NAACP and Urban League, as well as King's SCLC and CORE eschewed public cooperation and joint work with Marxists and socialists. In 1961, for example, the Louisville branch of the NAACP attacked Louisville's CORE chapter for working with Carl and Anne Braden, officers in the Southern Conference Educational Fund which was "widely charged" as a Communist organization. James Farmer and CORE's national leadership "dealt with the

Bradens most circumspectly, advising field personnel not to accept food or lodging from them."[27] Two years later, when Black activists were confronted with a desperate shortage of lawyers in Mississippi who would take civil rights cases, the National Lawyers Guild "aggressively volunteered its help to various civil rights groups." SNCC accepted the Guild's offer, but CORE's leaders rejected "cooperation with the Guild, fearing that its identification as a Communist front might damage the movement."[28] The Reverend Adam Clayton Powell, then the most influential Black elected official in the U.S., informed King in 1960 that he was willing to support him—on the condition that he fire Bayard Rustin, a moderate leftist, from his staff. Writing in *Harper's*, novelist James Baldwin charged that Martin "lost much moral credit . . . especially in the eyes of the young, when he allowed Powell to force Rustin's resignation. King was faced with the choice of defending his organizer, who was also his friend, or agreeing with Powell; and he chose the latter course."[29]

The explicit anticommunism of many Black ministers, the NAACP and even more liberal civil rights groups existed throughout the postwar period. In 1946, the NAACP rejected cooperation with the leftist Civil Rights Congress' campaign to oust the notorious racist, Mississippi Senator Theodore Bilbo, from office. Walter White, NAACP leader, argued that "it was imperative that this (campaign) be done under non-Communist auspices."[30] In 1948, CORE's Executive Committee issued a "Statement on Communism," ordering chapters not to affiliate with leftist organizations, and "enacted procedures for disaffiliating chapters which had fallen under Communist domination."[31] In a different way, a contempt for a materialist analysis was also expressed by Black, middle class student radicals in the 1960s. Julius Lester wrote in 1968 that "many Blacks view Marxism and Communism as foreign ideologies. Young Black militants do not consider Marxism relevant" since Marx "was a white man."[32] Liberal (and anticommunist) journalist Harry Golden suggested that Communists failed to attract Southern Blacks for two reasons. First, "they do not depend on nor incorporate Jesus and the Gospels." Second, "the great mass of the American Negroes do not reject the existing social order, they seek only to share fully in its bourgeois blessing."[33] More than other Blacks, the clergy commonly shared an unstated antipathy for atheism in any form, and possessed a class-oriented commitment to the acquisition of private property and Black petty capitalism.

"Historically, the Black preacher was the first member of the Black professional class, the Black elite," writes Robert Allen. "He frequently had some degree of education (and) enjoyed a semi-independent economic status."[34] The unwillingness to unite with Marxists and militant social democrats who expressed a sincere commitment to destroy racial segregation eliminated any possibility that the Civil Rights Movement would transcend its theoretical parochialism and develop a legitimate agenda to reconstruct the political economy of the United States.

Legitimate criticisms of King, coming from Black activists and sympathetic intellectuals, began as early as 1958. In *Présence Africaine*, Cruse charged that King's theoretical foundations for social protest exemplified "the confusion of the Negro middle-class mind on (the) question of racial integration." For Cruse, King's assertion that the civil rights struggle would allow Negroes to lose their "racial identity" was both tragic and absurd. "It requires neither intellect, education, nor morality these days to howl for civil rights," Cruse declared, "but it does require some profundity of insight and honesty in racial matters to know what to do with civil rights after they are achieved."[35] By late 1963, Rustin had begun to censure King for relying too heavily upon "the tactics of lying down in the streets to prevent the movement of trucks, and other forms of direct action." Rustin suggested that "heroism and ability to go to jail should not be substituted for an overall social reform program."[36] In 1963 Black writer LeRoi Jones was perhaps the first critic to draw the historical analogy between King and Booker T. Washington. In *Midstream* magazine, Jones noted that "Washington solidified the separate but equal lie, when that lie was of value to the majority of intelligent white men. King's lie is that there is a moral requirement to be met before entrance into the secular kingdom of plenty." For Jones, King was a model missionary who helped to perpetuate racist hegemony:

> In this sense King's main function (as was Washington's) is to be an agent of the middle-class power structure, Black and white. He has functioned in Montgomery, Albany, Birmingham, etc. (as has the Negro middle class in general) as a buffer, an informer, a cajoler against action not sanctioned by white Intelligence . . . He is screaming at the blimp with the loudspeaker of recent agonies. He is a hand-picked leader of the oppressed, but only the pickers are convinced.[37]

In the summer months of 1964 and 1965, the patience fostered by Black ministers within ghetto communities began to wear thin. The absence of any "national organization which could speak to the growing militancy of young Black people in the urban ghettos and the black-belt South," in SNCC leader Stokely Carmichael's words, undermined "the struggle against racism." When innercity Blacks watched the news and "saw Dr. King get slapped they became angry. When they saw little Black girls bombed to death in a church and civil rights workers ambushed and murdered, they were angrier."[38] The number of Black urban uprisings increased from nine in 1965, 38 in 1966, 128 in 1967, and 131 in the first six months of 1968. These urban disorders were not only a rejection of the Johnson Administration's limited "War on Poverty," but a break from the quiescence of Black middle class and Black preacher-dominated civil rights organizing efforts. The Black masses were prepared to "take to the streets and thereby declare their hatred for the bondage imposed on them."[39]

With the sudden renaissance of Black nationalism in the guise of Black Power, both King and his entire generation of activist-ministers received a profound jolt. SNCC activist Julius Lester's *Look Out, Whitey! Black Power's Gon' Get Your Mama!* repeated Jones' denunciation of King as merely the "successor of Booker T. Washington." King's message of "love" was hypocritical, Lester declared. "What is love supposed to do? Wrap a bullet in a warm embrace? Caress the cattle prod?" For Black activist veterans of the Albany, Birmingham and Selma campaigns, the spirituality and ethos of nonviolence was dead. "We used to sing 'I Love Everybody' as we ducked bricks and bottles," Lester reflected. "Now we sing: Too much love, Too much love, Nothing kills a nigger like too much love."[40] Robert Allen's *Black Awakening in Capitalist America* concluded that even the Black activist minister could not be expected to provide any effective, long-term leadership in the Black Movement. Although "the Black minister remains today an important, if not the most important, social force in most Black communities," he represents a prime "collaborator" and "force of conservatism." Allen noted:

> While it must be said that the Black church has performed an essential function in maintaining social cohesion in Black communities through decades of travail and suffering, it cannot be denied that the Black preacher is often identified as an 'Uncle Tom' . . . He is seen as a traitor to the best interest of his people

. . . The minister, in accepting Christianity, also in some degree identified with the major moral values and institutions of white society. Consequently it was relatively easy for him to work with whites, even though this sometimes amounted to a betrayal of Blacks.[41]

As for Martin himself, the young Black nationalists had little sympathy. "As the crisis of Black America deepened," Allen wrote, King was converted into "a reluctant accomplice of the white power structure." The white elites discovered that King was useful "to restrain the threatening rebelliousness of the Black masses and the young militants." Furthermore, "King could not repudiate this role because he was convinced that the establishment could be pushed and pressured to implement his program."[42] At a speech at the University of California-Berkeley in October, 1966, SNCC chairperson Stokely Carmichael expressed an ambiguous respect yet deep disillusionment toward King and his goals. Carmichael admitted that King was "full of love," "mercy and compassion," a man "who's desperately needed in this country. But every time I see (President) Lyndon (Johnson) on television, I say 'Martin, baby, you got a long way to go.' "[43]

King's final years provide some parallels with the last months of the major Black nationalist of the 1960s, Malcolm X. Like the former Muslim minister, King had begun to reevaluate the goals of the Black struggle from the simple demand for civil rights to the pursuit of "human rights." His first public speech on the Vietnam War, given at a Virginia statewide meeting of SCLC affiliates in Petersburg in July, 1965, was a mixture of anticommunism, moral suasion and passivism. "I am certainly as concerned about seeing the defeat of communism as anyone else," King stated, "but we won't defeat communism by guns or bombs or gasses. We will do it by making democracy work." He called for an immediate end to U.S. military involvement in Southeast Asia and a "negotiated settlement even with the Viet Cong."[44] By 1967 King was actively leading the U.S. peace movement, addressing rallies and proposing concrete details for U.S. disengagement from Vietnam. He became more concerned about the profound similarity between the oppressed material conditions of the unemployed, Blacks and whites, and proposed a "Poor People's March" on Washington, D.C. in October, 1967. Many of King's oldest friends rejected him, some visciously attacking his new political concerns in the media. Negro columnist Carl Rowan, who assisted King during the Montgomery Bus

Boycott, charged that the leader's peace activities have "alienated many of the Negro's friends and armed the Negro's foes, in both parties, by creating the impression that the Negro is disloyal." Conservative representatives of the Black middle class, such as Whitney Young of the Urban League, NAACP director Roy Wilkins and former socialist Ralph Bunche bitterly condemned King, as did the only Black in the U.S. Senate, Edward Brooke. Many Black ministers within the SCLC privately criticized King for moving too far left, and publicly separated themselves from any antiwar demonstrations and religious peace services. On April 4, 1968, King was assassinated while assisting 1,375 Black sanitation workers in Local 1733 of the American Federation of State, County, and Municipal Employees, AFL-CIO in a strike in Memphis, Tennessee. The middle class reformer had become a militant proponent of peace, economic democracy and Black working class interests.[45]

IV

King's strengths and weaknesses were not his alone, but those of his social group, the Black clergy. His moral appeals for nonviolence, racial harmony and desegregation were shared by previous generations of Black middle class reformers. His initial reluctance to emphasize economic issues, his implicit anticommunism and desire for compromise rather than confrontation with the white establishment was also the popular ideology of the Negro petty bourgeoisie. Where King departed from his contemporaries was his recognition that Black ministers as a group had to play a decisive role in the reconstruction of U.S. civil and political society. The greatest political contradiction confronting the masses of Blacks, the system of white supremacy, was of course the primary target of King's efforts. In the process of struggle, however, King concluded finally that the defeat of racial segregation in itself was insufficient for creating a just and decent society for all Americans. King followed the tradition of earlier Black activist-clergy—Henry Highland Garnet, Henry M. Turner, Nat Turner—by calling for radical and fundamental change. Without hesitation, he broke from many of his own advisors and supporters, and like Malcolm, raised many public policy issues which could not be easily resolved within the existing system. Congressperson Louis Stokes, chairperson of the U.S. House Select Committee on Assassinations, believes that

King was murdered because "he had begun to wake up poor people in this country, not only poor Black people but also poor white people. (In) entering this dangerous area," King had to be killed.[46]

Many of King's lieutenants in the Black clergy have failed to pursue King's vision. Abernathy, Hosea Williams and the brother of the martyred civil rights activist Medgar Evers, Charles Evers, endorsed the presidential candidacy of ultraconservative Ronald Reagan in 1980. Andrew Young, currently mayor of Atlanta, Georgia, served as U.N. ambassador in the Carter Administration.

Several ministers within the SCLC, including Fauntroy, have been elected to high office, and Jesse Jackson's Operation PUSH captures headlines with political maneuvers which are more style than substance. As a group, however, not a single member of King's generation has courageously pursued the logic of his final years. Part of their current dilemma is created by their conscious, class-oriented commitment to infuse the Negro middle class into the present economic order and to perpetuate the inert politics of bourgeois reform. They are not prepared to repudiate the system which rewards their own political accommodation at the expense of the continued exploitation of Black working class and poor people.

Even after the most detailed exploration of the politics of the Black Church, a series of contradictions remain. How has the Black Church as an institution failed repeatedly to evolve into a coherent agency promoting the liberation of Afro-American people, and why has it succeeded to reveal itself as an essential factor in Black struggles at certain difficult historical periods? Why is the stereotypical Black preacher the frequent object of embarrassment, ridicule and scorn for the Black petty bourgeoisie and to much of the Black working class, yet simultaneously he continues to be a critically important contributor to the total sum of Black social, cultural, economic and political life? How can such a church create Martin Luther King and Daddy Grace, Ben Chavis and Reverend Ike? Why, in short, does the Black Church continue to perform its fundamentally ambiguous role in the Black experience?

The insights of Marxist theorist Antonio Gramsci, and especially his critique of the role of Catholicism within Italian society and culture, have particular merit for our own situation. Religion for any society constitutes the most important element of the people's "common sense." But common sense "is not a single conception, identical in time and space: it is the folklore of philosophy . . . disintegrated, incoherent, inconsecutive." Organized religions attempt, first, to impose order out of the day-to-day chaos that is experienced in cultural, social and economic relations. Religion endeavors to transform "what the masses think embryonically and chaotically about the world and about life." Various social strata experience religion in diverse ways. "Every religion (is) a multiplicity of distinct and often contradictory religions: there is the Catholicism of the peasants, the Catholicism of the petty bourgeoisie and the town workers, the Catholicism of the women and the Catholicism of the intellectuals." The same could be claimed for Black America. The rural sharecroppers and urban poor are attracted to evangelical or fundamentalist denominations, with their physical and passionate expressions of faith and conversion. The Black working class for a century and more has consistently been Baptist and Methodist. The Black petty bourgeoisie are generally attracted to "high church" Anglicanism, Catholicism, Presbyterianism and Congregationalism. Substantial elements of the Black intelligentsia have been either Quakers, deists, agnostics or atheists. Nationalists have often been attracted to alternatives to Christianity, particularly Islam. Extreme integrationists have sometimes claimed Judaism. What unifies believers here is faith itself, "the most important element of a non-rational character" in all religious creeds.[47]

"But (faith) in whom and for what?" Gramsci asks. "The power of religion has consisted and does consist in the fact that they feel strongly the need for the doctrinal unity of the whole 'religious' mass, and struggle to prevent the superior intellectual elements detaching themselves from the inferior ones. The struggle has not always been fought without serious inconvenience for the church itself, but this inconvenience is connected with the historical process which transforms the whole of civil society and which *en bloc* contains a criticism destructive of religion."[48] Any and every religious organization is confronted with the problem of uneven ideological development and irregular commitments that the masses express toward the church and its dogma, an unevenness which is itself a direct product of class distinctions. Moreover, for historically oppressed groups, religion becomes a primary forum for the divisions that exploiters have pressed upon that people's socioeconomic reality. The church strives for unity in a material environment that cannot congeal itself.

The practical tasks of the Black Church have been (1) to provide an idealist, non-rational popular worldview to the Black masses, Christianity, which is achieved by the ritualistic acts of individuals who acknowledge Christ and the particular elements present within the theology of a denomination; (2) to preserve and to defend the actual material interests of one's congregation, and by extension, all Black people, by confronting the state apparatus, by taking calculated political risks, and by articulating the real grievances of Blacks from pulpits to public policy meetings; (3) to develop fraternal relations with white congregations and denominations, yet maintaining the unique character and independent spirit of the Black Church; and (4) to build cultural and social unity and a critical respect for Black history among Afro-Americans, while opposing the imposition of racial segregation, vigilante violence and racial hatred upon Blacks by whites. The Black Church is divided, because its *raison d'être* is divided. Confronting this nearly impossible challenge, Black churchmen have almost always set a series of priorities, either consciously or unconsciously. Those ministers who have emphasized material, day-to-day challenges of being Black in a racist/capitalist state, and those who have not hesitated to leave the cloistered halls of God to enter the turbulent and gritty realities of the streets are part of what I have called the tradition of Blackwater. Those ministers who emphasize prayer over politics, salvation over suffrage, the study of Ecclesiastes over the construction of economic cooperatives, represent the Other-Worldly position of Black faith. Both are legitimate and historically grounded within the Black Church, and are often expressed in contradictory ways by single individuals. The most conservative and accommodating Black itinerant preacher always has within him the capacity to become a Nat Turner.[49]

Both traditional perspectives within the Black Church are flawed, however. The basic contradiction evident within the most elementary kernel of Christian theology is that "despite everything," the evil of the world is rooted within man himself, "that is, (Christianity) conceives of man as a clearly defined and limited individual. Man is conceived of as limited by his individuality and his spirit as well." We are all our "brother's keepers;" neither "good works" nor our "faith" can erase the primal sin of another man/woman. Each individual who wishes to be "saved" must, through his /her own accord, confront Christ as his/her personal savior, or acknowledge that "there is but one God and that is Allah," etc. Gramsci argues, "it is precisely on this point that a change in the conception of man is required. It is essential to conceive of man as a series of active relationships (a process) in which individuality, while of the greatest importance, is not the sole element to be considered. . . . man changes himself, modifies himself, to the same extent that he is a nexus."[50]

The contemporary race/class crises within American society require that Black ministers confront the basic question that delienates humanity from all other forms of animal life—what is a human being, and what can hunanity become?[51] Man/woman is the product of many ideological, political and economic forces. But in the end, collectively, humanity creates itself, its institutions and its common sense. The internalized patterns of a people's history becomes the basis of their class consciousness. By transforming ourselves, and our consciousness, we begin to make history. The next great challenge, the battle for socialism, will force the Black Church to place the collective needs of Black humanity ahead of the narrow individual needs of any single person. Whether the Black Church, and those courageous ministers who embody the militant tradition of Blackwater, can face this test remains to be seen.

Black ministers all too often have been content to interpret the scriptures in various ways and to preach salvation to the masses. The real point of Black faith, and the fundamental meaning of King's evolution toward more militant politics, is to change the conditions of the oppressed Black majority for the better. If Black ministers fail to learn from their own mistakes, they may as a social group decline still further in the esteem of their own people. If they succeed, they have the potential to spark anew the moral and ethical commitment that remains essential within the struggle against racism and capitalist exploitation. It is entirely possible that the most decisive ally of the Black working class in its struggle for democratic socialism, at least among the Black elite, will be the Black Church.

CHAPTER EIGHT

THE DESTRUCTION OF BLACK EDUCATION.

The chief difficulty with the education of the Negro is that it has been largely imitation of his mind. Somebody outside of the race has desired to try out on Negroes some experiment which interested him and his coworkers; and Negroes, being objects of charity, have received them cordially and have done what they required. In fact, the keynote in the education of the Negro has been to do what he is told to do. Any Negro who has learned to do this is well prepared to function in the American social order as others would have him.

Carter G. Woodson, *The Mis-Education of the Negro* (Washington, D.C.: Associated Publishers, 1933), p. 134.

I

The demand for Black education has probably been the most enthusiastically supported political reform among Afro-American people, from slavery to the present. Unlike "Black Capitalism," which appealed only to the Negro entrepreneur and segments of the Black nationalist faction, the call for increased state support for Black educational institutions has been a universal concern among all classes. The historical reasons for this can be stated briefly. Less than 10 percent of all former slaves in 1865 were literate.[1] White racists

215

from George Fitzhugh in the 1850s to George Wallace in the 1960s saw the Blacks' demand for access to the schoolhouse as a threat to the preservation of white supremacy. Free Blacks in the antebellum South who learned to read by various means usually hid this explosive secret from their masters—for obvious reasons. After the Civil War, Black women, men and children recognized that their lack of education permanently restricted them to a life of agricultural penury and economic exploitation. As DuBois observed, "there is no doubt but that the thirst of the Black man for knowledge—a thirst which has been too persistent and durable to be mere curiosity or whim—gave birth to the public free-school system of the South. It was the question upon which Black voters and legislators insisted more than anything else."[2] Primary, secondary and university-level education was viewed as a decisive means to end the vicious cycle of racial underdevelopment.

Historically, the Black college is largely the direct product of racial segregation. Ninety-one of the 107 Black colleges were established before 1910. Generally underfinanced and inadequately staffed, Black higher education was permitted to exist only in skeletal form during the long night of white supremacy. As late as 1946, only four Black colleges—Howard University, Fisk University, Talladega College and North Carolina State—were accredited by the Association of American Universities. In the school year 1945–1946, Black undergraduate enrollment was 43,878 in the Black colleges. Less than 1,800 attended Black professional schools; only 116 were then training to become lawyers. Even after the passage of expanded educational legislation, the number of Afro-Americans who were financially able to attend universities was pitifully small. By 1950, 41,000 "minority" men and 42,000 "minority" women (Blacks, Asians, etc.) between ages 18–24 attended colleges, about 4.5 percent of the total Black age grouping. That same year, by way of contrast, 1,025,000 white males between 18–24 years old attended college, 15 percent of the total white age group. The function of the Black college was, at least from the view of white society, to train the Negro to accept a "separate and unequal" position within American life.[3] (See Table XXVII)

Despite these institutional barriers to quality education, the Black schools did a remarkable job in preparing Black youth for productive careers in the natural and social sciences, the trades and humanities. A brief review of one Black college, Fisk University, provides an illustration. Fisk was the home for a major number of Black intellectuals during the era of segregation: DuBois, historian John Hope Franklin; sociologist E. Franklin Frazier; artists/novelists James Weldon Johnson, Arna Bontemps, Sterling Brown, Nikki Giovanni, John Oliver Killens, and Frank Yerby. A number of other Fisk alumni joined the ranks of the Black elite in the twentieth century as decisive leaders in public policy, representing a variety of political tendencies: U.S. Representative William L. Dawson; **Marion Barry,** mayor of Washington, D.C.; Wade H. McCree, U.S. Solicitor General during the Carter Administration; U.S. district judge Constance Baker Motley; civil rights activist John Lewis; Texas State Representative Wilhelmina Delco; Federal judge James Kimbrough. Other Fisk graduates moved into the private sector to establish an economic program for Black development along capitalist lines, such as A. Maceo Walker, president of Universal Life Insurance Company. And, within the profressions, one out of every six Black physicians, lawyers and dentists in the United States today are Fisk graduates. A similar profile could be obtained from Atlanta University, Morehouse College of Atlanta, Spelman College of Atlanta, Tougaloo College of Mississippi, Tuskegee Institute of Alabama, Howard University of Washington, D.C., and other Black institutions of higher learning.

My point here is not that these schools ever developed a clear pedagogy for Black liberation, nor that they were organically linked to the daily struggles of the Black masses. The conservatism of many Black college administrators, as represented by Tuskegee's Booker T. Washington, is almost legend among Black people. These schools operated under the rigid constraints of race/class tyranny, and often suffered under benign-to-malignant administrations imposed by white trustees and state governments. But despite these and other contradictions, the Black universities have on the balance been much more open to progressive and liberal faculty—particularly during the period of the Cold War of the 1940s and 1950s. They created the intellectual and social space necessary for the development of militant political reformers, dedicated public school teachers, physicians, and other skilled professionals within the Black community. Without such institutions, the nightmare of Jim Crow might still exist, and the material conditions of the Black ghetto and working class would unquestionably be worse.

The Civil Rights and Black Power Movements, combined with a political shift of the U.S. government under the Johnson

Administration toward implementation of some affirmative action guidelines within white civil society, accelerated this educational process. By 1970, 192,000 Black men and 225,000 Black women between ages 18–24 attended college. The overall percentage of Black youth enrolled in college, 15.5 percent, contrasted with white attendance figures of 34 percent for males and 21 percent for females. Five years later, 294,000 Black men and 372,000 Black women between ages 18–24 were in college, respectively 20 and 21 percent of their age groups. The most recent available statistics, for the years 1976 and 1977, reveal a slight decline in Black college enrollment—a testament to the political assaults against Black educational opportunity of the 1970s. The total numbers of Black college youth slipped from 749,000 to 721,000, and the percentage of Black men who were college students within the 18–24 age group declined from 22.0 to 20.2 percent. Despite the desegregation of white universities, traditionally Black institutions, both private and public, continue to serve a majority of Blacks seeking college or professional training. Twenty-five percent of all Blacks in higher education attend the 35 state-supported Black colleges. Sixty-two percent of all Black M.D.'s and 73 percent of all Black Ph.D.'s are products of Black institutions.[4] (See Table XXVIII)

For those Black students who did not go on to Black colleges but who struggled within the white university, a number of searching political, historical and cultural questions were raised—inquiries that could not be easily answered by the sterile discourse or conservative pedagogy of these white institutions. The struggle from the streets of America suddenly scaled the walls of the academy. "In the mid- and late 1960s, at the height of the burnings and when the assassinations sent death and rage through each of our hearts, we said we knew that we were inseparable from the searing life of the Black community," reflected historian Vincent Harding. "When the students rose on the campuses and demanded our presence, or pressed for greater visibility and recognition for our work, we claimed, with them, indissoluble bonds to the heaving life of the Black masses."[5] The entire story of the Black Student Movement—the takeovers of computer centers, academic buildings and student unions; the creation of Black Student Unions and Black Cultural Centers; the emergence of Black nationalist ideology within the potential Black petty bourgeois stratum—remains to be told. It is sufficient to note that most white universities reacted first with fear, then anger, then finally with quiet calculation in the face of the Black revolt. Most white academicians viewed Black Studies as a tactical retreat on their part, an institutional maneuver to guarantee Black quiescence for a period of years. By the early and mid-1970s, many Black programs were reduced or eliminated entirely.[6]

The demand for Black Studies was also a call toward the systemic reconstruction of American learning. Its most advanced advocates understood that the study of the African diaspora and its people could not simply be "added" into the standard curricula, merged within the mainstream of white thought. Rather, the social science, literary and creative contributions of Blacks to the whole of human knowledge charted new and different directions of critical inquiry. First, Black Studies demanded a pedagogical approach toward learning that de-emphasized the "banking" concept of teaching, and advanced mixed methodological techniques, such as discussion, informal lecturing, debate and community studies. Black Studies theoreticians declared that interdisciplinary approaches toward learning were superior to narrow, selective teaching methods which concentrated on one single subject (e.g., history) at the exclusion of other related disciplines (sociology, political theory, political economy). Students were urged to devote some of their research activities towards the transformation and liberation of their own communities. Thus there was a basic relationship between theory and practice in the learning process that was missing from traditional white education. Students were urged to become active participants in their own education. For these theoretical and pedagogical reasons, therefore, Black Studies represented a basic and provocative challenge to the *raison d'être* of white universities.

But it was in the field of Black history that Black Studies evoked the greatest challenge to white bourgeois ideological hegemony. Prior to the 1960s, white historians approached the issue of race via two overlapping methods. The first approach, favored by ideological conservatives, could be termed "The Negro-as-Invisible Man." This school suggested that "the Negro had no history;" race relations studies, although interesting, properly belonged to the "secondary" discipline of sociology. Booker T. Washington and George Washington Carver were Negroes whose moderation merited some attention, but not W.E.B. DuBois, Henry Highland Garnet or Marcus Garvey. The Civil War was interpreted as a sectional conflict sparked by disagreements over tariff regulations. The second approach, advanced ideologically by Cold War liberals, argued that the Negro had always been part of the Great American Melting Pot. The "patriotic" exploits of Crispus Attucks, Salem Poor and Peter Salem were invariably mentioned in texts on the American Revolution. The historical fact that more Afro-Americans fought with the British than on the side of the colonial rabble, and that over 25,000 former slaves departed the U.S. with the British army in 1781–83, was relegated to the dusty footnotes. The liberals maintained that, despite slavery and segregation, the Negro people had proven themselves as loyal Americans. A testimony to the liberal belief in the "Americanization" of the Negro is provided in Kenneth Stampp's classic *The Peculiar Institution* (1956). With some pride, Stampp wrote, "I have assumed that the slaves were merely ordinary human beings, that innately Negroes *are,* after all, only white men with black skins, nothing more, nothing less."

From the late nineteenth century, Black historians challenged both positions with intellectual courage and historiographical skill. George Washington Williams' *History of the Negro Race in America,* published in 1882, was the first exhaustive critique of the inferior position of Blacks in the U.S. This pioneering study was followed by William T. Alexander, *History of the Colored Race in America* (1887); Harold M. Tarver, *The Negro in the History of the United States* (1905); Benjamin Brawley, *A Short History of the American Negro* (1913); and Willis D. Weatherford, *The Negro from Africa to America* (1924). The most important works were produced by Carter G. Woodson, *The Negro in Our History* (1922), and by DuBois: *The Negro* (1915); *Black Reconstruction in America* (1935); and *Black Folk, Then and Now* (1939). These works set the direction for a new generation of Black and white historians writing after World War II.

Thus, by the late 1950s many white historians had begun to view the Negro as "the creator of his own history." This recognition of the legitimacy of the Black past was fatally flawed by an idealistic approach toward historiography. Black "heroes" were popularized as contributors to American civilization. The pharoahs and the pyramids were illustrative of early Black genius—without the observation that these societies were based on slave labor and financed by the systematic plundering of the Black Sudan. Black inventors like Jan E. Matzeliger and Granville T. Woods were discussed as making "contributions toward the growing industrialization of America," in the words of John Hope Franklin—without the recognition of the role of modern industrial capitalism as a socially disruptive force. From this vantage point, the history of the Black national minority group becomes devoid of struggle as the central motif. It was the conceptual framework designed to serve the secular goal of integrating petty bourgeois Blacks into late capitalist civil and political society.

The Black Power Movement brought these schools of interpretation to a temporary halt. For young Black historians and social scientists—Vincent Harding, Lerone Bennett, Sterling Stuckey, David Lewis, Robert Allen, William Strickland, and many others—the history of Black people was a history of continuous struggle. Their research was rooted in the philosophical concept that human beings collectively made their own history. Always in the face of adversity, often betrayed by their own leaders and the petty bourgeoisie, the Black majority fought to maintain its unique identity as a people and to secure by whatever means the economic and political tools for self-determination and self-reliance. The chief shortcoming of this school of Black historiography was, in retrospect, its lack of institutionalization. Few Black publishing houses were created in the 1960s or early 1970s; the emergence of the Institute of the Black World in Atlanta was one of the rare instances where Black activist/intellectuals could find the creative space to produce their works. By the mid- to late 1970s many white publishers ceased to solicit Black manuscripts, and the number of Black Studies and Black historical journals began to recede. The Black petty bourgeois stratum, the chief beneficiary of the affirmative action quotes of the 1960s, failed to provide adequate material resources for Black intellectual and cultural workers. Many Black social scientists who vowed never to teach at white universities during the nationalistic era found themselves within the confines of the white academy by the 1980s.

Desegregation proved to be both a blessing and a curse. It created the conditions for a virtual revolution in Black educational opportunities. Simultaneously, the liberalization of white educational institutions permitted many of the best Black intellectuals to leave the South for more prestigious posts at Northern and West Coast universities. The generation of Black middle class professionals trained at Howard and Fisk in the 1940s sent their children to Harvard and Berkeley. The Black Power explosion of white campuses from the mid-1960s to early 1970s accelerated the crisis as the most militant and progressive Black professionals began to work in Afro-American studies departments on white campuses.

The rapid growth of state-supported, two-year colleges and vocational schools in the 1960s and 1970s also contributed to the financial crisis of private Black institutions. By 1978, 41.8 percent of all Blacks were enrolled in two-year degree programs, vs. 34 percent for whites. The number of white students transferring or applying to Black campuses jumped sharply. For example, by 1981 the white enrollment at the engineering school at previously all-Black North Carolina Agricultural and Technical State University in Greensboro reached 40 percent. On the other hand, first-generation college students from low-to-middle-income Black families could not afford to pay the higher tuitions at private Black colleges. Private foundations cut back sharply in their donations to Black schools after the recession of 1973–1974. By the late 1970s, the traditionally Black colleges were facing the mounting financial costs of even maintaining essential services and buildings without sufficient support within the Black community as a whole.[7]

II

One of the many promises made by Presidential-hopeful Ronald Reagan early in 1980 was a commitment "to improve and to defend" traditionally Black colleges. Unlike President Carter and independent candidate John Anderson, Reagan made substantial overtures to Black educators and administrators at predominantly Black Southern institutions. Reagan's chief Black aide, Art Fletcher, was the former executive director of the United Negro College Fund. The Republican nominee openly embraced the Black College Day demonstration held in Washington, D.C. on September 19, 1980, and charged that "the Carter Administration—in the name of desegregating Black colleges—is forcing them to become schools for training everybody but Blacks." Reagan also promised to encourage corporations to increase their financial support for Black universities and pledged "to work to increase the share of Title III budget allocated to Black colleges."

Under Carter's Administration, Black colleges received a smaller percentage of federal funds going to all universities than the Nixon-Ford years. Black educators had denounced Carter's intention to desegregate two Black Texas colleges, Southern and Prairie View. By late 1979, *Washington Post* columnist William Raspberry expressed the widely held view among Blacks that Administration officials "are unfamiliar with the historical role of these (traditionally Black) colleges and are indifferent to the vital service they perform." Given this recent history, many Black college administrators perceived that Reagan's election would mean a real advance for Black higher educational opportunities, despite his economic austerity program and conservative social policies.[8]

The Reagan Administration's first important announcement concerning the fate of Black colleges occurred, appropriately enough, at Tuskegee Institute. Institute President Luther Foster had invited Reagan to be the principal speaker at the April 12, 1981 "Founder's Day" program, marking the one-hundredth anniversary of Tuskegee. Reagan's hospitalization forced Vice President George Bush to substitute for the chief executive. Bush did not disappoint his Black audience. Before 3,000 people, the Vice President declared that his administration is "absolutely committed to supporting the nation's civil rights laws and to providing the resources necessary to make those laws work fairly and effectively for all Americans. We are committed to the principle of equal justice under the law." Interrupted repeatedly by loud applause, Bush promised to pressure public and private sources to grant greater financial support to traditionally Black universities. Bush was silent on whether the Reagan Administration would support the extension of the 1965 Voting Rights Act. But college administrators and local Black elected officials were generally pleased. Tuskegee mayor Johnny Ford stated that Bush's speech was "welcome by all of us who walked across the Edmund Pettus bridge" in nearby Selma, in the fight for Black equal rights and education.[9]

During the spring and summer, 1981, the Reagan Administration worked aggressively to draft less stringent terms for integration within state-funded higher education programs. By mid-August, agreement for Florida, North Carolina, South Carolina, Missouri, Louisiana, and West Virginia were completed which would leave the old segregation era Black and white institutions virtually intact. In general, the plans eased pressures on the formerly whites-only systems to hire additional Black faculty and staff, and cut back any additional Black supervision within the governance of state universities. They also included provisions to improve both the academic program and physical facilities available at formerly all-Black colleges. The announcement of the newly relaxed desegregation policies had an immediate impact upon several court cases. Louisiana and Mississippi had consistently refused to alter their dual college systems, and were sued by the Federal

Government for failing to enforce Title VI of the 1964 Civil Rights Act, barring racial discriminations. The Louisiana case was postponed as state and Federal officials were redrafting a settlement based on the North Carolina model.[10]

The North Carolina agreement which was approved by Federal District Judge Franklin Dupree in Raleigh on July 10, after eleven years of litigation, quickly became the basic document for all other Southern states. The plan kept the dual educational system intact, and had no provisions which would upgrade or expand master's or doctoral programs at Black universities. It ignored any quotas for the hiring of minority faculty and staff at North Carolina's white universities. The plan committed the state to allocate $80 million "to upgrade the physical plants and academic programs" at the Black institutions, and provided some modest affirmative action guarantees to expand the number of Black graduate students in both systems. The plan also forbade the Federal government from suing North Carolina officials over the agreement for five years.[11]

The North Carolina plan was quickly denounced as a return to "separate but equal" by the NAACP Legal Defense and Educational Fund, Inc., by former Carter Administration officials, and by Black alumni organizations from the traditional Black colleges in North Carolina. Leonard L. Haynes, director of the Office for the Advancement of Public Negro Colleges, informed the *New York Times* that the Reagan Administration "let North Carolina do whatever it wanted to do, thus abdicating its responsibility to enforce Title VI." Defenders of the agreement included all five Black chancellors of the state universities, and probably a majority of the Black college administrators and officials in the country. Clarence Thomas, a Black conservative attorney from Georgia who was appointed by Reagan as the Department of Education's Assistant Secretary for Civil Rights, justified the plan with the remark that "government fiat is not the only way to enforce civil rights laws." The road toward desegregation, initiated by the 1954 Brown decision, returned full circle to the Tuskegee-inspired dual educational structure.[12]

Yet Bush's address at Tuskegee Institute had a disturbing historical precedent. In November, 1898, another conservative Republican, William McKinley, made a political sojourn to that Black college community. Tuskegee Institute President Booker T. Washington had come to national prominence several years before by issuing his

"Atlanta Compromise" address which accepted the legal segregation of the races in return for Black economic and educational benefits. McKinley applauded Washington as "one of the great leaders of his race" and stated that Tuskegee Institute was a "generous and progressive" model for all Black education. McKinley's speech, like Bush's, was primarily symbolic, yet both provided political support for the construction and maintenance of all Black educational institutions. Within three years after McKinley's Tuskegee visit, Blacks were completely disfranchised in the state of Alabama, and the rule of "separate but equal" had become institutionalized throughout the South. The dual system of segregated higher education would exist for over sixty years. Would history repeat itself?[13]

III

It is from this perspective of history that the North Carolina agreement must be judged. The state acquired the reputation as the most "liberal" throughout the South in its policies on Black public education. The first Black colleges in North Carolina, Barber-Scotia in Concord, Shaw University and St. Augustine's in Raleigh, and Johnson C. Smith in Charlotte, were started immediately after the Civil War. The number of schools expanded rapidly with the emergence of Jim Crow laws. Today, there are more Black colleges in North Carolina with substantial state support than in any other state. Nevertheless, Southern liberals always justified the necessity for state-supported Black higher education as a defense of white supremacy. In 1903 Gustavus R. Glenn, former Georgia public schools superintendent and an administrator of the Peabody Fund, informed a joint session of the North Carolina legislature that "the colored man will only be a danger to us when we leave him to be educated by outside philanthropists. You need not be afraid of the negro boy. It will take him a thousand years to get where your boy is." This racist tradition was preserved into the 1950s, when North Carolina Senator Sam Ervin drafted a "Southern Manifesto," asserting the intention to use every legal tactic to halt public school desegregation.[14]

Caught in a seemingly hopeless dilemma, Black educators opted for what could be termed the lesser of two evils. An acceleration of the desegregation process would, in their view, simply transform traditionally Black colleges into majority white institutions. The North

Carolina agreement, and others like it, promised to halt the growing numbers of white faculty, administrators and students of Black campuses, while providing millions of dollars for sorely needed physical plant expansion and research. Like Booker T. Washington, these college administrators are political accommodationists, and insist that the national mood has become profoundly conservative on racial matters. When the House of Representatives voted 265 to 122 on June 9, 1981, to prohibit the Justice Department from pursuing court cases that would lead to the busing of school children to promote desegregation, for example, it had a direct impact upon Black higher education officials' willingness to conciliate with Reagan's agenda.[15]

The first real effects of the North Carolina agreement were a shock to Black college teachers. On August 24–25, 1981, between 70 to 90 instructors and assistant professors at North Carolina Central University were ordered to complete their doctoral degrees *by November 30, 1981.* Failure or inability to do so, under the terms of the consent decree, means that junior faculty members' contracts "would not be renewed and that they would not be considered for reappointment." The letter, signed by Vice Chancellor Charlie L. Patterson at Durham, was intended "to intensify the pressure" on mostly Black junior faculty members to complete their degree work. The agreement which promised to defend the legal and political stability of Black colleges quickly promised to radically transform them. As history professor Sylvia M. Jacobs complained, "I had no idea whatsoever that the results of a consent degree would be so extreme. It is feasible that under this policy, in the next two years we could have a predominantly white faculty" at North Carolina Central.[16]

The only possibility to save the traditionally Black institutions without another "Atlanta Compromise" would be to reject both the liberal integrationist approach and the neo-segregationist North Carolina agreement. It is imperative that white higher educational systems be forced to accept strict quotas in hiring Black faculty and administrators, and that duplicate programs offered at various schools be eliminated. At the same time, traditionally Black public institutions should not be forced to integrate faculty and student bodies at a rate faster than white state universities have done. Black private colleges *must remain Black,* to fulfill their historic mandate of providing quality education to Black people. Given the absence of a radical Black critique in Black higher education circles, however, the prospects for the destruction of the remaining Black universities and a concomitant drop in the total number of Blacks admitted to all colleges are now very real.

IV

Nonwhite education, whether within the colonial administrations of preindependent Africa, or in the United States, has expressed a consistent duality of purpose. Capital accumulation within the Black community required the training of a select number of Blacks to fill positions in the economy. But to guarantee that their essential authority over Blacks could not be challenged, white educators deliberately and systematically fostered a pedagogy for Black subservience to capitalism. This process of educational underdevelopment was never entirely successful. As Walter Rodney asserted:

> However much the colonialists tried, they could not succeed in shaping the minds of *all* the Africans whom they educated in schools. The most timid and the most brainwashed of educated Africans harboured some form of disagreement with the colonialists; and, in the pursuit of their own group or individual interests, the educated elite helped to expose and undermine the structure of colonial rule . . . (Colonial education) produced many 'loyal Kikuyu,' 'Capicornists,' (and) 'Anglophies' . . . but it also produced *in spite of itself* those Africans whom the colonialists called 'upstarts,' 'malcontents,' 'agitators,' 'communists,' 'terrorists,' etc. Students who were taken to universities in the metropoles were most favoured and the most pampered of Africans selected by the white colonial overlords to become Europeans; and yet they were among the first to argue vocally and logically that liberty, equality and fraternity about which they were taught should apply to Africa. [17]

The entire history of Black education is filled with examples which illustrate the central dynamic of Black civil society, the dual tendencies toward protest and accommodation. Washington and many Black educators consistently urged Black students and workers to "maintain peaceful and friendly relations with the best white people in the community who give our race employment and pay their wages."[18] Other Black educators such as DuBois "saw education (to be truly education) as partisan and—given the realities of the social order— fundamentally subversive," writes Herbert Aptheker.[19] Martin R. Delany was trained as a physician at Harvard; according to all white expectations, he should have become a non-threatening "credit to his race." Instead, this early nineteenth century product of the academy became an uncompromising abolitionist, a Black nationalist who declared that he "hoped the ground would refuse his body if a slaveholder crossed his threshold and he did not lay him a lifeless corpse at his feet."[20]

Thus the process of Black educational underdevelopment has returned in a fashion to its original premises: the overt suppression of independent Black educational institutions, and the elimination of Black educators who call for the transformation of the racist/capitalist order. This is the reason why Black Studies had to be uprooted; this is the motivation behind the liquidation of Black colleges and universities which were created, ironically, to perpetuate segregation and Black inferiority. The false boundaries of Western education, and the pedagogy for replicating bourgeois life and labor are a vital aspect of the hegemony of capital. When the Black student or scholar seeks "to build black institutions which maintain and press forward truth," in the words of Vincent Harding, he/she raises a problematic which cannot easily or quietly be resolved within the present, inhumane order. The Black school becomes the background for the construction of a new society.[21]

SECTION THREE

A QUESTION OF GENOCIDE.

CHAPTER NINE

THE MEANING OF RACIST VIOLENCE IN LATE CAPITALISM.

Fascism is a deformity of capitalism. It heightens the imperialist tendency towards domination which is inherent in capitalism, and it safeguards the principle of private property. At the same time, fascism immeasurably strengthens the institutional racism already bred by capitalism, whether it be against Jews (as in Hitler's case) or against African peoples (as in the ideology of Portugal's Salazar and the leaders of South Africa). Fascism reverses the political gains of the bourgeois democratic system such as free elections, equality before the law, parliaments, etc. . .

Walter Rodney, How Europe Underdeveloped Africa, p.216.

History has many cunning passages,
        contrived corridors
And issues, deceives with whispering ambitions,
Guides us by vanities. Think now
She gives when our attention is distracted
And what she gives, gives with such
        supple confusions
That the giving famishes the craving. Gives
        too late
What's not believed in, or is still believed,

In memory only, reconsidered passion. Gives too soon
Into weak hands, what's thought can be
  dispensed with
Till the refusal propagates a fear.

T. S. Eliot, "Gerontion," in *The Waste Land and Other Poems* (New York: Harcourt, Brace, Jovanovich, 1979), p. 20.

I

Throughout his long and brilliant career as both a social scientist and political militant, DuBois speculated that the final solution to racial conflict in America might be the complete extermination of the Black race. In "The Future of the Negro Race," published in January, 1904, DuBois thought that extinction or "migration to foreign lands" might await Afro-Americans.[1] Four decades later, in the pages of the *Amsterdam News,* DuBois shuddered at the horrors of the Nazi holocaust. "It is a case of race prejudice on a scale unknown and unconceived since the Emancipation Proclamation. What is happening to Jews," he warned, "may happen to us in the future. Unless (racism) is destroyed, rooted out, absolutely suppressed, modern civilization is doomed."[2] Black writers in the 1960s flirted with the possibilities of Black genocide and emigration from the United States, sometimes with a reluctant ambiguity. Harold Cruse wrote in *The Crisis of the Negro Intellectual* that Garveyism and "impractical Back-to-Africa" schemes were ventures into "romantic escapism; for if the Afro-American does not find his salvation in the United States he will find it nowhere." Yet in the same book, 104 pages later, Cruse asserted, "there may well come a time when the race question in Africa will have to be solved by admitting specified numbers of white Rhodesians, Angolans and South Afrikaners into the United States, in exchange for an equal number of Afro-Americans to take their places in Africa."[3] The most powerful thesis on the inevitability of whites' genocide of Blacks was Sidney M. Willhelm's *Who Needs The Negro?*

> The life situation of Black Americans deteriorates with the passing of each year . . . technological efficiency makes possible the full realization of the nation's anti-Negro beliefs. The arrival of automation eliminates the need for Black labor, and racist values call for the Negro's removal from the American scene. . . As the races pull apart into life styles with greater polarity, the

Black ghetto evolves into the equivalent of the Indian reservation. What is the point, demands White America, in tolerating an unwanted racial minority when there is no economic necessity for acceptance. With machines now replacing human labor, who needs the Negro?[4]

The historical predictions of race war, genocide and destruction, the darkest fears of previous Black generations, seemed to many to have become reality in the 1980s. Beginning with the public execution of five members of the Communist Workers Party by Ku Klux Klansmen and Nazis on November 3, 1979 in Greensboro, North Carolina, there was an acceleration of racist violence across the country.[5] Traditional leaders of the Black elite were convinced that "an informal coalition of white racist vigilantes, the police and government officials were conspiring to kill Blacks." Jesse Jackson declared to the *New York Times* in late November, 1980, that "there is almost a hysteria in Black communities because of the belief that there is a conspiracy. This country has taken a definite swing toward fascism."[6] Even Blacks who discounted the possibility of a "national conspiracy to murder Blacks" usually prefaced their statements with the admission that "racism in the form of violence is sweeping the country."[7]

Incidents of brutal violence against Blacks are reported infrequently. What usually is portrayed as an unusual or bizarre example of racism is only a small portion of the human tragedy. The lynching of nineteen-year-old Michael A. Donald in Mobile, Alabama, in March, 1981, was publicized as the first in the Deep South since the murder of Emmett Till in 1955.[8] Almost completely ignored or suppressed by the white media were a series of barbaric incidents that have occurred in that region since 1979. In May, 1981, the *Jackson Advocate* reported in Mississippi alone there have been twelve murders "in as many months which are suspected by Blacks of being (racially motivated)." The tortured body of one unidentified Black man was found floating down a river in Cleveland, Mississippi. The man's sex organs had been hacked off, and the coroner later reported finding his penis in his stomach. On January 11, 1981, the body of 45-year-old Lloyd Douglas Gray was found hanging from a tree in Tallahatchie County, Mississippi. A. W. Hulett, Tallahatchie coroner, pronounced Gray's death a suicide, and no autopsy was performed. On February 28, 1981, the body of 32-year-old Roy Washington was found in Cypress Creek, in Holmes County, Mississippi. Washington had been "badly beaten in the head and face," his hands bound behind him, and then shot in the head at point-blank range. The corpse was weighed down with a scissor jack and wrapped by barbed wire. Scars around his neck indicated that he had also been lynched. Local white newspapers were silent on the murder. Police did not aggressively pursue leads in the case, and even followed a Black reporter around while he conducted his own investigation. The majority of the other Black men who have been found beaten or hanging in Mississippi counties have also been officially labeled suicides. Familiar with the pattern of racial violence, one Black resident of Tallachatchie County declared, "if they say it was suicide, it was probably a lynching."[9]

Reaganites, Black and white, attempted to counter the growing perception that racism was out of control. Edwin Meese III, chief Presidential adviser, deplored the public statements of Jackson and others. "I guess what does disturb me, not from that standpoint of this administration as much as from society in general," he stated, "is that I think there are those people who are fomenting Black hysteria in order to preserve their own positions of so-called leadership." Many Black journalists agreed with Meese's condemnation of Black leadership. "The 1980 elections once again demonstrated that the group that designates itself as the Black leaders spent its political capital on a losing Democratic candidate and the failed politics of branding the winner as a warmongering racist," argued columnist Tony Brown. "As a result, there are fewer media opportunities, therefore a declining popularity for some of the traditional leaders." Both Brown and Meese concluded that "Black leaders were promoting hysteria for personal and selfish motives."[10]

Only one instance of random violence against Blacks in the early 1980s attracted international attention—the systemmatic murders of at least 28 young men and children in Atlanta. The immediate questions that virtually every American asked—Who are the killers? What has the city government and police done to thwart the murders?—became almost secondary considerations. Neither the conviction of Wayne Williams, charged with the murder of two Black youth, nor the entry of the FBI in the case reduced the anxiety of millions of Black parents for the safety of their children. Why was Atlanta the site of these bizarre and inexplicable deaths? Were the murders only one small part of a pattern of racial violence which constitutes a national conspiracy? How have different social strata within the Black community responded politically to the killings?

Modern Atlanta is the product of the infusion of monopoly capital into a rapidly changing racial and political milieu. Until the Civil Rights Movement, the piedmont and Blackbelt South's central means of production were predominantly agricultural, construction and light industry. During the 1950s and 1960s Georgia experienced a massive economic transformation. The number of Black-owned and operated farms in the state dropped from 12,049 to 4,450 between 1954 to 1969, as agribusiness increased. Atlanta became a glittering convention center, and headquarters for virtually every major corporation in the Southeast. Jim Crow was gradually abandoned as Blacks comprised 51 percent of the city's population by 1970. Atlanta's Black elite, allied with liberal elements of the city's white private sector, successfully challenged the older racist hierarchy to become the new managers of the political apparatus. Maynard Jackson was elected mayor in 1973. By the mid-1970s the city projected the image of a successful, pro-business, biracial community. [11]

Unresolved socioeconomic tensions created by the new realities of modern capital expansion and the older patterns of white Southern racism finally exploded in the late 1970s. Almost one quarter of Atlanta residents now exist below the poverty level. 26 percent of all households heads were unemployed in 1978. In recent years large numbers of middle-to-upper income whites fled to the suburbs. Between 1970-1980, 102,000 whites left Atlanta, and Blacks became two-thirds of the city's population. Incidents of violence between the remnants of the old segregationist police force and Blacks became more frequent. In 1973 and 1974, 23 Blacks were gunned down by police; 12 were under 14 years old. In the mid-1970s, Atlanta had the highest per capita police killings of civilians in the U.S. By 1979, Atlanta surpassed Detroit as the city with the highest murder rate in America. [12]

Black Atlantans were poorly prepared to deal with their childrens' murders. The Black ministers and religious leaders, the backbone of the Black community's Civil Rights Movement, at first showed little concern in the case. Community groups did nothing to help resolve local tensions until the summer and autumn months of 1980. As the number of victims mounted, criticisms were raised against the Black petty bourgeoisie, and observers commented that only poor Black children were being singled out by the killer or killers. The local white-owned media branded the Jackson Administration hopelessly inept and promoted the racial slur that Blacks were intellectually incapable of governing a major metropolis. Television stations competed with each other to project tactlessly the anguish of Black parents, turning funerals into circus sideshows. One group of white patrolmen leaked to the media their view that Black police and government officials were simply "too stupid to solve the case." By the winter of 1981 Atlanta was by all accounts "a city under seige." Small schoolchildren from poor and middle class Black neighborhoods were actually arming themselves in school with homemade weapons. The white business community was convinced that a "racial blow-up would occur if a white was charged with the murders." Promising over 8,000 more jobs for inner city youths, the Atlanta Chamber of Commerce actually delivered only 2,000. Police repression escalated everywhere. 1,500 children in February, 1981, and 4,670 children in March, 1981, were stopped by authorities for violating a 7 p.m. citywide curfew. Ordered to cooperate with local officials, the FBI promptly infuriated Blacks by suggesting that some of the victims' mothers may have been the killers. With the arrest of Williams, the FBI left the city, and the attention of white capitalist America moved elsewhere.[13]

Most Blacks recognized that the Atlanta murders signified a new level of terrorism which suppressed Black social and political development. Whether the racial identity of the killers was Black or white became secondary to what Jesse Jackson termed the conviction that "there is a cultural conspiracy to kill Black people."[14] Blacks in Atlanta's Techwood Homes public housing project, armed with baseball bats and revolvers, organized self-defense patrols. Techwood community leader Israel Green stated that patrols were needed to protect the project's youth from "the crazed racist killers."[15] Blacks and progressive whites organized solidarity demonstrations against the Atlanta murders across the nation. On March 13, 1981, almost 20,000 people marched down Harlem's Lenox Avenue in a candlelight demonstration. One reporter commented that "a certain religious atmosphere some organizers had called for, highlighted by candles, existed side by side with large pictures of Malcolm X, displays of revolutionary culture, and even an old 'Free the Panthers' banner from the sixties."[16] An Atlanta-based association of parents of murder victims, the Committee to Stop Children's Murders, held a protest rally at the Lincoln Memorial on May 25, 1981. The five thousand participants included Black and white hospital workers from District 1199 in New York City, members of the United Auto Workers Local 99, several locals of the American Federation of State, County and Municipal Employees, and the United Mine Workers. Significantly, neither Washington, D.C. mayor Marion Barry nor Atlanta's Black Brahmins attended the demonstration. Speakers at the gathering, from Jesse Jackson, Victor Goode, president of the National Conference of Black Lawyers, and Bernice Krawczwk of the UAW emphasized that Atlanta was "the product of a racist society."[17]

On several occasions Black speculation concerning the Atlanta crisis lapsed into a regrettable yet understandable (given the circumstances) level of paronoia. Social critic Dick Gregory developed a theory for the murders which asserted that "the missing children's bodies (are) drained of blood in order to create some miracle cure for cancer." Afro-Americans "have some special formula in their blood brought about because of the sickling traits which can be used in a formula to defeat cancer." Out of "sheer desperation," according to one Black source, some Blacks "have begun to accept Gregory's statement as fact and many (Black) Atlantans have begun to look strangely at all whites in the area."[18] At the Washington demonstration Ella Collins, the sister of Malcolm X, reiterated Gregory's theory. She charged that the murders were the "work of white scientists" who were "performing experiments to discover what made the Black man so superior that he was able to withstand the abuses of 400 years."[19] White journalists jumped at these and other statements to malign all progressive activities around the Atlanta murders. *Chicago Tribune* columnist Raymond Coffey denounced Collins' remarks as "dangerous, extremist, recklessly irresponsible, inflammatory, (and) abominably racist nonsense." The rally was a "political-racial-commercial jamboree," Coffey declared, dismissing the "End Genocide" placards carried by protestors as "preposterous." The Atlanta killings were not "racially motivated."[20] Without missing a beat, some influential Blacks parroted this line. *Big Red*, one of New York City's major Black newspapers' informed readers that "there is no reason to doubt that all that can be done is being done." Statements implying that "if those kids were white" that the crimes would be solved do "far more harm than good." Talk about Black armed self-defense or revolt "plays into the hands of right-wing and left-wing extremists, both of whom constantly seek ways to undermine democracy. We should avoid all the kind of loose talk which adds to the insanity which that tragedy represents."[21] Despite these arguments, the great majority of Blacks are now certain that the Atlanta murders will never be solved completely, and that the essense of the tragedy is both profoundly racial and political.

II

Atlanta represented the smallest fraction of random racist violence that had been mounting across the U.S. In every major city and small town, in virtually every part of the country, a shocking explosion of racist incidents occurred in the early 1980s. A small sample would include the following examples:

White police officers in New Orleans have shot at least 10 Blacks in 1980, killing eight. In one case, officers James Esposito and Robert Sedgeher shot Walter E. Brown on December 20, 1980, for cursing at them. They later resigned from the police force after admitting that they had planted a gun on Brown. An Orleans Parish grand jury cleared them of any wrong-doing.[22]

On March 16, 1981, police in Roseville, Michigan pursued three young Black men driving what the officers mistakenly believed to be a stolen automobile. After a highspeed chase, police officers Rafael Perez and Thomas Lavender pursued one of the Black men, 20 year old Theodoric Johnson. Both policemen fired, killing Johnson. According to the Reverend Timothy Chambers, who had witnessed the shooting, one of the policemen bragged to the other, "I blew that nigger's head off."[23]

Three Black women and one Black man were arrested in Summerville, South Carolina, on August 10, 1980, on shoplifting charges. The night of their transfer from the Summerville to Dorchester County Jail, police lieutenant Roger Hudson, 54 and white, forced the women "to perform sexual acts with and on him." The women filed charges through the sheriff's office charging Hudson with criminal sexual conduct, aggravated assault and official misconduct in office. A jury of ten whites and two Blacks acquitted Hudson. White jurors laughed and talked with Hudson, and the judge had told the jurors that "if (they) could not make up their minds, then the majority would rule." Two of the women and the man arrested for shoplifting were finally convicted and received sentences ranging from six to ten years.[24]

In early 1981, white police officers in northwest Florida and southeast Mississippi circulated a mock hunting regulation document announcing "open season" for shooting "Porch Monkeys." The flyer continued: "Regionally known as Negro, Nigger, Saucer Lips, Yard Apes, Jungle Bunnies, Spear Chunkers, Burr Heads, Spooks, and the Pittsburgh Pirates." It is "unlawful to shoot any Porch Monkey in a Cadillac," to "trap within 25 feet of watermelon patches, or to bait traps with "pork chops, watermelons, mangoes, collards, cheap whiskey, fried chicken, chitlings [sic] or flashy clothes."[25]

Cornelius Brown, a 42-year-old Black resident of Cleveland, was playing pool in a delicatessen on November 20, 1980. An off-duty white policeman, Napolean Dismuke, had left the pool table earlier and upon returning, demanded that Brown leave at once. Dismuke shot Brown with his .38 caliber revolver four times, killing him. Dismuke claimed that Brown had tried to assault him with a pool cue. In June, 1981, a jury found Dismuke innocent, and has since returned to active duty on the force.[26]

Leroy Perry, a 48-year-old Black resident of Annapolis, Maryland, was halted for suspected drunken driving on July 20, 1981, by a white officer, David Hodge. Hodge shot and killed Perry when the latter left his car and came out holding "an ice pick or a pistol." Actually Perry had been holding a screwdriver which he needed to pry open the trunk, in which the car's registration was kept.[27]

In Los Angeles, the police department was involved in a series of brutal citizen murders, where officers applied "chokeholds" across their victims' necks. In 1981 alone there were the following cases: Luel Marshall, 41 and Black, was stopped by police officers on February 3, 1981. While handcuffed, he was choked several times by police. Marshall suffered a massive heart attack, and died without gaining consciousness on March 17, 1981. Charles H. Hill, 40 and Black, was arrested after an altercation with police on March 14. Hill was beaten viciously with a baton and choked by officers. He subsequently stopped breathing in a Hollywood division cell tank prior to being booked, and was declared dead. The coroner's office declared that Hill had died from a "sickle cell crisis"! Arthur W. McNeil, 30 and Black, was arrested as a suspected prowler. Police choked McNeil, who died in a hospital on July 28. The coroner's inquest determined that McNeil died "at the hands of another, other than by accident," in February, 1982, and a $15 million lawsuit was filed against the city by McNeil's widow and daughter. When the press asked Daryl F. Gates, the police chief, why so many Blacks and Latinos were dying at the hands of his officers, he responded calmly that perhaps Blacks were not "normal people."[28]

There were also a series of inexplicable hangings in jails of perhaps four dozen Black men in 1981 alone. Three such examples include 19 year old Eric Boyd, charged with armed robbery, and lynched in a Chicago precinct jail cell on March 13; Cleophus Powell, 31, serving a 10 day sentence for shoplifting in Chickasaw, Alabama, on March 31; and Grant Lee, 19, arrested for driving a stolen car by Cleveland police, on April 22, and found strangled by his socks attached to a crossbar section of the jail cell door. In most cases, the Black men were in relatively good spirits when contacted by family or friends hours before their "suicides."[29]

Perhaps the largest number of racist incidents did not involve law enforcement officers at all, but were initiated by white youths. In 1981, there were at least 500 documented cases of random white teenage violence, including the following examples:[30]

The drowning of John Stencil, a Black freshman at Farleigh Dickenson University on April 11, 1981. Two white youths pushed Stencil into the Hackensack River as he sat on a bridge railing. Stencil reportedly "shouted to them that he could not swim but they went away." Hackensack prosecutor Roger Breslin, a white lawyer, termed the drowning an "accident."

Five white youths in a car attempted to run down three Black women in Far Rockaway, New York on February 28, 1981. Charged with attempted murder, the youths pleaded innocent and were released on only $5,000 bail.

Five young white men were arrested by Maryland State Police on June 1, 1981, and charged with conspiring to burn a cross on the lawn of Harford NAACP president Joseph Bond of Churchville.

Gary Allen Smith, a 24-year-old Black student at Morgan State University in Baltimore, was viciously attacked by eight white youths in June, 1981, after Smith had argued with a white female employee where he worked. Smith was beaten with pool cue sticks and suffered "a broken left arm, contusions and swelling of the brain."

Three white men, ages 19, 21, and 23 tossed a pipebomb into the house of a Black Detroit family. Mrs. Synthia Steele had seen the bomb crash through the bathroom window, picked it up and was attempting to throw it away when it exploded in her hand. Three fingers of her right hand were blown off. The attack was the last in a series lasting two and a half years. Previously, white youths had thrown baseballs through Mrs. Steele's windows and painted KKK signs on her garage.

Michael Jarrett, a Black youth of 19, was killed by a gunshot wound to the head in Steubenville, Ohio on April 17, 1981, for allegedly dating white girls. Police traced the murder weapon to a white youth, who was eventually released. Over 500 people marched to protest police inaction in the case.

White students at Cass Technical High School in Detroit began calling themselves "the Junior KKKs" and "Baby Hitlers." In March 1981, the juvenile racists circulated white supremacist literature, spraypainted lockers with swastikas and assaulted a student with a knife.

At Wesleyan College, Connecticut, a racist campaign of terror mounted for months. White youths posted a series of "Wanted—Dead or Alive" flyers throughout the campus, with an ugly, twisted sketch of a spear-carrying Black man portrayed. One flyer charged "Jigaboo" with a variety of crimes, including "rape, murder, robbery. He (is) led by Communist Jews in a conspiracy to destroy America and the White race." Another flyer taunted: "All you fuckin' black sambos think you own the fuckin' campus—well I've got news for you. . . I hate you, Mr. Fuckin' nigger. Oh yes I do . . . get that white man's cock outta your mouth—I'm talkin to you. Mr. Nigger, you suck. You call yourselves brothers . . . well you're brothers of the gorillas. I have a dream . . . you-all gonna die in pain." Still another racist tract promoting a fraternity informed prospective white members that it was "dedicated to wiping all goddamned niggers off the face of the earth." By late October, 1981, KKK members visited Wesleyan's campus to recruit young racists.[31]

The number of random racist incidents intensified to such an extent that it became a "normal" part of daily life for Blacks in the United States. Few Black parents were not concerned about the safety of their children during the 1980s. Few Black women did not worry about the possibility that their husbands, fathers, lovers and/or sons might be killed that horribly mutilated in Buffalo and dozens of other American cities. Even while writing this chapter in late 1981, I happened to return to my office at the Africana Center, Cornell University, early one morning. The windows on the first-floor of the building were punctured by an air-rifle. On the front door was printed clearly a single word—"NIGGER."

III

Simple recognition of the explosion in racially motivated random violence is no substitute for an analysis of the crisis. The current outbreak of racist attacks is a manifestation of a profound and fundamental crisis within the political economy of monopoly capitalism. Simultaneously it represents the logical culmination and popular expression of cultural/social patterns of race relations that increasingly pits the petty bourgeoisie, working class, and permanently unemployed of different ethnic groups against each other over increasingly scarce resources. What many Blacks perceive as a "white conspiracy," in the words of Jesse Jackson, is in reality the conjuncture of racist ideological hegemony in the U.S., an acceleration of the use of physical coercion and terrorism against Blacks by both the coercive apparatuses of the state (e.g., the police) and by paramilitary racist groups (the Ku Klux Klan, and many others), *and the absence of a powerful, democratic and progressive movement by Blacks which challenges racism in the streets as well as in the courts.*

In economic terms, the early 1980s are characterized in part by the crisis of capital accumulation and the steady erosion in the standard of living of the white petty bourgeoisie. The number of small business failures, to cite one example, reached epidemic proportions. During the first week of October, 1981, 468 U.S. companies—dry cleaners, lumber mills, restaurants, retail stores—closed permanently. From September, 1980 to September, 1981, commercial and industrial failures exceeded 12,600, a 250 percent increase over the bankruptcy rate of 1978. Median U.S. family incomes grew from $7,500 in the mid-1960s to over $22,000 in 1981. But inflation climbed from only 2 percent in 1965 to over 12 percent in 1980, negating any real income gains. As a result, many "middle class" whites believe that the Federal government's deficit spending, Keynesian economic policies since the Great Depression, and national, state and local taxes are the reasons for their economic plight.[32]

In 1950 the U.S. manufacturing output totaled 62 percent of the combined output of the ten major capitalist nations. By 1965 the percentage dropped to 50 percent, and was 43 percent by 1976. A series of major bankruptcies and near-bankruptcies threatened to produce a chain of economic disasters, from Penn Central in 1970 to Chrysler, First Pennsylvania Bank and the Hunt brothers in 1980.[33] For the automotive retail industry, including parts suppliers, service stations, new and used car dealers and repair shops, bankruptcies in 1980 rose more than 96 percent. Personal bankruptcies in the U.S. increased from 179,223 in 1977 to over 450,000 in 1981, with projected losses to creditors in excess of $6.4 billion. For white middle class families, even their solitary hedge against inflation, the home, ceased to provide any real security in the early 1980s. After adjustment for inflation and financing discounts, the average price of homes fell 10 percent in 1981, "the steepest drop since the Depression," according to the *New York Times.* The number of mortgage foreclosures instituted on homes financed by the Federal Housing Administration was over 2,000 each month in 1981, a 30 percent increase over 1980.[34]

The crisis within capitalism is expressed within racial relations as a public repudiation of civil rights legislation passed in the 1960s and a vicious posture towards health care, welfare, job training and social service programs which benefit large numbers of Blacks and Hispanics. A decade ago, even so malignant a politician as Richard Nixon was forced to promote "Black Capitalism" by releasing Federal Reserve funds to Black-owned banks, appointing a moderate civil rights leader, James Farmer, to his cabinet, and expanding welfare and some social service programs. Under Reagan, all stops have been pulled. Daniel Moynihan's infamous 1970 memorandum to Nixon, justifying "benign neglect" of Blacks, has succumbed to a public policy posture which threatens to smash affirmative action, vocational programs, food stamps and a host of democratic reforms won by the Black masses over a half century of struggle.[35]

Within civil and political society, a series of "Green Lights" has been signaled since 1978 which have been largely responsible for unleashing the racist terror. The first was the Bakke decision, which crystalized the anxieties of millions of whites of declining socioeconomic status to blame their misfortunes upon a scapegoat—Blacks and Hispanics. "The wide publicity given to the relatively small number of affirmative action programs instituted by government, by private corporations, and by unions, as well as the publicity given to Bakke, provided a highly distorted picture of undeserved Black gains to many white Americans," states Michael Reich in *Racial Inequality.* "The perception offended many white Americans' ethic of fair treatment and led to charges of 'racism in reverse.' It also provided a simple and emotionally appealing explanation of one of the principal causes of the economic deterioration that many households were experiencing in the 1970s."[36]

The second "Green Light" was the vicious execution of five members of the Communist Workers' Party in Greensboro, North Carolina, November 3, 1979. The coordinated efforts of the Ku Klux Klan, American Nazi Party, and in all probability, the FBI and local law enforcement officers, were needed to blunt the momentum of antiracist forces in that state. Only sixteen of the forty racists were indicted, and just six were tried. One year later, the six white supremacists were declared innocent by an all-white jury. The lesson of Greensboro was not lost by any observer on the left. Marxist-Leninist journal *Line of March* noted grimly that "the state had given the Klan a hunting license against the anti-racist movement, particularly against *any* forces who attempted to link that movement up to a broader political perspective." In *Monthly Review,* Michael Parenti and Carolyn Kazdin charged that "the Klan and Nazis could not have done what they did in Greensboro had they not enjoyed the active support and passive complicity of state officials and agents. . . The Klan and Nazis were doing the work of the state."[37]

The third "Green Light" was the election of Ronald Reagan in November, 1980, which represented the culmination of a sixteen year effort by the Right (beginning with Goldwater's Presidential campaign in 1964) to capture the executive branch of government. Reagan's campaign was based upon the same putrid ideology of racism, limited Federal government, sexism, anticommunism and states' rights that catapulted George Wallace to national prominence in the 1960s. Unlike Wallace, Reagan was able to win over Wall Street and monopoly capital, while maintaining his electoral base among small businessmen and sectors of labor. His greatest public relations victory in the area of race relations was the creation of "Black Reaganism," that tendency of the Black petty bourgeoisie which supported his election. Thus Reagan's Administration pursues what objectively amounts to an unprecedent, racist assault against national minorities while simultaneously appointing Blacks to prestigous positions and disclaiming any racist intentions. Thomas Sowell, Ralph D. Abernathy, Tony Brown, Walter Williams, Nathan Wright, *ad nauseum* therefore became essential to the destruction of the Black community.

The rise of Reaganism in electoral politics now has permitted the Right to openly question the utility of democracy for the 1980s.

Whether Reagan's supply side version of restoring corporate profits or an alternative state-directed/corporatist strategy emerges which calls for the state to regulate prices and allocate government contracts to corporations which agree to reorganize themselves is almost a mute question. Marxist economist Sam Bowles was one of the first observers to note that either public policy strategy would be forced to impose massive political repression and civil terror upon workers. Thomas Weisskopf, writing in *Socialist Review,* suggested that the restoration of "a system more palatable to corporate capitalists, it might well be necessary to undermine the ability of others to function within that political framework. Such an effort at political repression could take the form of growing authoritarianism—the removal of major decisions from arenas where they are subject to some degree of popular influence. . ."[38] Following this line of reasoning, California State Senator John Schmitz, a former Congressperson and colonel in the Marine Corps reserves, openly advanced the probability of a military coup in the U.S. as "the best we could hope for." In the October 30, 1981 issue of the *Los Angeles Times,* Schmitz sketched the following scenario: "Reagan's programs fail, the economy disintegrates, people are rioting in the streets, the Russians plan an invasion to take advantage of the domestic strife, the military recognizes the threat and the coup occurs." Schmitz stated that the coup will happen within several years, "definitely by 1986."[39]

Rightwing ideologues are usually more tactful than Schmitz, but nevertheless are drawing similar conclusions. In a critically important essay published in the *Wall Street Journal* in October, 1979, Irving Kristol admitted a year before Reagan's election that his policies would be inadequate to resolve the crisis of capitalism. Kristol noted that an "increase in the growth of the private sector can be achieved only by a cut in tax rates for business" and upper-income families. "Truly massive cuts" in social and educational programs, and a balanced Federal budget, would also help. In short, Kristol called for an austerity agenda "which will put America through the wringer. There is only one country," he noted, "where this economic policy seems to be working. *That is Chile,* where the nation has indeed been 'put through the wringer' these past couple of years and where the economic outlook is steadily improving." Commenting lightly upon Chile's bloody military junta, Kristol observed, "it would be ironic if it turned out that free-market economics . . . could only be achieved at the expense of a free society."[40]

The function of the rise of racist attacks is the preparation of the ideological and cultural foundations necessary for a potential "Chilean Solution" to resolve the crisis of U.S. capitalism. This is *not* to predetermine the course of history. The capitalist ruling classes have not yet reached a stable consensus in their search for a strategy to accumulate capital and reduce Federal government intervention into the economy and society. Conversely, the emergence of a democratic and progressive front of national minorities, working people and the oppressed could reverse the present balance of forces. Another more probable option available to the state is the selection of key aspects of the "Chilean Solution" (e.g., brutal state repression of leftists, labor union activities, minorities) without moving toward the complete domination of the political apparatus by the Joint Chiefs of Staff and their subordinates. The open encouragement of police brutalities against Blacks by law enforcement officials and elected politicians, plus the proliferating civil violence by white youths and adults against nonwhites, sets the social and cultural climate necessary to establish an authoritarian regime. Whether this regime is "fascist" in the classical model of Nazi Germany, or "authoritarian," which would permit some democratic rights, could be simply a question of semantics.

Therefore, the existence of random violence against Blacks and civil terrorism is no accidental phenomenon. It is a necessary element in the establishment of any future authoritarian or rightwing government. Attacks by political rightists, small property owners and the police against workers and peasants in Chile during the early 1970s disrupted civil society and established the possibility for the military's coup over the democratic government of Salvador Allende in 1973. The fascist terrorism of Patria y Libertad, the Comando Rolando Matus of the rightist National Party and other paramilitary groups in Chile closely parallel the Ku Klux Klan, the American Nazi Party and other more mainstream, conservative, mass based forces in the U.S.[41] In the United Kingdom, the rapid growth of the rightist National Front, founded in 1967, the neoNazi British Movement and other racist parties constituted the essential right tendency for the emergence of Thatcherism. In late June, 1979, the chair of the National Front, John Tyndall, toured the U.S. at the invitation of the National States Rights

Party. The "keynote of the tour," according to one British journalist, "was the unification of the far-right" in both English-speaking countries. Both the National Front and the U.S. Right are characterized by "authoritarianism, ethnocentrism, racism, biological naturalism and anti-intellectualism." Both have had recent success in attracting "white youngsters," have leaderships which are "firmly middle-class," and endeavor politically to appeal to both the white urban working class, petty enterpreneurs, and sections of the police.[42] Thatcherism, like Reaganism, is "conservatism no longer content with pragmatism and compromise, vying with a social-democratic Labour Party for a middle ground, or with piecemeal retrenchment in public spending in the face of economic crisis."[43] Both reactionary political movements unleash and rely upon the Klan and National Front/type movements to obliterate any possibility of unity between Black and white workers.

By late 1981 the State's repression of the Black Liberation Movement became conspiciously more overt than covert. The fourth "Green Light" was the arrest of Fulani Sunni Ali on October 27, 1981. Between 150 to 200 Federal agents, "a phalanx of four armored cars and a helicopter" descended on her farmhouse residence in Gallman, Mississippi. Charged with complicity in the New York robbery of a Brink's trunk, Ali was arrested and held under $500,000 bond by Federal magistrate John Countiss. Her arraignment to New York was under such intense security that one official described the courtroom as an "armed fortress." The FBI's "frameup" failed when witnesses testified that she was in New Orleans at the time of the holdup. Nevertheless immediately after Ali's release she was subpoenaed to appear before a federal grand jury on November 16. Federal Judge Irving Cooper, in an unprecedented move, granted the motion of U.S. Attorney John S. Martin to forbid one of Ali's attorney's, Chokwe Lumumba, to represent her in court. Although never accused or convicted of any crime, Lumumba's membership in the Republic of New Africa, [RNA] characterized by the FBI and media as a "terrorist organization," disqualified him as an attorney in the case. The New York Civil Liberties Union, the Center for Constitutional Rights, the National Lawyers Guild, the Central Committee of the National Black Independent Political Party (NBIPP), and other progressive groups denounced the FBI's attempt to smear Ali, the RNA and the State's efforts to bar Lumumba from representing his client.[44]

This blatant assault designed to discredit Black nationalist and progressive forces was by no means an isolated event. In early morning raids on October 16 and October 21, 1981, California Department of Corrections agents arrested four members of the Black August Organizing Committee, an "anti-imperialist and revolutionary prisoners' group" inspired by "the work of George Jackson and other martyrs of the prisoners' movement." The four Black men were charged with parole violations and conspiracy to assassinate California prison officials.[45] Four radical activists, Vera Michelson of Albany, Aaron Estis of Massachusetts, Mike Young of New York City and John Spearman of Kansas were arrested by police in Albany, New York on September 21, the night before the Springboks antiapartheid demonstration and march. The arrests were part of a well-publicized effort by Democratic Governor Hugh Carey and other administrators to diffuse criticism of the appearance of the South African regime's rugby team in the state capital.[46] In late October, 1981, the Youngstown, Ohio chapter of NBIPP was sued for $300,000 by the white owner of a local supermarket. Black Party members had organized a campaign to urge the Black community not to shop in stores where few or no Blacks were employed. The legal suit against NBIPP was curious in that the Party had previously achieved a tentative written agreement to hire more Black workers at the store in question. Charging that NBIPP was "conspiring to interrupt and destroy" his profits, the owner gave the Party no advance warning before filing the suit.[47]

The wave of random racist violence and "legal lynchings" can be placed in perspective only in the light of these fundamental factors—the socioeconomic instability within the white middle to upper classes, the rise of Reaganism, the recent surge of FBI and local police terrorism to suppress dissent, and the growing probability of some kind of "Chilean Solution" by the ruling class to resolve the crisis of capital accumulation. Any authoritarian or even fascist regime in the U.S. would conform to the basic definition given by Georgi Dimitrov in 1935: "the terroristic dictatorship of the most reactionary, most chauvinistic and most imperialistic elements of finance capital."[48] Reagan's base among white professionals and managers, the petty bourgeoisie and more affluent trade union members—and the emergence of virulent racist antagonisms which are manifested in their social and civil behavior towards Blacks—does not negate the basic and decisive corporate prerogatives behind Reaganism and contemporary racist violence. It is the interests of capital, in the final analysis, that permits the climate of racist terrorism to continue. It is the desire to restructure modern capitalism and to accumulate profits at the expense of Black, brown and white labor that is at the root of the current racial crisis.[49]

IV

It is impossible to detach oneself from the spectre of racist violence and the inevitable emotions of outrage it created within the Black community. So many millions of Afro-Americans have become convinced that a racist conspiracy exists that whether it is real or simply a political phantom may no longer matter. The question of an American conspiracy to destroy the Black community must be approached historically. Almost twenty years ago social historian Richard Hofstader first perceived that white American politics has been frequently "illuminated by the lurid glare of paranoid visions." The paranoid style was a standard "psychological device for projecting various symbols of evil on an opponent and for building emotional unity through a common sense of alarm and peril." Colonial historian Bernard Bailyn illustrated in *The Ideological Origins of the American Revolution* that the belief in a British conspiracy against American colonists was a powerful force in creating the foundations for war. David B. Davis' *The Slave Power Conspiracy and the Paranoid Style* carried the thesis into the Civil War. Some Northern abolitionists were convinced that the slaveholder was quite literally the "antichrist." Paranoid polemics "awakened millenarian fantasies of persecution and suffering, of absolute power and absolute emancipation."[50] Senator Joseph McCarthy and Vice President Richard Nixon manipulated the politics of postwar America through the demogoguery of the Red Scare in the late 1940s and 1950s. Black "paranoia" in the face of the white backlash against human dignity and civil rights, may be viewed as simply part of a largely American social/political response to fundamental change or conflict.

Perhaps a more productive approach to the problem of a racist conspiracy is suggested in the works of Louis Althusser. The solutions reached within any inquiry are predetermined by the paradigm from which one derives one's questions. A "problematic" exists, according to Althusser, "the objective internal reference system of its particular themes, the system of questions commanding the answers given." In

Reading Capital he asserts that a social scientist "can only pose problems on the terrain and within the horizon of a definite theoretical structure, its problematic, which constitutes its absolute and definite condition of possibility, and hence the absolute determination of the forms in which all problems must be posed, at any given moment."[51]

Using Althusser's problematic as a theoretical construct provides new insights into the contemporary reemergence of white racist atrocities. The theoretical common denominator of the variety of statements on Atlanta and other instances of violence raised by Blacks is the *a priori* assumption that whites as a group have adopted a more aggressive bigotry. The integrationist Old Guard (Vernon Jordan of the Urban League, Benjamin Hooks of the NAACP, Jesse Jackson, and others) relate the recent killings to a general political retreat of white American from the Great Society and Kennedy liberalism. This position suggests that a return to Keynesian economic policies, tougher affirmative action and civil rights legislation, and the successful election of a liberal Democrat into the White House would effectively reduce racial violence and social tensions—at best, an unlikely scenario. Black nationalists and community activists agree with the petty bourgeois integrationists that most whites are more overtly racist today than a decade ago, and that the current violence is a concrete manifestation of the level of racism tolerated by white civil society. But this approach starts from a false problematic that implies that *all whites*, to a greater or lesser extent, benefit materially from racism. Both problematics are profoundly superstructural—that is, the essential asssumptions made by both paradigms exclude any serious recognition of the current crisis of U.S. capital accumulation. Both approaches emphasize racism as an ideology or consciousness which directs or dictates certain behaviors or public policies. Their "structured fields" that define the problem do not provide answers which will effectively combat racism, or even explain adequately the central reasons for the relatively recent series of incidents in which Black workers, the unemployed and the elite alike have become seemingly random victims.

Constructing a Black socialist problematic for analyzing contemporary racism might begin with four critical observations. The first, which has been illustrated, is that there has been in recent years an extreme racial polarization within U.S. civil society, accompanied by a pervading climate of fear and terrorism which has reached into virtually every Black neighborhood. Second, many Black institutions which were either developed in the brutal crucible of antebellum slavery or in the period of Jim Crow segregation are rapidly being destroyed. Two of these are the Black educational systems, especially the traditional Negro private and public colleges, and Black-owned and operated businesses. Third, a growing number of Black workers have become irrelevant to the U.S. economy. The level of permanent unemployment for Blacks under the age of 25 has reached staggering levels, and continues to climb. Fourth, an urban "ghettoclass" or underclass has emerged since the recession of 1970, consisting largely of women and children, who survive almost totally on transfer payments and the illegal, subterranean economy of the inner city. Reagan's budget cuts in food stamps, medicaid, and other social services are in reality akin to capital punishment for the millions of ghettoclass Blacks. The root cause of the last three factors is generated by the crisis of capital accumulation, wherein major corporations must demand the restructuring of the capitalist economy in order to preserve it. The capitalist state must drastically reduce social expenditures, and pass legislation to permit a more favorable climate for higher profits and reinvestment. The first factor is both a manifestation of popular white working class anxiety which accompanies any basic restructuring of the economic order, and an expression of the New Right's ideological and cultural commitment to provide the final solution to the Negro Problem in America.

Genocide is usually defined as the systemic and deliberate destruction of a racial, political or cultural group. Blacks have been brutally oppressed, unquestionably, since 1619 as chattel slaves, sharecroppers and industrial laborers. But the dynamic of racial prejudice traditionally has not culminated into a political demand to exterminate Blacks. The most dogmatically racist Southerners at the height of Jim Crow would have found the idea of Black genocide unworthy of cursory debate. Lynchings and terrorism of all kinds were used to suppress the Negro, to "keep him in his place." The goal was to insure a continued supply of relatively cheap laborers who were politically docile. Whites could be prejudiced toward Blacks, but absolutely intolerant of Jews, for instance. Racists could admire the Hitlerian solution to the Jewish problem, while at the same time could recognize the necessity to sustain the Black U.S. community as a racially segregated entity for the systemmatic exploitation of its labor power.[52]

The scientific justification for the gradual eradication of "marginal" ethnic groups has been growing for two decades. In fall 1962 anthropologist Carleton Coon published *The Origin of Races* which proposed that Blacks were the youngest subspecies of *Homo sapiens* and therefore the least advanced intellectually and socially. In a similar vein, Dwight J. Ingle wrote a major article for the journal *Science* in October, 1964, entitled "Racial Differences and the Future." Ingles' thesis suggested that "equal representation of the Negro at the highest levels of job competence and in government will be deleterious to society." The greatest proponents of the neoracist scientific school are William Shockley and Arthur Jensen. Since 1965 Shockley has waged a relentless campaign, declaring that the soaring "crime and relief rates" are due to "some hereditary defect(s)." "The major deficit in Negro intellectual performance must be primarily of hereditary origin and thus relatively irremediable by practical improvements in environment," Shockley stated in 1968. Jensen's February, 1969 essay in *Harvard Educational Review*, "How much can we boost IQ and scholastic achievement?," was praised as "the most important paper in psychology since Pavlov and Freud, a masterful summary of evidence that has been gathering for several decades." Jensen's extension of Shockley's arguments was swiftly entered into the *US Congressional Record* by Louisiana Representative John R. Rarick. Copies of Jensen's polemic were sent to every member of the National Academy of Sciences with a letter from several prominent U.S. scientists, including Shockley, stating that "irrefutable evidence continues for the inheritance of genetically controlled, socially maladaptive traits. We fear that 'fatuous beliefs' in the power of welfare money, unaided by eugenic foresight, may contribute to the decline of human quality for both the Black and white segments of our society and that the fears of genetic deterioration expressed by Jensen are sound and significant."[53]

What is qualitatively *new* about the current period is that the racist/capitalist state under Reagan has proceeded down a public policy road which could inevitably involve the complete obliteration of the entire Black reserve army of labor and sections of the Black working class. The decision to save capitalism at all costs, to provide adequate capital for the restructing of the private sector, fundamentally conflicts with the survival of millions of people who are now permanently outside the workplace. Reagonomics must, if it intends to succeed, place the onerous burden of unemployment on the shoulders of the poor

(Blacks, Latinos and even whites) so securely that middle to upper income Americans will not protest in the vicious suppression of this stratum. Unlike classical fascism, Reaganism must pursue its policies without publicly attacking Blacks or Puerto Ricans by obvious racial slurs. The government's strategy must include a number of petty bourgeois minorities in responsible but low key positions to diffuse charges of white racism which would be levied by white liberal Democrats and progressives. But the final results of these socioeconomic policies, carried to their logical conclusions, would be the total destruction of all-Black institutions, the political separation of the Black elite and intelligentsia from the working class, and the benign but deadly elimination of the "parasitic" ghetto class that has ceased to be a necessary or productive element within modern capitalism.

Over a decade has passed since the Report of the *National Advisory Commission on Civil Disorders* published its devastating indictment against white racism. "What white Americans have never fully understood—but what the Negro can never forget—is that white society is deeply implicated in the ghetto. White institutions created it, white institutions maintain it, and white society condones it."[54] With the failure of the Black Power Movement and the political collapse of white liberalism, the direction of America's political economy and social hierarchy is veering toward a kind of subtle apocalypse which promises to obliterate the lowest stratum of the Black and Latino poor. For the Right *will not be satisfied* with institutionalization of bureaucratic walls that surround and maintain the ghetto. The genocidal logic of the situation could demand, in the not too distant future, the rejection of the ghetto's right to survival in the new capitalist order. Without gas chambers or pogroms, the dark ghetto's economic and social institutions might be destroyed, and *many of its residents would simply cease to exist.*

CHAPTER TEN

CONCLUSION: TOWARD A SOCIALIST AMERICA.

All phases of development are temporary and transient and are destined sooner or later to give way to something else . . . The capitalist epoch is not quite over and those who live at a particular point in time often fail to see that their way of life is in the process of transformation and elimination . . . Socialism has advanced on imperialism's weakest flanks—in the sector that is exploited, oppressed and reduced to dependency. Socialism aims at and has significantly achieved the creation of plenty, so that the principle of egalitarian distribution becomes consistent with the satisfaction of the wants of all members of society.

Walter Rodney, *How Europe Underdeveloped Africa*, pp. 18–20.

How Capitalism Underdeveloped Black America evolved from a concern with the contemporary race/class situation in the United States. Like Rodney's seminal work, I have attempted to delve "into the past only because otherwise it would be impossible to understand how the present came into being and what the trends are for the near future." As we have seen, the basic social division within the Black community, the Black worker majority vs. the Black elite, was an essential by-product of primitive capital accumulation in slave societies. This class division became more pronounced in the twentieth century, and represented a tendency among many "middle class" Blacks in electoral politics, the church, small business and education to articulate a "capitalist road" to Black liberation. With Rodney, I have argued the thesis that Black economic, political and social development is possible "only on the basis of a radical break with . . . the capitalist system, which has been the principal agency of underdevelopment." The data and historical examples I have collected, in my judgment, more than justify the thesis. What remains to be developed, however, is the "formulation of a strategy and tactics" implied within the historical evaluation, which will uproot the hegemony of American capitalism.[1] By necessity, such a strategy cannot be limited to Black Americans and their conditions, because the symbiotic processes of institutional racism and capital accumulation affect all American working and poor people.

The road to Black liberation must also be a road to socialist revolution. But what strategy is required, keeping in mind the special history of American society, and the convergence of racism, sexism and economic exploitation which comprises the material terrain of this nation? I would suggest ten points of departure, programmatically and theoretically, which may provide some tentative suggestions for social transformation and the end to the "underdevelopment" of Black America:

1) Any authentic social revolution in the United States must be both democratic and popular in character and composition. A majority of Americans, Black, Latino and white, must endorse socialism. By this statement, I do not imply that a majority of Americans will become socialists or Marxists. I mean that a clear majority of American people, with a large base in the working class, will support the general program of socialist construction. That expression of support may be electoral, but it should *not* be interpreted narrowly by social democrats to mean a constitutional majority within the electoral apparatus as it now exists. Visions of a revolutionary Black, radical feminist, or "Marxist President of the United States" are illusions fostered by the implicit acquisition of the logic of the bourgeois "democratic" process among some American progressives.

2) The American state apparatus is capitalist and racist in its operations and social trajectory, yet it also manifests the class

contradictions and struggles which are always present within bourgeois civil society as a whole. U.S. bourgeois "democracy" is oppressive
and under Reagan is even moving toward unambiguous authoritarianism, yet is not specifically fascist in the classical sense. Progressives
can have a direct impact upon public policies and the behavior of the
state in certain respects, via electoral participation, lobbying, civil
disobedience, mass demonstrations, etc. The state bureaucracy under
a bourgeois "democracy" often accommodates the demands of the left
into its own public policies. Progressives can gain positions within the
state, especially at municipal and state levels, which can help fund and
support grassroots interests and indirectly assist in the development of
a socialist majority.

Critical support for progressive and anticapitalist politicians (e.g.
Ronald Dellums) who run for office within the Democratic Party, *at the
present time,* may be a necessary and constructive activity in building an
anticorporate consensus within the working class. Yet to view either
major capitalist party as the *primary* or fundamental terrain for building
socialism would be to court disaster. The Democratic Party will never
be transformed into an appropriate vehicle for achieving the political
hegemony of Blacks, Latinos, feminists and the working class. This
requires the creation of an antiracist and antisexist political formation
which is distinctly anticapitalist, and represents the interests of
working and poor people.

3) Direct confrontations with the coercive agencies of state order
are inevitable in the future. Yet any socialist strategy which deliberately provokes the repressive powers of the capitalist/racist state
against working and poor people cannot win in the U.S. A series of
urban rebellions can shake the perception of the American working
class in capitalism as an inherently "fair" and "democratic" system, but
these will not topple the powers of the State. The U.S. government
cannot be directly equated, in short, with czarist Russia or Somoza's
Nicaragua. A putschist strategy by the left will not only fail in
overthrowing the racist/capitalist state, but will create the chaotic
political conditions essential for the installation of U.S. fascism. From
Gracchus Babeuf to Auguste Blanqui, ultraleftists have confused social
revolution with conspiratorial coups which implicitly express an
unstated distrust and even hatred for the people.[2] "When most Americans think about a revolution, all they can think of is a *coup d'état,*"
write James and Grace Lee Boggs. "But people do not make anything as

serious as a revolution to rub out a government or system. The only justification for a revolution is the fact that social, political and economic contradictions have accumulated to the point that the existing government and the existing institutions obviously cannot resolve them. Therefore it is not so much that the revolution overthrows the government and the system as that the government and the system, by their failure and their misdeeds, drive the people to rescind their mandate to rule."[3]

4) A long and painful ideological struggle must be mounted by progressives to create a "counter-hegemony" essential for socialism. Every aspect of the capitalist civil society—educational institutions, the church, the media, social and cultural organizations—must be undermined.[4] This "war of position," to use Antonio Gramsci's concept, must be viewed as the development of a popular "historic bloc" or "revolutionary social bloc" which is comprised of all progressive forces of divergent class and racial groups: women, Blacks, Hispanics, trade unions, Native Americans, antinuclear energy groups, environmentalists, anticorporate "populists," socialists, Communists, community and neighborhood associations, etc. A Common Program among these divergent forces would not be an informal alliance or a temporary convergence of formations as in a classical popular front. It would become the crystalization of a mass revolutionary bloc which would explicitly call for the transformation of the system as it now exists. It would wage a "war of position" for state legitimacy, for the majoritarian mandate to overturn the State. Within its structured forms, the embryonic models of what a socialist society would look like would be developed.[5]

5) The immediate and preliminary goal of this historic bloc would be the achievement of "nonreformist reforms" which can be won within the present capitalist state. These would include, for instance, the passage of: the Equal Rights Amendment; abortion rights; antidiscriminatory legislation against gays and lesbians; strict restrictions to halt plant closings; affirmative action; massive job training programs; universal health care; the abandonment of nuclear power plant construction, and so forth. The successful achievement of these legislative socioeconomic reforms does *not* create a socialist society or state. But combined with legislation which restricts the legal prerogatives of private capital, and a mass mobilization of popular forces in the streets as well as in the legislatures, it will create the social and material

foundations for a logical "alternative" to the bourgeois authority and hegemony. Throughout this initial process, a transitional program must be devised to divide and "win over" proletarian sections of the coercive apparatuses of the state, such as working class volunteers within the armed forces. The essential base of the historic bloc, however, must be the working class—not the petty bourgeoisie.[6]

6) Progressives can only succeed in constructing this historic bloc if they articulate their demands in a popular and historical discourse, in a language readily accessible to the majority of American workers and nonwhite people. This is not an issue of "public relations." The symbols of the American tradition of struggle from past generations must be planted deeply in the socialist praxis of the future. Thomas Paine's moving essays which denounced British tyranny must become our contemporary anti-imperialist vision. Frederick Douglass' belief in the humanity of Blacks and women must become our own worldview. Ida B. Wells' courage in the face of the Memphis lynch mob must become our inner strength. Osceola's fierce determination to fight for the preservation of the Seminole nation must become our will.

The "Other America" of Nat Turner, Malcolm X, Fannie Lou Hamer, Eugene V. Debs, Sojourner Truth, and Harry Bridges must be the historical starting point for our fresh efforts to build a genuine peoples' democracy, and a socialist economic system. We cannot create a revolution in the United States if we mistakenly view the enemy as Reagan alone, or all males, or all white people, rather than the *State*. In the midst of another social revolution, Amilcar Cabral observed that the people of Guinea-Bissau "criticise Salazar and say bad things about him. He is a man like any other. . . But we are not fighting against Salazar, we are fighting against the Portuguese colonial system. We don't dream that when Salazar disappears Portuguese colonialism will disappear."[7] The Boggs make the same observation somewhat differently. "A revolutionist does not hate the country in which the illegitimate and oppressive system and government continues to rule. Far less does the revolutionist hate the people of the country. On the contrary, a revolutionist loves the country and the people, but hates what some people are doing to the country and to the people."[8]

7) Any Common Program or set of "transitional demands" developed by the anticapitalist bloc must be based from the beginning on the basic contradictions which have dominated American political and civil societies throughout the twentieth century. This program must be

a) uncompromisingly antiracist b) antisexist c) anticorporate—that is, it must call for fundamental and powerful restrictions on the rights of private capital, and d) it must promote the necessity for world peace, and advocate an end to the escalating conventional and nuclear arms race with the Soviet Union. Support must be given to all legitimate national liberation struggles, and opposition to any wars of imperialist aggression waged by Western capitalist nations and their clients against the Third World (e.g., the El Salvadorian junta's bloody suppression of that nation's peasantry and working class); the South African reich's terror against the peoples of Angola, Namibia and Azania. In short, the bloc must commit itself in theory and practice to struggle against racism, sexism, U.S. imperialism and capitalism. The principal force for oppression in the world is not the Soviet Union: it is the racist/capitalist state, best represented by the United States and South Africa.

8) Racism and patriarchy are both *precapitalist* in their social and ideological origin. The successful seizure of state power by the U.S. working class and the creation of workers' democracy within the economic sphere would destroy the *modern* foundations for racial prejudice and sexism; however, it would not obliterate the massive ideological burden of either form of oppression in the practices of millions of whites and males. Separate and even autonomous apparatuses must be created after the revolution to effectively uproot racism and patriarchy. In practice, this means that the historic bloc in the presocialist period, the war of position, must build antiracist and antisexist structures within their own organizations. Organizations comprised solely of Blacks, Hispanics, and/or women must be an essential part of the struggle to build a new society.

9) Every decisive gain achieved by the anticapitalist forces will be countered by the state against the working class. This repression will be significantly greater against Blacks and other national minorities than experienced by other sectors of the working class. Socialists must come to the conclusion at the outset that there will be no peaceful culmination in the achievement of state power. If every Congressional district elected a socialist, and if the executive and judicial branches of government were dominated by Marxists, capital would not sit by benignly and watch its

power erode or be destroyed through legal measures. Chile illustrated this feature of capitalist "democracy" decisively. Major corporations will not turn over the keys to their factories willingly to the workers.

The final question of power will be determined in a "war of maneuver," at a point in history wherein the capitalist ruling class will find no alternatives left except raw coercion. C.L.R. James makes his point in his brief discussion of the past European revolutions. "Why did not Charles I and his followers behave resonably to Cromwell? As late as 1646, two years after Marston Moor, Mrs. Cromwell and Mrs. Ireton had tea with Charles at Hampton Court. Cromwell, great revolutionary but great bourgeois, was willing to come to terms. Why did not Louis and Marie Antoinette and the court behave reasonably to the moderate revolutionaries?" James asked. "Why indeed? The monarchy in France had to be torn up by the roots."[9] The racist/capitalist ruling elite in this country will do *whatever is necessary to stay in power.* Today it uses racist ideology to divide Blacks and whites, relies upon patriarchy to perpetuate males' suppression of women, and urges white workers to literally destroy a half century of labor reforms in the workplace through unionization by the relocation of factories and by pressuring the rank-and-file to accept contractual "give-backs" to corporate directors and owners. Tomorrow it may cloak itself in the flag and the Constitution while negating the civil liberties of millions of nonwhite, poor and working people.

There can be no long term "Historic Compromise" with capitalism. The choice for Blacks is either socialism or some selective form of genocide; for the U.S. proletariat, workers' democracy or some form of authoritarianism or fascism.

10) We must always remind ourselves that history is an organic process, the evolution of the forces of production as they affect and in turn are influenced by the civil and political institutions, ideologies and the cultures of human beings. Nothing in Black history, American history, or world history has ever been predetermined by any single factor or force. "Underdevelopment" and "socialism," when reduced to bare economic categories, outside of a particular history, become meaningless abstractions. The socialism we construct will have to encounter racial, sexual, and class components which do not exist anywhere else in the world, exactly as they appear here. If we apply some rigid "iron laws" of revolution gleaned from the dusty textbooks of other revolutionaries, in the name of Marxism, we will not only

succumb to a left form of economic determinism but will fail to build an alternative to the oppressive state which we seek to overturn. "Men make their own history," Marx observed in *The Eighteenth Brumaire of Louis Bonaparte,* "but they do not make it just as they please; they do not make it under circumstances chosen by themselves, but under circumstances directly encountered, given and transmitted from the past."[10] I have devoted a great deal of space in these pages toward analyzing Black history, therefore, because the transition to socialism and an end to Black underdevelopment did not begin in the 1980s, but in the racial and class struggles of past generations.

Our challenge is to interpret society in order to change it. But we must grasp that the particular manifestations of the American war of maneuver, the transition to socialism, will not be fixed or predetermined. C.L.R. James emphasized this point in his discussion of the Russian revolution. "The thing that we have to remember" about the development of the Petrograd's Soviet or workers' council of 1905, James noted, "is that nobody invented it. Nobody organized it. Nobody taught it to the workers. It was formed spontaneously. . ."[11] A workers' democracy in America will not look precisely like anything we can ever imagine at this moment. A revolutionary rupture with the petty bourgeoisie's tendencies toward accommodation within Black America will generate new Black social organizations, new Black political institutions and workers' councils which many Marxists and revolutionary Black nationalists will not comprehend, and may at some point even oppose as "deviations" from their "master plan." We must consciously learn from other peoples' revolutionary experiences without reifying them into a pseudo-revolutionary catechism.

A final word: progressive white Americans must succeed in overturning their own racism, in theory and practice, if a successful revolution can be achieved in this country, which will in the process write the final page on Black underdevelopment. Nothing short of a commitment to racial equality and Black freedom such as that exhibited by the militant white abolitionist John Brown will be sufficient. Nothing less than the political recognition that white racism is an essential and primary component in the continued exploitation of all American working people will be enough to defeat the capitalist class. And to the Black working class, the historic victim of slavery and sharecropping, rape and lynching, capital punishment and imprisonment, I leave the advice of C.L.R. James:

> Marxism is the doctrine which believes that freedom, equality and democracy are today possible for all mankind. If this (book) has stimulated you to pursue the further study of Marxism, we will have struck a blow for the emergence of mankind from the darkness into which capitalism has plunged the world.[12]

"INEQUALITY AND THE BURDEN OF CAPITALIST DEMOCRACY."

Author's Note: Sections from this introduction were published previously in "The Contradictory Legacy of American Democracy," *Socialist Review*, Vol. 43 (January-February, 1979), pp. 114-120.

1. Fred R. von der Mehden, *Politics of the Developing Nations* (Englewood Cliffs, New Jersey: Prentice-Hall, 1964), p. 43.

2. *Ibid.*, p. 6.; David E. Apter, *The Politics of Modernization* (Chicago: University of Chicago Press, 1965), p. 43.

3. Robert L. Heilbroner, *The Great Ascent: The Struggle for Economic Development in Our Time* (New York: Harper and Row, 1963), p. 10.

4. Frank Tachau, ed., *The Developing Nations: What Path to Modernization?* (New York: Dodd, Mead, 1972). Other liberal perspectives on development include C. E. Black, *The Dynamics of Modernization* (New York: Harper and Row, 1966); Irving Louis Horowitz, *Three Worlds of Development* (Oxford University Press, 1966).

5. Von der Mehden, *Politics of the Developing Nations*, p. 3.

6. Harry Magdoff, *The Age of Imperialism: The Economics of U.S. Foreign Policy* (New York: Monthly Review, 1969), p. 23.

    Karl Marx recognized the central role of slavery in the development of world capitalism. "Without slavery, no cotton; without cotton, no modern industry. Slavery has given value to the colonies; the colonies have created world trade; world trade is the necessary condition of large-scale machine industry. Thus before the traffic in Negroes began, the colonies supplied the Old World with only very few products and made no change in the face of the earth. Slavery is therefore an economic category of the highest importance." Karl Marx, in Marx, Frederich Engels, and V. I. Lenin, *On Historical Materialism* (New York: International Publishers, 1974), p. 279.

7. Many Marxists tend to underestimate the role of civil society in the perpetuation of economic exploitation. The cultural chaos spawned by capitalists' disruption of traditional societies is in many respects the most apparent and decisive characteristic of underdeveloped societies. Under capitalist domination, as Noam Chomsky observers, "civil society is hardly more than a conspiracy by the rich to guarantee their plunder." Chomsky, *For Reasons of State* (New York: Vintage, 1973), p. 390.

8. See Staughton Lynd, "Slavery and the Founding Fathers," in Melvin Drimmer, ed., *Black History: A Reappraisal* (Garden City, New York: Anchor, 1969), pp. 117-131.

9. Richard Price, ed., *Maroon Societies: Rebel Slave Communities in the Americas* (Baltimore: Johns Hopkins Press, 1979), p. 150; Herbert Aptheker, *To Be Free: Studies in American Negro History* (New York: International Publishers, 1948), pp. 11-30.

10. See Price, *Maroon Societies;* C. L. R. James, *The Black Jacobins: Toussaint L'Ouverture and the San Domingo Revolution* (New York: Vintage, 1962). One illustration of the bravery of African people will suffice. James writes: "Far from being intimidated, the civil (Haitian) population met the terror with such courage and firmness as frightened the terrorists. Three blacks were condemned to be burnt alive. A huge crowd stood round while two of them were consumed, uttering horrible cries. But the third, a boy of 19, called to them in creole, 'You do not know how to die. See how to die.' By a great effort he twisted his body in his bonds, sat down and, placing his feet in the flames, let them burn without uttering a groan." p. 361.

11. *Ibid.;* Kenneth Stampp, *The Peculiar Institution: Slavery in the Antebellum South* (New York: Vintage, 1956), pp. 180-181, 185-186.

12. W.E.B. DuBois, "Opinion," *Crisis,* Vol. 21 (March, 1921), p. 197.

13. DuBois, "The Negro in America Today," *National Guardian* (January 16, January 23, January 30, February 13, March 5, 1953).

14. DuBois, "Opinion," *Crisis,* Vol. 28 (June, 1924), pp. 55-56.

    The legal end of slavery in 1865 did not terminate the "peculiar institution" in the U.S. According to the *New York Times,* Federal authorities discovered a slave smuggling ring operating on the West Coast in early 1982 that sold 30 Indonesian adults to wealthy residents of Los Angeles and Beverly Hills. In North Carolina, three men were convicted of kidnapping, slavery and holding farm workers in "involuntary servitude" on February 2, 1982. Judith Cummings, "U.S. Says 30 Asians Were Sold as Slaves By Los Angeles Ring," *New York Times* (January 28, 1982); "Three Bosses of Migrant Crews Get Long Terms in Carolina Slavery Case," *New York Times* (February 3, 1982); Judith Cummings, "Recruiter Suspect in 'Slave' Case is Arrested," *New York Times* (February 4, 1982).

15. DuBois, "The Election and Democracy," *Crisis,* Vol. 21 (February, 1921), pp. 156-160.

    This is not to suggest, by any means, that the various legal victories achieved by Blacks and their progressive white allies during the period of Reconstruction (e.g., the thirteenth, fourteenth, and fifteenth amendments to the U.S. Constitution; the Freedman's Bureau; the Civil Rights Act of 1875) were unimportant or undemocratic, or that the U.S. is a mirror image of Nazi Germany. "Democracy" for the majority of Afro-Americans has not and does not now exist because the political apparatus is a "bourgeois parliamentary democracy" and not a proletarian or "workers' democracy." Ernest Mandel noted that the majority of working people in the West usually "identify their democratic freedoms with the bourgeois-democratic, parliamentary state institutions." As a result, "the characteristic feature of bourgeois democracy is the tendency towards atomization of the working class—it is individual voters who are counted, and not social groups or classes who are consulted. Moreover, the economic growth of the last twenty-five years has brought into the heart of the working class consumption habits—most serve to reprivatize leisure activity and thus to reinforce the atomization of the class." Within public discourse, socialism is usually identified with dictatorship and the loss of civil liberties; capitalism is portrayed as the ultimate in freedom (i.e., "free enterprise") and democratic decision-making. By attacking the consensus notion that real democracy exists for the American masses, DuBois established the possibility of elevating to national discussion the idea of socialist democracy. See "Ernest Mandel: a Political Interview," *New Left Review*, No. 100 (November, 1976-January, 1977), pp. 108-109.

16. DuBois, "Is Man Free?" *Scientific Monthly*, Vol. 66 (May, 1948), pp. 432-433.

17. DuBois, "The Winds of Time," *Chicago Defender* (August 17, 1946).

18. DuBois, "The Winds of Time," *Chicago Defender* (September 15, 1945).

19. DuBois, "Opinion," *Crisis*, Vol. 23 (March, 1922), pp. 199-200.

20. DuBois, "The Case of Samuel Moore," *Crisis*, Vol. 23 (April, 1922), pp. 249-250.

21. DuBois, "Postscript," *Crisis*, Vol. 38 (January, 1931), pp. 29-30.

22. DuBois, "As the Crow Flies," *Crisis*, Vol. 26 (September, 1929), p. 293.

23. C. Vann Woodward, *The Strange Career of Jim Crow* (New York: Oxford Unviersity Press, 1954).

24. W. E. B. DuBois, *The Autobiography of W. E. B. DuBois*, (New York: International Publishers, 1968), pp. 304-305.

25. DuBois, "Woman Suffrage," *Crisis*, Vol. 6 (May, 1913), pp. 28-29.

26. DuBois, "As the Crow Flies," *Amsterdam News* (April 26, 1941).

27. DuBois, "On the Right to Express and Hear Unpopular Opinion," *National Guardian* (May 25, 1953).

28. DuBois, "Public School," *Crisis*, Vol. 12 (May, 1916), p. 32.

29. DuBois, "As the Crow Flies," *Amsterdam News* (January 9, 1943).

30. DuBois, "As the Crow Flies," *Amsterdam News* (September 11, 1943).

31. DuBois, "Opinion," *Crisis*, Vol. 24 (August, 1922), pp. 154–155.

32. DuBois, "As the Crow Flies," *Amsterdam News* (September 7, 1940).

33. Julius K. Nyerere, *Ujamaa: Essays on Socialism* (London: Oxford University Press, 1968), pp. 38–39.

Nyerere's essential point is that "socialism is not for the benefit of black men, nor brown men, nor white man, nor yellow men. The purpose of socialism is the service of man. The man or woman who hates "Jews," or "Asians," or "Europeans," or even "Western Europeans and Americans" is not a socialist. "He is trying to divide mankind into groups . . . In either case he is denying the equality and brotherhood of man."

34. W.E.B. DuBois, *The Education of Black People* (New York: Monthly Review Press, 1973), pp. 118–119.

35. DuBois, "Socialism and Democracy," *American Socialist*, Vol. 4 (January, 1957), pp. 6–9.

36. DuBois, "There Must Come a Vast Social Change in the United States," *National Guardian* (July 11, 1951).

"THE CRISIS OF THE BLACK WORKING CLASS."

Author's Note: Sections of this chapter were read in a paper at an international conference of political economists and social theorists at the Institute De Investigaciones Sociales, Universidad Nacional Autonoma De Mexico, Coyoacan, Mexico, July 29, 1981. A section of this paper was also published under the title, "The Crisis of the Black Working Class," in *Science and Society*, Vol. 46 (Summer, 1982), pp. 130-161.

1. Malcolm X, *By Any Means Necessary* (New York: Pathfinder, 1970), p. 183.
2. Antonio Gramsci, *Prison Notebooks* (New York: International Publishers, 1971), p. xciii.
3. W.E.B. DuBois, *The Souls of Black Folk* (Greenwich, Connecticut: Fawcett, 1961), p. 20.
4. Afro-American writers have made this point repeatedly, in various ways. James Baldwin explains: "The history of the American Negro is unique also in this: that the question of his humanity, and of his rights therefore as a human being, became a burning one for several generations of Americans, so burning a question that it ultimately became one of those used to divide the nation. It is out of this argument that the venom of the epithet *Nigger!* is derived . . . In America, even as a slave, he was an inescapable part of the general social fabric and no American could escape having an attitude toward him." James Baldwin, *Notes of A Native Son* (New York: Bantam, 1964), pp. 144–145.
5. Amilcar Cabral, *Revolution in Guinea: Selected Texts* (New York: Monthly Review Press, 1969), p. 86.
6. Philip S. Foner, *Organized Labor and the Black Worker, 1619–1973* (New York: International Publishers, 1976), Chapter 22.
7. Manning Marable, *From the Grassroots: Social and Political Essays Towards Afro-American Liberation* (Boston: South End Press, 1980), pp. 144–146.
8. Clayborne Carson, *In Struggle: SNCC and The Black Awakening of the 1960s* (Cambridge, Massachusetts: Harvard University Press, 1981), p. 104.
9. *Ibid.*, p. 172.
10. Foner, *Organized Labor and The Black Worker, passim.*
11. Philip S. Foner, "Organized Labor and The Black Worker in the 1970s," *Insurgent Sociologist*, Vol. 8 (Fall, 1978), pp. 87–95.
12. Harold M. Baron, *The Demand for Black Labor: Historical Notes on the Political Economy of Racism* (Boston: New England Free Press, 1972), p. 39.
13. Bureau of the Census, *The Social and Economic Status of the Black Population in the United States: An Historical View, 1790–1978* (Washington, D.C.: Government Printing Office, 1980), pp. 30, 72. Hereafter this source will be cited as *The Social and Economic Status of the Black Population.*
14. *Ibid.*, p. 15.

15. Victor Perlo, *Economics of Racism USA: Roots of Black Inequality* (New York: International Publishers, 1975), pp. 198–201. Also see Philip S. Foner and Ronald L. Lewis. *The Black Worker from 1900–1919*, Vol. 5 (Philadelphia: Temple University Press, 1980).

16. Horace R. Cayton and George S. Mitchell, *Black Workers and the New Unions* (Chapel Hill: University of North Carolina Press, 1939), pp. 317–320; George Brown Tindall, *The Emergence of the New South, 1913–1945* (Baton Rouge: Louisiana State University Press, 1967), p. 337.

17. Robert L. Allen, *Black Awakening in Capitalist America: An Analytic History* (Garden City, New York: Anchor Books, 1969), pp. 237–238.

18. Tindall, *The Emergence of the New South*, p. 572.

19. Dan Georgakas and Marvin Surkin, "Niggermation in Auto: Company Policy and the Rise of Black Caucuses," *Radical America*, Vol. 8 (January/February, 1975), pp. 31–57.

20. Baron, *The Demand for Black Labor*, pp. 38–39.

21. George Morris, *CIA and American Labor: The Subversion of the AFL-CIO's Foreign Policy* (New York: International Publishers, 1967), pp. 88–91, 149–150.

22. *Ibid.*, pp. 100–105.

23. Allen, *Black Awakening in Capitalist America*, pp. 237–238.

    Lack of union support for on-the-job training programs for Blacks and other national minorities is another sensitive issue for Black civil rights proponents. There is substantial evidence that federally supported corrective programs have reduced the income gap between Black and white workers, particularly for Black male workers with some secondary school education and with less than six years of actual work experience. See Daniel Taylor, "Education, On-The-Job Training, and the Black-White Earnings Gap," *Monthly Labor Review*, Vol. 104 (April 1981), pp. 28–34.

24. Paul Johnston, "The Promise of Public-Service Unionism," *Monthly Review*, Vol. 30 (September 1978), pp. 9–10.

25. Marable, *From The Grassroots*, pp. 42–43. The perception among some Blacks that unions were inherently racist was reinforced by the failure of AFSCME secretary-treasurer William Lucy to gain the presidency of the union upon Wurf's death in December, 1981. Although AFSCME's membership is estimated to be between 25 and 40 percent nonwhite, only three Blacks, one Hawaiian and one Native American served on the union's 25-member board. One AFSCME leader observed that "Lucy most likely would have gotten the job if he had been white." Ben Bedell, "AFSCME Elects New President," *Guardian* (December 30, 1981).

26. Walter E. Williams, Loren A. Smith and Wendell W. Gunn, *Black America and Organized Labor: A Fair Deal?* (Washington, D.C.: Lincoln Institute for Research and Education, 1980).

    With the exception of Thomas Sowell, Williams has become the most prominent Black apologist for the Reagan Administration and right-wing political causes. Not only is Williams a staunch defender of the open shop, but he also advocates the abolition of the minimum wage. The "minimum wage law systematically discriminates against the most disadvantaged members of the labor force," he argued in late 1980. Blacks, teenagers, and "any worker who cannot produce $3.10-an-hour's worth of goods and services" should have the "right" to work at jobs which pay below government wage mandates. See Walter E. Williams, "Legal Barriers to Black Economic Gains: Employment and Transportation," in Institute for Contemporary Studies, ed., *The Fairmont Papers: Black Alternatives Conference, December, 1980* (San Francisco: Institute for Contemporary Studies, 1981), pp. 26–27.

27. Williams' statements that high Black unemployment rates are a product of Blacks' lack of skills, an inability to work productively, and/or because of poor educational backgrounds, is absurd. Historically, Black males and females *at all ages and in almost all sectors of employment* have been *overqualified.* In 1976, the high school overqualification rate for Black males and females was 52 percent, and 27 percent higher than the rate for whites. For jobs requiring a college-level education, the Black male overqualification rate was 23 percent higher than for white males. U.S. Commission on Civil Rights, *Social Indicators of Equality for Minorities and Women* (Washington, D.C.: Government Printing Office, 1978), pp. 18–20.

28. Paul L. Riedesel, "Racial Discrimination and White Economic Benefits," *Social Science Quarterly,* Vol. 60 (June, 1979), pp. 120–129.

29. Michael Reich, *Racial Inequality: A Political-Economic Analysis* (Princeton: Princeton University Press, 1981), p. 271.

30. Albert Szymanski, "Response to Reidesel," *Social Science Quarterly,* Vol. 60 (June 1979), pp. 130–134.

31. See William Serrin, "Labor Group Girds For Capital Rally," *New York Times* (September 18, 1981).

32. Perlo, *Economics of Racism USA,* pp. 206–207; see Table 31. "Median Income of Persons 14 Years Old and Over With Income, by Sex and Work Experience, for Selected Years: 1956 to 1974," in *The Social and Economic Status of the Black Population,* p. 47.

33. U.S. Bureau of the Census, *Social and Economic Status of Blacks in the United States, 1972,* (Washington, D.C.: Government Printing Office, 1973), p. 55.

34. Richard Freeman, "Unionism and the Dispersion of Wages," *Industrial and Labor Relations Review,* Vol. 34 (October, 1980), pp. 3–23.

35. Richard Freeman, "The Effect of Unionism on Fringe Benefits," *Industrial and Labor Relations Review,* Vol. 34 (July, 1981), pp. 489–509; Duane Leigh, "The Effect of Unionism on Workers' Valuation of Future Pension Benefits," *Industrial and Labor Relations Review,* Vol. 34 (July 1981), pp. 510–521.

36. *The Social and Economic Status of the Black Population,* pp. 214–215.

37. Ray Marshall, *Labor in the South* (Cambridge: Harvard University Press, 1965) and J. Wayne Flint, *Dixie's Forgotten People: The South's Poor Whites* (Bloomington: Indiana University Press, 1979).

38. Reich, *Racial Inequality: A Political-Economic Analysis,* p. 269.
    The U.S. Department of Labor reported in 1974 that nonagricultural

membership in unions was 26.2 percent in 1974. In the Southeast, the figure was 14 percent. Mississippi's union membership in 1974 was 12.1 percent, and North Carolina's rate of 6.8 percent was the lowest in the U.S. See Douglas Sease, "Many Northern Firms Seeking Sites in South Get Chilly Reception," *Wall Street Journal* (February 10, 1978).

39. Marable, *From The Grassroots*, p. 141. On the plight of Black and white textile workers in the South, see Ed McConville, "The Southern Textile War," *Nation* (October 2, 1976), and *The Struggle for Economic Justice at J. P. Stevens* (New York: Amalgamated Clothing and Textile Workers Union, 1977).

40. Bureau of the Census, *Characteristics of Households and Persons Receiving Noncash Benefits: 1979* (Washington, D.C.: Government Printing Office, 1981), pp. 2–3. On January 2, 1982, the Reagan Administration announced plans to count food stamps as part of the income of poor people, a decision which would increase rents for families by 10 percent or more. Black Republican Samuel R. Pierce, Secretary of Housing and Urban Development, explained to the press that "food stamps should be counted as income. If somebody buys my food for me, that's income to me." Robert Pear, "Food Stamp Plan Could Increase Rents for The Poor," *New York Times* (January 3, 1982).

41. *Ibid.*, pp. 4–7.

42. *Ibid.*, pp. 7–9.

Studies completed by the National Center for Health Services Research indicates that the Federal government spends as much, if not more, to subsidize the health care of the rich than it does to assist lower-income people. In 1981 alone, the U.S. government lost between $17.5 billion and $24 billion in potential taxes on health insurance premium deductions. Sixty percent of the money, in the form of tax breaks, was received by the upper two percent of U.S. taxpayers. Only one percent of the tax deductions are received by the poor. "Report Finds High U.S. Aid for Health Care of Wealthy," *New York Times* (January 1, 1982).

43. Georg Lukács, *History and Class Consciousness: Studies in Marxist Dialectics* (Cambridge: MIT Press, 1971), p. 133.

44. Jean-Paul Sartre, *Anti-Semite and Jew* (New York: Grove Press, 1960), pp. 26–27.

45. Frantz Fanon, *Black Skin, White Masks: The Experiences of a Black Man in a White World* (New York: Grove Press, 1967), pp. 177, 180.

46. "America's Restructured Economy," *Business Week* (June 1, 1981), pp. 56–100. *Business Week* is not alone in its predictions. The recession of 1981–82 will create permanently high unemployment rates for employees in the rubber, construction, lumber, auto and steel industries. Any economic "recovery" after 1982, in the opinion of many Wall Street analysts, will not restore these jobs. Winston Williams, "The Jobs That Won't Come Back," *New York Times* (December 12, 1981). Liberal political economists, notably Robert Heilbroner and Lester Thurow, have also concluded that capitalism has entered a long period of deep structural recession. See Robert Heilbroner,

"The New Economics: A Guide to Post-Keynesian Economics." *New York Review of Books,* Vol. 28 (February, 1980), pp. 19–22; Lester Thurow, *The Zero-Sum Society: Distribution and the Possibilities for Economic Change* (New York: Basic Books, 1980).

47. "America's Restructural Economy," *Business Week.*

48. *Ibid.*
    The literature on the flight of capital from the industrial Northeast and Midwest is growing. Some excellent monographs and articles include *Business Closing Legislation Won't Place Ohio at A Disadvantage* (Cleveland: Ohio Public Interest Campaign, 1977); Stephen Mick, "Social and Personal Costs of Plant Shutdowns," *Industrial Relations,* Vol. 14 (May, 1975), pp. 203–208; Barry Bluestone and Bennett Harrison, *Capital and Communities: The Causes and Consequences of Private Disinvestment* (Washington, D.C.: The Progressive Alliance, 1980); *Reclaiming Our Future: A Citizen's Conference on The Crisis of the Industrial States* (Washington, D.C.: Conference on Alternative State and Local Policies, 1979); and Edward Kelley, *Industrial Exodus: Public Strategies for Control of Corporate Relocation* (Washington, D.C.: Conference for Alternative State and Public Policies, 1977).
    The Reagan-inspired strategy to save industrial and commercial jobs in urban areas, the so-called "free enterprise zones"—where corporations receive massive tax reductions, zoning laws are relaxed, and minimum wage laws are perhaps suspended—is advanced in Stuart M. Butler, *Enterprise Zones: Pioneering in the Inner City* (Washington, D.C.: Heritage Foundation, 1980).

49. *Ibid.*

50. *The Social and Economic Status of the Black Population,* pp. 218–219.

51. *Ibid.*

52. Ray Marshall and Virgil L. Christian, *Employment of Blacks in the South: A Perspective on the 1960s* (Austin and London: University of Texas Press, 1978).

53. Paul M. Sweezy, "The Present Global Crisis of Capitalism," *Monthly Review,* Vol. 29 (April, 1978), pp. 1–12; and Paul Sweezy and Harry Magdoff, "Debt and the Business Cycle," *Monthly Review,* Vol. 30 (June, 1978), pp. 1–11.

54. *Ibid.*

55. See Bluestone and Harrison, *Capital and Communities;* Peter Dreier, "Plant closings are good business, but bad news," *In These Times* (February 13, 1980); Thomas Bodenheimer, "Taxes Do Not Cause Runaways," *Our Socialism,* (Spring, 1981); Douglass R. Sease and Robert L. Simison, "UAW Switch on Revising Contracts Reflects Growing Concern for Jobs," *Wall Street Journal* (December 21, 1981).

56. The thesis expressed in this paper is not a new idea. In 1911, W.E.B. DuBois observed that the liberation of Black Americans was basically an economic, and not simply a political, question. He believed that the material interests of white workers objectively favored Black equality. DuBois stated that the goal of international capital was "to reduce human labor to the lowest depth in order to derive the greatest personal profit." DuBois, "The Economics of

Negro Emancipation in the United States," *Sociological Review,* Vol. 4 (October, 1911), pp. 303–313.

"THE BLACK POOR: THE HIGHEST STAGE OF UNDERDEVELOPMENT."

1. Bureau of the Census, *Characteristics of the Population Below the Poverty Level: 1978* (Washington, D.C.: Government Printing Office, 1980), pp. 1–2, 50; John Herbers, "Poverty Rate on Rise Even Before Recession," *New York Times* (February 20, 1982).

    Perhaps the most obvious manifestation of "lumpenization" in the 1980s was the growing army of homeless women and men who live on America's alleys, sidewalks and gutters. Gentrification in urban core areas has sharply reduced the number of single-room occupancy hotels for unemployed and poor persons. When the poor are locked out of their boarding houses, they often have nowhere else to turn except to the street. By 1982, New York City had an estimated 24,000 men and 6,000 women who were homeless. Chicago has an estimated 8,000 people homeless; Los Angeles, 7,500; and Washington, D.C., more than 6,000. Mary Ellen Schoonmaker, "Home on the Curb," *In These Times* (April 28–May 4, 1982).

2. *Ibid.,* p. 10.

3. Bureau of the Census, *Social Indicators III: Selected data on social conditions and trends in the United States* (Washington, D.C.: Government Printing Office, 1980), p. 417.

4. *Ibid.,* p. 491.

    The poverty index was adopted in 1969 to reflect the sex and age of the householder, family size, urban or rural residence and family composition. Rural standards for poverty are figured at 85 percent of urban or suburban living levels. A number of persons, including prison inmates, are not counted in poverty statistics.

    Embarrassed by the recently growing number of poor Americans, the U.S. Commerce Department began to explore statistical maneuvers to redefine "poverty." On April 14, 1982, in what the Bureau of the Census admitted was a "highly exploratory procedure," the government suggested that many noncash benefits might be calculated in the determination of the poverty level. Such benefits under consideration are: Food Stamps, Medicaid, Medicare, subsidized school lunches, and public housing. The implications of this latest bureaucratic manipulation are alarming. For example, the number of poor persons in 1979 was 23.6 million, 11.1 percent of the total population. If assigned values of noncash government benefits were included in determining poverty status, the number of poor persons would drop between 13.6 million (6.4 percent) and 20.7 million (9.8 percent). For Black Americans, the number of persons classified as being poor would plummet from 7.5 million (30.8 percent of all Blacks) to as low as 3.7 million (15.1 percent). "Including Government Noncash Benefits Would Reduce Number of Poor," Bureau of the Census, *U.S. Department of Commerce News* (April 14, 1982).

5. Bureau of the Census, *Characteristics of the Population Below the Poverty Level: 1978*, pp. 2–4, 6.

6. Bureau of the Census, *Social Indicators III*, pp. 491–493.

7. Bureau of the Census, *The Social and Economic Status of the Black Population*, p. 201.

8. Bureau of the Census, *Social Indicators III*, p. 483.

9. *Ibid.*, pp. 486–487.

10. Bureau of the Census, *Characteristics of the Population Below the Poverty Level: 1978*, p. 97.

11. *Ibid.*, pp. 51, 101, 103.

12. *Ibid.*, pp. 54, 82.

13. *Ibid.*, pp. 56, 58.

14. Bureau of the Census, *Social Indicators III*, p. 490.

15. Bureau of the Census, *The Social and Economic Status of the Black Population*, pp. 69–71; and Bureau of the Census, *Characteristics of the Population Below the Poverty Level: 1978*, p. 71.

16. Conservative estimates of the number of "discouraged workers" ranged from the Bureau of Labor Statistics' figure of 1.2 million in 1981 to over 2 million by independent observers of the labor force. The Federal government's number would still represent the largest total of discouraged workers in the U.S. since the mid-1940s. About one-third of this group is nonwhite, and almost two-thirds are females.

17. Bureau of the Census, *Characteristics of the Population Below the Poverty Level: 1978*, p. 180.

18. Douglas G. Glasgow, *The Black Underclass: Poverty, Unemployment and the Entrapment of Ghetto Youth* (New York: Vintage, 1981), pp. 1–9.

19. *Ibid.*, pp. 10–11. There is a regrettable oversimplification of the dynamics of racism within the structural realities of late capitalism that mars what is otherwise an important contribution to the field of race relations. At one point, for instance, Glasgow issues this undocumented assertion: "In this country Blacks as a group represent the have-nots, whites the haves. The conflict between the two, although it has shifted from the open confrontation of the sixties, remains constant." This viewpoint all but negates the class component in the racial equation, which in turn creates sharply divergent interests within both the whites and Blacks as groups. (p. 31).

20. Stephen Birmingham, *Certain People: America's Black Elite* (Boston: Little, Brown and Company, 1977), p. 127.

21. *Ibid.*, pp. 127, 192–193, 288.

"GROUNDINGS WITH MY SISTERS: PATRIARCHY AND THE EXPLOITATION OF BLACK WOMEN."

1. Angela Davis, "Reflections on the Black Woman's Role in the Community of Slaves," *Black Scholar,* Vol. 3 (December, 1971), p. 7.
2. John Hope Franklin, *From Slavery to Freedom: A History of Negro Americans* (New York: Vintage, 1969), p. 179; Herbert Gutman, *Slavery and the Numbers Game* (Urbana: University of Illinois Press, 1975) pp. 102–103, 112, 126, 128.
3. Kenneth M. Stampp, *The Peculiar Institution,* pp. 245–247.
4. *Ibid.,* p. 249.
5. Frances Anne Kemble, *Journal of a Residence on a Georgian Plantation in 1838–1839* (New York: New American Library, 1975), pp. 76, 245.
6. Ulrich B. Philips, *Life and Labor in the Old South,* (Boston: Little, Brown and Company, 1963), p. 204.
7. Gutman, *Slavery and the Numbers Game,* p. 98.
8. Davis, "Reflections on the Black Woman," p. 13.
9. Gilberto Freyre, *The Masters and the Slaves* (New York: Alfred A. Knopf, 1971), p. 324.
10. *Ibid.,* pp. 325–326.
11. *Ibid.,* pp. 74–75.
12. Davis, "Reflections on the Black Woman," p. 13.
13. Franklin, *From Slavery to Freedom,* p. 205.
14. Gerald W. Mullin, *Flight and Rebellion: Slave Resistance in Eighteenth Century Virginia* (New York: Oxford University Press, 1972), pp. 103–105.
15. Jane Blake, *Memoirs of Margaret Jane Blake* (Philadelphia: Innes and Son, 1897), p. 13.
16. Jane Brown, *Narrative of the Life of Jane Brown and Her Two Children* (Hartford: G.W. Offley, 1860), pp. 47–49.
17. Louisa Picquet, *Louisa Picquet, the Octoroon; or, Inside Views of Southern Domestic Life* (New York: the author, 1860), pp. 50–52.

    Other slave narratives written by Black women include Annie L. Burton, *Memories of Chidhood's Slavery Days* (Boston: Ross Publishing Company, 1919); Elizabeth Keckley, *Behind the Scenes* (New York: G.W. Carlton, 1868); Sylvia Dubois, *A Biography of the Slave Who Whipt Her Mistress and Gained Her Freedom* (New Jersey: C.W. Larison, 1883).
18. Lawrence W. Levine, *Black Culture and Black Consciousness: Afro-American Folk Thought From Slavery To Freedom* (New York: Oxford University Press, 1977), pp. 392–393.
19. Quoted in John Bracey, August Meier, and Elliott Rudwick, eds., *Black*

Nationalism in America (Indianapolis and New York: Bobbs-Merrill, 1970), pp. 70–71, 75–76.

20. *Ibid.*, pp. 215–216.

21. *Ibid.*, pp. 140–141.

22. *Ibid.*, p. 62.

23. Benjamin Ouarles, *Frederick Douglass* (New York: Atheneum, 1969), pp. 131–136, 244–247.

   Bell Hooks' treatment of Douglass in *Ain't I A Woman* seems somewhat monolithic. She argues that Douglass "saw the entire racial dilemma as a struggle between white man and black men. . . . By emphasizing that the right to vote was more important to men than [to] women, Douglass and other Black male activists allied themselves with white male patriarchs on the basis of shared sexism." Hooks does not discuss Douglass' significant role in the early evolution of the suffragist cause, and does not mention DuBois even once in her study.

   The record of white feminists and early supporters of women's suffrage on racism is more contradictory than Hooks suggests. In 1851, white suffragists protested the appearance of Sojourner Truth at an Ohio women's convention because they opposed both "abolition and niggers." In her debate with Douglass, Elizabeth Cady Stanton asserted that she would not trust "the colored man with my rights; degraded, oppressed himself, he would be more despotic with the governing power than even our Saxon rulers are. If women are still to be represented by men, then I say let only the highest type of manhood stand at the helm of State." Robert L. Allen, *Reluctant Reformers: Racism and Social Reform Movements in the United States* (Garden City, New York: Anchor Books, 1975), pp. 141, 153–154; Hooks, *Ain't I A Woman* (Boston: South End Press, 1981), pp. 89–90.

24. Hooks, *Ain't I A Woman*, pp. 44–45.

26. Joan R. Sherman, *Invisible Poets: Afro-Americans of the Nineteenth Century* (Urbana: University of Illinois Press, 1974), pp. 62–74.

27. John E. Fleming, "Slavery, Civil War and Reconstruction: A Study of Black Women in Microcosm," *Negro History Bulletin*, Vol. 38 (August-September, 1975), pp. 430–433; Hertha Ernestine Pauli, *Her Name Was Sojourner Truth* (New York: Appleton-Century Crofts, 1962); Sojourner Truth, *Narrative of Sojourner Truth* (Battle Creek, Michigan: the author, 1878); Marie Harlowe, "Sojourner Truth, the First Sit-In," *Negro History Bulletin*, Vol. 29 (Fall, 1966), pp. 173–174; E. Jay Ritter, "Sojourner Truth," *Negro History Bulletin*, Vol. 26 (May, 1963), p. 254; Arthur H. Fausett, *Sojourner Truth: God's Faithful Pilgrim* (New York: Russell and Russell, 1971).

28. David M. Tucker, "Miss Ida B. Wells and the Memphis Lynching," *Phylon*, Vol. 32 (Summer, 1971), pp. 111–122; Alfreda M. Duster, ed., *Crusade for Justice: The Autobiography of Ida B. Wells* (Chicago: University of Chicago Press, 1969).

29. Elizabeth Chittenden, "As We Climb: Mary Church Terrell," *Negro History Bulletin*, Vol. 38 (February-March, 1975), pp. 351–354; August Meier, *Negro*

Thought in America, 1880–1915 (Ann Arbor: University of Michigan Press, 1963), pp. 239–241; Gladys B. Shepperd, *Mary Church Terrell* (Baltimore: Human Relations Press, 1959); Mary Church Terrell, *A Colored Woman in a White World* (Washington, D.C.: Ransdell Publishing Company, 1940); Terrell, "Lynching From a Negro's Point of View," *North American Review,* Vol. 178 (July, 1904), pp. 853–898.

30. Franklin, *From Slavery to Freedom,* pp. 505–506, 511.

A *caveat* must be registered concerning Hurston's views on politics. At the end of her career, Hurston drafted a letter attacking the 1954 *Brown* decision of the Surpeme Court as an "insult" to all Blacks. "Since the days of the never-to-be-sufficiently-deplored Reconstruction, there has been currently the belief that there is no greater delight to Negroes than physical association with whites . . . It is to be recalled that Moscow made it the main plank in their campaign to win the American Negro from 1920s on. It was the come-on stuff. Join the party and get yourself a white wife or husband." Not surprisingly, the viciously racist Mississippi State Sovereignty Commission reprinted and widely distributed her remarks. James Graham Cook, *The Segregationists* (New York: Appleton-Century Crofts, 1962), p. 311.

31. *Ibid.,* pp. 511, 532, 601-602; Rackham Holt, *Mary McLeod Bethune: A Biography* (New York: Doubleday, 1964); C.O. Pearce, *Mary McLeod Bethune* (New York: Vanguard Press, 1951); "Life of Mary McLeod Bethune," *Our World,* Vol. 5 (December, 1950), pp. 32–35; Bethune, "Clarifying Our Vision With the Facts," *Journal of Negro History,* Vol. 23 (January, 1938), pp. 12–15.

32. W.E.B. DuBois, editorial, *Fisk Herald,* Vol. 5 (December, 1887), p. 9.

33. DuBois, "Fifty Years Among the Black Folk," *New York Times* (December 12, 1909).

34. DuBois, "Postscript," *Crisis,* Vol. 40 (February, 1933), p. 45.

35. DuBois, "As the Crow Flies," *Crisis,* Vol. 41 (January, 1934), p. 5.

36. DuBois, *Disfranchisement* (New York: National American Woman Suffrage Association, 1912).

37. DuBois, "Suffering Suffragettes," *Crisis,* Vol. 4 (June, 1912).

38. DuBois, "As the Crow Flies," *Amsterdam News* (March 22, 1941); DuBois, "The Winds of Time," *Chicago Defender* (January 25, 1947).

39. DuBois, "Ohio," *Crisis,* Vol. 4 (August, 1912), p. 182.

40. DuBois, "Opinion," *Crisis,* Vol. 19 (March, 1920), p. 234.

DuBois' writings on women's rights and Black women include: *An Attack* (Atlanta: Published by author, 1906); "The Work of Negro Women in Society," *Spelman Messenger,* Vol. 18 (February, 1902), pp. 1–3; "Suffrage Workers," *Crisis,* Vol. 4 (September, 1912); "The Burden of Black Women," *Crisis,* Vol. 9 (November, 1914), p. 31; "A Question of Facts," *Crisis,* Vol. 21 (February, 1921), p. 151; *The Gift of Black Folk: Negroes in the Making of America* (Boston: Stratford Company, 1924); "Greetings to Women," *Women of the Whole World* (1959), p. 24.

41. Amy Jacques-Garvey, ed., *The Philosophy and Opinions of Marcus Garvey* (New York: Reprinted, Atheneum, 1977), p. 7.

42. *Ibid.*, p. 9.
43. John Henrik Clarke, ed., *Marcus Garvey and the Vision of Africa* (New York: Vintage, 1974), pp. 309–310.
44. Garvey, ed., *The Philosophy and Opinions of Marcus Garvey*, p. 348.
45. Robert G. Weisbord, *Genocide? Birth Control and the Black American* (Westport, Connecticut: Greenwood Press, 1975), p. 43.

This criticism of the sexist character of the Universal Negro Improvement Association's program should not be construed as a condemnation of the legitimate achievements of Garveyism. C.L.R. James is correct in his characterization of this Black nationalist leader: "Garvey is the only Negro who has succeeded in building a mass movement among American Negroes. Garvey never set foot in Africa. He spoke no African language . . . but Garvey managed to convey to Negroes everywhere (and to the rest of the world) his passionate belief that Africa was the home of a civilisation which had once been great and would be great again. When you bear in mind the slenderness of his resources, the vast material forces and the pervading social conceptions which automatically sought to destroy him, his achievement remains one of the propagandistic miracles of this century." James, *The Black Jacobins*, p. 396.

46. W.E.B. DuBois, "Black Folk and Birth Control," *Birth Control Review* (June, 1932), pp. 166–167; Margaret Sanger, "The Case for Birth Control," *Crisis*, Vol. 41 (June, 1934).
47. Weisbord, *Genocide?*, pp. 52–53.
48. *Ibid.*, pp. 141–142.

In some Southern counties, doctors refused to deliver a third or even a second child of a welfare mother unless she agreed to be sterilized. In a number of U.S. hospitals, particularly those with large numbers of Black and Latino patients, white doctors still perform sterilizations "without bothering to get permission." Linda Jenness, "Black Women Fight Sterilization," in Willie Mae Reid, ed., *Black Women's Struggle For Equality* (New York: Pathfinder Press, 1980), pp. 9–10.

49. *Ibid.*, pp. 96–104.

A note on the intimate relationship between religion and patriarchy is appropriate here. The ancient Jews stoned young brides to death "if the village elders agreed" with their husbands' charges that they were not virgins. The Orthodox Jewish prayer—"Blessed art Thou O Lord our God, King of the Universe who has not made me a woman"—speaks for itself. Muhammad taught his disciples, "When Eve was created, Satan rejoiced." The Hindu Code of Manu states: "In childhood a woman must be subject to her father; in youth to her husband; when her husband is dead, to her sons. A woman must never be free of subjugation." From its origins, Christianity promulgated misogyny. The Holy Bible taught that "all wickedness is but little to the wickedness of a woman." The woman was "an unescapable punishment" and "a necessary evil." In his correspondence to the Corinthians, St. Paul declared that "the head of every man is Christ, and the head of the woman is the man."

St. Augustine commented that women were as a temple built over a sewer. Later-day Christian leaders were generally worse than their forefathers. John Calvin, the Protestant patriarch, argued that the sole function of women was to bear as many offspring as possible. Political responsibilities for females were a "deviation from the original and proper order of nature." Martin Luther "thought that sexual relations carried on Original Sin." In colonial America, evangelical ministers delivered solemn prayers while burning "witches" and "adulteresses" at the stake. At the level of popular ideology and cultural tradition, therefore, the various rituals of faith have often dictated an overtly hostile policy of suppressing women. The "good Christian" could beat his wife in "the name of the Father." The crude and often vicious practices of many Black male Christians and Muslims toward Afro-American women historically is to a degree an expression of a much older cultural heritage. See Lucy Komisar, *The New Feminism* (New York: Warner, 1972), pp. 69–72, 111–112.

50. Hooks, *Ain't I A Woman*, pp. 85–86.

51. *Ibid.*, pp. 91, 93.

52. Bureau of the Census, *The Social and Economic Status of the Black Population*, pp. 67, 74.

53. *Ibid.*, pp. 124, 131.

Considerable sociological evidence exists indicating that Black women wanted to bear fewer children than white women. This was particularly true for low- to lower-middle-income Black women, even in the 1950s and 1960s. Researchers Adelaide Cromwell Hill and Frederick S. Jaffe point to a 1960 national survey demonstrating that "the average number [of children] wanted by nonwhite [women] was 2.9, compared to 3.3 by the white wives . . . Furthermore, 46 percent of nonwhites said they wanted no more than 2 children, compared to 29 percent of whites." They also noted a Chicago study in which "twice as many nonwhites as whites said they wanted only two children, and 90 percent of a group of A.F.D.C. mothers of out-of-wedlock children said they did not want to have the child." See Hill and Jaffe, "Negro Fertility and Family Size Preferences—Implications for Programming of Health and Social Services," in Talcott Parsons and Kenneth Clark, eds., *The Negro American* (Boston: Beacon Press, 1967), pp. 160–204.

54. Nikki Giovanni, "The True Import of Present Dialogue: Black vs. Negro," in Dudley Randall, ed., *The Black Poets* (New York: Bantam, 1972), pp. 318–319.

55. Giovanni, "Beautiful Black Men," in *Ibid.*, pp. 320–321.

56. Sonia Sanchez, "Homecoming," in Don L. Lee, ed., *Dynamite Voices* (Detroit: Broadside Press, 1971), p. 48.

57. Alice Lovelace, "Wedding Song," *Gumbo Literary Anthology*, Vol. 1 (Winter, 1978–1979); p. 46.

58. Carolyn Rodgers, "For Some Black Men," in Lee ed., *Dynamite Voices*, p. 57.

59. Ann DuCille, "Lady in Waiting," in Pat Crutchfield Exum, ed., *Keeping the*

Faith: Writings by Contemporary Black American Women (Greenwood, Connecticut: Fawcett, 1974), pp. 70–71.

60. Lucille Clifton, "Apology (to the panthers)," in *Ibid.*, pp. 67–68.

61. Robert Staples, "The Myth of the Black Matriarchy," *Black Scholar,* Vol. 1 (January-February, 1970), p. 16.

62. Sonia Sanchez, "to all brothers," in Randall, ed., *The Black Poets,* p. 231.

63. Nikki Giovanni, "Woman Poem," in Lee, ed., *Dynamite Voices,* pp. 70–71.

64. Ntozake Shange, poem in *Black Scholar,* Vol. 12 (November-December, 1981), p. 61.

65. Stokely Carmichael, *Stokely Speaks: Black Power Back to Pan-Africanism* (New York: Vintage, 1971), p. 23.

66. Malcolm X, *The Autobiography of Malcolm X* (New York: Grove Press, 1965), p. 454.

67. Hooks, *Ain't I A Woman,* p. 109.

68. Malcolm X, *The Autobiography of Malcolm X,* pp. 389–390.

    Following his second journey to Africa in 1964, Malcolm X began to question his profoundly sexist education via the Nation of Islam, and was gradually embracing more progressive thoughts on the role of women in political struggle. In a Paris interview in November, 1964, he contended: "The degree of progress (in the Third World) can never be separated from the woman. If you're in a country that's progressive . . . the woman is progressive . . . One of the things I became thoroughly convinced of in my recent travels is the importance of giving freedom to the woman, giving her education, and giving her the incentive to get out there and put that same spirit and understanding in her children." Despite the political advance, the discourse on women is still framed in a primarily patriarchal caste. Malcolm X, *By Any Means Necessary,* p. 179.

69. Carmichael, *Stokely Speaks,* p. 114.

70. *Ibid.,* pp. 64–65.

71. *Ibid.,* p. 73.

72. Weisbord, *Genocide?,* pp. 94–95.

73. Haki R. Madhubuti, *Enemies: The Clash of Races* (Chicago: Third World Press, 1978), p. 188.

74. In *Soul on Ice* (New York: Delta, 1968), Cleaver described homosexuality as "a sickness, just as are baby-rape or wanting to become the head of General Motors . . . Many Negro homosexuals are outraged and frustrated because in their sickness they are unable to have a baby by a white man. . . . The fruit of their miscegenation is not the little half-white offspring of their dreams, though they redouble their efforts and intake of the white man's sperm. (pp. 102, 110).

75. Eldridge Cleaver, *Soul on Ice,* pp. 206–209.

76. *Ibid.,* p. 61.

77. Robert Staples, "Mystique of Black Sexuality," *Liberator,* Vol. 7 (March, 1967), pp. 8–10.

78. Staples, ed., *The Black Family: Essays and Studies* (Belmont, California: Wadsworth Publishing Company, 1971), p. 74.

Not surprisingly, Staples also justified the sexual relations between Black males and white females. "Since the interracial sex taboo is mostly centered around Negro men/white women, it is not strange that these two groups may have a certain curiosity about the sex ability of each other. Inflaming their curiosity" is the "common stereotype" that the Black man "possesses an overly large penis and has an abnormal sex drive." Many Black men "are preoccupied with the sexual conquest of women . . . Sexual conquest of women is generally seen as a sign of masculinity in American culture . . . being masculine, in a sexual sense, is very important to Negro males because the ordinary symbols of masculinity have often been denied them in the past." Staples, "Negro-White Sex: Fact and Fiction," *Sexology Magazine*, Vol. 35 (August, 1968), pp. 46–51.

79. Quoted in Hooks, *Ain't I A Woman*, pp. 92–93.

80. Bureau of the Census, *The Social and Economic Status of the Black Population*, pp. 70, 103, 106, 107, 109.

81. Helen King, "The Black Woman and Women's Lib," *Ebony* (March, 1971), pp. 68–76.

82. Elizabeth Hood, "Black Women, White Women: Separate Paths to Liberation," *Black Scholar*, Vol. 9 (April, 1978), pp. 45–46.

83. Staples, "The Myth of the Black Matriarchy," pp. 15–16.

84. Linda LaRue, "The Black Movement and Women's Liberation," *Black Scholar* Vol. 1 (May, 1970), pp. 36–42.

One root cause for dissention between elements of the Black activist intelligentsia and feminists was competition for white-collar jobs. Throughout the 1970s, many Black women and men argued that white women were seizing many of the avenues for upward mobility within the corporate and political hierarchies that had been offered originally as concessions to the Black Movement. Between 1966 and 1979, the percentage of total professional jobs that various groups held were: white women, 13 percent in 1966 to 31.6 percent in 1979; white men, 83.5 percent to 58.9 percent; Black women, 0.6 percent to 2.2 percent; Black men, 0.7 percent to 1.9 percent; and others (including Latinos, Asians, and Native Americans), 2.2 percent to 5.4 percent. White corporate executives and employment experts interviewed by the *New York Times* suggested several factors for the apparent preference for white women over Black women/men in executive hiring practices. "The white men who control advancement are more at ease with white women than with Blacks of either sex," some pointed out. Others noted that Blacks had a disturbing "lack of faith in the fairness" of capitalism whereas the majority of white middle-class females did not. See Sheila Rule, "Blacks Believe White Women Lead in Job Gains," *New York Times* (March 25, 1982).

85. Bibi Amina Baraka, "Coordinator's Statement," in Imamu Amiri Baraka, ed., *African Congress: A Documentary of the First Modern Pan-African Congress* (New York: William Morrow, 1972), pp. 177–178.

86. Akiba ya Elimu, "The Black Family," in *Ibid.*, pp. 179–180.
87. Kasisi Washao, "Marriage Ceremony," in *Ibid.*, pp. 181–186.
88. Madhubuti, *Enemies: The Clash of Races*, pp. 139–158.

The academic interest in polygyny transcended the Black Movement in the 1970s. Other works on the subject as it relates to Blacks include Jacquelyne Jackson, "But Where Are the Men?" *Black Scholar*, Vol. 2 (December, 1971), pp. 30–41; Melvin Ember, "Warfare, Sex Ratio, and Polygyny," *Ethnology*, Vol. 8 (1974), pp. 197–206; Joseph W. Scott, "Polygamy: A Futuristic Family Arrangement for African Americans," *Black Books Bulletin* (Summer, 1976), pp. 13–19; Leachim T. Semaj, "Male/Female Relationships: Polygamy Reconsidered," in Semaj, *Working Papers in Cultural Science* (Ithaca, New York: the author, 1980).

89. Joint Center for Political Studies, *National Roster of Black Elected Officials* (Washington, D.C.: Joint Center, 1976), pp. xliii–li.

Works by or about Black women politicians include Shirley Chisholm *Unbought and Unbossed* (Boston: Houghton and Mifflin, 1970); Chisholm, *The Good Fight* (New York: Harper and Row, 1973); Herrington J. Bryce and Allan E. Warrick, "Black Women in Elective Offices," *Black Scholar*, Vol. 6 (October, 1974), pp. 17–20; Jewel L. Prestage, "Political Behavior of American Black Women: An Overview," in La Frances Rodgers-Rose, ed., *The Black Woman* (Beverly Hills and London: Sage Publications, 1980), pp. 233–245.

90. Cathy Sedgewick and Reba Williams, "Black Women and the Equal Rights Amendment," *Black Scholar*, Vol. 7 (July-August, 1976), pp. 24–29.
91. Michele Wallace, *Black Macho and the Myth of the Superwoman* (New York: Warner Books, 1980), pp. 52–53.
92. *Ibid.*, pp. 103–104, 118.

Predictably, the reviews of *Black Macho* were mixed. The bourgeois press embraced Wallace's analysis with gusto. "With this rude, witty polemic—part political broadside, part personal memoir—a 26–year-old Black writer makes a striking debut," declared *Newsweek* (February 5, 1979). The *Library Journal* (March 1, 1979, p. 616) was impressed with Wallace's "simple yet brilliant thesis . . . laser-like in its probing of Black sexual politics. Wallace ranges easily over a vast array of contemporary thought and culture." *Kirkus Reviews* judged *Black Macho* as "thoughtful and temperate." Former SNCC activist Julius Lester wrote in the *Nation* (February 17, 1979, pp. 181–182) that he liked "the book and agree with its thrust and energy when she calls for a Black feminism that is not imitative of what white feminists have done before." Most Black intellectuals' responses to Wallace were divided along feminist lines. Black males who were explicitly sexist provided the most caustic commentary. Harvard psychiatrist Alvin F. Poussaint bristled that "the Black macho response during the Black Liberation Movement was primarily and appropriately a response to white macho and was only secondarily directed at women." In Poussaint's view, Wallace and other Black women had now joined "with whites to destroy the number one object of racism—the Black male."

(Poussaint, "White Manipulation and Black Oppression," *Black Scholar* (May/June, 1979), p. 54.) Robert Staples' response was loaded with sexist stereotypes. "The attack on Black men is occurring when Black women threaten to overtake them, in terms of education, occupation, and income," he wrote. "True, lower-class Black women are not faring well. But lower-class Black men are in even worse condition." (Staples, "The Myth of Black Macho," *Black Scholar* (May/June, 1979), pp. 24–33.) Antisexist Black males such as Kalamu ya Salaam recognized the problems with Wallace's polemic, but also insisted that a feminist perspective was imperative for progressive struggle. Salaam stated that "regardless of our [Black men's] power, the fact remains that we routinely act our sexist behavior and the controllers of society at large condone, seldom punish, and even sometimes reward such sexist behavior." (Salaam, "Revolutionary Struggle/Revolutionary Love," *Black Scholar* (May/June, 1979), p. 21.) Black women intellectuals Sherely A. Williams, Pauline Terrelonge Stone, Sarah Webster Fabio, and Julianne Malveaux critiqued both *Black Macho* and the obvious sexism inherent in Staples' and Poussaint's analysis of the Black community.

93. In 1977, for example, Black women workers in sales jobs suffered more than twice the unemployment rate of Black men, 19.6 percent v. 9.2 percent. Black women in blue-collar jobs had an overall unemployment rate of 16.9 percent v. 11.8 percent for men. Bureau of the Census, *The Social and Economic Status of the Black Population*, p. 214.

94. Cindy Jaquith, "Joanne Little's Victory," in Reid, ed., *Black Women's Struggle For Equality*, pp. 10–13.

95. Sedgewick and Williams, "Black Women and the Equal Rights Amendment."

96. Hooks, *Ain't I A Woman*, p. 151.

97. *Ibid.*, pp. 152.

98. Michele Barrett, *Women's Oppression Today: Problems in Marxist Feminist Analysis* (London: Verso Editions, 1980), pp. 258–259.

Sheila Rowbotham also provides some insights on the continuing contradictions between socialism and feminist politics: "Marxists have in general assumed that the overthrow of capitalist society will necessitate the fundamental transformation in the organization and control of production and the social relations which came from the capitalist mode of production. Women's liberation implies that, if the revolutionary movement is to involve women . . . as equals, then the scope of production must be seen in a wider sense and cover also the production undertaken by women in the family and the production of self through sexuality . . . The connection between the oppression of women and the central discovery of Marxism, the class exploitation of the worker in capitalism, is still forced. I believe the only way in which their combination will become living and evident is through a movement of working-class women, in conscious resistance to both, alongside black, yellow and brown women struggling against racialism and imperialism." Rowbotham, *Women, Resistance and Revolution: A History of Women and Revolution in the Modern World* (New York: Vintage, 1972), pp. 246–247.

"BLACK PRISONERS AND PUNISHMENT IN A RACIST/CAPITALIST STATE."

1. Stampp, *The Peculiar Institution*, pp. 2, 24–25.

2. *Ibid.*, pp. 174–175; Eugene D. Genovese, *Roll, Jordan, Roll: The World The Slaves Made* (New York: Pantheon, 1974), pp. 36–37, 66–67.

3. Leon Litwack, *North of Slavery: The Negro in the Free States, 1790–1860* (Chicago: University of Chicago Press, 1961), pp. 97–99.

4. Eric Foner, *Free Soil, Free Labor, Free Men: The Ideology of the Republican Party before the Civil War* (New York: Oxford University Press, 1970), pp. 263, 286.

5. Vernon Lane Wharton, *The Negro in Mississippi, 1865–1890* (Chapel Hill: University of North Carolina Press, 1964), pp. 227–233.

6. Pete Daniel, *The Shadow of Slavery: Peonage in the South, 1901–1969* (New York: Oxford University Press, 1972), pp. 23–25.

7. C. Vann Woodward, *Origins of the New South, 1877–1913* (Baton Rouge: Louisiana State University Press, 1951), pp. 3–5, 213–215.

8. Fletcher M. Green, "Some Aspects of the Southern Convict Lease System in the Southern States," in Fletcher M. Green (ed.), *Essays in Southern History* (Chapel Hill: University of North Carolina Press, 1949), p. 122.

9. Woodward, *Origins of the New South*, pp. 397–398.

10. *Ibid.*, pp. 213–214.

11. Walter Wilson, "Twilight of the Chain Gang," *Nation*, Vol. 150 (1940), pp. 44–46; George Brown Tindall, *The Emergence of the New South*, pp. 214–215.

12. Allison Davis, Burleigh B. Gardner, Mary R. Gardner, *Deep South: A Social Anthropological Study of Caste and Class* (Chicago: University of Chicago Press, 1941), pp. 297–301.

13. Richard Wright provides a typical illustration of this in *Black Boy*:
    "Do you want this job?" the woman asked.
    "Yes, ma'am," I said, afraid to trust my own judgment.
    "Now, boy, I want to ask you one question and I want you to tell me the truth,"
        she said.
    "Yes, ma'am," I said, all attention.
    "Do you steal?" she asked me seriously.
    I burst into a laugh, then checked myself.
    "What's so damn funny about that?" she asked.
    "Lady, if I was a thief, I'd never tell anybody."
    "What do you mean?" she blazed with a red face.
    I had made a mistake during my first five minutes in the white world. I hung my
        head.
    "No, ma'am," I mumbled. "I don't steal."

Richard Wright, *Black Boy: A Record of Childhood and Youth* (New York: Harper and Row, 1945), p. 160.

14. Davis, Gardner, and Gardner, *Deep South,* pp. 302, 310–311.
15. Woodward, *The Origins of the New South,* p. 160.
16. Even at the height of "gangland" killings in Chicago, immediately after World War I, the murder rate in that major Midwest city averaged a mere 11.8, slightly above the national homicide rate. Memphis' average homicide reached 88.2 in 1915. Walter White, *Rope and Faggot: A Biography of Judge Lynch* (New York: 1929, reprinted, Arno Press, 1969), pp. 238–244. Also see James H. Chadbourn, *Lynching and the Law* (Chapel Hill: University of North Carolina Press, 1933) and Arthur F. Roper, *The Tragedy of Lynching* (Chapel Hill: University of North Carolina Press, 1932).
17. White, *Rope and Faggott,* pp. 83–87.
18. Genovese, *Roll, Jordan, Roll,* p. 32; Stampp, *The Peculiar Institution,* p. 191.
19. Manning Marable, *Blackwater: Historical Studies in Race, Class Consciousness and Revolution* (Dayton, Ohio: Black Praxis Press, 1981), p. 15.
20. Genovese, *Roll, Jordan, Roll,* p. 33.
21. Stampp, *The Peculiar Institution,* p. 191.
22. White, *Rope and Faggott,* pp. 232–236, 252–259.
23. Tindall, *The Emergence of the New South, 1913–1945,* pp. 170–171.
24. Davis, Gardner, Gardner, *Deep South,* p. 25.
25. White, *Rope and Faggott,* pp. 35–36.
26. *Ibid.,* pp. 27–29.
27. "Surprising Facts About the Death Penalty," (Durham, North Carolina: Institute for Southern Studies, 1981). Other monographs cited on the death penalty and related data is collected from the Institute of Southern Studies, unless otherwise noted.
28. *Ibid.*
29. Anthony G. Amsterdam, "The Case Against the Death Penalty," and "The Bible and the Death Sentence," Institute for Southern Studies, 1981.
30. "Common Misconceptions About the Death Penalty," Institute of Southern Studies, 1981.
31. Hans W. Mattick, "An Unsentimental View of Capital Punishment," *Community,* Vol. 36 (Summer, 1977), p. 11.
32. "Common Misconceptions About the Death Penalty."
33. Amsterdam, "The Bible and the Death Sentence."
34. "Surprising Facts About the Death Penalty."
35. *Ibid.,* and Clare Jupiter, "Lost Lives? A Profile of Death Row," Institute of Southern Studies monograph, 1981.

U.S. politicians have been forced recently to resort to outright lies in order to justify the death penalty. One small but typical example occurred in April, 1982, when President Ronald Reagan asserted to the press that Great Britain once hanged people if they used a gun in the commission of a crime, whether or not the gun was used. Reagan declared that this was a "cruel but effective system" that ended only when Britain ended capital punishment in 1965. Within days, a spokesperson for Britain's Law Society responded that the presidential assertion was "absolutely wrong." Researchers at the Library of Congress checked records dating back to the fourteenth century, and found nothing to support Reagan's brutal statement. When a White House press secretary was challenged for an explanation, he admitted that the story was untrue. He added for the record, "Well, it's a good story, though." "Briton Rebuts Reagan on Use of Guns and the Death Penalty," *New York Times* (April 17, 1982).

36. Table 5/1, "Persons Afraid To Walk Alone at Night, Selected Years: 1965–1977," and Table 5/2, "Attitudes Toward Treatment of Criminals by the Courts, Selected Years: 1965–1978," in Bureau of the Census, *Social Indicators III.*, p. 237.

37. Table 5/3, "Public Safety Expenditures, by Function and Level of Government: 1952–1977;" Table 5/4, "Per Capita Expenditures for Police Protection, Selected Cities: 1974," in *Ibid.*, pp. 238–240.

38. Table 5/6, "Violent Crimes by Type: 1960–1978;" Table 5/7, "Property Crimes by Type, 1960–1978;" Table 5/8, "Victims of Homicide, by Race and Sex: 1940–1977," in *Ibid.*, pp. 206, 241–243.

39. Table 5/8, "Victims of Homicide," and Table 5/10, "Personal Crimes of Violence and Theft: 1973–1978;" in *Ibid.*, pp. 243–244. Black women are also more likely to be victims of violent crime than whites or Hispanics.

40. *Ibid.*, pp. 207, 246–247. Black families who rent their homes or apartments are also more likely to experience burglaries than all whites and those Blacks who own their own residences. Between 1973 and 1978, the instances of burglaries per 1,000 households for Black renters was between 139 to 154 annually.

41. *Ibid.*, p. 247. Between 1973 and 1978, white families earning $25,000 a year or more experienced household burglaries at a rate of 80 to 113 per 1,000. Black families in the same income bracket were victims of burglaries at a rate of 82 to 214 per 1,000 households annually.

42. "Crisis and Cutbacks Stirring Fresh Concern on State of the Nation's Prisons," *New York Times* (January 5, 1982).

43. *Wall Street Journal* (December 17, 1981).

Caught in a major crisis of capital accumulation, the corporations eagerly seized upon Burger's proposal as a step forward in penal reform. If one carries this model to its logical conclusions, half of all U.S. prisoners (250,000) could be employed in existing blue-collar jobs. At least 250,000 persons currently not in prison would no longer be necessary in the workplace. A sizeable number of now-unemployed Blacks, Hispanics and poor whites would have to commit petty crimes simply to survive. Once convicted, they could be added to the ever-expanding penal workforce at lower wage levels. Perhaps the final solution would simply be to imprison the entire working class, cutting wages in half, and turning the entire society into a kind of permanently armed camp. No proposal is too "extreme" in the pursuit of profits!

44. Hinds, *Illusions of Justice*, pp. 36, 44.

45. There is an unbroken political correlation between extreme bigotry and an opposition to socialism and communism. A fierce anticommunism was an integral part of white racist political culture by the Great Depression. At the famous trial of Black activist Angelo Herndon in 1937, the Georgia prosecutor informed the all-white jury that class played an equally important role with race in the conviction of alleged Black leftists. "This is not only a trial of Angelo Herndon, but of Lenin, Stalin, Trotsky and Kerensky, and every white person who believes that black and white should unite for the purpose of setting up a nigger Soviet Republic in the Black Belt . . . As fast as the Communists come [into Georgia], we shall indict them and I shall demand the death penalty in every case." Angelo Herndon, *Let Me Live* (New York: Reprinted from 1937 edition, Arno Press, 1969), p. 228.

46. United States Senate, *Final Report of the Select Committee to Study Governmental Operations with Respect to Intelligence Activities, Book III* (Washington, D.C.: Government Printing Office, 1976), pp. 6, 40, 56, 57, 187–188.

    The "long-range goals" of the "Black Nationalist-Hate Groups" program were outlined on March 4, 1968, and forwarded to 41 FBI offices nationwide:

    "(1) to prevent the 'coalition of militant black nationalist groups' which might be the first step toward a real 'Mau Mau' in America;

    (2) to prevent the rise of a 'messiah' who could 'unify, and electrify,' the movement, naming specifically Martin Luther King, Stokely Carmichael, and Elijah Muhammad;

    (3) to prevent violence on the part of black nationalist groups, pinpointing 'potential troublemakers' and neutralizing them 'before they exercise their potential for violence';

    (4) to prevent groups and leaders from gaining 'respectability' by discrediting them to the 'responsible' Negro community, to the white community (both the responsible community and the 'liberals') . . . and to Negro radicals; and (5) to prevent the long-range growth of these organizations, especially among youth, by developing specific tactics to 'prevent these groups from recruiting young people.' " (pp. 21–22)

47. On December 4, 1981, "two FBI agents entered the home of black writer Sonia Sanchez and belligerently interrogated her . . . [and] threatened her with imprisonment for her alleged acquaintance with black militants, declaring that 'there will be no imprisonment; there will be no jail for them. We will kill." "FBI threatens Black writer," *Militant* (January 1, 1982).

48. "Federal grand jury investigates Black groups," *Portland Observer* (December 31, 1981). One Black woman in New York City, Yaasmyn Fula, was sentenced in 1981 to an 18–month jail sentence because she refused "to tell a grand jury about her group."

49. Eric Mann, *Comrade George: An Investigation into the Life, Political Thought, and Assassination of George Jackson* (New York: Harper and Row, 1974), pp. 21, 25.

50. *Ibid.*, p. 114.

"BLACK CAPITALISM: ENTREPRENEURS, CONSUMERS AND THE HISTORICAL EVOLUTION OF THE BLACK MARKET."

1. One of the best critiques of Gold Coast economic development is provided in Bob Fitch and Mary Oppenheimer, *Ghana: End of an Illusion* (New York: Monthly Review Press, 1966).

2. Chinweizu, *The West And The Rest of Us: White Predators, Black Slavers and the African Elite* (New York: Vintage, 1975), pp. 355–356.

3. *Ibid.*, p. 382.

4. *Ibid.*, p. 385.

5. Frantz Fanon, *The Wretched of the Earth* (New York: Grove Press, 1968), p. 167.

6. I am tempted to assert that the most decisive "intellectuals" within Black history have always been found among the entrepreneurs. A solid argument could be made that racial segregation and an aggressive capitalist political economy fashioned the conditions for upwardly mobile, Black intellectuals in the traditional sense to flock to the marketplace instead of the academy. Gramsci's observation of Italian entrepreneurs provides a rough parallel to those in Black America: "The entrepreneur himself represents a higher level of social elaboration . . . he must have a certain technical capacity, not only in the limited sphere of his activity and initiative but in other spheres as well, at least in those which are closest to economic production. He must be an organizer of masses of men; he must be an organizer of 'confidence' of investors in his business, of the customers for his products, etc. If not all entrepreneurs, at least an elite amongst them must have the capacity to be an organizer of society in general, including all its complex organism of services, right up to the state organism, because of the need to create the conditions most favorable to the expansion of their own class . . . " Gramsci, *Prison Notebooks*, pp. 5–6.

7. August Meier and Elliott Rudwick, *CORE: A Study in the Civil Rights Movement, 1942–1968* (New York: Oxford, 1973), p. 423; Benjamin Quarles, *Frederick Douglass*, pp. 269–270. Also see Roy Innis, "Separatist Economics: A New Social Contract," in G. Douglass Pugh and William F. Haddard, eds., *Black Economic Development*, (Englewood Cliffs, New Jersey: Prentice-Hall, 1969).

8. E. Franklin Frazier, *Black Bourgeoisie* (Glencoe, Illinois: Free Press, 1957).

9. Abram L. Harris, *The Negro As Capitalist: A Study of Banking and Business Among American Negroes* (New York: Haskell, 1936: Reprinted 1970), pp. 4–24.

10. *Ibid.*, pp. 8–9.

11. *Ibid.*, 12, 17–18.

12. Booker T. Washington and W.E.B. DuBois, *The Negro In The South* (New York: Reprinted from 1907 edition, Citadel Press, 1970), pp. 26–28.

13. Roger L. Ransom and Richard Sutch, *One Kind of Freedom: The Economic Consequences of Emancipation* (Cambridge: Cambridge University Press, 1977), p. 35.

14. W.E.B. DuBois, *The Negro Artisan: A Social Study* (Atlanta: Atlanta University Press, 1902), p. 22.

15. Ransom and Sutch, *One Kind of Freedom*, p. 36.

16. *Ibid.*, pp. 37–38, 228–229.

17. Bureau of the Census, *The Social and Economic Status of the Black Population*, p. 78.

18. Meier, *Negro Thought in America*, pp. 140–141.

19. *Ibid.*, pp. 144–145, 148; Timothy Bates, *Black Capitalism: A Quantitative Analysis* (New York: Praeger, 1973), p. 9; Earl Ofari, *The Myth of Black Capitalism* (New York: Monthly Review Press, 1970), p. 30.

20. Louis R. Harlan, *Booker T. Washington: The Making of a Black Leader, 1856–1901* (New York: Oxford University Press, 1972), pp. 254, 266–270.

21. Henry G. La Brie, III, *A Survey of Black Newspapers* (Kennebunkport, Maine: Mercer House, 1979), pp. 10–11.

22. Meier, *Negro Thought in America*, pp. 225–228.

23. Bates, *Black Capitalism*, p. 9.

24. John Henrik Clarke, ed., *Marcus Garvey and the Vision of Africa* (New York: Vintage, 1974), pp. 89–91.

25. *Ibid.*, p. 207.

26. W.E.B. DuBois, "The Upbuilding of Black Durham," *World's Work*, Vol. 13 (January, 1912), pp. 334–338.

27. DuBois, "The Business League," *Crisis*, Vol. 6 (October, 1913), p. 289.

28. DuBois, "The Negro Bank," *Crisis*, Vol. 23 (April, 1922), pp. 253–254; DuBois, "Black Banks and White in Memphis," *Crisis*, Vol. 35 (May, 1928), pp. 154, 173–174.

29. DuBois, "Opinion," *Crisis*, Vol. 29 (April, 1925), p. 252.

30. DuBois, "As the Crow Flies," *Amsterdam News* (October 10, 1942).

31. DuBois, "As the Crow Flies," *Amsterdam News* (May 1, 1943).

32. Harris, *The Negro As Capitalist*, p. 55.

33. *Ibid.*, pp. 145, 153, 60–61.

34. Bates, *Black Capitalism*, pp. 10–13.

35. David Caplovitz, *The Poor Pay More: Consumer Practices of Low-Income Families* (New York: The Free Press, 1963), pp. 4–5.

36. Harris, *The Negro As Capitalist*, pp. 180–181.

37. *Ibid.*, p. 183; Paul Jacobs, "Negro and Jew," in Shlomo Katz (ed.), *Negro and Jew: An Encounter in America* (New York: MacMillan, 1967, pp. 74–80.
    It would be a distortion of Black social history not to admit that many Blacks were profoundly influenced by the deep antisemitism of the dominant civil

society. Richard Wright asserts: "All of us black people who lived in the neighborhood hated Jews, not because they taught at home and in Sunday school that Jews were 'Christ killers.' With the Jews thus singled out for us, we made them fair game for ridicule . . . No one ever thought of questioning our right to do this; our mothers and parents generally approved, either actively or passively. To hold an attitude of antagonism or distrust toward Jews was not merely racial prejudice, it was a part of our cultural heritage." Richard Wright, *Black Boy*, pp. 70–71.

38. Flournoy A. Coles, Jr. *Black Economic Development* (Chicago: Nelson Hall, 1975), pp. 177–181.

39. Meier, *Negro Thought in America*, pp. 124–177.

40. Coles, *Black Economic Development*, p. 185; LeRoy W. Jeffries, *Facts About Blacks, 1980–81* (Los Angeles: Jeffries and Associates, 1980), pp. 11–14.

41. D. Parke Gibson, *$70 Billion in the Black* (New York: MacMillan, 1978), p. 11.

42. Another method to test the thesis that racially segregated cities help to support the development of Black Capitalism can be illustrated by a brief comparison between Dayton, Ohio (Black population 103,380 in 1977) and Raleigh-Durham, North Carolina (Black population 107,104). Dayton has 735 Black-owned firms, 130 of which (17.7 percent) have a total of 403 employees. Total gross receipts in Dayton, a Midwestern city with a strong Black petty bourgeoisie and a Black mayor, were $20.9 million in 1977. Raleigh-Durham has 921 Black-owned firms, 192 (20.8 percent) with 1826 workers. Gross receipts for Raleigh-Durham's firms without employees were $6.1 million. Black businesses with paid employees grossed $69.1 million, for a combined total of $75.2 million. See Bureau of the Census, *1977 Survey of Minority-Owned Business Enterprises* (Washington, D.C.: Government Printing Office, 1979), pp. 129, 142–143.

43. *Ibid.*, pp. 169–173.

44. *Ibid.*, p. 169; Bates, *Black Capitalism*, pp. 24–25.

The real status of the Black entrepreneur within the proletarian periphery is not unlike that of a factory foreman. As Lenin observed, a foreman is not a boss; he/she is a worker who controls only a minute aspect of the process of production. His/her status, at least in the estimation of those who own the plant, is not as an equal partner or investor. The intermediate entrepreneur, only one out of every six Black businesspersons, is not a worker, but is also not part of the capitalist class. The periphery is sustained by "bourgeois illusions," whereas intermediate entrepreneurs do have a real material interest in private enterprise.

45. LeRoy W. Jeffries, *Facts About Blacks, 1980–81*, pp. 11–14, 21–23.

46. Gibson, *$70 Billion in the Black*, pp. ix, 108–109, 152–153.

There is a substantial amount of research on the impact of advertising on Black consumers since 1970. Some informative sources are: T.R. Donohue, "Effect of Commercials on Black Children," *Journal of Advertising Research* (December, 1975), pp. 41–47; "Ethnic Marketing—So Much Opportunity,

So Much To Learn," *Product Marketing Magazine* (June, 1977), pp. 29–34; "Selling to the Black Consumer: A Roundtable Discussion of the Increasing Black Impact on Corporate Economies," *Black Enterprise* (November, 1973), pp. 31–33; Thaddeus H. Spratlen, "The Black Consumer Response to Black Business," *Review of Black Political Economy* (Fall, 1973), pp. 73–105; Donald E. Sexton, "Black Buyer Behavior," *Journal of Marketing* (October, 1972), pp. 36–39; A.G. Woodside, "Credibility of Advertising Themes Among Blacks and Whites," *Marquette Business Review* (Fall, 1975), pp. 134–142; John H. Johnson, "Greening of the Black Consumer Market," *Crisis* (March, 1976), pp. 92–95; C. Marticorena, "Ethnic Market: Biggest Potential for Growth . . . " *Chemical Marketing Reporter* (June 23, 1975), pp. 37–39; "New Look at the Black Consumer," *Sales Management* (August 6, 1973), p. 13; C. Orphen, "Reactions to Black and White Models," *Journal of Advertising Research* (October, 1975), pp. 75–79.

47. *Ibid.*, pp. 132, 134–136.

Coca Cola launched a counterattack against Pepsi by hiring soul artists Ray Charles and the Supremes. Coke's advertising agency, McCann-Erickson, convinced the Atlanta-based billion dollar multinational that a blacker-than-thou approach was needed to boost profits at Pepsi's expense. Commercial tapes were cut and aired only on "Black-oriented" radio stations. Within a few months, Coke gross profits earned from Black consumers increased sharply. "The Charles commercial even got fan mail and consumer requests of stations for its play." Gibson, *$70 Billion In the Black*, pp. 90–91.

48. *Ibid.*, pp. 40, 41, 202.

49. *Ibid.*, 89–90, 95–97.

50. *Ibid.*, pp. 4, 85, 159–162. Also see Gil Scott, "Blacks in the Liquor Industry," *Black Enterprise* (September, 1975), pp. 33–37.

By the mid–1970s Black entertainers and athletes were standard spokespersons for corporate products, something that would have been unthinkable twenty years before. A few on this ever-expanding list include: singer Nancy Wilson, Johnson and Johnson Disposable Diapers; Wilt Chamberlin, Deacon Jones, and Bubba Smith for Miller Lite beer; Pearl Bailey for Greyhound; O.J. Simpson for Hertz; Muhammad Ali for Brut; and Lou Rawls for Budweiser beer. Gibson, *$70 Billion In the Black*, p. 92.

51. Caplovitz, *The Poor Pay More*, p. 126.

52. *Ibid.*, p. 96.

53. Gibson, *$70 Billion in the Black*, pp. 34, 44, 250.

54. Jeffries, *Facts About Blacks*, pp. 18–20.

55. *The Social and Economic Status of the Black Population*, p. 175; *Ibid.*, 21.

56. *The Social and Economic Status of the Black Population*, p. 17; Jeffries, *Facts About Blacks*, pp. 11–14.

Since 1960, Brimmer has emerged as one of the ruling class' most prominent spokespersons on economic issues. Some of his essays include "Economic Trends in the Negro Market," *Marketing Guide* (May, 1964), pp. 2–7; "The Negro in the American Economy," monograph (Durham, North Carolina:

North Carolina Life Insurance Company, 1966); "Outlook for Black Business," *Black Enterprise* (June, 1976), pp. 26–30; Brimmer and Henry Terrell, "The Economic Potential of Black Capitalism," *Public Policy,* Vol. 19 (Spring, 1971).

57. Coles, *Black Economic Development,* p. 88.

58. *Ibid.,* pp. 88–89; Richard F. America, Jr., "What Do You People Want?" *Harvard Business Review,* Vol. 47 (March-April, 1969), pp. 103–112.

Economists who have proposed similar programs to aid in the development of Black Capitalism include Robert B. McKensie, "Vitalize Black Enterprise," *Harvard Business Review,* Vol. 46 (September, 1968); James M. Hund, *Black Entrepreneurship* (Belmont, California: Wadsworth, 1970); Theodore L. Cross, *Black Capitalism* (New York: Atheneum, 1969); Richard S. Rosenbloom, "Business, Technology, and the Urban Crisis," in Richard S. Rosenbloom and Robin Marris, eds. *Social Innovation in the City* (Cambridge, Mass.: Harvard University Press, 1969), pp. 51–61; George S. Odiorne, *Green Power* (New York: Pitman, 1969).

Other recent sources on Black Capitalism include Courtney N. Blackman, *Black Capitalism in Economic Perspective* (New York: Economic Research Department, Irving Trust Company, 1973); Edward D. Irons, "Black Entrepreneurship: Its Rationale, Its Problems, Its Prospects," *Phylon* (March, 1976), pp. 12–25; Arthur L. Tolson, "Historical and Modern Trends in Black Capitalism," *Black Scholar* (April, 1975), pp. 8–14.

59. *The Social and Economic Status of the Black Population,* pp. 78–79; Jeffries, *Facts About Blacks,* p. 21.

60. An ominous example is provided by Floyd McKissick, a prominent Black Powerite, supporter of Richard Nixon in 1972, and architect of Soul City, North Carolina. Defending Black Capitalism, McKissick justified his autocratic political practice by declaring his affinity with Marcus Garvey. In his view, Garvey "was not a democratic leader; in fact, he was a dictator." McKissick stated, "we need to study his style." Meier and Rudwick, *CORE,* p. 422.

Reaganism as a social and political force is clearly authoritarian, but is not fascist. The Reaganites' desire for law and order at any cost to civil liberties, extreme racism, the rightist libertarian demand to reduce the size of the welfare state, and the call for a balanced federal budget, do not constititute fascism. Moreover, the politically conservative wing of Black Capitalism obviously would have nothing in common with the racist maneuvers of a Jesse Helms. Nevertheless, by calling for state intervention to assist in the development of a Black capitalist class, they must also embrace critical elements of an authoritarian and even proto-fascist ideology—crushing labor unions, passing right-to-work laws, increasing police in urban areas to protect Black-owned private property, reducing business taxes at the expense of higher taxes for Black workers, etc. As the most insecure and marginal element of the petty bourgeoisie and aspiring capitalist class, Black Reaganites and Black Capitalists alike have already repudiated the interests of the Black working class and the unemployed; whether their repudiation of Black liberation festers into an aggressive authoritarian political posture will only be decided by history.

"BLACK BRAHMINS: THE UNDERDEVELOPMENT OF BLACK POLITICAL LEADERSHIP."

Author's Note: A section of this chapter was published as "Black Conservation and Accommodation: Of Thomas Sowell and Others," *Negro History Bulletin*, Vol. 45 (April-June, 1982), pp. 32-35.

1. Frantz Kafka, "Couriers," in Walter Kaufman, ed., *Existentialism From Dostoevsky to Sartre* (New York: New American Library, 1956), p. 130.
2. Gordon Crovitz, "Black Community Reviews Life With Reagan," *Wall Street Journal* (September 4, 1981).
3. "NAACP Asserts Reagan Budget Profits the Rich at Expense of Poor," *New York Times* (April 14, 1981).
4. Joyce Daniels Phillips, "Reaganomics Call For Values," *Jackson Advocate* (September 17–23, 1981).
5. Crovitz, "Black Community Reviews Life with Reagan."
6. Ivory Phillips, "Reaganism, Americanism and the Future," *Jackson Advocate* (September 17–23, 1981).
7. Marable, *Blackwater*, pp. 160–161.
8. Lee A. Daniels, "The New Black Conservatives," *New York Times* (October 4, 1981); Nathan Wright, Jr., "Dilemma of Black Republicans," *Pensacola Voice* (May 30–June 5, 1981).
9. See Colin Campbell, "Conservative Economist Rides With the Reagan Tide," *New York Times*, (September 18, 1981).

    Sowell's unbridled sycophancy was strikingly revealed in an October 12, 1981 interview in *U.S. News and World Report*. Beneath a large portrait of slaves laboring in the cotton fields, Sowell stated, "Blacks who suffered from slavery also suffered from its aftermath, in that many became hypersensitized against menial jobs. That's tragic." Sowell asserted that racial discrimination plays only a minor role "in holding back ethnic groups in America." Sowell's bankruptcy as a social theorist is matched only by his ability to debase himself as the witless tool of racist reactionaries.
10. "Top Black Reagan Appointees Honored At Hill Reception," *Pensacola Voice* (June 6–12, 1981); "White House Names Minority Liaisons," *Civil Rights Update* (May, 1981), p. 4.

11. Tony Brown, "NAACP Shuns Denver Blacks, Part II," Fort Lauderdale *Westside Gazette* (August 30, 1981).

    Another prominent fellow traveler is Percy Sutton, former attorney for the family of Malcolm X and past Manhattan Borough president. At the San Francisco conference of Black conservatives, Sutton attacked "the environmental movement" and praised the Federal deregulation of corporations. Reagan's policy of urban enterprise zones, a massive corporate rip-off of taxpayers and inner city residents, received Sutton's endorsement with one qualification. "Free enterprise zones" will work, he declared, only if the state "[gave] us a lot [more] policemen." "Percy Sutton Calls For Help To 'Help Ourselves,' " *Milwaukee Courier* (June 13, 1981).

12. Marguerite Ross Barnett, "The Congressional Black Caucus: Illusions and Realities of Power," in Michael B. Preston, Lenneal J. Henderson, Jr. and Paul Puryear, eds., *The New Black Politics: The Search For Political Power* (New York and London: Longman, 1982), pp. 28–54.

13. Frank Elam, "Marchers Back Voting Rights," *Guardian* (May 6, 1981); "3,000 March in Montgomery," *Guardian* (August 19, 1981).

    Jackson also led a major march in Natchez, Mississippi on May 31, 1981, in support of the Voting Rights Act. "Natchez March Begins Struggle," *Jackson Advocate* (June 4–10, 1981). Julian Bond hosted a Black conference on the significance of the Voting Rights Act in Jackson, Mississippi, on October 10, while Yolanda King, Martin's daughter, led a rally of over 1,000 people to defend a group of poor Black workers attempting to organize in Tylertown, Mississippi, on October 3, 1981. "Bond in Jackson for Voting Confab," and "Mass March At Tylertown," *Jackson Advocate* (October 8–14, 1981).

14. "Bond Accuses Greensboro Police of 'Negligence,' " *Atlanta Constitution* (October 3, 1981).

15. William Serrin, "Labor Group Girds For Capital Rally," *New York Times* (September 18, 1981); Seth S. King, "240,000 in Capital Rally For Protest of Reagan Policies," *New York Times* (September 20, 1981).

16. William Raspberry, "Coke Deal: Reciprocity Rather Than Generosity," *Miami Times* (September 3, 1981).

    Despite Jackson's failures, the Black capitalists' strategy continues on. In March, 1982, Heublein, Inc., a multi-billion-dollar beverage and food corporation, announced a $180 million program to develop Black business, in conjunction with Jackson and Operation PUSH Heublein's plans provided for $20 million in minority oriented programs in 1982, rising to about $50 million within five years. The program included: "$10 million in capital assistance to enable blacks to open 24 Kentucky Fried Chicken stores, with an additional 88 franchises to be made available to qualified investors who want to become owner-operators; a 50 percent increase (in 1982) in black ad agency expenditures; and increase in loan agreements with black-owned banks to at least $20 million; the placing of 15 percent of Heublein's group life insurance with a black-owned company; a plan to hire black-owned law and accounting firms; and a plan to spend $75 million in goods and services under a minority purchasing program." "Heublein Plan on Blacks," *New York Times* (March 17, 1982).

17. *Ibid.;* and "Coke Covenant Brings King Followers Back Together," *Miami Times* (September 3, 1981).

   The Black Brahmins joined forces once more when Ralph Abernathy, a prominent supporter of Reagan in 1980, and "Daddy" King endorsed the mayoral candidacy of Andrew Young in Atlanta, Georgia. Carole Ashkinaze, "Abernathy Endorses Young," *Atlanta Constitution* (October 3, 1981).

18. Tony Brown, "The newest twist in the Coke Deal," *Pensacola Voice* (September 26–October 2, 1981).

19. Sheila Rule, "Black Caucus in Capital Works to Develop Communal Leadership," *New York Times* (September 30, 1981).

20. Gus Savage, syndicated column, *Pensacola Voice* (September 26–October 2, 1981).

21. Reginald Stuart, "Georgia Blacks Join Battle on Legislative Redistricting," *New York Times* (September 28, 1981); Vernon Jarrett, "Black Democrats turn to the Republicans for help," *In These Times* (September 16–22, 1981).

   The attitude of white Reaganites toward the Black Old Guard leadership was one of bitter denunciation. Richard Richards, Reagan's personal selection as national GOP chairperson, complained that his party did not win many Black votes because of "the so-called Black leaders, the so-called civil rights leaders, [and] the Black ministers." Richards attacked Benjamin Hooks by name, stating that "the NAACP hasn't been our friend at all," and declared that Reagan and other Republican politicians would go "around, through and over" traditional Black leaders to win a conservative Black constituency. Adam Clymer, "Black Leaders Criticized by GOP Chairman," *New York Times* (September 20, 1981).

22. Stokely Carmichael's 1966 definition of integration, published in the *New York Review of Books,* represents the popular expression of Black nationalism during the Black Power period: "Integration speaks not at all to the problem of poverty—only to the problem of blackness. Integration today means the man who "makes it," leaving his black brothers behind in the ghetto. It has no relevance to the Harlem wino or to the cotton-picker making three dollars a day . . . integration is a subterfuge for the maintenance of white supremacy." It is based on a "lie: that black people inherently can't do the same thing white people do, unless white people help them." Carmichael, *Stokely Speaks,* p. 27.

23. Meier, *Negro Thought in America,* pp. 32–33, 50–51.

   DuBois' views on Price are unclear. In *The Souls of Black Folk,* he relates that "Price and others had sought a way of honorable alliance with the best of the Southerners," thus paving the way for Booker T. Washington. In an unsigned editorial in the *Crisis,* Price is called a relatively progressive and successful educator who possessed "the quality of grit." Had Washington not existed, however, it seems likely that Price could have emerged in his place as the leading Black accommodationist. See DuBois, *The*

Souls of Black Folk, p. 42; "The Ruling Passion," *Crisis*, Vol. 23 (March, 1922), pp. 224–225.

24. *Ibid.*, pp. 26, 27, 36, 45.
25. *Ibid.*, pp. 31, 38, 46–47, 128–129, 173–174, 228.
26. DuBois' criticism of the Tuskegee philosophy remains the best analysis of the failures of accommodation: " . . . the way to truth and right lies in straightforward honesty, not in indiscriminate flattery; in praising those of the South who do well and criticising uncompromisingly those who do ill. . . . the way for a people to gain their reasonable rights is not be vulantarily throwing them away and insisting that they do not want them; the way for a people to gain their respect is not by continually belittling and ridiculing themselves." DuBois, *The Souls of Black Folk*, pp. 50–51.
27. Lawrence W. Levine makes this connection between the Tuskegee philosophy and the blues: "It was not coincidental that a new emphasis upon the individual and individual expression was taking hold in black song at the very time that Booker T. Washington's philosophy was taking hold among black intellectuals and the black middle class. The individualist, ethos [influenced] the black school teachers produced by such new institutions as Hampton and Tuskegee, the popular press, and . . . preachers, businessmen, and leaders of every sort. This is not to suggest that the blues mirrored the moral and economic lessons of the [Horatio] Alger message; the opposition would be closer to the truth. But there was a direct relationship between the national ideological emphasis upon the individual, the popularity of Booker T. Washington's teachings, and the rise of the blues." Levine, *Black Culture and Black Consciousness*, pp. 222–223.
28. James, *The Black Jacobins*, pp. 127–128.

Black accommodationists and conservatives alike suffer from what Walter Rodney described as "a cultural and psychological crisis" of doubt, a failure to believe in the effective capacity of nonwhites to direct their own societies. "That means that the African himself has doubts about his capacity to transform and develop his natural environment. With such doubts, he even challenges those of his brothers who say that Africa can and will develop through the efforts of its own people." In a biracial capitalist social order, Black conservatives tacitly acknowledge the "higher" intellectual and cultural level of whites, identify with Western thought, and attempt to out-excel whites in the mental gymnastics that they have established for themselves. Rodney, *How Europe Underdeveloped Africa* (London: Bogle l'Ouverture, 1972), p. 30.

29. Meier, *Negro Thought In America*, pp. 72, 110, 209–210; Harlan, *Booker T. Washington*, pp. 168-169.
30. K.L. Walgemoth, "Wilson and Federal Segregation," *Journal of Negro History* Vol. 44 (April, 1959), pp. 158–173; Andrew Buni, *The Negro in Virginia Politics, 1902-1965* (Charlottesville, Virginia: University of Virginia Press, 1967); Zane Miller, *Boss Cox's Cincinnati: Urban Politics in the Progressive Era* (New York: Oxford University Press, 1968); Lyle W. Dorsett, *The Pendergast*

Machine (New York: Oxford University Press, 1968); Herbert Aptheker, *A Documentary History of the Negro People in the United States* (New York: Citadel Press, 1969), pp. 819–820.

31. Chuck Stone, *Black Political Power in America,* Revised Edition (New York: Delta, 1970), pp. 177–179; Hanes Walton, Jr., *Black Politics: A Theoretical and Structural Analysis* (Philadelphia: J.B. Lippincott, 1972), pp. 67, 107, 111, 116.

32. Henry Lee Moon, *Balance of Power: The Negro Vote* (Garden City, New York: Doubleday, 1948), pp. 35–36.

33. Stone, *Black Political Power in America,* p. 52.

34. *Ibid.,* pp. 192–207.

   Even Malcolm X was favorably impressed with Powell. In 1963 he informed Alex Haley, "I'd think about retiring if the black man had ten like him in Washington." Malcolm X, *The Autobiography of Malcolm X,* p. 402.

35. *Ibid.,* pp. 174–175.

36. Rodney, *How Europe Underdeveloped Africa,* p. 280.

37. See George Schuyler, *Black and Conservative* (New Rochelle, New York: Arlington House, 1966).

38. See Thomas Sowell, "The Uses of Government for Racial Equality," *National Review,* Vol. 33 (September 4, 1981), pp. 1009–1016; "Myths About Minorities," *Commentary,* Vol. 68 (August, 1979), pp. 33–37; *Ethnic America: A History* (New York: Basic Books, 1981); *Markets and Minorities* (New York: Basic Books, 1981); "Affirmative Action Reconsidered," *Public Interest,* Vol. 42 (Winter, 1976), pp. 47–65; *Race and Economics* (New York: McKay, 1975).

39. Kwame Nkrumah, *Class Struggle in Africa* (New York: International Publishers, 1970), p. 56.

"THE AMBIGUOUS POLITICS OF THE BLACK CHURCH."

Author's Note: Sections of this chapter were published under the title, "King's Ambiguous Legacy," in *WIN* magazine, Vol. 18 (April 15, 1982), pp. 15–19.

1. Meier, *Negro Thought in America,* pp. 6, 30, 49, 55–66; Lerone Bennett, Jr., *Black Power USA: The Human Side of Reconstruction 1867–1877* (Baltimore: Penguin, 1967), p. 102.

2. "Black Persons Employed in Selected Professional Occupations for Selected Years: 1890 to 1970," and "Black Elected Officials," in Bureau of the Census, *The Social and Economic Status of the Black Population,* pp. 76, 156.

3. *Ibid.*

4. W.E.B. DuBois, "The Religion of the Negro," *New World*, Vol. 9 (December, 1900), pp. 614–625.

5. DuBois, "The Negro Church," book review of Carter G. Woodson's *The History of the Negro Church* in *The Freeman*, Vol. 6 (October 4, 1922), pp. 92–93; editorial on "The Negro Church," in *Crisis*, Vol. 4 (May, 1912), pp. 24–27.

6. "The Baptist Controversy," *Crisis*, Vol. 11 (April, 1916), pp. 314–316.

7. "Postscript," *Crisis*, Vol. 35 (June, 1928), p. 203. Also see "Postscript," *Crisis*, Vol. 38 (June, 1931), pp. 207–208, in which DuBois critiques the religious views of Darrow and Bishop R.E. Jones.

8. "The Three Wise Men," *Crisis*, Vol. 7 (December, 1913), pp. 80–82.

9. W.E.B. DuBois to the Reverend John R. Timpany, January 17, 1945, in Herbert Aptheker, ed., *The Correspondence of W.E.B. DuBois: Volume III* (Amherst, Massachusetts: University of Massachusetts Press, 1978), pp. 26–27.

10. W.E.B. DuBois to the Reverend William Crowe, Jr., August 9, 1939, in Herbert Aptheker, ed., *The Correspondence of W.E.B. DuBois: Volume II* (Amherst, Massachusetts: University of Massachusetts Press, 1976), pp. 144–145.

11. "The Failure of the Negro Church," *Messenger*, Vol. 2 (October, 1919), p. 6.

12. V.F. Calverton, "Orthodox Religion, Does It Handicap Negro Progress?" *Messenger*, Vol. 9 (July, 1927), pp. 221–236.

13. LeRoi Jones, *Home: Social Essays* (New York: William Morrow, 1966), pp. 94–95.

14. Harold Cruse, *The Crisis of the Negro Intellectual* (New York: William Morrow, 1967), p. 90.

15. When the Truman Administration attempted to convict DuBois on the charge that he had "[failed] to register as agent of a foreign principal," the response of the Black Church was divided. The National Baptist Convention "took no action," but Black Baptists in Philadelphia voiced strong support for DuBois. Most AME and AMEZ church leaders were silent out of "the wide fear and intimidation" of the McCarthy period. However, Reverdy C. Ransom, former board trustee president of Wilberforce University and senior bishop of the AME Church publicly supported DuBois as "one of the best-known Negroes in America or for that matter in the world. This blow at him looks like a strike at the intelligentsia of Negro Americans and the millions who trust and follow their leadership." See Reverdy C. Ransom to the National Council of the Arts, Sciences and Professions, October 26, 1951, copy of DuBois, in Aptheker, ed., *The Correspondence of W.E.B. DuBois, Volume III*, pp. 317–318; also see DuBois, *The Autobiography of W.E.B. DuBois*, p. 391.

16. E. Franklin Frazier, *The Negro Church in America* (New York: Schocken Books, 1964), pp. 51, 72, 73; Benjamin E. Mays and Joseph W. Nicholson, *The Negro's Church* (New York: Arno Press, 1969), p. 59.

17. Daniel C. Thompson, *The Negro Leadership Class* (Englewood Cliffs, New Jersey: Prentice-Hall, 1963), p. 37.

18. Numan V. Bartley, *Massive Resistance: Race and Politics in the South During the 1950s* (Baton Rouge: Louisiana State University Press, 1969), pp. 294–301.

   Not a few Black ministers in the South, accommodationist in outlook, quickly joined forces with the white supremacists. The Reverend Dr. M.L. Young of Memphis was praised by the racists as a staunch opponent to integration and "one among the first of his race to combat communism." Young explained his political poverty in this fashion: "When the Supreme Court came out with its decision and the word was handed down that everybody's gonna be integrated now, a lot of these folks like to had a baby. But I want to know: will desegregation be the answer to the progress of the Negro universlly? . . . My approach is like that of Booker T. Washington. In no section of the country does the Negro enjoy the education, employment, and economic opportunities which the Negroes in the South enjoy." James Graham Cook, *The Segregationists* (New York: Appleton-Century-Crofts, 1962), p. 322.

19. William Robert Miller, *Martin Luther King, Jr.: His Life, Martyrdom And Meaning for The World* (New York: Avon Books, 1968), pp. 46–56.

20. *Ibid.*, pp. 56–58.

21. *Ibid.*, pp. 104, 109, 150, 191; Hannah Lees, "Boycott in Philadelphia," Jay David, ed., *Black Defiance: Black Profiles in Courage* (New York: William Morrow, 1972), pp. 162–169.

22. Miller, *Martin Luther King, Jr.*, p. 103.

23. August Meier, "On the Role of Martin Luther King," *New Politics*, Vol. 4 (Winter, 1965), pp. 52–59.

24. Martin Luther King, Jr., "Letter from Birmingham Jail," *The Christian Century* (June 12, 1963); *Liberation* (June, 1963); also see King, *Why We Can't Wait* (New York: Harper and Row, 1964), chapter five.

25. Miller, *Martin Luther King, Jr.* pp. 66, 108, 137, 260.

26. Cruse, *The Crisis of the Negro Intellectual*, p. 322.

27. Meier and Rudwick, *CORE*, p. 120.

28. *Ibid.*, pp. 270–271.

29. James Baldwin, "The Dangerous Road Before Martin Luther King," *Harper's Magazine* (February, 1961), p. 42; Miller, *Martin Luther King, Jr.*, pp. 107–108.

   King's rejection of communism was based on his religious conviction that divine laws set all standards of justice. A Marxist society, he believed, is based on "no divine government, no absolute moral order." As a result, "almost anything—force, violence, murder, lying—is a justifiable means to the 'millenial' end." See Martin Luther King, *Strength to Love*, (New York: Pocket Books, 1964), pp. 114–118.

30. Steven F. Lawson, *Black Ballots: Voting Rights in the South, 1944–1969* (New York: Columbia University Press, 1976), pp. 104–105.

31. Meier and Rudwick, *CORE*, pp. 64–65.

"It was the liberals," Hugh T. Murray argues, "who refused to compromise on the Communist issue. Liberals might compromise with anyone else, sheriffs of Mississippi, bombers of Vietnam, blockaders of Cuba, invaders of Santo Domingo, anyone else except Communists." Middle-class Blacks excluded "Communists and then anyone suspected of being one, even when the result was bitterness, dissension . . . or denial of needed aid." See Murray's review essay of Meier and Rudwick, *CORE*, in *Freedomways*, Vol. 14 (First Quarter, 1974), pp. 62-66.

32. Julius Lester, *Look Out, Whitey! Black Power's Gon' Get Your Mama!* (New York: Grove Press, 1968), p. 79.

33. Harry Golden, *Mr. Kennedy And The Negroes* (Greenwich, Connecticut: Fawcett, 1964), p. 43.

34. Allen, *Black Awakening in Capitalist America*, p. 12.

35. Harold Cruse, *Rebellion Or Revolution?* (New York: William Morrow, 1968), pp. 60–62.

36. *Ibid.*, p. 128.

37. Jones, *Home: Social Essays*, pp. 138–139.

38. Stokely Carmichael and Charles V. Hamilton, *Black Power: The Politics of Liberation in America* (New York: Vintage, 1967), p. 50.

39. Allen, *Black Awakening in Capitalist America*, pp. 126–127.

40. Lester, *Look Out, Whitey! Black Power's Gon' Get Your Mama!* pp. 79, 106–107.

Until 1966, King continued to consider the Johnson Administration, liberal corporate contributions to SCLC, NAACP, and other Black groups as allies in the desegregation struggle. SNCC, on the other hand, viewed "the liberal corporate Establishment as the main but often faraway enemy," and accepted Malcolm's definition of America as simply "one large Mississippi." See Paul Jacobs and Saul Landau, eds. *The New Radicals* (New York: Vintage, 1966), p. 17.

41. Allen, *Black Awakening in Capitalist America*, p. 12.

42. *Ibid.*, p. 111.

43. Carmichael, *Stokely Speaks*, p. 58.

44. Miller, *Martin Luther King, Jr.*, p. 236.

45. *Ibid.*, pp. 267, 272, 280; Carl T. Rowan, "Martin Luther King's Tragic Decision." *Reader's Digest* (September, 1967), p. 42.

46. "Interview with Louis B. Stokes," in Emily Rovetch, ed., *Like It Is* (New York: E.P. Dutton, 1981), p. 42.

47. Antonio Gramsci, *The Modern Prince and Other Writings* (New York: International Publishers, 1970), pp. 90–91.

48. *Ibid.*, pp. 63, 72.

49. Marable, *Blackwater*, pp. 14–50.

50. Gramsci, *The Modern Prince*, p. 77.

51. *Ibid.*, p. 76.

The great danger in Christianity as in all forms of human spirituality is that it all too often blocks the ability for the oppressed to comprehend the political and economic reasons for their victimization. A vivid and particularly sad example of this is illustrated in a letter of one Black man on Death Row in Mississippi, written to the *Jackson Advocate*: "I've been here at Parchman Prison on Death Row for five months and fifteen days. Twelve human beings sentenced me to the penalty of Death for a crime that I did not commit. And today I found out the true and real reason I'm here on Death Row. It's really a good reason; the reason has brought so much joy unto me this very day. I've found God. Yes, God sent me to Death Row so that I may see His light because but through Him only can a person be born again. I'm here in prison because I failed to see my true job in life and that job is to help God in the work that will never be finished and that is saving souls of lost sinners. Praise the Lord." *Jackson Advocate* (January 28-February 3, 1982).

"THE DESTRUCTION OF BLACK EDUCATION."

1. DuBois' estimate of the number of Blacks who were literate in 1865 was 5 percent. DuBois, *Black Reconstruction in America, 1860–1880* (New York: Atheneum, 1971), p. 638.

2. DuBois, "Reconstruction and Its Benefits," *American Historical Review*, Vol. 15 (July, 1910), p. 797.

3. "Table 66, Persons 18 to 24 Years Old Enrolled in College,"; and Table 72, Historically Black Colleges and Universities by Region and Period Founded," in *The Social and Economic Status of the Black Population*, pp. 90, 96; W. Hardin Hughes, "The Negro and Education," in Jessie P. Guzman, ed., *Negro Year Book: A Review of Events Affecting Negro Life 1941–1946* (Tuskegee Institute: Tuskegee Institute Department of Records, 1947), pp. 54–108.

4. Marable, *From The Grassroots*, p. 194.

5. Vincent Harding, "The Vocation of the Black Scholar," in Institute of the Black World, ed., *Education and Black Struggle: Notes from the Colonized World* (Cambridge: Harvard Educational Review, 1974), pp. 3–29.

6. The inevitable retrenchment of the white university establishment against Black studies programs was not entirely unanticipated. In June, 1970, historial Eugene Genovese observed that "most campus liberals who were falling all over themselves to placate . . . Black students were unprincipled scoundrels whose fancy rhetoric disguised an overriding commitment to peace and quiet at any price. As soon as they realized their error in thinking that doles, third-rate educational programs, and fireworks would buy peace—as soon as they learned that black students wanted a serious education ., . . then

these same liberals would send for troops to restore the peace and quiet that alone interest them." Eugene D. Genovese, *In Red and Black: Marxian Explorations in Southern and Afro-American History* (New York: Vintage, 1971), pp. 228–229.

7. Reginald Stuart, "New Trend in College Desegregation Emerges," *New York Times* (September 3, 1981).

8. Marable, *Blackwater,* pp. 151–152.

9. "Bush At Tuskegee," *Black Belt Journal* (April 20, 1981).

10. Stuart, "New Trend in College Desegregation Emerges."

11. *Ibid.;* and "Teachers on Mainly Black Campus Warned to Earn Doctorates," *New York Times* (August 26, 1981).

12. Stuart, "New Trend in College Desegregation Emerges."

13. Harlan, *Booker T. Washington,* p. 286.

14. Louis R. Harlan, *Separate and Unequal: Public School Campaigns and Racism in the Southern Seaboard States, 1901–1915* (Chapel Hill: University of North Carolina Press, 1958), pp. 104–105; Mary Berry, *Black Resistance, White Law: A History of Constitutional Racism in America* (Englewood Cliffs, New Jersey: Prentice-Hall, 1971), p. 180.

15. Steven Roberts, "House, by 265 to 122, Votes to End Justice Department Role in Busing Case," *New York Times* (June 10, 1981).

16. "Teachers on Mainly Black Campus Warned to Earn Doctorates."

17. , Rodney, *How Europe Underdeveloped Africa,* pp. 300–303.

18. Thomas A. Brooks, *Toil and Trouble: A History of American Labor* (New York: Dell Publishing Company, 1971), p. 245.

19. DuBois, *The Education of Black People,* p. xi.

20. Benjamin Quarles, *Black Abolitionists* (New York: Oxford University Press, 1969), p. 201. Also see Martin R. Delaney, *The Condition, Elevation, Emigration and Destiny of the Colored People of the United States* (New York: Arno Press, Reprint of the 1852 edition, 1968).

21. Harding, "The Vocation of the Black Scholar," p. 25.

"THE MEANING OF RACIST VIOLENCE IN LATE CAPITALISM."

1. W.E.B. DuBois, "The Future of the Negro Race in America," *East and the West,* (January, 1904), pp. 4–19.

2. DuBois, syndicated column, *Amsterdam News* (September 18, 1943).

3. Cruse, *The Crisis of the Negro Intellectual,* pp. 344, 448.

4. Sidney M. Willhelm, *Who Needs the Negro?* (Garden City, New York: Anchor Books, 1971), pp. 332–334.

5. Paul C. Bermanzohn and Sally A. Bermanzohn, *The True Story of the Greensboro Massacre*, (New York: Cesar Cause Publishers, 1980).

6. Marable, *Blackwater*, p. 151.

7. Vincent Baker, "Racism and Violence," *Big Red* (March 21, 1981).

8. Frank Elam, "Mobile lynching: White men cleared," *Guardian* (June 17, 1981).

9. "Lynchings in the Mississippi Delta, 1980–1981," *Racially Motivated Random Violence*, (May/June, 1981). Tallachatchie County was also the site of the famous Emmitt Till murder. The town of Tutwiler, where Gray's body was found, has no active NAACP chapter. No Blacks serve on the city council or the school board.

10. Tony Brown, "57 Percent Say Some Black Leaders Selfishly Formented Hysteria," *Jackson Advocate* (September 17–23, 1981).

11. See Mack Jones, "Black Political Empowerment in Atlanta: Myth and Reality," *Annals* (September, 1978), pp. 90–117.

12. Stanley Crouch, "Atlanta Reconstructed," *Village Voice* (April 29, 1981), pp. 17–18; *New York Daily News* (May 3, 1981).

13. "Atlanta Officials Harass Victims," *Guardian* (June 17, 1981); "Fear Alters Atlantans' Summer Plans," *New York Times* (June 5, 1981); interview with Jan Douglas, director, Community Relations, Atlanta, Georgia, September 30, 1981.

14. Raymond Coffey, "Racial views on Atlanta killings," *Chicago Tribune* (May 29, 1981).

15. Tom Fiske, "Atlanta Blacks assert right to self-defense," *Militant* (April 3, 1981).

16. "Profound Outrage, Revolutionary Stirrings Over Atlanta," *Revolutionary Worker* (March 20, 1981); Lionel Cuffie, "Who's killing Atlanta Children?" *Militant* (April 3, 1981).

17. Frank Elam, "5000 rally in D.C. to defend Atlanta's children," *Guardian* (June 3, 1981); Suzanne Haig, "D.C. rally: stop racist terror in Atlanta," *Militant* (June 5, 1981).

18. James H. Cleaver, "Dick Gregory's Theory in Atlanta Deaths Gains Credence," *Charleston Chronicle* (May 30, 1981)

19. Wendell Rawls, Jr., "Washington Rally Marks Atlanta Murders," *New York Times* (May 26, 1981).

20. Coffey, "Racial Views on Atlanta Killings."

21. Editorial, "If Those Kids Were White," *Big Red* (March 28, 1981).
    Columnist William Raspberry also denounced the Washington, D.C. rally as a "display of futility." *Washington Post* (June 1, 1981).

22. *Southern Advocate* (April, 1981).

23. Kevin O. Fitzpatrick, "Serious Questions Raised in Police Slaying Investigation," *Michigan Chronicle* (March 28, 1981).

24. Barney Blakeney, "Minister Concerned With Lack of Local Interest for Charleston Women in Sex Abuse Case in Summerville," *Charleston Chronicle* (March 7, 1981).

25. *Racially Motivated Random Violence,* (September/October, 1981), pp. 5–6.

26. *Cleveland Call and Post* (June 27, 1981).

27. Patricia Tatum, "FBI, NAACP enter case of county man slain by cop." Baltimore *Afro-American* (August 1, 1981).

28. James H. Cleaver, "Chief Daryl Gates Must Go—Right Now!" *Los Angeles Sentinel* (May 13, 1982); Charles P. Wallace, "Blacks More Susceptible to Chokeholds?" *Los Angeles Times,* (May 8, 1982); David Johnston, "Bradley Orders Probe of Statements by Gates," *Los Angeles Times* (May 11, 1982).

   Gates ordered his department's personnel and training division to determine if Blacks were more vulnerable to injury from chokeholds than whites. Gates declared to the press, "We may be finding that in some Blacks when it is. applied the veins or arteries do not open up as fast *as they do on normal people.* There may be something arresting the ability of the blood to flow again (after the hold is applied)."

29. *Chicago Defender* (March 16, 1981); Pat Bryant, "Racism Swings in Mobile Trees," *Atlanta Voice* (April 25, 1981); *Cleveland Call and Post* (May 2, 1981).

30. The following examples above are documented in *Racially Motivated Random Violence* (November, 1981).

31. Tom Hentoff, "200 rally against racism and rightism," *Wesleyan Argus* (October 13, 1981); Mary Beth Bruno, "KKK reported on campus" and "Campbell addresses assembly on racism," *Wesleyan Argus* (November 3, 1981); Mark Sirota, Susan Lepselter and Melissa Hendricks, "Campus reacts to racist poster," *Wesleyan Argus* (October 27, 1981).

   The events at Wesleyan were mirrored at dozens of other college campuses. In the winter of 1979, a group of white students at the University of San Francisco launched the "Society of White Students," a campus group dedicated to preserve and defend "white culture." Whites defaced Black students' posters with the racist epithets "nigger" and "jungle bunny." A series of cross burnings occurred at Purdue University in 1980, and the funds for Black Student Unions were reduced or eliminated at many institutions. See Manning Marable, "Neo-Racism: The White Shadow," *Politics and Education,* Vol. 2 (Spring, 1980), pp. 19–22; Marable, *Blackwater,* p. 151.

32. Alexander L. Taylor, "Hard Times on Main Street," *Time* (October 26, 1981).

33. Paul Sweezy and Harry Magdoff, "The Deepening Crisis of U.S. Capitalism," *Monthly Review* (October, 1981), pp. 12, 15.

34. Kenneth B. Noble, "The Surge in Business Failures," *New York Times* (November 18, 1981); Thomas L. Friedman, "Sag in Home Prices May Affect Families' Investing," *New York Times* (November 16, 1981); Robert Lindsey, "More Families Losing Homes as Inflation and Jobless Rate Soar," *New York Times* (November 28, 1981.)

35. Daniel Patrick Moynihan, "Memo to Nixon on the Status of Negroes, January 16, 1970." *New York Times* (March 1, 1970); U.S. Department of Labor,

Bureau of Labor Statistics, *The Social and Economic Status of Negroes in the United States, 1970,* Report no. 394 (Washington, D.C.: Government Printing Office, 1971).

The urban fiscal crisis within the framework of a racist/capitalist state also manifests itself as a *racial* crisis. In New York City, for example, 3.5 million jobs were destroyed between 1953 and 1973, primarily in manufacturing. Significantly, the prime sectors of job growth during these two decades were in government and highly skilled selected services. The dual labor market process meant that whites continued to occupy positions in the most highly paid sectors, while Puerto Ricans and Afro-Americans assumed the burden of burgeoning unemployment in manufacturing. As petty bourgeois whites and the "professional-managerial class" fled to the suburbs, city tax revenues declined. New businesses that relocated in New York tended to be capital intensive, not labor intensive. The result of the transformation of the city's labor market meant higher Black-on-Black crime, diminished city services for minority communities, and an increased polarization between the races. See Arthur Paris, "Hidden Dimensions of the New York City Fiscal Crisis," *Review of Black Political Economy,* Vol. 10 (Spring, 1980), pp. 262–278; William K. Tabb. "The New York City Fiscal Crisis," in William K. Tabb and Larry Sawers, eds., *Marxism and the Metropolis: New Perspectives in Urban Political Economy* (New York: Oxford University Press, 1978), pp. 241–266; Charles Brecher, *Where Have All the Dollars Gone? Public Expenditures for Human Resource Development in New York City, 1961–1971* (New York: Praeger, 1974).

36. Reich, *Racial Inequality,* p. 6.

37. "A Communist Proposal for a United Front Against War and Racism," *Line of March,* Vol. 1 (March-April, 1981), p. 24; Michael Parenti and Carolyn Kazdin, "The Untold Story of the Greensboro Massacre," *Monthly Review,* Vol. 33 (November, 1981), pp. 42–50; Bermanzohn and Bermanzohn, *The True Story of the Greensboro Massacre.*

The closest historical parallel to the Greensboro slayings might be the execution of Leo Frank in Georgia, August 16, 1915. Frank, a Jew, was accused and convicted of slaying a white fourteen-year-old girl, in a trial characterized by the cry for the blood of the "Jew pervert." Governor John M. Slaton commuted the death sentence on the day before his term in office ended. Twenty five armed men entered the state prison, took Leo Frank out, and hanged him. "A heel was repeatedly ground into the dead man's face, and bits of his clothing and of the rope were distributed as souvenirs." The new Georgia governor and mayor of Atlanta defended the lynching. Former Populist Tom Watson declared, "The next Jew who does what Frank did is going to get exactly the same thing that we give to Negro rapists." The Frank case was a key reason for the resurrection of the Ku Klux Klan in 1915, and formed the ideological basis for the infamous "Red Summer of 1919." See C. Vann Woodward, *Tom Watson: Agrarian Rebel* (New York: Oxford University Press, 1970), pp. 435–450.

38. Thomas Weisskopf, "The Current Economic Crisis in Historical Perspec-
tive," *Socialist Review* (May-June, 1981), p. 49; Sam Bowles, "The Trilateral
Commission: Have Capitalism and Democracy Come to a Parting of the
Ways?" URPE, ed., *U. S. Capitalism in Crisis* (New York: URPE, 1978). Also
see Terry Cannon, "Reviving McCarthyism in Washington," *Political Affairs*,
Vol. 60 (October, 1981), pp. 20–25.

39. Harry Ring, "A Military Coup the best we could hope for?" *Militant*
(November 27, 1981).

40. Irving Kristol, "Will Conservative Economics Work?" *Wall Street Journal*
(October 24, 1979). Yale professor James Tobin, the 1981 winner of the Nobel
Prize, has predicted that Reaganomics "will have devastating effects on the
finances of many state and local governments and on the services they render,
especially to the poor. In the end, I think, a democratic policy will not tolerate
in its government and central bank an economic strategy of indifference to the
real state of the economy." This articulates the assumption, held by many
liberal Democrats and democratic socialists in the U.S., that the capitalist
state will not resort to extralegal or extraordinary means to discipline labor or
to restore capitalist profits at the expense of the democratic process. James
Tobin, "Reaganomics and Economics," *New York Review of Books*, Vol. 28
(December 3, 1981) p. 14.

41. Les Evans, ed. *Disaster in Chile: Allende's Strategy and Why it Failed* (New York:
Pathfinder, 1974), pp. 104–105; Paul E. Sigmund, *The Overthrow of Allende
and the Politics of Chile, 1964–1976* (Pittsburgh: University of Pittsburgh
Press, 1977), p. 212; Luis Corvalan, "The Unarmed Road of the Revolution:
How It Worked Out in Chile," *Political Affairs*, Vol. 58 (July, 1978), pp.
21–29.

It is of some importance to American progressives to analyze critically the
U.S. state's role in the brutal murder of Allende, the military overthrow of
Chile's democratic socialist government, and the subsequent installation of a
pro-American, fascist regime. From the moment Allende achieved the
presidency in a democratic election on September 4, 1970, U.S. ambassador
Edward Korry wrote frantically to the Nixon administration: "Chile voted
calmly to have a Marxist-Leninist state, the first nation in the world to make
this choice freely and knowingly . . . It will have the most profound effect on
Latin America and beyond; we have suffered a grievous defeat; the consequences will be domestic and international." Henry Kissinger, then Nixon's
National Security Adviser, later wrote that "Allende's election was a challenge
to our national interest. We did not find it easy to reconcile ourselves to a
second Communist state in the Western Hemisphere." Covert action by the
CIA was required to check Allende's "hostility to the United States and his
patent intention to create in effect another Cuba . . . Allende's success would
have had implications also for the future of Communist parties in Western
Europe, whose policies would inevitably undermine the Western Alliance
whatever claims of respectability." Kissinger, *White House Years* (Boston:
Little, Brown, 1979), pp. 653, 654, 656–657.

42. Michael Billig and Andrew Bell, "Fascist Parties in Post-War Britain," *Race Relations Abstracts*, Vol. 5 (February, 1980), pp. 1–30; G. Weightman, "Red roses and drums," *New Society* (April 28, 1977); "Right, righter, rightest," *The Economist* (April 14, 1979); "Tyndall's Sentimental Journey," *Searchlight*, No. 53 (September, 1979), pp. 3–5.

   The politics of Reaganism and the New Right is a phenomenon of political retrenchment, crude racism and capitalist reaction that is evident not only in the U.K. and the U.S., but across Western Europe. In the Netherlands, Italy, France, West Germany and Switzerland, the extreme right since the late 1960s has been organized specifically against nonwhite or colored immigrants and migrant workers. The cutting edge of neoconservatism is not Nazism or fascism in the classical sense, but white supremacy. See Christopher T. Husbands, "Contemporary Right-Wing extremism in *Western European Journal of Political Research*, Vol. 9 (March, 1981), pp. 75–99.

43. Peggy Kahn, "Thatcher's Assault on the Unions," *Socialist Review*, Vol. 10 (September-October, 1980), p. 55.

   Thatcher's Conservative government has even gone as far as to deny that the racial uprisings in south London's Brixton neighborhood in April, 1981, were caused by racism. British police are "not on the whole racist." "London Melee Not Race Riot, Study Says," *New York Times* (November 26, 1981).

44. Scott Anderson, "Black Liberation Army, White Left Ties Used to Justify Government Crackdown, Obadele Says," *Milwaukee Courier* (November 7, 1981); "Conflicts, Brinks, Boston and RNA," *Jackson Advocate* (November 5–11, 1981); "Case Against Fulani Ali Collapses," *Mississippi Enterprise* (November 14, 1981); Wes Miller, " Sunni-Ali Blames 'Fascist State' for Her Arrest," *Jackson Advocate* (November 12–18, 1981); Nelson Gonzalez, "Black Leaders Condemn FBI Terrorism Smear," *Militant* (November 13, 1981); Nelson Gonzales, "Black Activist released, terrorism smear continues," *Militant* (November 20, 1981).

45. Mike Wyman, "Black August Activists Raided," *Guardian* (November 11, 1981).

46. Michael Kozak, "Anti-Apartheid activists framed up in Albany," *Militant* (October 30, 1981); William Robinson, "Springboks Hounded Out of U.S.," *Guardian* (October 7, 1981).

47. Malik Miah, "Black Party Sued in Affirmative-Action Fight," *Militant* (November 27, 1981).

48. Georgi Dimitrov, Report to Seventh Comintern Congress, 1935, quoted in Palmiro Togliatti, *Lectures on Fascism* (New York: International Publishers, 1976), pp. 1–2.

49. It is paramount to distinguish between the traditional racism of Jim Crow and Southern segregation of the late nineteenth to mid-twentieth century with the new racist "counter-revolutionary" movement that exists now. James Boggs correctly characterizes the current mood: "Every day that the crisis of inflation, mass unemployment and barbarism in all our social relationships grows worse, more and more Americans are joining or following these

counter-revolutionary organizations. These organizations are led by very calculating and political individuals who are skillfully playing on the fears, frustrations and prejudices of middle America. There are a lot of white Americans who have the illusion that America can go back to where it used to be . . . just as there are a lot of Black Americans who have the illusion that we can go back to struggling only against racism when the only solution to our problems has become the struggle against capitalism." James Boggs, "From Racism to Counter-Revolution," speech in Milwaukee, Wisconsin, November 1, 1980.

50. Bernard Bailyn, *The Ideological Origins of the American Revolution* (Cambridge: Harvard University Press, 1967), pp. 144–159; David B. Davis, *The Slave Power Conspiracy and the Paranoid Style* (Baton Rouge: Louisiana State University Press, 1969), pp. 3–5, 76.

51. Louis Althusser, *For Marx* (New York: Vintage, 1970), p. 67; Louis Althusser and Etienne Balibar, *Reading Capital* (London: Verso, 1979), p. 25.

52. Marable, *Blackwater*, pp. 69–77.

53. See Jerry Hirsh, "To 'Unfrock the Charlatans'," *Race Relations Abstracts*, Vol. 6 (May, 1981), pp. 1-65.

54. The National Advisory Commission on Civil Disorders, *Report of the National Advisory Commission on Civil Disorders*, (New York: Bantam Books, 1968), p. 2.

"CONCLUSION: TOWARD A SOCIALIST AMERICA."

1. Rodney, *How Europe Underdeveloped Africa*, p. 7.

2. The extreme left wing of the French Revolution, the Babouvists, mapped out a plan to seize control of society without any real democratic participation of the working class. A half century later, the Blanquists argued that a militant vanguard should seize state power in the name of the masses. See Blanqui, *Textes Choisis* (Paris: Editions Sociales, 1955); Babeuf, *Textes Choisis* (Paris: Editions Sociales, 1965); David McLellan, *Karl Marx: His Life and Thought* (New York: Harper and Row, 1973), pp. 155, 168, 170, 187. An elitist dictatorship which exercises authority in the "name of the people" has no relationship with genuine socialist democracy or workers' power.

3. Boggs and Boggs, *Revolution and Evolution in the Twentieth Century*, p. 260.

4. Carl Boggs, "Gramsci and Eurocommunism," *Radical America*, Vol. 14 (May-June, 1980), pp. 15–16.

5. Marable, *Blackwater*, pp. 171–186.

6. This point cannot be overemphasized. Social democrats tend to substitute white students and professionals for the traditional working class. They develop reformist programs which concentrate on "quality of life concerns," such as the environment and the issue of nuclear power, which are valid issues, but not of the nature which can generate the immediate and profound concern of Blacks, Latinos and blue-collar workers. Neo-Bakuninists make the same error in the opposite direction by glorifying the "lumpenproletariat" as the motivative factor in socialist revolution.

7. Cabral, *Revolution in Guinea*, p. 79.

8. Boggs and Boggs, *Revolution and Evolution in the Twentieth Century*, pp. 260–261.

9. James, *The Black Jacobins*, p. 127.

10. Karl Marx, *The Eighteenth Brumaire of Louis Bonaparte* (New York: International Publishers, 1975), p. 15.

11. C.L.R. James, *Modern Politics* (Detroit: Bewick, 1973), p. 46.

12. *Ibid.*, p. 155.

Tables

Author's note
Census data on Black Americans is notoriously unreliable in many respects. Yet when taken into perspective with other factors, it can provide critical insights into the material conditions of Blacks in the United States. The social scientist who tacitly accepts the quantitative research of the U.S. government without this *caveat* will inevitably succumb to the ideological hegemony of the state vis-a-vis any alternative framework of analysis.
—M.M.

Table I
Urban-rural residence: 1890-1970
Total population (thousands)

	Black	Urban	Rural total	Rural farm	Foreign born
1890	7,489	20	80	(N)	20
1910	9,828	27	73	(N)	40
1940	12,866	49	51	35	84
1950	15,045	62	38	21	114
1960	18,849	73	27	8	125
1970	22,539	81	19	2	253

(N) = no information

Source: Bureau of the Census, *The Social and Economic Status of the Black Population in the United States: An Historical View, 1790-1978* (Washington, D.C.: U.S. Government Printing Office, 1980), p. 14.

Table II
Occupations of Black workers 14 years old and over, 1940, 1960, 1970.
Percentages

	1940	1960	1970
Total employed	4,479	6,097	7,420
Percent	100	100	100
White-collar workers	**6**	**13**	**24**
Professional, technical	3	5	8
Nonfarm managers, administrators	1	2	2
Sales, clerical	2	7	14
Blue-collar workers	**28**	**38**	**37**
Craft	3	6	8
Operatives, transport	10	19	21
Nonfarm laborers	14	13	8
Farm workers	**32**	**8**	**3**
Farmers, managers	15	3	
Farm laborers	17	5	2
Service workers	**34**	**32**	**25**
Private household	22	15	7
Other	12	17	18
Occupation not reported	1	8	12

Source: Bureau of the Census, *The Social and Economic Status of the Black Population*, p. 74.

Table III
Black civilian labor force, by industry: 1977
Numbers in thousands. Annual averages.

Construction[a]	404
Manufacturing	2,254
Nondurable goods	996
Transportation, communications, public utilities	658
Wholesale, retail trade	1,260
Finance, insurance, real estate	369
Service industries	3,276
Agriculture[a]	146
Government	703

[a] total for Black men only

Source: Bureau of the Census, *The Social and Economic Status of the Black Population*, p. 249.

Table IV
Unemployment rates for Black workers, by industry and sex: 1977
Annual averages in percentages

	Black men	Black women
Total	13.1	14.8
Construction	**18.6**	**B**
Manufacturing	**9.7**	**15.6**
Durable goods	8.7	12.9
Primary metal industries	10.2	B
Fabricated metal industries	13.6	B
Machinery	5.9	B
Electrical equipment	B	14.3
Motor vehicles, equipment	5.6	B
Other transportation equipment	8.8	B
Other durable goods	9.4	15.5
Nondurable goods	**11.4**	**17.6**
Food products	11.6	19.7
Textile mill products	8.6	B
Apparel and other finished textile products	B	15.6
Other nondurable goods	11.3	19.6
Transportation, communication and public utilities	**7.2**	**6.7**
Communication and public utilities	6.1	3.7
Service industries	**11.5**	**11.7**
Government wage and salary workers	**7.1**	**9.4**
Agricultural wage and salary workers	**11.1**	**B**
Wholesale and retail trade	**15.9**	**21.6**
Finance, insurance, real estate	**10.7**	**9.0**

B = less than 75,000 workers.

Source: Bureau of the Census, *The Social and Economic Status of the Black Population*, p. 215.

Table V
Age and sex—poverty status in 1978 of persons, by family relationship, sex of head, race, and Spanish origin
Numbers in thousands. Persons as of March, 1979.

Age and sex	All races Total	All races Below poverty level Number	% of total	White Total	White Below poverty level Number	% of total	Black Total	Black Below poverty level Number	% of total	Spanish origin Total	Spanish origin Below poverty level Number	% of total
All persons												
Both sexes, total	**215,656**	**24,497**	**11.4**	**186,450**	**16,259**	**8.7**	**24,956**	**7,625**	**30.6**	**12,079**	**2,607**	**21.6**
Under 14 years	46,070	7,583	16.5	38,052	4,467	11.7	6,907	2,898	42.0	4,021	1,115	27.7
14 to 17 years	16,241	2,348	14.5	13,617	1,364	10.0	2,322	932	40.1	991	269	27.2
18 to 21 years	16,375	2,036	12.4	13,967	1,346	9.6	2,097	632	30.1	1,020	211	20.6
22 to 24 years	11,674	1,151	9.9	10,017	787	7.9	1,403	323	23.0	679	101	14.8
25 to 34 years	34,052	2,783	8.2	29,574	1,931	6.5	3,644	761	20.9	1,926	344	17.9
35 to 44 years	24,611	1,860	7.6	21,534	1,286	6.0	2,577	512	19.9	1,367	229	16.8
45 to 54 years	22,826	1,638	7.2	20,145	1,154	5.7	2,277	455	20.0	961	125	13.0
55 to 59 years	11,211	900	8.0	10,070	664	6.6	972	226	23.3	341	56	16.5
60 to 64 years	9,420	964	10.2	8,525	729	8.6	804	224	27.9	233	32	13.9
65 years and over	23,175	3,233	13.9	20,950	2,530	12.1	1,954	662	33.9	539	125	23.1
Median age, years	30.1	22.7		30.9	25.9		24.5	17.9		22.0	16.8	
Male, total	**104,480**	**10,017**	**9.6**	**90,781**	**6,648**	**7.3**	**11,625**	**3,078**	**26.5**	**5,922**	**1,186**	**20.0**
Under 14 years	23,511	3,779	16.1	19,474	2,207	11.3	3,477	1,460	42.0	2,043	586	28.7
14 to 17 years	8,253	1,138	13.8	6,938	667	9.6	1,161	448	38.6	513	138	26.8
18 to 21 years	8,010	803	10.0	6,894	519	7.5	966	252	26.1	511	105	20.5
22 to 24 years	5,719	447	7.8	4,972	337	6.8	627	92	14.7	322	34	10.5
25 to 34 years	16,718	926	5.5	14,712	713	4.8	1,607	181	11.3	917	118	12.9
35 to 44 years	11,940	656	5.5	10,578	498	4.7	1,124	126	11.2	640	82	12.9
45 to 54 years	11,036	646	5.8	9,804	486	5.0	1,053	148	14.0	457	44	9.6
55 to 59 years	5,342	304	5.7	4,815	225	4.7	438	73	16.7	169	19	11.1
60 to 64 years	4,402	367	8.3	3,996	282	7.1	359	81	22.6	101	9	9.1
65 years and over	9,548	951	10.0	8,598	714	8.3	812	217	26.7	250	52	20.9
Median age, years	29.0	18.5		29.8	21.5		23.0	14.7		21.2	14.2	

Female, total	**111,175**	**14,480**	**13.0**	**95,669**	**9,610**	**10.0**	**13,332**	**4,547**	**34.1**	**6,156**	**1,420**	**23.1**
Under 14 years	22,558	3,804	16.9	18,578	2,260	12.2	3,430	1,438	41.9	1,979	528	26.7
14 to 17 years	7,988	1,210	15.1	6,679	697	10.4	1,161	484	41.7	477	132	27.6
18 to 21 years	8,365	1,233	14.7	7,073	827	11.7	1,131	380	33.6	510	106	20.7
22 to 24 years	5,955	704	11.8	5,045	451	8.9	775	231	29.8	358	67	18.7
25 to 34 years	17,334	1,857	10.7	14,861	1,219	8.2	2,037	580	28.5	1,009	226	22.4
35 to 44 years	12,671	1,204	9.5	10,956	788	7.2	1,453	386	26.6	728	147	20.2
45 to 54 years	11,790	993	8.4	10,341	668	6.5	1,225	307	25.1	503	81	16.1
55 to 59 years	5,869	596	10.2	5,255	438	8.3	534	153	28.7	173	38	21.8
60 to 64 years	5,018	598	11.9	4,529	447	9.9	445	143	32.2	131	23	17.6
65 years and over	13,627	2,282	16.7	12,352	1,816	14.7	1,142	445	38.9	289	72	25.1
Median age, years	31.2	26.6		32.0	29.7		25.8	21.7		22.9	19.9	

Source: Bureau of the Census, *Characteristics of the Population Below the Poverty Level: 1978* (Washington, D.C.: Government Printing Office, 1980), p. 51.

Table VI

Earners per family, by race: 1967-1978

Data as of March of the year following the income year.

Race and number of earners	1967	1968	1969	1970	1971	1972	1973	1974	1975	1976	1977	1978
White												
Number, thousands	44,814	45,437	46,022	46,535	47,641	48,477	48,919	49,451	49,161	49,378	49,898	50,312
Percent	100.0	100.0	100.0	100.0	100.0	100.0	100.0	100.0	100.0	100.0	100.0	100.0
No earners	8.2	8.0	8.3	8.7	9.1	9.3	10.0	10.5	11.7	11.8	11.9	11.8
1 earner	39.5	38.8	38.2	37.4	38.1	37.5	35.6	35.1	35.1	33.6	32.8	31.7
2 earners or more	52.3	53.1	53.5	53.8	52.9	53.2	54.4	54.3	53.1	54.7	55.3	56.5
2 earners	38.4	39.0	39.0	39.3	38.8	39.4	40.2	39.8	38.9	39.9	40.3	41.6
3 earners	10.0	10.0	10.1	10.1	9.9	9.6	9.5	9.6	9.8	9.5	10.0	9.7
4 earners or more	3.9	4.1	4.4	4.4	4.2	4.2	4.7	4.9	4.4	5.3	5.0	5.2
Persons per family	3.59	3.56	3.54	3.52	3.47	3.42	3.38	3.36	3.32	3.31	3.28	3.25
Earners per family	1.67	1.68	1.68	1.68	1.67	1.67	1.68	1.68	1.63	1.66	1.67	1.69
Ratio of persons to earners per family	2.15	2.12	2.11	2.10	2.08	2.05	2.01	2.00	2.04	1.99	1.96	1.92
Black												
Number, thousands	4,589	4,646	4,774	4,928	5,157	5,265	5,440	5,403	5,512	5,692	5,699	5,824
Percent	100.0	100.0	100.0	100.0	100.0	100.0	100.0	100.0	100.0	100.0	100.0	100.0
No earners	10.2	10.0	10.5	11.9	14.4	15.1	15.3	17.0	17.7	18.1	18.5	17.2
1 earner	31.6	32.9	32.3	33.5	34.4	35.4	35.3	34.1	35.5	34.7	35.6	36.2
2 earners of more	58.2	57.1	57.3	54.5	51.2	49.5	49.5	48.9	46.8	47.3	45.9	46.6
2 earners	41.8	41.2	41.7	40.4	37.4	38.0	36.3	36.5	34.8	35.6	34.2	34.6
3 earners	11.1	10.1	10.2	9.3	9.8	7.9	9.2	8.2	7.9	8.2	7.8	8.1
4 earners or more	5.3	5.8	5.4	4.8	4.0	3.6	4.0	4.2	4.1	3.5	4.0	3.8
Persons per family	4.35	4.36	4.31	4.26	4.05	4.01	3.92	3.90	3.90	3.78	3.77	3.74
Earners per family	1.76	1.72	1.73	1.67	1.58	1.53	1.55	1.52	1.52	1.50	1.51	1.54
Ratio of persons to earners per family	2.47	2.53	2.49	2.55	2.56	2.62	2.53	2.57	2.57	2.52	2.50	2.43

Source: Bureau of the **Census**, *Social Indicators III: Selected data on social conditions and trends in the United States* (Washington, D.C.: Government Printing Office, 1980), p. 490:

Table VII
Unemployment rates for persons 16 years old and over:
1948 to 1975
Annual averages

Year	Unemployment rate		Ratio: Black and other races to White
	Black and other races	White	
1948	5.9	3.5	1.7
1949	8.9	5.6	1.6
1950	9.0	4.9	1.8
1951	5.3	3.1	1.7
1952	5.4	2.8	1.9
1953	4.5	2.7	1.7
1954	9.9	5.0	2.0
1955	8.7	3.9	2.2
1956	8.3	3.6	2.3
1957	7.9	3.8	2.1
1958	12.6	6.1	2.1
1959	10.7	4.8	2.2
1960	10.2	4.9	2.1
1961	12.4	6.0	2.1
1962	10.9	4.9	2.2
1963	10.8	5.0	2.2
1964	9.6	4.6	2.1
1965	8.1	4.1	2.0
1966	7.3	3.3	2.2
1967	7.4	3.4	2.2
1968	6.7	3.2	2.1
1969	6.4	3.1	2.1
1970	8.2	4.5	1.8
1971	9.9	5.4	1.8
1972	10.0	5.0	2.0
1973	8.9	4.3	2.1
1974	9.9	5.0	2.0
1975	13.9	7.8	1.8

Source: Bureau of the Census, *The Social and Economic Status of the Black Population*, p. 69.

Table VIII
Percent of the population gainfully employed by age and sex: 1890 and 1930

Age and sex	Black		White	
	1890[1]	1930	1890	1930
Male				
Total, 10 years old and over	80	80	77	76
10 to 14 years	30	17	8	3
15 to 19 years	73	65	56	46
20 to 24 years	94	94	92	89
25 to 34 years	97	97	97	97
35 to 44 years	98	97	98	98
45 to 54 years	98	97	96	96
55 to 64 years	97	94	92	90
65 years and over	88	75	72	57
Age unknown	83	70	74	57
Female				
Total, 10 years old and over	36	39	14	20
10 to 14 years	20	10	3	1
15 to 19 years	43	30	25	26
20 to 24 years	47	46	28	42
25 to 34 years	37	47	15	26
35 to 44 years	37	48	10	20
45 to 54 years	38	46	10	18
55 to 64 years	37	41	10	15
65 years and over	26	24	7	7
Age unknown	41	47	26	29

[1] Data include persons of "other" races.

Source: Bureau of the Census, *The Social and Economic Status of the Black Population*, p. 66.

Table IX
Occupation of the gainfully employed population 10 years old and over by sex: 1890, 1910, and 1930

Occupation and sex	Black			White		
	1890	1910	1930	1890	1910	1930
Both sexes						
Total, gainful workers, thousands	3,073	5,193	5,504	19,542	32,774	42,584
Percent	100	100	100	100	100	100
Agriculture, forestry, and fishing[1]	57	55	37	37	30	20
Manufacturing and mechanical	6	13	19	25	30	30
Transportation and communication[2]	5	5	7	16	7	8
Domestic and personal service	31	22	29	17	8	8
Other occupations[3]	1	6	9	5	25	34
Male						
Total, gainful workers, thousands	2,101	3,179	3,663	16,603	26,730	33,767
Percent	100	100	100	100	100	100
Agriculture, forestry, and fishing[1]	63	57	42	42	33	24
Manufacturing and mechanical	7	18	25	24	31	33
Transportation and communication[2]	7	8	11	18	9	9
Domestic and personal service	22	8	12	13	3	4
Other occupations[3]	1	8	10	4	24	30
Female						
Total, gainful workers, thousands	972	2,014	1,841	2,939	6,044	8,818
Percent	100	100	100	100	100	100
Agriculture, forestry, and fishing[1]	44	52	27	9	12	4
Manufacturing and mechanical	3	3	5	34	29	20
Transportation and communication[2]	-	-	-	8	2	3
Domestic and personal service	52	42	63	39	28	23
Other occupations[3]	1	2	5	10	29	50

- Represents or rounds to zero.

[1] Includes the occupation "mining" for 1890.

[2] Includes the occupation "trade" for 1890.

[3] Includes the occupation "professional service" for 1890. Includes the following occupations for 1910 and 1930—extraction of minerals, trade, public service, professional service, and clerical occupations.

Note: In tables 51 and 52, occupational statistics for the census years 1890, 1910, and 1930 are not strictly comparable due to changes in definition.

Source: Bureau of the Census, *The Social and Economic Status of the Black Population*, p. 72.

Table X

Black women ever married by number of children ever born, by age for selected years: 1910 to 1975

Age of women and year	Total, women ever married (thousands)	Percent distribution by specified number of children ever born					Children ever born per woman ever married
		Total	0	1	2 to 4	5 or more	
1910							
Total, 15 to 49 years	1,820	100	18	18	33	31	3.5
15 to 19 years	103	100	40	42	18	-	0.8
20 to 24 years	356	100	24	28	43	5	1.7
25 to 29 years	378	100	20	19	41	21	2.6
30 to 34 years	299	100	16	16	33	35	3.5
35 to 39 years	292	100	13	13	29	45	4.5
40 to 44 years	212	100	11	11	26	52	5.5
45 to 49 years	180	100	9	10	24	58	6.2
1940							
Total, 15 to 49 years	2,655	100	29	21	32	18	2.3
15 to 19 years	127	100	42	41	17	-	0.8
20 to 24 years	405	100	35	28	34	2	1.3
25 to 29 years	491	100	32	21	36	11	1.8
30 to 34 years	454	100	29	20	32	18	2.3
35 to 39 years	476	100	27	18	32	23	2.7
40 to 44 years	381	100	24	16	33	27	3.1
45 to 49 years	322	100	22	15	34	29	3.3
1960							
Total, 15 to 49 years	3,312	100	20	19	39	22	2.8
15 to 19 years	125	100	25	41	33	1	1.3
20 to 24 years	413	100	17	25	51	7	2.0
25 to 29 years	536	100	14	17	47	22	2.8
30 to 34 years	597	100	16	16	41	28	3.2
35 to 39 years	599	100	20	17	36	27	3.1
40 to 44 years	540	100	25	18	33	25	2.9
45 to 49 years	502	100	28	19	31	22	2.8
1970							
Total, 15 to 49 years	3,639	100	14	19	43	24	3.0
15 to 19 years	141	100	32	43	24	1	1.0
20 to 24 years	536	100	21	33	43	4	1.6
25 to 29 years	608	100	13	20	52	15	2.5
30 to 34 years	598	100	9	14	48	29	3.4
35 to 39 years	596	100	10	12	42	35	3.8
40 to 44 years	604	100	13	14	38	34	3.8
45 to 49 years	557	100	18	16	36	29	3.4

Table X (continued)

1975

Total, 15 to 49 years	3,841	100	12	20	46	21	2.9
15 to 19 years	108	100	28	47	25	-	1.0
20 to 24 years	514	100	20	37	42	-	1.4
25 to 29 years	706	100	16	25	53	6	2.0
30 to 34 years	689	100	8	17	55	20	3.0
35 to 39 years	605	100	6	11	46	36	3.9
40 to 44 years	634	100	11	11	42	35	3.9
45 to 49 years	587	100	10	17	40	34	3.7

- Represents or rounds to zero.

Source: Bureau of the Census, *The Social and Economic Status of the Black Population*, p. 128.

Table XI
Children ever born per women ever married 35 to 44 years old, by years of school completed: 1940, 1960, 1970, and 1975

Subject, by years of school completed	1940[1]	1960[2]	1970	1975
Black				
Total, women ever married, thousands	857	1,231	1,197	1,239
Total, children ever born per woman ever married	[3]2.9	3.1	3.8	3.8
Elementary: 8 years or less	3.1	3.6	4.6	4.8
High school: 1 to 3 years	2.3	3.0	4.2	4.4
4 years	2.0	2.4	3.3	3.4
College: 1 to 3 years	1.7	2.1	2.9	3.5
4 years or more	1.2	1.7	1.8	2.1
White				
Total, women ever married, thousands	6,266	10,356	9,824	9,659
Total, children ever born per woman ever married	[3]2.6	2.6	3.0	3.1
Elementary: 8 years or less	3.1	3.1	3.6	3.9
High school: 1 to 3 years	2.3	2.6	3.2	3.5
4 years	1.8	2.4	2.9	3.0
College: 1 to 3 years	1.8	2.4	2.9	2.9
4 years or more	1.5	2.3	2.6	2.4

[1] Data for White exclude foreign-born population.
[2] Data for Black include persons of "other" races.
[3] Includes a small number of persons not reporting their educational attainment.

Note: Average number of children ever born per woman ever married for 1940 are based on women reporting number of children ever born; in 1960, 1970, and 1975, women who did not report the number of children ever born were allocated a number.

Source: Bureau of the Census, *The Social and Economic Status of the Black Population*, p. 129.

Table XII
States with 100 or more lynchings in the period 1882-1927, in numerical order

State	Total	Whites	Blacks
Mississippi	561	44	517
Georgia	549	39	510
Texas	534	164	370
Louisiana	409	62	347
Alabama	356	52	304
Arkansas	313	69	244
Florida	275	28	247
Tennessee	268	55	213
South Carolina	174	9	165
Kentucky	233	79	154
Oklahoma (Indian Territory)	141	97	44
Missouri	117	51	66
Virginia	109	24	85
North Carolina	100	20	80
Total number of lynchings in the U.S., 1882-1927	**4951**	**1438**	**3513**

Source: Walter White, *Rope and Faggot* (New York: Arno Press, 1969), pp. 254-56.

Table XIII
U.S. capital punishment for all offenses, murder, and rape, by race (excluding other ethnic groups), 1930-1959

	All offenses		Murder		Rape	
	White	Black	White	Black	White	Black
1930-1939	827	816	803	687	10	115
Percent of totals for whites/blacks	(100.00)	(100.00)	(97.1)	(84.2)	(1.2)	(14.1)
1940-1949	490	781	458	595	19	179
Percent of totals for whites/blacks	(100.00)	(100.00)	(93.5)	(76.2)	(3.9)	(22.9)
1950-1959	336	376	316	280	13	89
Percent of totals for whites/blacks	(100.00)	(100.00)	(94.0)	(74.5)	(3.9)	(23.7)
Total executed, 1930-1959	**1653**	**1973**	**1577**	**1562**	**42**	**383**
Percent of totals for whites/blacks	(100.00)	(100.00)	(95.4)	(79.2)	(2.5)	(19.4)

Source: Lennox S. Hinds, *Illusions of Justice: Human Rights Violations in the United States* (Iowa City: School of Social Work, University of Iowa, 1978), pp. 46-47.

Table XIV
Number of death row inmates, by race, June, 1981

State	Total	Black	White	Spanish Surname	Native American	Unknown	% Nonwhite
Alabama	37	23	14	-	-	-	62%
Arkansas	17	9	7	1	-	-	59
Florida	163	63	97	3	-	-	40
Georgia	106	55	51	-	-	-	52
Kentucky	8	-	8	-	-	-	0
Louisiana	27	15	12	-	-	-	56
Mississippi	17	12	5	-	-	-	70
North Carolina	16	6	10	-	-	-	36
South Carolina	20	7	13	-	-	-	35
Tennessee	23	6	16	-	1	-	30
Texas	139	51	74	14	-	-	47
Virginia	16	11	5	-	-	-	69
West Virginia	-	-	-	-	-	-	-
South	589	258	312	18	1	0	47%
U.S.	827	337	446	37	4	3	46%

Source: Institute for Southern Studies, Durham, North Carolina, 1981.

Table XV
Victims in death penalty cases, by race, in the South, February, 1978

State	White	Black	Other	Unknown	% White
Alabama	38	3	-	2	87%
Arkansas	2	-	-	8	20
Florida	149	30	3	4	80
Georgia	99	18	-	-	84
Kentucky	3	-	-	-	100
Louisiana	15	1	-	-	93
Mississippi	9	-	-	3	75
North Carolina	11	1	-	1	84
South Carolina	7	3	-	-	70
Tennessee	5	-	-	-	100
Texas		not available			
Virginia	9	-	-	-	100
West Virginia	-	-	-		-
South	347	56	3	18	85%

Source: Institute for Southern Studies, 1981.

Table XVI
Race of defendant matched to race of victim in the South, February, 1978

State	White Defendant/ White Victim	White Defendant/ Black Victim	Black Defendant/ White Victim	Black Defendant/ Black Victim	Unknown
Alabama	20	-	18	3	2
Arkansas	1	-	-	3	8
Florida	95	2	54	28	-
Georgia	52	3	47	15	-
Kentucky	2	-	1	-	-
Louisiana	10	-	5	1	-
Mississippi	4	-	5	-	3
North Carolina	6	-	5	1	2
South Carolina	7	3	-	3	1
Tennessee	3	1	1	-	-
Texas		not available			
Virginia	4	-	5	2	-
West Virginia	-	-	-	-	-
South	204	9	141	56	16

Source: Institute for Southern Studies, 1981.

Table XVII
Demographic profile of U.S. convict population in state correctional facilities, 1974

Characteristic	Number of inmates	% of inmates	Characteristic	Number of inmates	% of inmates
Sex			**Armed forces service**		
Total	191,400	100	Total[a, d]	187,500	100
Male	185,000	97	Served	51,200	27
Female	6,300	3	Never served	136,400	78
Race					
Total[a]	191,400	100	**Personal income**		
White	97,700	51	(year prior to arrest)		
Black	89,700	47	Total[a,d]	168,300	100
Other	3,400	2	No income	7,600	5
Not reported	600	([b])	Less than $2,000	32,400	19
Age			$2,000 to $3,999	30,700	18
Total[a]	191,400	100	$4,000 to $5,999	30,400	18
Under 18	1,800	1	$6,000 to $9,999	29,900	18
18	5,500	3	$10,000 or more	23,000	14
19	7,900	4	Amount not known	12,600	8
20 to 24	57,100	30	Not reported	1,800	1
25 to 29	44,900	23	**Length of time on last job**		
30 to 34	27,300	14	Total[a,d]	168,300	100
35 to 39	16,300	9	Less than 5 weeks	16,900	10
40 to 49	19,600	10	5 to 26 weeks	61,100	36
50 and over	10,300	5	27 to 104 weeks	55,100	33
Not reported	600	([b])	105 to 260 weeks	21,500	13
			261 or more weeks	13,700	8

[a] Detail may not add to totals because of rounding. Percent distribution based on unrounded figures.
[b] Less than 0.5 percent.
[c] Includes sentenced inmates only.
[d] Includes only those inmates who had held a full-time job after December,1968 or who had been employed during most of the month prior to their arrest.

Data does not include juvenile offenders.

Source: U.S. Department of Justice, Law Enforcement Assistance Administration, *Survey of Inmates of State Correctional Facilities, 1974* (Washington, D.C.: Government Printint Office, 1976), pp. 24-25.

Table XVIII
Demographic profile of U.S. convict population in state correctional facilities, 1974

Characteristic	Number of inmates	% of inmates	Characteristic	Number of inmates	% of inmates
Level of educa-tional attainment			**Occupation** (at time of arrest)		
Total[a,c]	187,500	100	Total[a,d]	168,300	100
Eighth grade or less	49,000	26	Professional and technical workers	4,900	8
1-3 yrs high school	65,900	35			
4 yrs high school	52,200	28	Managers and administrators	9,500	6
1-3 yrs college	14,300	8	Salesworkers	3,900	2
4+ yrs college	1,500	1	Clerical workers	7,000	4
Not reported	4,700	2	Craftsmen and kindred workers	39,300	23
Employment status (month prior to arrest)			Carpenters	4,400	3
Total[a]	191,400	100	Auto mechanics	4,100	2
Employed	131,000	68	Painters	4,300	3
Full time	117,100	61	Other craftsmen	26,500	16
Part time	13,800	7	Operatives	48,100	29
Unemployed	59,000	31	Welders	3,700	2
Looking for work	23,800	12	Machine operators	3,800	2
Not looking for wk	35,200	18	Truck drivers	9,200	5
Wanting work	9,100	5	Other operatives	31,400	19
Not wanting wk	26,100	14	Nonfarm laborers	29,200	17
Not reported	1,400	1	Construction labor	8,200	5
Marital status			Freight and materi-al handlers	7,100	4
Total[a,c]	187,500	100	Other nonfarm labor	13,800	8
Married	44,300	24	Farmers and farm managers	400	(')
Widowed	5,800	3			
Divorced	31,900	17	Farm laborers and supervisors	4,000	2
Separated	15,200	8			
Never married	89,900	48	Service workers	19,200	11
Not reported	300	(')	Others	500	(')
			Not reported	2,500	1

[a] Detail may not add to totals because of rounding. Percent distribution based on unrounded figures.
[b] Less than 0.5 percent.
[c] Includes sentenced inmates only.
[d] Includes only those inmates who had held a full-time job after December, 1968 or who had been employed during most of the month prior to their arrest.

Data does not include juvenile offenders.

Source: U.S. Department of Justice, Law Enforcement Assistance Administration, *Survey of Inmate State Correctional Facilities, 1974*, pp. 24-25.

Table XIX
Arrests, by offense charged: whites and blacks in the United States, 1975

Offense charged	Total arrests			Percentage	
	Total	White	Black	White	Black
Total	7,671,230	5,538,890	1,935,422	72.2	25.2
Criminal homicide					
Murder and nonnegligent manslaughter	15,173	6,581	8,257	43.4	54.4
Manslaughter by negligence	2,971	2,316	555	78.0	18.7
Forcible rape	19,920	10,414	9,050	52.3	45.4
Robbery	110,411	43,598	64,867	39.5	58.8
Aggravated assault	180,668	105,226	71,360	58.2	39.5
Burglary	422,032	294,779	119,853	69.8	28.4
Larceny—theft	923,127	620,618	282,297	67.2	30.6
Motor vehicle theft	110,320	78,029	29,145	70.7	26.4
Violent crime	326,172	165,819	153,534	50.8	47.1
Property crime	1,455,479	993,426	431,295	68.3	29.6
Subtotal for above offenses	1,784,622	1,161,561	585,384	65.1	32.8
Other assaults	338,441	217,481	113,608	64.3	33.6
Arson	13,667	10,843	2,618	79.3	19.2
Forgery and counterfeiting	53,692	35,615	17,470	66.3	32.5
Fraud	141,866	99,972	40,476	70.5	28.5
Embezzlement	8,809	6,030	2,691	68.5	30.5
Stolen property: buying, receiving, possessing	93,148	60,444	31,462	64.9	33.8
Vandalism	165,846	138,107	25,149	83.3	15.2
Weapons: carrying, possessing, etc.	123,114	69,843	51,028	56.7	41.4
Prostitution and commercial vice	46,727	21,030	25,032	45.0	53.6
Sex offenses (except forcible rape and prostitution)	47,901	37,635	9,259	78.6	19.3
Narcotic drug laws	487,287	383,649	96,660	78.7	19.8
Gambling	47,798	11,960	34,424	25.0	72.0
Offenses against family and children	52,199	36,751	14,616	70.4	28.0
Driving under the influence	893,798	751,024	117,105	84.0	13.1
Liquor laws	263,051	233,061	21,337	88.6	8.1
Drunkenness	1,161,140	883,383	224,417	76.1	19.3
Disorderly conduct	578,630	390,194	174,517	67.4	30.2
Vagrancy	58,228	34,010	22,897	58.4	39.3
All other offenses (except traffic)	986,652	696,160	267,294	70.6	27.1
Suspicion	27,133	16,105	10,665	59.4	39.3
Curfew and loitering law violations	111,167	80,517	28,499	72.4	25.6
Runaways	186,314	163,515	18,814	87.8	10.1

Note: Arrests for other ethnic minority groups (e.g. Native Americans) are excluded from list. Percentages are based on the percent of White or Black arrests compared to the total number of all arrested for specific offenses.

Source: Hinds, *Illusions of Justice*, pp. 42-43.

Table XX
Selected statistics by industry division for cities with 100 or more Black-owned firms: 1977-Con.

City and industry, South	All firms		With paid employees				Without paid employees	
	Firms (number)	Gross receipts ($1,000)	Firms (number)	Employees for week including March 12 (number)	Annual payroll ($1,000)	Gross receipts ($1,000)	Firms (number)	Gross receipts ($1,000)
Chattanooga, Tenn.	**344**	**8,719**	**71**	**288**	**948**	**6,056**	**273**	**2,663**
Construction	26	472	9	8	69	244	17	228
Manufacturing	1	(D)	1	(D)	(D)	(D)	-	-
Transportation and public utilities	42	272	1	(D)	(D)	(D)	41	(D)
Wholesale trade	2	(D)	-	-	-	-	2	(D)
Retail trade	108	5,319	29	84	368	4,058	79	1,261
Finance, insurance, and real estate	6	21	-	-	-	-	6	21
Selected services	151	2,152	29	127	374	1,334	122	818
Other industries	-	-	-	-	-	-	-	-
Industries not classified	8	(D)	2	(D)	(D)	(D)	6	112
Greenville, Miss.	**247**	**12,765**	**68**	**182**	**1,202**	**10,045**	**179**	**2,720**
Construction	39	856	15	39	285	669	24	187
Manufacturing	2	(D)	1	(D)	(D)	(D)	1	(D)
Transportation and public utilities	23	649	9	(D)	(D)	(D)	14	(D)
Wholesale trade	1	(D)	-	-	-	-	1	(D)
Retail trade	80	3,360	19	26	127	1,821	61	1,539
Finance, insurance, and real estate	6	(D)	1	(D)	(D)	(D)	5	25
Selected services	87	1,734	19	47	243	964	68	770
Other industries	2	(D)	2	(D)	(D)	(D)	-	-
Industries not classified	7	(D)	2	(D)	(D)	(D)	5	105
Pensacola, Fla.	**175**	**4,334**	**49**	**118**	**576**	**2,778**	**126**	**1,556**
Construction	29	697	10	36	183	492	19	205
Manufacturing	4	198	2	(D)	(D)	(D)	2	(D)
Transportation and public utilities	9	149	3	5	11	105	6	44
Wholesale trade	1	(D)	1	(D)	(D)	(D)	-	-
Retail trade	45	1,508	10	23	120	867	35	6,411
Finance, insurance, and real estate	3	(D)	-	-	-	-	3	(D)
Selected services	72	1,640	22	46	222	1,108	50	42
Other industries	6	(D)	1	(D)	(D)	(D)	6	42
Industries not classified	6	43	-	-	-	-	6	43

D=withheld to avoid disclosing figures for individual companies.

Source: Bureau of the Census, *1977 Survey of Minority-Owned Business Enterprises* (Washington, D.C.: Government Printing Office, 1979).

Table XXI
Selected statistics by industry division for cities with 100 or more Black-owned firms: 1977

City and industry, North	All firms Firms (number)	Gross receipts ($1,000)	With paid employees Firms (number)	Employees for week including March 12 (number)	Annual payroll ($1,000)	Gross receipts ($1,000)	Without paid employees Firms (number)	Gross receipts ($1,000)
Bridgeport, Conn.	**144**	**3,289**	**23**	**66**	**323**	**1,789**	**121**	**1,500**
Construction	12	199	2	(D)	(D)	(D)	10	(D)
Manufacturing	1	(D)	1	(D)	(D)	(D)	-	-
Transportation and public utilities	2	(D)	-	-	-	-	2	(D)
Wholesale trade	2	(D)	1	(D)	(D)	(D)	1	(D)
Retail trade	28	983	5	10	32	346	23	637
Finance, insurance, and real estate	4	23	-	-	-	-	4	23
Selected services	87	1,410	14	32	143	780	73	630
Other industries	1	(D)	-	-	-	-	1	(D)
Industries not classified	7	24	-	-	-	-	7	24
Akron, Ohio	**490**	**7,666**	**64**	**140**	**794**	**4,623**	**426**	**3,043**
Construction	35	816	9	16	199	582	26	234
Manufacturing	6	48	-	-	-	-	6	48
Transportation and public utilities	42	762	8	(D)	(D)	(D)	34	(D)
Wholesale trade	2	(D)	-	-	-	-	2	(D)
Retail trade	94	3,027	17	43	150	· 2,211	77	816
Finance, insurance, and real estate	25	177	1	(D)	(D)	(D)	24	(D)
Selected services	258	2,590	27	74	320	1,330	231	1,260
Other industries	8	(D)	2	(D)	(D)	(D)	6	33
Industries not classified	20	144	-	-	-	-	20	144
Harrisburg, Penn.	**224**	**5,729**	**34**	**109**	**618**	**3,352**	**190**	**2,377**
Construction	15	572	6	27	180	484	9	88
Manufacturing	1	(D)	-	-	-	-	1	(D)
Transportation and public utilities	15	264	3	(D)	(D)	(D)	12	(D)
Wholesale trade	2	(D)	-	-	-	-	2	(D)
Retail trade	57	2,919	11	38	185	1,885	46	1,034
Finance, insurance, and real estate	8	255	1	(D)	(D)	(D)	7	(D)
Selected services	120	1,643	13	37	219	865	107	778
Other industries	1	(D)	-	-	-	-	1	(D)
Industries not classified	5	17	-	-	-	-	5	17

D=withheld to avoid disclosing figures for individual companies.

Source: Bureau of the Census, *1977 Survey of Minority-Owned Business Enterprises.*

Table XXII
Selected statistics by industry division for cities with 100 or more Black-owned firms: 1977

City and industry, West	All firms Firms (number)	All firms Gross receipts ($1,000)	With paid employees Firms (number)	With paid employees Employees for week including March 12 (number)	With paid employees Annual payroll ($1,000)	With paid employees Gross receipts ($1,000)	Without paid employees Firms (number)	Without paid employees Gross receipts ($1,000)
Austin, Texas	**533**	**10,047**	**83**	**322**	**1,576**	**6,269**	**450**	**3,778**
Construction	41	1,613	10	41	333	1,239	31	374
Manufacturing	3	(D)	-	-	-	-	3	(D)
Transportation and public utilities	51	994	7	(D)	(D)	(D)	44	(D)
Wholesale trade	4	(D)	1	(D)	(D)	(D)	3	(D)
Retail trade	108	2,977	28	46	169	1,783	80	1,194
Finance, insurance, and real estate	23	376	4	6	37	185	19	191
Selected services	217	3,401	31	216	896	2,426	186	975
Other industries	12	(D)	2	(D)	(D)	(D)	10	87
Industries not classified	74	179	-	-	-	-	74	179
Sacramento, Cal.	**402**	**6,920**	**65**	**149**	**762**	**4,195**	**337**	**2,725**
Construction	20	728	7	(D)	(D)	(D)	13	(D)
Manufacturing	2	(D)	-	-	-	-	2	(D)
Transportation and public utilities	22	511	5	6	34	221	17	290
Wholesale trade	5	(D)	1	(D)	(D)	(D)	4	(D)
Retail trade	76	1,551	13	32	140	1,025	63	526
Finance, insurance, and real estate	38	663	1	(D)	(D)	(D)	37	(D)
Selected services	216	3,161	37	75	429	2,093	179	1,068
Other industries	10	47	-	-	-	-	10	47
Industries not classified	13	(D)	1	(D)	(D)	(D)	12	64
Phoenix, Arizona	**374**	**11,132**	**68**	**242**	**1,535**	**8,218**	**306**	**2,914**
Construction	34	2,245	18	73	469	1,975	16	280
Manufacturing	3	(D)	1	(D)	(D)	(D)	2	(D)
Transportation and public utilities	20	201	-	-	-	-	20	201
Wholesale trade	9	2,313	5	38	316	2,214	4	99
Retail trade	91	3,034	15	35	211	2,047	76	987
Finance, insurance, and real estate	23	312	3	9	27	151	20	161
Selected services	163	2,557	21	74	415	1,635	142	922
Other industries	16	(D)	4	(D)	(D)	(D)	12	145
Industries not classified	15	117	1	(D)	(D)	(D)	14	(D)

D=withheld to avoid disclosing figures for individual companies.

Source: Bureau of the Census, *1977 Survey of Minority-Owned Business Enterprises.*

Table XXIII

Selected statistics by industry division and employment size for Black-owned firms: 1977 and 1972

	1977, with paid employees				1972 (revised), with paid employees		
Industry	Firms (number)	Employees for week including March 12 (number)	Annual payroll ($1,000)	Gross receipts ($1,000)	Firms (number)	Employees for week including March 12 (number)	Gross receipts ($1,000)
All industries	39,968	164,177	1,135,444	6,396,850	24,509	147,184	3,466,898
1 to 4 employees	32,581	47,225	315,885	2,242,573	16,654	36,315	1,104,430
5 to 9 employees	4,556	28,985	163,267	958,158	4,782	30,924	667,932
10 to 19 employees	1,771	23,231	143,007	728,161	1,984	25,827	496,511
20 to 49 employees	717	21,229	166,122	914,010	852	25,371	546,911
50 to 99 employees	230	15,540	125,358	542,319	163	10,619	264,148
100 employees or more	113	27,967	221,505	1,011,629	74	18,128	386,966

Source: Bureau of the Census, *1977 Survey of Minority-Owned Business Enterprises.*

Table XXIV

Concentration of wealth index: statistics by selected industries and receipts of $1,000,000 or more for Black firms: 1977

All industries	Firms	Percent of total	Gross receipts ($1,000)	Percent of total	Employees	Percent of total
Total	231,203	(100.)	8,645,200	(100.)	164,177	(100.)
$1,000,000 or more	716	(00.3)	2,580,041	(29.8)	47,129	(28.7)
Construction: total	21,101	(100.)	757,691	(100.)	17,199	(100.)
$1,000,000 or more	48	(00.2)	115,223	(15.2)	2,365	(13.8)
Manufacturing: total	4,243	(100.)	613,665	(100.)	15,790	(100.)
$1,000,000 or more	103	(02.4)	412,718	(67.3)	9,081	(52.8)
Wholesale trade: total	2,212	(100.)	664,052	(100.)	4,534	(100.)
$1,000,000 or more	110	(05.0)	500,122	(75.3)	2,642	(58.3)
Finance, insurance, real estate: total	9,805	(100.)	641,372	(100.)	15,361	(100.)
$1,000,000 or more	90	(00.9)	443,994	(69.2)	11,850	(77.1)

Source: Bureau of the Census, *1977 Survey of Minority-Owned Business Enterprises.*

330

Table XXV
Spending patterns for Black families with incomes $15,000 and above compared to total U.S. spending patterns, 1980

Commodity purchases in 1980	Middle income Blacks (percent)	U.S. total population (percent)
U.S. Treasury notes	1.1	0.9
Travel insurance	3.2	3.1
Gold jewelry	7.9	7.4
Diamond rings	4.2	3.7
Jazz records/tapes	8.2	4.4
Soul records/tapes	15.9	4.8
Televisions, black/white, table model	9.7	4.7
Wall-to-wall carpeting	8.9	6.9
Cigarettes	44.6	40.1
Encyclopedias	4.5	2.0
Orange juice	46.7	40.8
Designer jeans/men	6.2	5.6
Sweaters/men	25.2	18.5
Overcoats/men	11.8	6.5
Tennis clothing/men	5.2	2.8
Skirts/women	39.5	28.5
Designer jeans/women	18.5	14.2
Fur coats/women	4.9	4.3
Tennis clothing/women	5.1	2.2
Brandy and cognac	15.5	12.3
Scotch	17.8	15.6
Malt liquor	14.0	6.7
Bedroom furniture	5.4	4.5
Weekly groceries @ over $100/week	11.1	10.7

Source: LeRoy W. Jeffries, *Facts About Blacks, 1980-81* (Los Angeles: Jeffries and Associates, 1980), pp. 18-21.

Table XXVI
Black political and economic tendencies since the Civil War

	Black nationalist Racial separatist/ Crummell's "race love"	Cultural pluralist double consciousness	Integrationist cultural identification with dominant culture
Revolution Radical transformation of means of production and political apparatus	Malcolm X S. Carmichael Revolutionary Action Movement African Blood Brotherhood	DuBois (1940s- 1963) Angela Davis	A.P. Randolph (1914-1918)
Militant reform Progressive transferral of power to oppressed without a seizure of state power	Martin Delany H.H. Garnet Alex Crummell Black Panther Party (post 1970) National Black Indepen- dent Political Party	DuBois (1905- 1940s) W.M. Trotter	Julian Bond R. Bunche (1930s) M.L. King, Jr. Randolph (1919-1930s) Ron Dellums John Conyers F. Douglass
Gradual reform Pragmatism, slow and steady change within existing system	Black Cultural Nationalists (1970s) "Buy Black" campaigns T. Thomas Fortune (post 1900)	Kelly Miller E.F. Frazier	Majority of Congres- sional Black Caucus NAACP (post 1934)
Accommodation Tactical compromises, conciliatory rhetoric, covert activities against racial prejudice	Booker T. Washington National Negro Business League		Urban League Black Republicans
Conservatism Acceptance of status quo, defense of existing capitalist economic and political system	Roy Innis Floyd McKissick		George Schuyler (1960s) Thomas Sowell Walter Williams Black Reaganites

Table XXVII

Percent of persons 5 to 29 years old enrolled in school, by age and sex: 1950, 1960, 1970, and 1975

Age and sex	Black[1]				White			
	1950	1960	1970	1975	1950	1960	1970	1975
Male								
Total, 5 to 29 years	56	66	69	69	55	69	70	64
5 to 13 years	87	92	96	98	89	96	97	98
14 to 17 years	79	88	92	93	85	92	95	95
18 and 19 years	20	37	41	50	37	49	56	50
20 to 24 years	11	9	17	21	15	21	31	27
25 to 29 years	6	4	6	12	6	9	11	13
Female								
Total, 5 to 29 years	47	62	64	63	49	61	62	59
5 to 13 years	87	93	96	98	89	95	98	99
14 to 17 years	72	85	92	91	84	90	94	93
18 and 19 years	26	32	39	45	24	30	42	44
20 to 24 years	3	6	12	19	5	8	15	19
25 to 29 years	1	2	4	8	-	2	4	7

- Represents or rounds to zero.

[1] Data for 1950 and 1960 include persons of ''other'' races.

Source: Bureau of the Census, *The Social and Economic Status of the Black Population*, p. 89.

Table XXVIII
Persons 18 to 24 years old enrolled in college or below college level, by sex: 1950, 1960, 1970, and 1975

Numbers in thousands

Enrollment status, sex, and race	1950[1]	1960[1]	1970	1975
Black				
Total men, 18 to 24 years	839	887	1,220	1,451
Number enrolled in college	41	63	192	294
Percent of total	5	7	16	20
Number enrolled below college level	95	131	116	148
Percent of total	11	15	10	10
Total women, 18 to 24 years	965	978	1,471	1,761
Number enrolled in college	42	66	225	372
Percent of total	4	7	15	21
Number enrolled below college level	74	111	77	106
Percent of total	8	11	5	6
White				
Total men, 18 to 24 years	6,856	6,688	9,053	11,050
Number enrolled in college	1,025	1,267	3,096	3,326
Percent of total	15	19	34	30
Number enrolled below college level	622	664	429	420
Percent of total	9	10	5	4
Total women, 18 to 24 years	7,118	6,921	10,555	11,653
Number enrolled in college	558	811	2,209	2,790
Percent of total	8	12	21	24
Number enrolled below college level	425	474	246	250
Percent of total	6	7	2	2

[1] Data for Black include persons of ''other'' races.

Source: Bureau of the Census, *The Social and Economic Status of the Black Population*, p. 90.

Index

Abbot, Robert S., 145
Abernathy, Ralph D., 29, 30, 31, 202, 203, 205, 211, 244
Advertising, 159-162
Affirmative action, 95, 172-173, 174, 250, 258; Bakke decision, 243; and Black education, 218; and Black elite, 136; "North Carolina Agreement", 222-227; and the right, 175
Ali, Fulani Sunni, 247
Allen, Robert, *Black Awakening in Capitalist America*, 37, 207, 208-209
Allende, Salvador, 246
Althusser, Louis, *Reading Capital*, 249, 250
America, Richard, 165-166
American Federation of State, County and Municipal Employees (AFSCME), 30, 36
American Institute for Free Labor Development, 36
Anderson, Ida, 81
Anthony, Susan B., 77
Anticommunism, 205-207, 209, 210, 249
Anti-Semitism, 47, 150, 166, 232, 251
Aptheker, Herbert, 227
Arms Race, 260
Atkins, Hannah, 99
Authoritarianism, 166-167, 245, 246, 261

Bailyn, Bernard, *Ideological Orgins of the American Revolution*, 249
Baldwin, James, 206
Baraka, Bibi Amina, 97
Baron, Harold, 32, 36
Barrett, Michele, 103
Barry, Marion, 237
Bartley, Numan V., 201
Bennett, Reverend L. Roy, 202
Bethel, Lorraine, "What Chou Mean We, White Girl? Or, The Cullud Lesbian Feminist Declaration of Independence," 102
Bethune, Mary McLeod, 81, 82
Bevel, James, 204
Birmingham, Stephen, *Certain People: America's Black Elite*, 65
Birth control, 83-85, 92
Blac, Fred, 175
Black August Organizing Commitee, 248

Black capitalism: authoritarian, 166-167; and Black press, 145-146; Black vs. white labor, 149-150; and boycott of Coca-Cola, 178; and B.T. Washington, 144-145; prior to civil war, 141-142; after the civil war, 142-148; concentration of wealth, 155-156; corporate core, 157-158; decline of, 163-166; depression, 147-148; history of, 139, 140-148; and migration, 148-149; in the 1980s, 156-158; and paradox of desegregation, 163-166, 158-159; profile of, 153-158; and racial chauvinism, 149-150; and segregation, 144, 153; support by corporate leaders, 150-152; and underdevelopment, 152-158
Black clergy: and accommodation, 205; and civil rights movement, 196-197; criticism of, 199-200, 210-214; decline in number, 198-199; decline in political influence, 196, 197-199; definition of, 137; and the left, 205-207; during reconstruction, 197
Black codes, 109, 142
Black colleges: decline in enrollment, 218; and desegregation, 225-227; financial crisis of, 222; product of segregation, 216; progressive faculty, 217-218; and the Reagan Administration, 222-225; and White universities, 218-222
Black conservatives: 173, 176; and accommodation, 186-192; history of, 182-193; ideology of, 182; and White supremacy, 183-184
Black consumer market, 164; theory of, 139-140; trends in, 159-160; white corporate interest in, 158-163
Black educators, 137-138
Black labor: in agriculture, 33, 34, 51; and boycotts, 149-150; crisis of, 32, 33, 52-53; and economic transformation, 53; income, 34, 57, 59; and industrial decline, 50-51; in industry, 33-34; job accident and death rates, 36; migration after 1915, 34; public sector employment, 35, 37-38; and segregation, 143-144; and technology, 36; unemployment, 39, 51; and unions, 34-35, 37-38, 42-44; vs. white, 13, 37-38

335

ABOUT THE AUTHOR

Born in 1950, Professor Marable received his Ph.D. from the University of Maryland-College Park in 1976. He has served as chairperson of Tuskegee Institute's political science department, and was associate professor of political economy and history at Cornell University's Africana Studies Center. In 1982, Professor Marable was appointed professor of economics and history and Director of the Race Relations Institute, Fisk University.

Professor Marable is the author of *From The Grassroots: Social and Political Essays Toward Afro-American Liberation* (1980) and *Blackwater: Historical Studies in Race, Class Consciousness and Revolution* (1981). His weekly syndicated column on Black politics appears in over 135 newspapers in the United States and the United Kingdom. He has also contributed over seventy major articles to *The Nation, Science and Society, Socialist Review, Negro History Bulletin, Social Text, Radical America*, and many other journals.

Professor Marable is involved in Black political activities across the country. He is also a Vice Chairperson of the Democratic Socialists of America (DSA).